THE GREAT RECESSION

THE GREAT RECESSION

David B. Grusky, Bruce Western, and
Christopher Wimer
EDITORS

Russell Sage Foundation • New York

The Russell Sage Foundation

The Russell Sage Foundation, one of the oldest of America's general purpose foundations, was established in 1907 by Mrs. Margaret Olivia Sage for "the improvement of social and living conditions in the United States." The Foundation seeks to fulfill this mandate by fostering the development and dissemination of knowledge about the country's political, social, and economic problems. While the Foundation endeavors to assure the accuracy and objectivity of each book it publishes, the conclusions and interpretations in Russell Sage Foundation publications are those of the authors and not of the Foundation, its Trustees, or its staff. Publication by Russell Sage, therefore, does not imply Foundation endorsement.

Library of Congress Cataloging-in-Publication Data

The great recession / David B. Grusky, Bruce Western, and Christopher Wimer (editors).
  p. cm.
  Includes bibliographical references and index.
  ISBN 978-0-87154-421-6 (pbk. : alk. paper) — ISBN 978-1-61044-750-8 (ebook) 1. Recessions—United States. 2. Financial crises—United States. 3. Global Financial Crisis, 2008-2009. 4. United States—Economic conditions—2009– 5. United States—Economic policy—2009– I. Grusky, David B. II. Western, Bruce, 1964– III. Wimer, Christopher.
  HB3743.G74 2011
  330.973'0931—dc23   2011022413

Text design by Suzanne Nichols.

RUSSELL SAGE FOUNDATION
112 East 64th Street, New York, New York 10065
10 9 8 7 6 5 4 3 2 1

Contents

Contributors vii

Preface ix

PART I   INTRODUCTION   1

Chapter 1   The Consequences of the Great Recession   3
David B. Grusky, Bruce Western, and
Christopher Wimer

Chapter 2   The Roots of the Great Recession   21
Neil Fligstein and Adam Goldstein

PART II   ECONOMIC EFFECTS: THE LABOR
MARKET, INCOME AND POVERTY,
AND WEALTH AND HOUSING   57

Chapter 3   Job Loss and Unemployment   59
Michael Hout, Asaf Levanon, and
Erin Cumberworth

Chapter 4   Poverty and Income Inequality in the
Early Stages of the Great Recession   82
Timothy M. Smeeding, Jeffrey P. Thompson,
Asaf Levanon, and Esra Burak

Chapter 5   How Much Wealth Was Destroyed in the
Great Recession?   127
Edward N. Wolff, Lindsay A. Owens, and
Esra Burak

PART III   SOCIAL EFFECTS: CONSUMPTION,
                ATTITUDES, AND FAMILY   159

Chapter 6   An Analysis of Trends, Perceptions, and
                Distributional Effects in Consumption   161
                *Ivaylo D. Petev, Luigi Pistaferri, and Itay
                Saporta-Eksten*

Chapter 7   The Surprisingly Weak Effect of Recessions
                on Public Opinion   196
                Lane Kenworthy and Lindsay A. Owens

Chapter 8   The Great Recession's Influence on Fertility,
                Marriage, Divorce, and Cohabitation   220
                *S. Philip Morgan, Erin Cumberworth, and
                Christopher Wimer*

PART IV   THE COLLECTIVE RESPONSE: THE
                GOVERNMENT AND CHARITABLE
                GIVING   247

Chapter 9   The Federal Stimulus Programs and
                Their Effects   249
                Gary Burtless and Tracy Gordon

Chapter 10   Has the Great Recession Made Americans
                Stingier?   294
                *Rob Reich, Christopher Wimer, Shazad
                Mohamed, and Sharada Jambulapati*

Index   315

Contributors

David B. Grusky is professor of sociology at Stanford University.

Bruce Western is professor of sociology at Harvard University.

Christopher Wimer is associate director of the Collaboration for Poverty Research and senior editor of *Pathways* at the Stanford Center for the Study of Poverty and Inequality.

Esra Burak is a graduate student at Stanford University.

Gary Burtless is senior fellow, Economic Studies, and the John C. and Nancy D. Whitehead Chair at the Brookings Institution.

Erin Cumberworth is a graduate student at Stanford University.

Neil Fligstein is Class of 1939 Chancellor's Professor and director of the Center for Culture, Organization, and Politics at the Institute of Industrial Relations at the University of California, Berkeley.

Adam Goldstein is a graduate student at the University of California, Berkeley.

Tracy Gordon is fellow in the Economic Studies program at the Brookings Institution.

Michael Hout is the Natalie Cohen Sociology Chair at the University of California, Berkeley.

Sharada Jambulapati is a student at Stanford University.

Lane Kenworthy is professor of sociology and political science at the University of Arizona.

Asaf Levanon is researcher in the department of sociology and anthropology at the University of Haifa.

Shazad Mohamed is a graduate of Stanford University.

S. Philip Morgan is Norb F. Schaefer Professor of International Studies and professor of sociology at Duke University.

Lindsay A. Owens is a graduate student at Stanford University.

Ivaylo D. Petev is researcher at the Laboratoire de Sociologie Quantitative of the Centre de Recherche en Economie et Statistique.

Luigi Pistaferri is professor of economics at Stanford University.

Rob Reich is associate professor of political science at Stanford University.

Itay Saporta-Eksten is a graduate student at Stanford University.

Timothy M. Smeeding is Arts and Sciences Distinguished Professor of Public Affairs, La Follette School of Public Affairs, and director of the Institute for Research on Poverty at the University of Wisconsin, Madison.

Jeffrey P. Thompson is assistant research professor at the University of Massachusetts, Amherst Political Economy Research Institute.

Edward N. Wolff is professor of economics at New York University.

Preface

DAVID B. GRUSKY, CHRISTOPHER WIMER,
AND BRUCE WESTERN

T HE GREAT RECESSION, as it has come to be called, has been covered
relentlessly in conventional print, radio, and television media as
well as by bloggers and the sprawling network of less conventional media. If the Second Gulf War of 2003 was the first Internet-cov-
ered war, arguably the Great Recession is the first major recession covered in real time by the new media. The sheer volume of commentary on
the Great Recession is, as a result, dauntingly large. Although the coverage has been diverse and varied, even a cursory search reveals that the
"dramatic fallout" storyline has been especially popular. The consensus
view is that the Great Recession has not only recast the economic landscape but has also affected marriage and divorce rates, social and political attitudes, lifestyles and consumption practices, and much more.

In many cases, such conclusions have been based on preliminary and
limited evidence, and an understandable interest in the quick and
splashy story appears to have carried the day. The purpose of this book
is to reexamine the economic and social effects of the Great Recession
using the very best systematic and rigorous data available. We have
drawn on top experts to provide a considered answer to a simple question: How is the Great Recession changing our lives, and who is bearing
the brunt of those changes? This is not another whodunit about what
caused the Great Recession. Rather, this volume is about the economic
and social fallout of the Great Recesssion, about the so-called collateral
effects of a financial crisis that, according to some, pushed modern capitalism to the precipice.

Is it too early to weigh in definitively on these questions? Absolutely.
The available data are often too thin and the lagged effects of the reces-

sion too long to pretend that the reading provided here is anything more than a preliminary one. Because the recession's effects are still unfolding, the Stanford Center for the Study of Poverty and Inequality is partnering with the Russell Sage Foundation to provide continuing coverage of its effects via a new website, www.recessiontrends.org, that updates and extends the analyses reported here. This site provides not just expert coverage of the effects of the Great Recession but also a new graphing tool that allows users to access a comprehensive database of recession time series and to create their own customized graphs and charts. We invite journalists, students, scholars, and the general public to visit this website regularly to find out the latest about the effects of the recession on labor-market outcomes, housing and consumption, social and political attitudes, family and communities, and many other institutions and domains.

We thank the Russell Sage Foundation and the Elfenworks Foundation for supporting the Great Recession initiative. The Russell Sage Foundation funded the conference in which initial results for each of the chapters were presented and is also supporting the continuing coverage of recession developments via www.recessiontrends.org. The Elfenworks Foundation funded the innovative Collaboration for Poverty Research (see www.cpr.org), of which the Great Recession initiative is a part, and further supported the many postdoctoral, graduate, and undergraduate research assistants who carried out the hard labor behind this book. These two foundations are committed to the premise that good policy and a strong civil society rests on providing high-quality data to scholars, politicians, and the general public.

We are grateful as well to the many individuals and organizations that supported this effort in other important ways. The Stanford Institute for Economic Policy Research generously allowed us to host the Great Recession conference in their facility; the Stanford Center for the Study of Poverty and Inequality (www.inequality.com) and the Department of Sociology at Stanford University funded the work of some of the research assistants who participated in the Great Recession initiative; and the book manuscript profited from insightful comments from participants at the Social Stratification Dynamics Conference at the Swedish Institute for Social Research at Stockholm University (December 14 to 15, 2010), the Tohoku University Center for the Study of Social Stratification and Inequality Conference at Stanford University (July 26 to 30, 2010), and the Russell Sage Foundation board meeting (June 18, 2010). We also profited from comments from Swethaa Ballakrishnen, Koji Chavez, LaToya Baldwin Clark, Anna Comerford, Brooke Conroy, Tristan Ivory, Sharon Jank, Tamar Kricheli Katz, Manwai Candy Ku, Rachel Lindenberg, Krystale Littlejohn, Yujia Liu, Laura Lopez-Sanders, Alex Makarevich, Stephen Nunez, Beth Red Bird, Emily Ryo, Jordan Dentler Segall, and Traci Tucker. The anonymous Russell Sage Foundation reviewers also provided particularly valuable comments despite working within a short time frame.

The last paragraph in any self-respecting acknowledgments should be reserved for praising the especially praiseworthy. And ours is no exception. We thank Alice Chou for so patiently herding our many contributors, for formatting the final document so expertly, and for keeping the trains running (more or less!) on time. We thank Suzanne Nichols for overseeing a talented publication team and for tolerating one broken promise after another when it came to delivering the final manuscript. We're grateful to Eric Wanner for helping us think through the book's motivation as well as our response to the many excellent criticisms of the reviewers. We must also single out Lauren Speeth for her especially fruitful suggestions early in the project that shaped the topics that were (and were not) covered. Finally, Michelle Jackson offered up an unusually sharp and attentive reading of the manuscript, the type of close reading that only angels, altruists, or spouses provide.

The careful reader of acknowledgments, the one who codes up disciplinary affiliations, might note the strongly interdisciplinary cast of this book. Although the Great Recession initiative isn't exactly "big science" in terms of its size or funding, it nonetheless draws on a wide and broad network and thus reveals how even midrange initiatives in the study of poverty and inequality are now routinely interdisciplinary. We'd like to dedicate this book to the emergence of a truly interdisciplinary field committed to understanding how labor markets work and how poverty and inequality are generated.

PART I

INTRODUCTION

Chapter 1

The Consequences of the Great Recession

DAVID B. GRUSKY, BRUCE WESTERN,
AND CHRISTOPHER WIMER

AFTER EIGHTEEN MONTHS of recession, the longest since the Great
Depression of the 1930s, growth returned to the U.S. economy
in the summer of 2009. The recession may now be officially over,
but its effects live on in the form of high unemployment, a host of associated labor-market problems, and the ongoing threat of a double-dip
recession. For the 13.9 million Americans who were still out of work as
of May 2011, the recession continues and economic recovery remains
elusive.

The purpose of this book is to describe the various and manifold consequences of the recession, not just the direct and ongoing consequences
for the labor market but also the indirect, and possibly more subtle, consequences for how we live our lives, the beliefs and commitments that
we've come to hold, and the ways our institutions have evolved. The
questions we ask are whether and to what extent the Great Recession
has transformed the social and economic life of the country. We look for
answers by exploring recent trends in employment, poverty, income,
wealth, consumption, fertility, mortality, marriage, attitudes, charitable
giving, and much more.

Why might one believe that the Great Recession has been transform-
ative? The simplest answer to that question is that it's the longest postwar recession and the associated labor-market dislocations have been
especially severe, and remain so. The 1981-to-1982 recession, which was
previously regarded as the most severe in postwar history, lasted only
sixteen months and didn't bring about labor-market disruptions as pro-

found as those we are currently experiencing. In comparison to past recessions, the increase in joblessness has been greater, the long-term unemployed are a larger fraction of total employment, and the recovery of the labor market, in terms of job growth and falling unemployment, has been very slow. From May 2007 to October 2009, the labor force lost over 7.5 million jobs, and the unemployment rate climbed from 4.4 to 10.1 percent. At the same time, long-term unemployment increased sharply, and by 2010 over 40 percent of the unemployed had been looking for work for more than six months. Because discouraged workers withdraw from the labor force in bad economic times, and because some workers are forced to work part-time even though they want full-time jobs, the conventional unemployment rate understates the magnitude of the employment problem. A broader measure of slack in the labor market, one that counts both discouraged workers and involuntary part-timers, hovered between 16 and 18 percent throughout 2010.

A further distinguishing feature of the Great Recession is its origins in an unusually dramatic financial crisis. As occurred at the outset of the Great Depression, the crisis began with a financial collapse that erased more than half the capitalization of the stock market. The Dow Jones Industrial Average dropped in a mere nineteen months from a high of 14,165 in October of 2007 to a low of 6,547 in March of 2009. In March 2008, the former labor secretary Robert Reich warned of "a 20 percent chance of a depression" (Poor 2008, para. 2), revealing the crisis mentality of the time. Although complete disaster has seemingly been averted, the financial sector is now more concentrated, reform has been limited, and bank failures continue.

Another reason why the Great Recession differs from many other postwar recessions is the deep housing crisis that both precipitated and sustained the financial and labor-market crises. The housing market began a sustained rise in the late 1990s and gathered momentum through 2004 and 2005. Just before the fall, real home prices increased by 49 percent in Las Vegas in 2004, by 43 percent in Phoenix in 2005, and by over 60 percent in Miami throughout 2004 and 2005 (Shiller 2007). The bubble burst the following year as home prices around the country plunged. From their peak in May 2006 to their trough in May 2009, real housing prices fell by about one-third across the nation, and in some cities, such as Las Vegas and Phoenix, they fell by more than 50 percent. The collapse of housing prices was of course associated with delinquencies in mortgage payments. Property foreclosures more than doubled through 2007, and foreclosure activity continued to increase through 2008 and 2009.

The Great Recession is distinguished, finally, by the multipronged government response elicited by both the initial crisis and the recession it engendered. The initial response took the form of equity or asset purchases of troubled financial institutions. When the housing bubble burst, investors found that mortgage-backed securities were much riskier than advertised, and both European and American financial markets tightened as these toxic assets quickly became untradable. The investment houses that were heavily invested in these assets foundered as a result. In March 2008, Treasury Secretary Henry Paulson, in collaboration with Fed Chairman Ben Bernanke and New York Fed President Timothy Geithner, engineered a rescue of the Bear Stearns investment house. The quasi-governmental mortgage brokers Fannie Mae and Freddie Mac were then taken over in August of 2008. On September 15, the investment bank Lehman Brothers fell into bankruptcy, unable to borrow or to sell its toxic assets. The international insurance firm AIG was nationalized the next day as panic spread. At this point, credit markets became entirely frozen, and the stock market crashed. On October 3, Congress enacted the Troubled Asset Relief Program, or TARP, which aimed to keep troubled financial institutions solvent by purchasing equity or assets from them.

The second wave of government response was directed toward the labor-market consequences of the financial crisis. As the recession unfolded, February 2009 saw passage of the American Recovery and Reinvestment Act (ARRA), a stimulus package that took the form of fiscal relief for state governments, benefit increases and tax cuts for households, and investments in infrastructure and technology. In December 2010, President Barack Obama signed into law another large stimulus package, the Tax Relief, Unemployment Insurance Reauthorization, and Job Creation Act of 2010. This package focused on extending temporary income and payroll tax cuts and providing additional funding for emergency unemployment compensation.

The Great Recession thus stands out because it was brought on and prolonged by an unusually dramatic housing crisis; because this housing crisis in turn engendered a financial crisis that evoked memories of the Wall Street Crash of 1929; because the associated financial problems triggered a deep labor-market crisis that continues to this day; and because the federal government's response to these housing, financial, and labor-market crises was both substantial and multipronged. Taken together, all of these factors make it at least plausible that the Great Recession will prove to be an event that transforms beliefs, behaviors, and even institutions. To regard the recession as a purely economic event—even one of historic severity—may well be to underestimate its impact on U.S. society.

The purpose of this book is to provide the first general assessment of precisely such far-flung social and economic consequences of the Great Recession. Whereas other scholars have turned to the important question of the causes of the Great Recession (see, for example, Posner 2009;

Lounsbury and Hirsch 2010), our volume assembles some of the first social science research on the consequences of the recession for individuals, families, public policy, and private organizations. Drawing on a varied array of recently released data, we consider not only the narrow range of indicators referenced in technical definitions of recession but also a wider band of social variables, such as marriage, fertility, attitudes, and politics. The most authoritative technical definition of recession, that used by the Business Cycle Dating Committee of the National Bureau of Economic Research (NBER), is a "significant decline in economic activity spread across the country, lasting more than a few months, normally visible in real gross domestic product (GDP), real income, employment, industrial production, and wholesale-retail sales" (NBER 2010). In our labor-market analyses we examine many of these variables (including income and employment), but we also consider the broader and more distal social effects of the recession.

Why are such social effects of interest? It's partly that the economic costs of recession, such as loss of income or wealth, cannot fully capture the social costs and hardships that individuals and families must endure in hard times. These social costs of the recession may be in the form of divorce, delayed or forgone fertility, foreclosures and homelessness, postponed consumption, despair and pessimism, and much more. We will report on a variety of social and economic costs and how they are distributed among different social groups. That is, we care not just about whether, and how much, the recession is imposing extra stress and hardship on the population but also about which groups are especially at risk of bearing those costs. Has the recession hit the already-disadvantaged especially hard? Or have its effects been unusually far-reaching and thus harmed the middle class and even the rich nearly as much as the poor?

This dual focus on the extent and distribution of costs plays out across the three lines of analysis pursued in this book. In part I we inquire into the extent and distribution of the economic costs of the recession, as revealed in trends in employment, poverty, income, and wealth. In part II we inquire into the extent and distribution of the social and cultural fallout in areas such as consumption, family behavior, and political attitudes. In the final section we examine governmental and nongovernmental efforts to cushion the recession's negative effects and how these efforts helped some groups more than others. We turn next to describing these themes in more detail for each section.

Economic Effects

Our first task is to document trends in employment, earnings, poverty, income, and wealth during the recession and its aftermath. The employment trends, with which we begin, are especially fundamental because they underlie trends in other important outcomes, such as poverty. We ask a variety of questions pertaining to the distinctiveness of the Great Recession relative to prior recessions. To what extent are the unemployment trends consistent with those of prior recessions? Have the ranks of the long-term unemployed grown more quickly than in prior recessions and created a new jobless underclass (Burtless 2009)? Is the number of discouraged workers especially large? Has there been a substantial increase in poverty? Or have automatic stabilizers and the government's stimulus package worked as intended and moderated the rise in poverty? How much wealth was lost in the early stages of the recession, and how much has since been regained? For many of these questions, it is too early to secure any definitive reading, and our efforts can only provide the first round of evidence on the severity and distinctiveness of the Great Recession. Indeed, because employment is a lagging indicator, it adds an especially long tail to the recession and makes it impossible at this early point to understand the full storyline.

We will also be asking whether certain groups and subpopulations have borne the brunt of these effects. Because the stimulus and automatic stabilizers serve to preserve employment and income at the bottom of the economic ladder, it's possible that the poor and disadvantaged have to some extent been protected from the fallout. Furthermore, given the extensive wealth destruction at the start of the recession, one might expect a temporary or even long-term closing of the gap between rich and poor. We will likewise examine trends in employment and income across racial, gender, education, and occupation groups. We will ask, for example, whether we're experiencing a "man-cession," in which unemployment has especially increased for men (see Nancy Folbre, "The Declining Demand for Men," *New York Times*, December 13, 2010), whether the college-educated are indeed having difficulties finding jobs (see Sara Murray, "The Curse of the Class of 2009," *Wall Street Journal*, May 9, 2009, p. A1), and whether certain occupational sectors have experienced unusually high levels of unemployment and job loss (Autor 2010). The simple question behind these analyses is whether we're experiencing an inequality-increasing recession in which those who were poor or disadvantaged prior to the recession's onset were also the ones most harmed.

Social and Cultural Effects

Such economic effects may be understood in part as exogenous shocks experienced by individuals who had few alternatives but to bear them. In many cases, economic catastrophe is deeply disempowering, as workers find themselves subject to impersonal economic forces that bring about a loss in employment or in the value of their real estate or stock market holdings. When we shift our attention to the social and cultural fallout from the crisis, a more complicated behavioral model is required. Whereas layoffs or stock market losses are largely thrust on individuals who must simply bear them, other types of behaviors and outcomes are less determinate and subject to more subtle psychological and sociological forces. We might expect, for example, that individuals who are pessimistic about the economy and their own future would be more likely to delay a major purchase, to forgo or delay marriage or childbearing, or to opt to live with their parents or to cohabit with others. Likewise, individuals living in hard-hit regions or neighborhoods will observe others engaging in such cautious behaviors, and their own behavior may then fall in line as a result of usual mimetic and social network dynamics.

We know surprisingly little as yet about the extent and variation in such behavioral and attitudinal responses to the recession. To be sure, there's a growing scholarly and journalistic literature about possible social effects, a literature suggesting, for example, that "conspicuous consumption is now out of favor" (Flatters and Willmott 2009, 112), that the crisis will have a "devastating impact on American families" (Greenstone 2010, para. 6), that it will plunge many into "despair and dysfunction" (Peck 2010, para. 6), and that it is "rejiggering our lives by elevating experiences over things" ("Recession Impact: Americans Spending Less, Doing More," *Economic Times*, January 5, 2010). These types of stories may well be true: after all, the Great Depression entailed social and cultural effects of precisely this sort (see, for example, Elder 1974), although typically they revealed themselves over a longer time horizon than we can yet observe. So far, the case for similarly strong effects of the Great Recession has yet to be convincingly made, and not simply because deadline-pressed journalists are sometimes obliged to craft stories on the basis of relatively weak evidence. It's additionally worrying that well-known selective processes will bias readers of popular media toward the conclusion that social effects are indeed profound. In deciding what stories to run, editors presumably find a tagline of "no effects" rather the hard sell, and a steady diet of stories about how the crisis is instead "rejiggering our lives" may be a built-in outcome of journalistic decisionmaking. Although we can hardly claim to provide a definitive analysis at this early point, we can at least supplement the existing journalistic accounts with more rigorous quantitative evidence.

Collective Responses

To understand the Great Recession it's important to attend not just to the ways in which individuals were affected but also to the ways in which governmental and nongovernmental groups sought to manage it. The modern view is that recessions can be managed not just via the conventional weaponry of macroeconomic policy but also, in more extreme crises, by recasting existing institutions and developing new ones. In the past, economic crises have sometimes given rise to institutions that redistributed rewards in a lasting way, rewriting the economic rules to reduce the population's vulnerability to the business cycle. The Depression of the 1930s provides the key example here. Many pillars of American social policy, such as the National Labor Relations Act, the minimum wage, and Social Security, were instituted in response to the Depression and have moderated economic inequality and the effects of recessions throughout the postwar period. These institutional changes were as important to the post-Depression decline in inequality—the so-called "great compression"—as were the fortunes destroyed by the plunging stock market. In the late nineteenth century, the landscape of social provision was again reshaped by institutional change, although in this case more by private organizations than governmental reform. For example, amid the economic instability of that era, settlement houses and mutual aid societies promoted social welfare under conditions of mass migration and rapid urbanization.

Thus, the twofold question we take on is whether the collective response, in its governmental and nongovernmental forms, has (1) blunted at least some of the labor-market fallout and (2) sown the seeds of more fundamental institutional reform. The latter question is arguably the more complicated and speculative one. It might on the face of it appear that major institutional reform, even a fundamental rewriting of the rules of economic distribution, would be in the offing. The crisis exposed stratospheric Wall Street bonuses, cast high CEO pay in especially sharp relief, and called all such remuneration into question insofar as it was paid out despite seemingly poor performance. It now appears, however, that Depression-style institutional reform is unlikely, at least in the short run. Although a new Democratic administration came to office in 2009 with commanding majorities in the Congress, other currents were flowing in the opposite direction. The labor movement was in decline, the social safety net had frayed under Democratic and Republican administrations alike, and congressional Republicans became more conservative as the Tea Party movement emerged and gained influence.

The role of the nonprofit sector must also be considered as we gauge the collective response to the recession. Compared to other countries, the United States is exceptional in the extent to which it relies on charitable giving and the nonprofit sector to provide for the most needy and to protect people from the consequences of hard times. The nonprofit sector is of interest because we depend upon it to respond to rising need, although the obvious catch-22 here is that such need emerged precisely as endowments were plunging in value and the capacity for charitable giving was being undermined by unemployment, declining income, and declining wealth. Our first question: Did the nonprofit sector manage to withstand such problems and continue delivering aid even as it was seemingly weakened by the recession?

The nonprofit sector is of further interest because it sheds light on the resilience of civil society under economic stress. Have Americans stepped up to the plate during a moment of crisis and worked together to assist others? Or have they withdrawn into a self-protective and individualistic cocoon? Although American society has characteristically been understood as overcoming rank individualism through civic associations and mutual aid, there is evidence that at least some forms of civil society have been eroding over the previous two to three decades (see, for example, Putnam 2000). Indeed, some critics associate the conservative turn in American politics with a burgeoning individualism that offers little sense of fellow-feeling or shared fate, a sensibility that then culminates in a declining commitment to volunteering or a redistributive social policy. The resurgent debates about the legitimacy of federal spending on the safety net and health care are the most recent expression of this long-standing tension between our nation's collectivist and individualist commitments.

Our Analytical Approach

The foregoing analyses are carried out by examining each of the main social and economic domains in which substantial recession effects might be anticipated. We recruited leading scholars in the relevant disciplines to analyze how the recession affected the labor market, the distribution of income, the distribution of wealth, consumption behavior, the family, political and social attitudes, public policy, and charitable giving. In chapter 2 we asked Neil Fligstein and Adam Goldstein to set the stage for these analyses with an account of the events that led up to the crisis as well as the larger social and economic forces behind it.

We charged the contributors with examining the depth of social and economic effects of the Great Recession and investigating how such effects were experienced by different groups. This is a broad task that allowed the contributors to focus on the most important results within their respective domains. The chapters on the labor market, income, and wealth pertain mainly to economic effects; the chapters on consumption, the family, and attitudes pertain mainly to social and cultural effects; and the final chapters, on public policy and charitable giving, relate mainly to the collective response to the recession. These are, of course, just rough-and-ready classifications, and some chapters touch on several areas.

The virtue of recruiting a cast of experts is that a wide range of data sets could be analyzed by those who know them best. In some cases the contributors were allowed special access to advance releases of survey data, thus allowing us to produce and release this book in a relatively timely way (at least by the slow-as-syrup standards of conventional academic research). Our contributors relied primarily on the Current Population Survey (CPS), the American Community Survey (ACS), the Survey of Consumer Finances (SCF), the National Income and Product Accounts (NIPA), the Index of Consumer Sentiments (ICS), the Consumer Expenditure Survey (CEX), the Panel Study of Income Dynamics (PSID), the annual Capgemini and Merrill Lynch World Wealth Report, the RealtyTrac foreclosure data, the National Vital Statistics Reports, the General Social Survey (GSS), the Political Values and Core Attitudes Survey, and Giving USA.

Whenever possible, the analyses not only cover the Great Recession (and the years immediately preceding it) but also make comparisons to earlier recessions. To maintain uniformity, our graphs and figures will adopt the six recession periods identified by the NBER Business Cycle Dating Committee: 1973 to 1975, 1980, 1981 to 1982, 1990 to 1991, 2001, and 2007 to 2009.[1] In all of the book's graphs, we adopt the NBER end date of June 2009 for the current recession, but obviously our graphs reveal that severe labor-market disruptions continue on well past that conventional end date.

Overview of Volume

In the first analytic chapter, "The Roots of the Great Recession," Neil Fligstein and Adam Goldstein review the most important signposts of the Great Recession and lay out a new synthetic account of how it came about. The main competing stories on offer have been quite aggressively marketed and now enjoy the status of conventional wisdom. For example, the "hot potato" story has it that mortgage brokers and originators engaged in reckless underwriting because they were merely collecting fees and could quickly sell off to packagers, while the packagers in turn could pass off the "hot potato" bonds to unwitting investors. According to the "complexity" story, however, the financial instruments were too opaque or complicated to be fully understood and consequently risk was underestimated. In debunking these and other conventional stories, Neil Fligstein and Adam Goldstein show instead that the subprime crisis may have had its roots in early decisions to stimulate the housing market, decisions that then were fatefully coupled with an unwillingness to regulate the new financial instruments devised to exploit this stimulus. Although the roots of the crisis extend back to early housing policy, it was not until quite recently that banks in search of a new source of cash aggressively expanded into the subprime market, one that ultimately came to play a central role in the financial system. At every turn, Fligstein and Goldstein show that the government and regulators promoted this expansion, all operating with an abiding faith in a self-equilibrating market. The banks, having ready access to cheap money, thus fueled a housing price bubble, fed on that bubble, and ultimately brought about the financial crisis when the bubble burst.

The financial crisis quickly infected the wider economy. In chapter 3, "Job Loss and Unemployment," Michael Hout, Asaf Levanon, and Erin Cumberworth show how the financial collapse brought about job losses and unemployment on a scale not experienced since the early 1980s. Over the course of the crisis, the United States lost some 8.5 million jobs. The peak employment level (138.1 million jobs) occurred in December 2007 and the trough (129.6 million jobs) arrived twenty-six months later, in February 2010. During the same period the unemployment rate increased from 5.0 percent to 10.4 percent, and it remains very high as of this writing. The plunge in jobs and the spike in unemployment were much sharper in the current recession than in the previous three recessions (1981 to 1982, 1990 to 1991, 2001). Moreover, the spectacular rise in long-term unemployment is, the authors contend, a "defining difference" between the Great Recession and all previous recessions, with unemployed Americans in January 2010 finding themselves out of work for twenty-one weeks on average. The comparable average in the four recessions from 1977 to 2001 is a mere nine weeks at the depth of each of those recessions. The authors' stark conclusion: "The Great Recession of 2007 to 2009 was a jobs disaster that took unemployment to historic heights."

Is this also an inequality-generating recession in which the most disadvantaged are the most harmed? The evidence suggests that it's not entirely so. For example, Hout and his coauthors report that unemployment increased most in the construction and manufacturing sectors, whereas job loss was comparatively limited in some of the lower-paid service industries. Moreover, because of the types of industries affected, unemployment also increased more among men (approximately 7.5 percentage points) than among women (approximately 4.2 points). At the same time, the disadvantaged do fare worse with respect to education, which is perhaps surprising in light of frequent media reports of the travails of the college-educated (Sara Murray, "The Curse of the Class of 2009," *Wall Street Journal*, May 9, 2009, p. A1). Although unemployment did increase at all levels of schooling, including the college level, the size of the increase was roughly proportionate to the base rate. It follows that the unemployment increase among college graduates was less in absolute terms than that experienced by workers with a high school education (as their base rate is quite high). The larger story, then, is that many disadvantaged groups are suffering disproportionately, yet some of the

recession's effects also reached up to somewhat more privileged workers. This complication emerges because, as with past recessions, the
Great Recession has been a vehicle for industrial restructuring and thus
affects industrial sectors that have been the province of white unionized
males.

In chapter 4, Timothy M. Smeeding, Jeffrey P. Thompson, Asaf Levanon, and Esra Burak explore the extent to which the Great Recession increased poverty and reduced income. The official poverty rate for 2009,
14.3 percent, is slightly less than the peak poverty rates of the recessions
of the 1980s and 1990s, but simulations show that poverty may rise to
well over 15 percent by 2012. This recession-induced increase in poverty
is especially prominent among young unskilled men and children.

The labor-market data also reveal an increase in inequality from 2007
to 2009, with incomes falling for the bottom 60 percent of Americans
while holding steady or rising for those at the top. If one takes into account income generated by wealth, this takeoff in inequality is moderated because wealth-generated income fell off substantially at the top
and middle of the distribution. This is likely to be just a temporary falloff
given that the stock market has since rebounded and will allow those at
the top to continue to regain some of their wealth-generated income. In
contrast to the great compression of incomes that followed the 1930s, so
far the Great Recession has done little to reduce the gap between rich
and poor.

The distribution of wealth is the topic of chapter 5, "How Much
Wealth Was Destroyed in the Great Recession?," by Edward N. Wolff,
Lindsay A. Owens, and Esra Burak. As expected in a "financial recession," the destruction of wealth has been profound, as high-net-worth
individuals (those with over $1 million in investable assets) lost $2.6 trillion in wealth between 2007 and 2008. Of course this destruction was
also experienced by the middle class. By the end of 2009, 16.4 percent of
all homeowners were "underwater" with their mortgages, meaning that
they had negative net home equity, and 14.1 percent of American homeowners were delinquent or soon to be delinquent on their mortgage payments. The share of households with negative net worth also increased
to 24.8 percent by the end of 2009.

There was clearly much pain to be spread around, but the question
arises as to whether certain groups experienced losses disproportionately. The rich lost wealth, especially early in the recession, but their
wealth has been partly recouped as the stock market has recovered. The
middle class, whose wealth tends to consist mostly of housing and retirement accounts, have suffered as well and may not rebound as quickly.
Some of the biggest relative losses have occurred among the disadvantaged. Indeed, African Americans and Hispanics are especially likely to

be underwater with their mortgages, and poor and minority neighborhoods are experiencing the highest probabilities of foreclosure.

In part III of the book the social and cultural effects of the recession are addressed. Chapter 6 provides an analysis of consumption, a properly transitional topic insofar as consumption is rooted not only in financial and labor-market forces, but also subjective perceptions of the economy and its future path. In "An Analysis of Trends, Perceptions, and Distributional Effects in Consumption," Ivaylo D. Petev, Luigi Pistaferri, and Itay Saporta-Eksten document that the decline in consumption has been unusually steep and enduring when compared to the declines of past recessions. Consumption declined sharply in 2008 and the first half of 2009 but has since recovered somewhat, although even now it hasn't regained pre-recession levels.

Which groups were behind this decline? In a financial recession, one might expect the rich to reduce spending dramatically in response to their declining wealth and the poor to be protected from equally severe cuts by transfer payments and other social programs. There is indeed some evidence of just such an asymmetric effect. Although this early evidence is important, the compression at the top may of course be short-lived as stocks and other sources of wealth make a sustained recovery and induce the well-off to begin spending again.

In "The Surprisingly Weak Effect of Recessions on Public Opinion," Lane Kenworthy and Lindsay A. Owens examine long-term trends in public opinion. The key question: Did the Great Recession produce enduring shifts in opinion of the sort that the Great Depression quite famously precipitated? The answer is largely no. Although confidence in banks and financial institutions did suffer during the Great Recession, the authors find no evidence of lasting change in confidence in nonfinancial corporations, the tendency to blame the government or to support government activism, perceptions of fairness and social justice, or support for redistributive policies or policies aimed at helping the poor. They conclude that "recessions have not produced lasting changes—scarring effects—in attitudes throughout the full population." It's nonetheless possible, they point out, that the economic downturn could protract or deepen and ultimately bring about more fundamental changes than have yet surfaced.

There's somewhat more evidence of a demographic response to the recession. In chapter 8, "The Great Recession's Influence on Fertility, Marriage, Divorce, and Cohabitation," S. Philip Morgan, Erin Cumberworth, and Christopher Wimer explore the effects of the recession on family life, an analysis that's motivated in part by the many journalistic suggestions that such effects are substantial. The authors find little change in patterns of marriage, divorce, or cohabitation, but they do find a decline in fertility rates, a decline that's rather stronger in Republican ("red") states than in Democratic ("blue") states. Although the source of such state-level differences cannot be definitively established, the authors provide preliminary evidence suggesting that blue-state residents are relatively optimistic about the economy and hence more inclined to go forward and have children, whereas red-state residents are quite pessimistic about the economy, and such pessimism induces them to delay childbearing until the future appears more certain. Because these results hold even when objective differences in state-level economic circumstances are controlled, they are suggestive of politically colored variability in how couples view the economy and their capacity to afford a child. The authors also report that young adults are increasingly "returning to the nest" and moving in with parents or grandparents. Young adults have good reason to fall back on relatives for housing because they are more likely to lose their jobs, to fail to find jobs, or to fear that they may soon lose their jobs.

In part IV, "The Collective Response," we explore how the government and the nonprofit sector have responded to the recession. Gary Burtless and Tracy Gordon provide a comprehensive description of the government's response and a preliminary assessment of its effectiveness in "The Federal Stimulus Programs and Their Effects." The discussion focuses on the four main features of the response: extension of unemployment benefits and social transfers, provision of tax cuts and credits, support for state and local governments, and new spending on infrastructure projects.

Although some of these measures, such as the extension of unemployment benefits and the expansion of Food Stamps, are standard antirecession policy, the federal response was also innovative in several ways, including its subsidy of state governments and of individual health insurance for those who lost their jobs and benefits. Was this aggressive and (somewhat) innovative response effective? The most striking result in this regard is that, despite the large recession-induced decline in personal income, disposable income (which takes account of taxes and transfer payments) held steady through 2009 and 2010. The implication is that the stimulus prevented what would have otherwise been a more substantial decline in consumption and well-being.

The concluding chapter, "Has the Great Recession Made Americans Stingier?," by Rob Reich, Christopher Wimer, Shazad Mohamed, and Sharada Jambulapati, examines whether Americans continue to be a particularly charitable people even in times of economic duress. Has the Great Recession induced us to hunker down, tend to our own needs, and scale back our well-known generosity? The answer to this question is largely no. Although total giving declined by 2.4 percent between 2007 and 2008 and fell even more dramatically in 2009, Americans are still giving at high levels and at nearly the same proportion of their total income as before the recession. This giving, while slightly reduced in amount, also appears in some cases to be more efficiently channeled to those in need; that is, there's evidence of a shift in giving priorities toward contributing to benefit organizations, food banks, and other charitable causes serving the truly needy. The authors note, however, that some charities serving the needy, such as human services organizations, have suffered steep declines in donations. The slight decline in monetary giving is somewhat offset by a continuing growth in volunteering. This may in part reflect an increase in free time resulting from rising unemployment, but the authors also consider whether the increased volunteering arises from an authentic response to escalating poverty and need.

How Does It All Add Up?

We began this chapter by asking whether the Great Recession stands out relative to prior postwar recessions. The clear, if unsurprising, conclusion is that it has indeed been distinctively severe. Although previous postwar recessions have also been labeled *the* Great Recession (David Wessel, "Did 'Great Recession' Live Up to the Name?" *Wall Street Journal*, April 8, 2010, online), our view is that the label is especially warranted now. The results in this book show that the recession of 2008 to 2009 is distinguished from all prior recessions by the rise of long-term unemployment, the profound destruction of wealth (and housing wealth in particular), and the deep and long-lasting decline in consumption.

The travails in the U.S. labor market are especially troubling and reflect an increasingly tenuous relationship between economic growth and the labor market. Although growth in GDP and productivity once straightforwardly improved circumstances for U.S. workers, it's now no longer the case that they invariably deliver gains in employment or income (Levy and Temin 2007; Elsby, Michaels, and Solon 2009). This tenuous relationship will evidently continue for the near term: the Congressional Budget Office predicts that even as GDP continues to grow, the unemployment rate will remain over 8 percent at least until 2012. The present recession adds an especially high rate of long-term unemployment to the jobless mix and hence raises the new specter of a more permanent jobless underclass.

Another conclusion of interest pertains to changes in the distribution of income and valued goods. The key question is whether the Great Recession has the potential to slow down the historic increase in economic inequality in recent decades. In the recessions of the twentieth century, those at the bottom of the distribution were hit hardest, and inequality increased. The Great Depression, by contrast, triggered a small income compression in 1929 that was followed by a far more substantial compression in the 1940s, brought about in part by the New Deal and World War II. The question that arises, then, is whether the Great Recession is just another inequality-increasing recession or whether it may instead bring decades of increasing inequality to a close, just as the Great Depression and its aftermath ultimately ended the Gilded Age of the late nineteenth and early twentieth centuries.

It is too early to answer this question with confidence, but our preliminary conclusion is that we haven't yet witnessed fundamental institutional changes of the New Deal variety that made the post-Depression period redistributive and inequality-reducing. The stimulus program is extensive, but it is only a temporary initiative and it principally works to buttress existing programs rather than establish new institutions or rules for economic redistribution. At the same time, health-care reform as embodied in the Patient Protection and Affordable Care Act may ultimately have equalizing effects for the distribution of health and life chances, but it's not a reform directed toward the labor market and it doesn't address the economic restructuring that the Great Recession appears to have accelerated. In the absence of fundamental labor-market or social policy reform, it's unlikely that the Great Recession will permanently reverse the ongoing increase in income inequality, and indeed the analyses in chapter 4 by Timothy M. Smeeding and his coauthors suggest just that.

This is not to imply that the Great Recession has been straightforwardly and exclusively inequality-increasing. Although there have been some compressive features to the recession, we're suggesting that they're likely to be transitory because they're not undergirded by major institutional change. For example, the stock market decline brought about a transitory reduction in wealth-based income and consumption at the top of the income distribution, and the government subsequently acted to extend unemployment benefits and other programs for the purpose of temporarily propping up income and spending at the bottom of the income distribution. These two compressive effects are likely to be short-lived. The stock market has partly recovered and restored wealth-based income at the top, while the prospects for a major stimulus that would continue to prop up incomes at the bottom seem, at present, unlikely.

This conclusion leads us quite directly to our line of inquiry on the extent of cultural and social effects. It bears recalling that the Depression was distinctive not just because it was compressive but also because it ultimately ushered in fundamental social and cultural change. Here again, it's far too early to attempt any definitive statement on the extent of such change, and indeed any conclusions we can offer are more hypotheses than statements of fact. The evidence does nonetheless suggest a largely negative conclusion on the matter of early collateral change.

With a few notable exceptions, there is no evidence of sizable recession effects on attitudes or behaviors, a result that led Lane Kenworthy and Lindsay A. Owens to conclude in their chapter that recessions have not produced lasting "scarring effects." Even where we do find social effects, such as the decline in fertility or the downturn in charitable giving, the magnitude of these effects is arguably on the small side.

Why, one might ask, are the social and cultural effects of the recession seemingly so small? The institutionalist response to this question is that major behavioral or cultural transformations don't typically occur in the absence of new institutions that support such transformations. We're unlikely, for example, to witness any sea changes in attitudes toward regulating CEO pay in the absence of new and well-publicized measures that institute such regulation, that susequently come to be accepted and taken for granted, and that ultimately change the discourse on regulation. It's likewise unlikely that attitudes about the legitimacy of unions will change without first changing the rules by which unions can be organized and thereby reintegrating unions into the fabric of American life (Rosenfeld 2010). By this logic, the question "Will major social and cultural changes emerge?" becomes "Will major institutional reform occur?" The answer appears to be no.

The more obvious point is that we're still on the leading edge of the crisis, and any attempt to judge its impact now is quite heroic. This does not necessarily invalidate the institutionalist position. For example, Tea Party activism may in the end precipitate a backlash (such as that seen in the Wisconsin protests) and lead to increased support for fundamental reform, while some of the more austere economic pathways might bring about Greek-style agitation and ultimately institutional reform. It's surely too early to rule out a prolonged economic downturn of the sort that Japan continues to experience. It's possible that severe unemployment will persist or even worsen, that consumption will recover only slowly, and that the housing sector will continue to contract over the long term. If the anticipated recovery is indeed long in coming (or, worse yet, a new crisis emerges), then support for Roosevelt-style reform might ultimately surface and we might observe more substantial social and cultural change.

This volume should be viewed as an early reading of an unusually volatile economic and political landscape. It is no less foolhardy, some might argue, to attempt to weigh in a mere three years after the market's crash than it would have been to attempt to write a book in 1932 on the social fallout from the 1929 crash. This ill-fated book would have been written before President Franklin Roosevelt's election, before any major institutional reforms were undertaken, and hence before the real fallout could have been observed. Since a thorough-going assessment is not yet feasible, we plan to produce a second volume on the Great Recession, also to be published by the Russell Sage Foundation, after some of the volatility has played out and a clearer economic and political course has been charted.

Note

1. Occasionally we refer to the 1980 and 1981-to-1982 recessions as a combined early-1980s "recessionary period."

References

Autor, David. 2010. "The Polarization of Job Opportunities in the U.S. Labor Market: Implications for Employment and Earnings." A paper jointly released by The Center for American Progress and The Hamilton Project. Washington, D.C.: Brookings Institution. Available at: www.brookings.edu/papers/2010/04_jobs_autor_aspx; accessed June 29, 2011.

Burtless, Gary. 2009. "The 'Great Recession' and Redistribution: Federal Anti-poverty Policies." *Fast Focus* 4(December): 1–6. Available at: http://www.irp.wisc.edu/publications/fastfocus/pdfs/FF4-2009.pdf ; accessed May 19, 2011.

Elder, Glen H., Jr. 1974. *Children of the Great Depression: Social Change in Life Experience*. Chicago: University of Chicago Press.

Elsby, Michael W. L., Ryan Michaels, and Gary Solon. 2009. "The Ins and Outs of Cyclical Unemployment." *American Economic Journal: Macroeconomics* 1(1): 84–110.

Flatters, Paul, and Michael Willmott. 2009. "Understanding the Post-Recession Consumer." *Harvard Business Review* 87(7 and 8): 106–12.

Greenstone, Michael. 2010. "From Recession to Recovery to Renewal." Proceedings of the Hamilton Forum, Washington, D.C. (April 20). Washington, D.C.: Brookings Institution. Available at: http://www.brookings.edu/~/media/Files/events/2010/0420_economic_recovery_biden/20100420_thp.pdf; accessed May 19, 2011.0

Levy, Frank S., and Peter Temin. 2007. "Inequality and Institutions in 20th Century America." MIT Department of Economics Working Paper No. 07-17. Cambridge, Mass.: MIT and National Bureau of Economic Research.

Lounsbury, Michael, and Paul Hirsch, eds. 2010. *Markets on Trial: The Economic Sociology of the U.S. Financial Crisis*. Bingley, U.K.: Emerald Group Publishing.

National Bureau of Economic Research. 2010. "Business Cycle Dating Committee, National Bureau of Economic Research." Available at: http://www.nber.org/cycles/Sept2010.html; accessed September 14, 2011.

Peck, Don. 2010. "How a New Jobless Era Will Transform America." *The Atlantic*. Available at: http://www.theatlantic.com/magazine/archive/2010/03/how-a-new-jobless-era-will-transform-america/7919; accessed May 19, 2010.

Poor, Jeff. 2008. "Not Just Recession, Clinton Appointee Talking 'Depression.' " *Business and Media Institute*, March 14, 2008. Available at: http://www.businessandmedia.org/articles/2008/20080314131851.aspx; accessed May 19, 2011.

Posner, Richard A. 2009. *A Failure of Capitalism: The Crisis of '08 and the Descent into Depression*. Cambridge, Mass.: Harvard University Press.

Putnam, Roberto. 2000. *Bowling Alone: The Collapse and Revival of American Community*. New York: Simon and Schuster.

Rosenfeld, Jake. 2010. "Little Labor: How Union Decline Is Changing the American Landscape." *Pathways*, Summer 2010, 3–6.

Shiller, Robert J. 2007. "Understanding Recent Trends in House Prices and Home Ownership." NBER Working Paper No. 13553. Cambridge, Mass.: National Bureau of Economic Research.

Chapter 2

The Roots of the Great Recession

Neil Fligstein and Adam Goldstein

THE PROXIMATE CAUSE of the "Great Recession" was the unraveling of the mortgage securitization industry beginning in 2007. What had been a relatively small niche market at the beginning of the 1990s was, from 1993 to 2007, transformed into the core activity of the rapidly expanding financial sector. At the peak of the mortgage business, in 2003, the financial sector, comprising about 10 percent of the labor force, was generating 40 percent of the profits in the American economy (Fligstein and Shin 2007; Krippner 2010). These profits were mostly being made from businesses engaged in selling mortgages and creating various forms of mortgage-backed securities and related financial products. In 2003, the mortgage business represented a $4 trillion industry. Beginning in late 2006 and early 2007, the housing and mortgage-backed securities markets began to collapse, taking the larger financial sector down with them by the end of 2008. That crisis threatened the existence of the entire banking system in America. As banks and other financial institutions panicked, the system of granting access to short- and long-term credit for both businesses and consumers appeared to seize up and threatened to shut the economy down. In response to this uncertainty, consumers and businesses stopped buying. This created a downward spiral in the economy, and the most severe crisis in American capitalism since 1929 rapidly took hold.

Our basic argument in this chapter is that the Great Recession happened because the growing American financial sector sought to base its business on selling risky mortgages to individuals. These mortgages were risky both because of the questionable creditworthiness of the borrowers to whom they were sold and because key features of the mortgages made them dependent on continued growth in housing prices (Mian and Sufi 2010; Bhardwaj and Sengupta 2009a; Demyanyk and Van Hemert 2009). Over $5.2 trillion worth of these "unconventional," subprime, Alt-A, and home equity loans were sold to residential borrowers in the United States between 2003 and 2007. Banks and other financial institutions made money from the fees generated by selling the mortgages, packaging them into bonds, and selling the bonds to investors. They also often retained a significant portion of the securities in order to profit from the lucrative spreads on high-yield bonds that could be funded through cheap capital in the period from 2001 to 2006. By aggressively pumping so much credit into housing markets, the banks helped fuel a housing price bubble on which the boom in mortgage-based securities in turn fed (Nadauld and Sherlund 2009). The bursting of this bubble after it peaked in late 2006 set off a wave of mortgage defaults that reverberated back through the mortgage industry and global financial markets.

The purpose of this book is to document the recession's wide-ranging effects in various spheres of social life. This chapter helps set the stage for that discussion by tracing the roots of the recession in developments within the mortgage-finance industry. We have two main aims. The first is to answer the question of what happened and how. We begin by recounting the key events and examining how a drop in housing prices could catalyze a wholesale implosion of the financial economy. We outline the sequencing of these events and connect them to the broader economic downturn they created. We then go back and document the history of how the mortgage finance industry expanded during the 1990s and how the character of this expansion fed the housing bubble that ultimately led to the near collapse of the economy.

The second aim is to explore some of the commonly voiced explanations for *why* the crisis happened. Was it a perfect storm that nobody could have seen coming? Or was it simply that the incentives in the securitization process were misaligned, such that mortgage originators and securitizers had little reason to care about borrowers' ability to repay, since they were passing the risk off onto others? To what extent can we see the crisis as a result of Wall Street's infatuation with mathematical models and securitization technologies whose complexity concealed risks and eventually outstripped the ability of people to understand them? We evaluate the strengths and limits of these explanations of the crisis in light of the evidence we will present. What we find is that the most conventional explanations commonly heard in the media and in academic discussions fail. What becomes clear is that the mortgage industry had become a system that linked all of the financial institutions in the economy and made them dependent on the continued increase in U.S. housing prices. It was this dependency on the part of Wall Street and the rest of the banking system that eventually made the downfall seem so surprising. Most regulators never saw the crisis coming precisely because they did not see the interconnectedness of the different elements of the system. One could argue that this systemic understanding is still lacking.

We concentrate here on the crisis in the United States; an analysis of how it played out around the world is beyond the scope of this chapter. Suffice it to say that the U.S. housing crash had both direct and indirect effects on the world economy (for some accounts of this see Rose and Siegel 2010; Claessens et al. 2010). Banks around the world held large volumes of mortgage-backed securities. Those banks experienced stress and many countries had some form of a banking crisis as a direct result of holding these dubious securities, but all in all, the indirect effects of the U.S. crisis were probably larger than the direct ones.[1] Here, we stick with what happened in the United States.

The Events of the Great Recession

What were some of the main events that marked the rise and fall of the mortgage sector and, with it, the economy? At the core of the crisis was the rapid increase in house prices that fueled the economy from 1997 to 2007 and then just as suddenly plunged. Figure 2.1 shows the unprecedented rise in house prices that accompanied the securitization craze. Throughout the postwar era house prices fluctuated around an inflation-adjusted constant. Indeed, housing prices on an adjusted-for-inflation scale remained more or less constant from 1950 to as late as 1997. Beginning in 1997, house prices rose dramatically, to peak in 2006 at nearly 160 percent of their long-run average.

In some parts of the country housing prices rose even more dramatically. Figure 2.2 presents data that show that the states of California, Nevada, Arizona, and Florida experienced price increases at or above the rate of 15 percent a year from 2004 to 2006. Beginning at the end of 2006, housing prices started to drop precipitously in those four states, and in 2008 the prices fell a whopping 25 percent. The rest of the country experienced some of the bubble, but nowhere as extremely as those four states. Housing prices also decreased in the rest of the country, but around 5 percent, not 25 percent. In the face of these price declines, foreclosure rates rose dramatically. Figure 2.2 shows that the states that saw the greatest appreciation in housing prices—California, Nevada, Ari-

Figure 2.1   Inflation-Adjusted National House Price Index (1995 = 100).

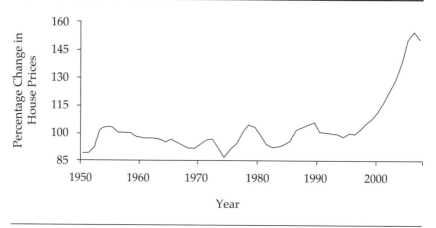

Source: Wilcox (2008).
Note: Prices are based on the Case-Shiller Home Value Index from 1950 to 1974 and the Office of Federal Enterprise Oversight (OFHEO) Index from 1975 to 2007. Prices are deflated using the Consumer Price Index.

zona, and Florida—had dramatic increases in rates of foreclosures. Foreclosure rates in those states went from less than 0.5 percent at the beginning of 2006 to almost 3 percent of all mortgages by 2008. Foreclosure rates increased across the country, but not as dramatically as in those four states.

The increase and subsequent drop in housing prices might not have had such a large overall effect on the economy if it had not been for the way mortgages were being sold and financed in this period. Between 2003 and 2007, the number of mortgages issued that were subprime went from being about 30 percent to almost 70 percent of the total. These subprime mortgages were more likely to have adjustable rates that would reset to dramatically higher rates after twenty-four to thirty-six months. People who had such mortgages made it a practice to refinance their mortgages before these resets occurred, and they did so mainly on the basis of the appreciation in the value of their homes. But the appreciation in the value stopped and the values started to fall just as mortgage rates adjusted, and now people found themselves with unsustainably high payments for houses that were not worth as much as their mortgages (Bhardwaj and Sengupta 2009a, 2009b). Figure 2.3 captures this dynamic by comparing the rates of adjustable-rate mortgages either in arrears or in default alongside an index of the increase in housing prices. Subprime adjustable-rate mortgages had relatively high default rates of around 8 to 10 percent. In 2006, when the appreciation in

Figure 2.2   Housing Price Appreciation and Foreclosures, by Region

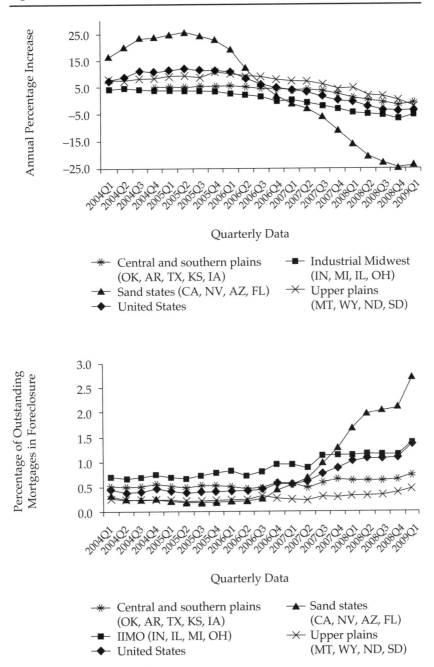

Quarterly Data

Central and southern plains (OK, AR, TX, KS, IA)

Industrial Midwest (IN, MI, IL, OH)

Sand states (CA, NV, AZ, FL)

Upper plains (MT, WY, ND, SD)

United States

Quarterly Data

Central and southern plains (OK, AR, TX, KS, IA)

Sand states (CA, NV, AZ, FL)

IIMO (IN, IL, MI, OH)

Upper plains (MT, WY, ND, SD)

United States

Source: U.S. Department of Housing and Urban Development (2009).
Note: Housing price changes are based on averages of Federal Housing Finance Agency's state-level price indices. Mortgage foreclosure rates are based on the Mortgage Bankers Association's widely used delinquency survey (2010).

**Figure 2.3   Mortgage Delinquency Rates (left scale) and House Price
Appreciation (right scale)**

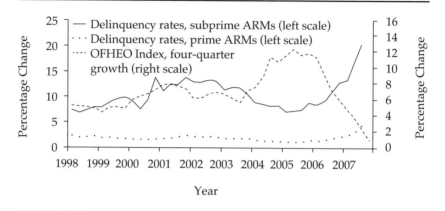

Source: Furlong (2008).
Note: Delinquency rates here combine mortgages two months and more delinquent and mortgages in foreclosure.
ARM = adjustable-rate mortgage
OFHEO = Office of Federal Enterprise Oversight

house prices slowed dramatically, the default rates skyrocketed to over 20 percent.

Banks who were heavily exposed to mortgage-backed securities based on subprime mortgages came under financial pressure beginning in the spring of 2007. New Century Financial, the largest subprime lender in the country, filed for bankruptcy on April 2, 2007. Over the next year the Federal Reserve began to intervene in the market to help banks refund and reorganize themselves. In the spring of 2008, the investment bank Bear Stearns was forced into a merger with JP Morgan. The financial crisis accelerated in the summer of 2008. IndyMac, one of the largest savings and loans banks, went bankrupt in July, and the federal government took over the two government-sponsored housing enterprises, Freddie Mac and Fannie Mae, in August. Instead of calming the markets, events accelerated in September with Bank of America's purchase of Merrill Lynch and Wells Fargo's of Wachovia, and of course, the collapse of Lehman Brothers on September 15, 2008. The federal government began to support AIG on September 17, 2008. As the crisis gathered momentum, the federal government undertook a set of dramatic moves, including passing the legislation known as the TARP (Troubled Asset Relief Program), which authorized the use of $700 billion to help resolve the crisis. In late 2008, both the automobile and large insurance companies requested access to the TARP money, and eventually many of these companies were granted monies.

Figure 2.4   Recession Indicators: Monthly Net Job Growth and Consumer Confidence

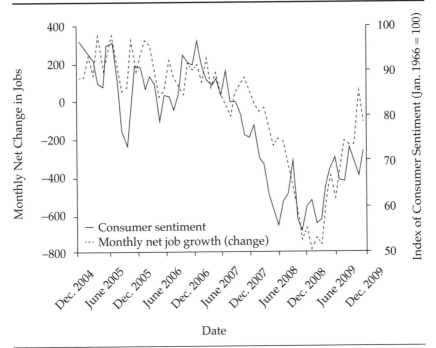

Source: Authors' compilation based on data from U.S. Bureau of Labor Statistics (2010) and University of Michigan (2010).

Of course losses were not confined to investors and the large banks that had caused the meltdown. Even before the historic implosion and hasty bailout of the financial system in September 2008, the rising tide of foreclosures and financial-sector losses was beginning to put downward pressure on the real economy. The severity of the resulting recession reflected the fact that it was not a typical business cycle downturn but a major crisis in an economy that had become increasingly centered on financial markets. According to the National Bureau of Economic Research's Business Cycle Dating Committee, the recession officially began in December 2007, midway through the financial meltdown.

Figure 2.4 displays two indicators of the downturn's reverberation through the real economy: consumer sentiment and job losses. The darker line plotted on the right axis shows the index of consumer sentiment, which is based on a monthly survey and often viewed as a leading indicator that presages more systemic economic trends. The index peaked in July of 2007 and began a steady freefall thereafter. By the summer of 2008 it had reached its lowest level in twenty-eight years. The lighter line shows that the economy began shedding jobs six months later, in January 2008. The rate of job losses accelerated throughout the next year. All told, the economy lost a net total of over 4.3 million jobs in 2008 and 2009. The worst months were between November 2008 and March 2009, when 700,000 to 800,000 jobs were lost each month; the bleeding continued at a slower rate through the rest of 2009. Despite a highly touted job turnaround, only 4 percent of total losses from the recession had been regained during the first quarter of 2010 (U.S. Bureau of Labor Statistics 2010). In response to this growing crisis, the Dow Jones Industrial Average peaked at 14,164 on October 9, 2007, and it reached its low point of 6,547 on March 9, 2010, a decline of 53 percent. In the midst of this crisis, on February 17, 2009, President Barack Obama got the Congress to pass a $987 billion stimulus package.

The economic crisis remained even more persistent in the housing sphere. Mounting job losses and waves of distressed home sales in 2008 put continued negative pressure on housing prices. By the end of 2009 national composite price indices had fallen 29 percent from their May 2006 high. In some bubble areas such as Las Vegas and Phoenix, house prices were less than 50 percent of what they had been at the peak of the bubble. The continued drop in prices spread the foreclosure crisis well beyond the subprime borrowers who were its initial victims. Many homeowners with conventional mortgages found their houses worth less than what they owed on them. If they should be unable to pay their mortgages because of unemployment, they would be inclined to walk away from their homes. As of the end of 2009, the combined percentage of outstanding mortgages that were either delinquent or in foreclosure exceeded 15 percent, which was an all-time high (Mortgage Bankers Association 2010). Over 40 percent of subprime loans were over three months delinquent. Furthermore, an additional 11.3 million households owed more on their mortgages than the value of the properties, a situation referred to as an underwater mortgage. This amounted to over 24 percent of all outstanding mortgages. In Arizona and Florida over 50 percent of mortgages were underwater, and in Nevada an astonishing 70 percent or more were underwater (First American CoreLogic 2010). Negative equity tends to be associated with heightened likelihood of default and foreclosure. Yet policy initiatives to staunch the rising tide of foreclosures have had minimal success. The most up-to-date data as of this writing come from the widely reported RealtyTrac, which shows that the number of homes foreclosed by banks increased 7 percent during the first quarter of 2010 to reach an all-time high ("Foreclosure Activity Increases 7 Percent in First Quarter," RealtyTrac, press release, April 14, 2010). Such data dim any hopes that the fallout of the crisis will soon subside without more aggressive governmental actions to force lenders into renegotiating mortgage terms.

Mortgage Finance and the Financial Meltdown: What Happened?

The "facts" of the Great Recession are quite daunting. The depth and rapidity of the decline is astounding. But, these events also spur us to wonder why this happened. How did housing become so important to the American economy? Why did the trading of mortgage-backed securities become such a fundamental business in the United States? Why did the market for subprime mortgages expand so quickly, and how did their decline come to be able to bring down the entire system of finance? Finally, how did mortgage finance come to be so intimately connected to the overall health of the American economy to such a degree that its decline cascaded through all of American business? To understand how a decline in house prices could catalyze a national and then a worldwide recession, it is necessary to understand the profound transformations in the structure, size, and significance of the housing finance sector in the United States during the previous three decades.

Background and Structure of Mortgage Securitization

The mechanics of mortgage finance remained relatively simple through the 1980s. Individuals would find a house to buy. They would go to their local bank (most likely a savings and loan association) and apply for a mortgage. The bank would agree to lend the funds and then hold on to the mortgage until it was paid off or the house was sold. Mortgages were geographically dispersed and held by local banks. This system was upheld by a set of regulatory laws that protected local savings associations from competition and treated them as socially beneficial instruments for promoting the American dream of home ownership.

Now, this scenario has changed markedly. After mortgages are issued, they migrate to a few square miles of Manhattan where in the offices of the major banks and government-sponsored enterprises (GSEs) such as Fannie Mae or Freddie Mac, the mortgages are packaged into bonds called mortgage-backed securities. These securities can be bought and sold on the market by investors and are sold and resold to investors all over the world. Figure 2.5 describes the way the mortgage industry was organized by the 1990s. Here, the borrower goes to a lending company (frequently but not necessarily a bank), which now is called an "originator" of a mortgage because it makes the initial loan. Unlike the original savings and loans banks, these companies do not want to hold on to the mortgages they sell but instead want to sell them off to others. Their

Figure 2.5   A Mortgage Securitization Package

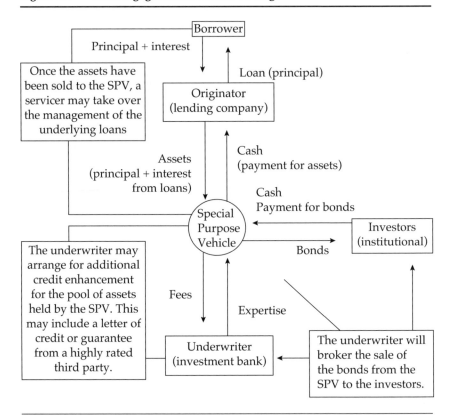

Source: Authors' adaptation of Kendall (1996, 3).

business basically is organized to make fees as an intermediary broker, not, as an old-fashioned banker would, by collecting a modest interest on the mortgage. Instead, they sell the mortgages, thus recapturing their capital so they have the money they need to move back into the market by making further loans. If they were to hold on to the mortgages, they would be unable to lend money again and generate more fees.

The mortgages are bought by the GSE or private banks, who "package" them into a type of bond called a "special-purpose vehicle." By being packaged into this "vehicle" the pools of mortgages are transformed into an asset that pays a fixed rate of return generated from income streams on the underlying mortgages. These bonds are then rated by bond-rating agencies in terms of their riskiness and sold by investment banks to various classes of investors. Once issued, mortgage-backed securities are managed by trustees, who perform administrative tasks, and servicers, who collect the monthly mortgage payments and disburse them to the bond holder in return for a fee.

There are several ways the issues of a mortgage-backed security (sometimes shortened to MBS) can structure the securities, which over time became more varied and complex. By the 2000s most MBS deals were divided up into risk-stratified securities called "tranches." Although backed by common pools of mortgages, the various tranches provide different risk profiles. In this way investors can buy riskier bonds that pay a higher rate of return but are the first to default in the event of losses, or they can buy less risky bonds that pay a lower rate of return. The rationale for these securities is that they could be engineered to manage risk; even though there is always a chance that an individual borrower might default on his or her mortgage, pooling and packaging of mortgage debt meant that investment banks and other issuers could create supposedly safe AAA-ranked securities from risky mortgage debts. These MBS packages that were divided up into tranches were called collateralized debt obligations, or CDOs.

Pricing a CDO can be a complex process because of the disparate income streams from which it is constituted, yet in essence a CDO is simple: a claim on income from mortgage payments made by homebuyers. By the middle of 2007, there was between $6.7 trillion and $9.1 trillion in outstanding bonds and derivatives backed by American mortgages (Inside Mortgage Finance 2009; Securities Industry and Financial Markets Association 2010). Banks and other financial institutions, mostly on Wall Street, began to construct new forms of derivatives based on existing CDOs called synthetic CDOs (Tett 2009). Housing finance had not only become an enormously complex enterprise, it had taken up residence at the epicenter of the nation's, and the world's, financial structure.

How did we move from a world where the local buyer went to her sleepy local bank to get a loan to one where most of the mortgages in the country are now packaged into mortgage-backed securities and are sold into a broad national and international market? It will surprise most readers that the origins of the mortgage-backed security and the complex financial structure depicted in figure 2.5 were not invented by the financial wizards of Wall Street but instead were invented by the federal government. The mortgage-backed security had its genesis in an off-balance-sheet accounting maneuver: During the 1960s federal officials were interested in expanding home ownership as part of President Lyndon B. Johnson's Great Society agenda. They wanted to find a way for the federal government to help pump credit into mortgage finance. But they were also worried about the size of the budget deficit. Because of the Vietnam War and the recent expansion of Medicaid, Medicare, and other social benefits, the government was running large and persistent debts. An expensive housing program where the government provided funds for mortgages would add to the deficit, because the government would have to borrow money for the mortgages and hold those mortgages for up to thirty years.

To overcome this problem the government created the quasi-public GSEs Fannie Mae, Freddie Mac, and Ginnie Mae to issue mortgage-backed securities and insure them (Sellon and VanNahmen 1988; Quinn 2008).[2] The GSEs would take conventional mortgages—mortgages where the buyer would put 20 percent down and pay a fixed interest rate for thirty years—and package them into mortgage-backed securities. The first mortgage-backed security was issued on April 24, 1970, by Ginnie Mae ("Ginnie Mae Offers First Mortgage Backed Bond," *Wall Street Journal*, April 24, 1970). By turning mortgage debt into bonds and selling them to investors, the GSEs could recirculate the proceeds back into the mortgage markets and thus maximize the availability of funds to lend and thus of credit. And by insuring these so-called "agency-backed" bonds against default, the government could encourage private capital to purchase them (Barmat 1990).

The Housing Boom and the Securitization of Subprime Mortgages

Mortgage securitization grew slowly during the 1970s. Part of the problem was regulatory in nature. In order for many investors to hold mortgage-backed securities, the tax status of such bonds needed to be dealt with. The 1986 tax reform legislation, which was written by Louis Ranieri of the Wall Street investment bank Salomon Brothers and was supported by the GSEs, allowed many new investors to enter the market (Nocero and McLean 2010). The financial crisis of the savings and loans banks during the mid-1980s caused them to sell hundreds of millions of dollars worth of mortgages to investment banks for packaging into mortgage-backed securities (Lewis 1989). Salomon Brothers grew rich and expanded on the business. The GSEs took over from the savings and loans the main role of mortgage provider in the economy (Fligstein and Goldstein 2010). They also operated as the ultimate guarantor of mortgage-backed securities.

By the early 1990s, investment bankers came to see that mortgages could be a profit center for them; the loans could be packaged and sold as bonds just like their corporate and government bonds (Jungman 1996). The potential size of these markets was huge. The market for mortgages in the United States increased from $458 billion in 1990 to nearly $4 trillion at its peak in 2003. Most of these mortgages were packaged into mortgage-based securities, and although most of them were still sponsored by the GSEs, commercial or investment banks played an

Figure 2.6   Residential Mortgage Origination in the United States by
Type, 1990 to 2008

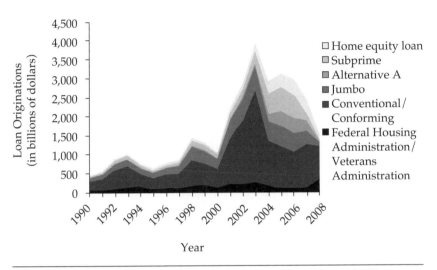

Source: Authors' calculations based on data from Inside Mortgage Finance (2009).

increasingly prominent role in putting these packages together and helping the government to sell them.

Then a new twist came along: subprime and other unconventional
mortgages. The nonconventional mortgage market contained a number
of products that allowed people with less-than-perfect credit or who
needed help in qualifying for loans to get mortgages. Such mortgages
included those that required less than 20 percent down payment, had
variable interest rates, or had different term lengths. Because of regulatory restrictions, the GSEs could not enter the subprime market. That
market started small, but after 2003 the big private banks created a massive market segment for those unconventional mortgages that the GSEs
could not back.

It is useful to document the growth of the mortgage origination market since the early 1990s. Figure 2.6 presents data on total loan originations from 1990 to 2008 and breaks down the loan types into various
products. The American mortgage market was about $500 billion in
1990. In the course of the 1990s it went up to nearly $1 trillion, in 1993,
and peaked at around $1.5 trillion, in 1998. In 2000, it stood at $1 trillion.
The real surge in the mortgage market began in 2001 (the year of the
stock market crash). From 2000 to 2003, residential originations in the
United States climbed from about $1 trillion to almost $4 trillion. About

70 percent of this rise was accounted for by people refinancing their conventional mortgages at lower interest rates.

One much-discussed set of factors behind the housing credit boom was low interest rates in the United States coupled with a glut of capital savings around the world in search of safe yet high-yielding assets. The availability of cheap, plentiful capital was an important macro-economic background condition of the housing bubble. The other major factor in the housing boom was the proliferation of mortgage securitization tools and the increased participation of the bigger banks in these processes. The large banks entered these markets with the goal of growing them and growing their market share in them. Table 2.1 shows how the top players in various parts of the mortgage market changed over time as those markets grew. It shows that in 1996, the largest players in the mortgage market were mostly either mortgage-lending specialists such Countrywide or NW Mortgage or regional commercial banks such as Fleet Financial or PNC. But by the end of the bubble in 2007, the identities of the largest loan originators had changed. Now the largest mortgage originators were the large national bank holding companies such as Wells Fargo, Citibank, and Bank of America. Countrywide had turned itself into a national bank, as had Chase, Wachovia, and Washington Mutual. These large players grew larger as the national market expanded.

The table also shows a similar process for the packagers of mortgage-backed securities—in the industry jargon these packagers are often called conduits. In 1996, two large firms, Salomon Brothers (now part of Citibank) and Merrill Lynch, were on the list of packagers, but aside from these, the packagers of MBSs were generally smaller firms that tended to be focused on the mortgage market, rather than investment banks. By 2007, the list of MBS conduits is dominated by investment banks: Lehman Brothers, Bear Stearns, JP Morgan, Morgan Stanley, Deutsche Bank, and Merrill Lynch. Several of the largest originators of mortgages—Countrywide, Washington Mutual, IndyMac, and Wells Fargo—had taken advantage of deregulatory changes in the Glass-Steagall Act, passed during the Bill Clinton administration, that allowed them to move into the investment banking business. Now they not only make mortgage loans but also act as packagers of those loans into mortgage-backed securities.

The table highlights not only the shifting composition of the group of dominant players in the mortgage-finance field but also the increasing concentration of the whole field. The market share of the top five originators stood at 16.3 percent in 1996, a remarkably low concentration ratio, whereas in 2007 the top five originators accounted for 52.5 percent of a much larger market. Table 2.1 shows a similar process of concentration for the conduit market. In 1996, the top five packagers of mortgage-

Table 2.1 Dominant Firms in Selected Mortgage Finance Segments, 1996 and 2007

Top Overall Mortgage Originators and Their Market Share				Top Subprime Originators and Their Market Share			
1996		2007		1996		2007	
Norwest	6.6	Countrywide Financial	16.8	Associates Capital	7.0	Citibank	10.2
Countrywide	4.9	Wells Fargo	11.2	Money Store	4.3	Household Finance	9.3
Chase	4.3	Chase	8.6	ContiMortgage	3.5	Countrywide	8.8
Fleet Financial	2.3	Citibank	8.1	Beneficial Mortgage	2.8	Wells Fargo	8.0
Bank America	2.0	Bank of America	7.8	Household Finance	2.6	1st Franklin	7.0
NationsBank	1.5	Washington Mutual	5.7	United Co.	2.3	Chase	6.0
WaMu	1.4	Wachovia	4.0	Long Beach Mortgage	2.2	Option 1	5.8
Standard Federal	1.3	IndyMac	3.9	Equicredit	2.1	EMC	4.1
FT Mortgage	1.3	Residential Capital	3.2	Aames Capital	2.0	Ameriquest	3.3

Top Nonagency Mortgage-Backed Securities Issuers and Their Market Share				Top Subprime Mortgage-Backed Securities Issuers and Their Market Share			
1996		2007		1996		2007	
GE Capital	8.4	Countrywide	13.6	Money Store	10.3	Merrill Lynch	10.1
Independent National	5.0	Wells Fargo	7.8	United Co.	6.4	Countrywide	7.9
NW Assets	4.5	Lehman Brothers	7.1	ContiMortgage	5.3	Morgan Stanley	7.8
Merit	3.6	Bear Stearns	6.8	Beneficial	5.0	Lehman Brothers	5.5
Prudential	3.3	Washington Mutual	5.7	AMRESO	4.5	Bear Stearns	4.3
Salomon Bros.	3.3	JP Morgan	5.7	Aames	4.3	Barclays	3.4
Merrill Lynch	3.1	Merrill Lynch	5.6	Household Finance	4.2	Citibank	3.3
Donaldson et al.	2.0	Morgan Stanley	4.8	Residential Finance	4.2	Deutsche Bank	3.2
Structural Assets	2.0	Deutsche Bank	4.4	Associates Mutual	4.1	Washington Mutual	2.7

Source: Authors' calculations based on data from Inside Mortgage Finance (2009).

backed securities held a 24.5 percent market share, whereas in 2007 this rose to 41 percent. The top ten conduits' market share in 2007 was 71 percent. So in addition to a rapid growth in the size of these markets, there was also a rapid concentration of activities in a fewer larger and more nationally oriented banks. The significance of these trends is that the dynamics of mortgage-finance markets increasingly became a function of the strategies that these few leading firms pursued.

After 2003, the major banks' strategies pointed increasingly toward subprime and other nonconventional segments of the mortgage market. Figure 2.6 highlights the remarkable degree and rapidity with which firms gravitated toward nonprime lending (we discuss the reasons for this shift in a later section). The growth of this multi-trillion-dollar shoulder on the upper-right part of the graph would prove pivotal in unleashing the meltdown. It is useful to discuss the components of figure 2.6 in greater detail in order to fully understand the implications of this transformation of the mortgage market. At the bottom of the graph are home loans originated by the Federal Housing Administration and the Veterans Administration. These were never a large portion of the total originated loans, although the segment did increase slightly after 2001. The largest components of the market were conventional, or "conforming," mortgages: prime fixed-rate mortgages for people who made down payments of 20 percent of the sale price for their houses and whose loan values did not exceed the size limitations imposed by the government for inclusion in GSE loan pools. The loans were generally securitized into low-risk agency-backed mortgage-backed securities, which were insured against default and thus paid relatively lower rates of return. We can see that the bulk of the mortgage market from 1990 until 2003 consisted of these two categories of loans.

Beginning in 2003, however, we begin to see a rapid shift toward nonconventional loans. In contrast to conventional loans, securitization of most nonconventional mortgages was done by private-sector banks rather than GSEs. The term "jumbo loans" refers to loans that exceed government-set size limits and hence are not eligible to be in GSE pools. Jumbos are used to purchase expensive real estate, and many but not all are sold to affluent persons with strong credit. Home-equity loans are loans secured by the value of the equity in a house. These were frequently in the form of a line of credit or a second mortgage and were usually sold to persons who had equity but required additional income. Predatory origination practices were especially prevalent within the home-equity loan segment. Alt-A and subprime mortgages (sometimes called "B/C" mortgages to denote their lower credit quality) were sold to people with impaired credit history, or people who lacked the ability to make a large down payment, or people who did not have verification of their income. Alt-A is not strictly defined but is generally viewed as an intermediate category that encompasses borrowers whose credit scores would qualify them for a prime mortgage but may not fully qualify them for a conventional mortgage. The term "subprime" actually has a set of formal definitions. To qualify for a prime or conventional mortgage, a person needed 20 percent down and a credit FICO score of 660 or above (the average score is 710 on a scale from 450 to 900). Mortgagees who did not have these qualifications were not eligible for prime or conventional mortgages.

What constituted impaired credit? Some of the conditions that could qualify a mortgagee as a candidate for a subprime mortgage were as follows: two or more late payments in the previous twelve months; one or more sixty-day payment delinquencies in the previous twenty-four months; a judgment, foreclosure, or repossession in the prior twenty-four months; bankruptcy in the previous five years; a FICO score less than 660; and debt-service-to-income ratio of 40 percent or greater (in other words, monthly loan payments totally more than 40 percent of the gross income of the household).

In 2004, for the first time, loan to borrowers who fell into nonconventional mortgages exceeded the number of borrowers in the prime market or conventional market. In 2001, the largest conventional (prime, government-insured) loan originator did 91 percent of its origination business in the conventional market and only 9 percent in the nonconventional market. By 2005 the largest conventional originator was doing less than half of its origination business within the conventional sector (Inside Mortgage Finance 2009). At the peak of the mortgage craze, in 2006, fully 70 percent of all loans made were unconventional mortgages. Thus, in a very short period of time banks reoriented housing finance— one of the largest industries in the economy—around securitizations of highly risky loans. This astounding change in the character of the mortgage market was noticed by regulators and Congress, but the Federal Reserve chose to ignore what was going on. Former Federal Reserve Chairman Alan Greenspan famously testified before Congress in October 2008 that the reason he did nothing to stop this rapid growth in unconventional mortgages was that he believed banks would not have made these loans if they thought they were too risky (Edmund L. Andrews, "Greenspan Concedes Error on Regulation," New York Times, October 24, 2008, p. B1).

There were two main reasons banks pursued these risky subprime loans so aggressively. First, there were fewer and fewer loans left to sell in the saturated prime market. Almost everyone who wanted to refinance their house had done so by 2003, and in order to keep their businesses going, banks and other financial institutions needed to find a new source of mortgages. Second, subprime origination and securitization turned out to be enormously profitable. According to a study by the consulting firm Mercer Oliver Wyman, nonconventional lending accounted for approximately half of originations in 2005 but over 85 percent of profits ("Taking It Seriously," *National Mortgage News*, March 21, 2005, p. 4). Once lenders figured this out they often tried to sell subprime loans even to persons who qualified for cheaper prime loans. The repackaging of nonconventional mortgages into bonds also became the largest fee-generating business for many investment banks, including Lehman Brothers, Bear Stearns, Merrill Lynch, Morgan Stanley, and Goldman Sachs. Commercial banks and bank holding companies such as Bank of America, Wells Fargo, Citibank, and Countrywide Financial also became deeply involved in all stages of the market, from origination to packaging to servicing loans.

The major firms employed strategies to profit from mortgage-backed securities in multiple ways simultaneously, earning money both from fees and from income on retained MBS assets. Bank originators could use either their own capital or cheap borrowed capital to make loans to home buyers (Ashcroft and Scheuermann 2008 take up this story). Then, they could turn around and sell those loans to conduits. If they used someone else's money (borrowed at, say, 1 or 2 percent interest), then they could essentially do the entire transaction with very low cost and relatively high fees. Conduit banks could also borrow money cheaply. They would buy up the mortgages with cheap money, package them, and sell them to investors.

Beginning sometime around 2002, both commercial and investment banks began to realize that they could borrow money at 1 to 2 percent interest, create mortgage-backed securities, and then hold on to them— these securities might pay as much as 6 to 7 percent in interest. This allowed the banks to make a profit using other people's money and without risking their own capital. The low interest rates in the United States and the world encouraged banks of all kinds to borrow as much as they could to make as many subprime loans as they could, earn fees from packaging them into mortgage-backed securities, and then also hold on to a portion of the securities as investments. The massive amounts of money banks borrowed to fund this strategy are the reason they were so highly leveraged when the liquidity crisis hit in 2008.

Figure 2.7 shows holdings of unconventional-mortgage-related security assets for several major banks and thrifts. Unlike data of investment banks and private mortgage companies, firm-level data on holdings of commercial bank and thrifts are publicly available. Each of the firms shown in the figure was among the top fifteen private-label issuers of mortgage-backed securities at the peak of the market. Each was also among the top fifteen subprime originators (Inside Mortgage Finance 2009). Several things are worth noting here. First, the graph shows that the firms issuing mortgage-backed securities were holding on to a sig-

Figure 2.7   Nonagency Mortgage-Backed Securities Holdings of Selected Issuers

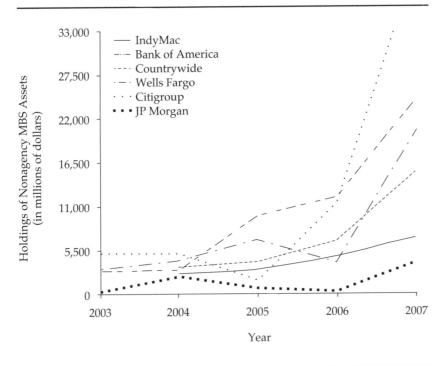

Source: Authors' calculations based on data from Inside Mortgage Finance (2009).

nificant portion of the bonds. Second, they were rapidly increasing their positions even as the bubble grew. IndyMac, which shows the lowest increase on the graph, actually increased its holdings by over 50 percent per year on average during this period. Citibank increased its MBS holdings by almost 400 percent, to $41 billion, during 2007. The company subsequently took a $35 billion loss on these assets. Although consistent company-level data for investment banks are not available, the same pattern of growth is evident among them. As a group they increased their nonconventional-mortgage holdings from $5 billion in 2002, to $60 billion in 2005, to $180 billion by June 2008 (Inside Mortgage Finance 2009).

The Housing Bubble

The massive growth of unconventional-mortgage securitizations fueled and fed on an unprecedented housing price bubble during this period.

The year 2000 will be remembered as the year of the crash in "dot-com" stocks. As that crash began, the Federal Reserve, to make sure that there was substantial credit in the economy and that lending would continue, essentially lowered interest rates to zero. Their actions were met by similar actions in central banks around the world. But there was an unintended effect of lowering interest rates so far: it encouraged the housing bubble in the United States. The rapid expansion of that bubble was astonishing: mortgage origination rose 400 percent in four years, and prices followed a similar pattern. That the Federal Reserve knew this and did not take any actions to stop it is one of the critical facts to be explained. Alan Greenspan has testified that he did not believe this was a bubble because housing prices are a local affair in the United States—a house in Boston is not the same as a house in Phoenix. In fact, quite a few markets—Atlanta and Denver are two of them—experienced population increases without housing bubbles.

But Greenspan chose to ignore the role of securitization in creating causally linked bubbles in many markets. A good deal of research suggests that the low interest rates across the country and strong demand from investors in the mortgage-backed securities market encouraged banks to pump as much credit into housing markets as they could (Mian and Sufi 2010; Herbert and Apgar 2010). Bankers could borrow money at around 1 percent interest and lend it at 5 to 7 percent. Where housing was scarce and population was growing, prices rose, encouraging banks to focus on those markets. This in turn encouraged further price increases, as borrowers could use access to plentiful credit to bid up prices. In 2004, the investment banks convinced the Security and Exchange Commission (SEC) to allow them to increase their ability to borrow money against their capital reserves. This allowed them to buy securities worth as much as forty times those reserves. As a result, they dramatically increased the amount of subprime credit being pumped into zip codes where housing prices were rising (Nadauld and Sherlund 2009).

Part of the reason banks focused on these markets was that the upward price trends fit the models used by the banks and credit ratings agencies to gauge default risks (Demyanyk and Van Hemert 2009). MBS issuers could attain safer credit ratings for securities by including in them a larger proportion of mortgages from zip codes with high price appreciation, since these were thought to be less prone to default. Subprime securitization thereby fed itself forward in the aggregate as the aggressive provision of credit in selected markets helped further inflate prices. All of the top thirteen subprime metropolitan statistical areas (MSAs) by this metric were located in the boom states of Arizona, California, Florida, and Nevada. Housing markets in these states effectively became linked through the common strategies banks adopted toward them. It is not surprising, then, that Arizona, Florida, Nevada, and parts of California turned out to be ground zero of the subprime lending boom, the housing price bubble, and the subsequent foreclosure crisis.

The Bubble Pops and Defaults Increase

The meltdown was precipitated by the bursting of the securitization-fueled housing bubble. Slowing house appreciation led to rising mortgage defaults, which in turn led to far larger than expected losses on mortgage-backed securities (Mayer, Pence, and Sherlund 2009). The stall in housing prices activated all the latent risks of subprime lending that the persistent rise had repressed. We have already detailed the link between the peaking of the housing bubble and the rise in defaults as well as its pattern of regional concentration. We have also shown how defaults were concentrated within the subprime segment, which had grown rapidly from 2003 to 2007.

The more fundamental reason subprime mortgages were at the epicenter of the rising defaults in 2007 was that their basic design was predicated on a housing bubble. Traditionally the rationale for subprime loans was that borrowers with impaired credit could get a loan at a relatively high rate for a few years, build their credit with steady payments, and then refinance at a better rate. In other words, it was risk-based pricing for under-served borrowers who needed credit but were considered risky by financial institutions. But as the bubble grew, the underlying logic and structure of subprime loans became less about building borrowers' creditworthiness and more about making speculative bets on the housing market (Gorton 2008; Davis 2009). One of the underexplored issues of the financial crisis is: Exactly who was taking out subprime mortgages? We know that some of these borrowers had little income and no money for a down payment (Bhardwaj and Sengupta 2009b). Some were real estate speculators. And some were middle-class families who found themselves priced out of conventional mortgages because of rapid price increases in housing.

The shift into subprime mortgages led to increasing use of hybrid adjustable-rate mortgages (ARMs), which were mortgages that started at a low rate for a fixed period of time but then adjusted to a higher rate (Mayer, Pence, and Sherlund 2009, 31). Hybrid ARMs became popular because lenders could sell more loans by charging less interest initially—a predatory marketing ploy. But two-year "teaser" rates on ARMs were not simply a predatory marketing ploy to draw uncanny consumers and then lock them into high rates. Lenders were betting that house prices would continue to rise in the short term, offsetting other credit risks and justifying a somewhat lower initial interest rate. Borrowers could then refinance using quickly accumulated home equity before the mortgage reset to the higher adjustable rate. This incentive to refinance every two years is why approximately two-thirds of subprime originations from 2000 to 2006 were refinances rather than new purchases.

Once housing prices stopped appreciating, however, the design of subprime loans made them especially prone to default. Borrowers who had been promised that they would be able to refinance in two years suddenly found it much more difficult to do so once the downturn spurred lenders to rapidly contract subprime credit availability. Instead of the lower payments that had been anticipated, borrowers faced a reset shock as their monthly payments ballooned to the higher adjustable rate (Demyanyk and Van Hemert 2009). Thus the fact that defaulting subprime loans sparked the financial crisis was due not only to the heightened risk profile of subprime borrowers but to the fact that subprime ARM loans even more than others were premised on the dynamic of a bubble that could not last.

Financial Meltdown

By the beginning of 2007 the massive growth of unconventional-mortgage securitization had spread at least $3.8 trillion of assets directly linked to these mortgages to financial institutions around the world. Nonetheless it is clear that the markets, the credit ratings agencies, regulators, and most of the large banks all registered comparatively little response when housing prices started to stall out and mortgage default rates began to rise in late 2006. Several large banks such as Merrill Lynch and Citibank continued expanding their subprime businesses aggressively during the first two quarters of 2007. In March of 2007 Fed Chairman Ben Bernanke stated in congressional testimony that "at this juncture, the impact on the broader economy and financial markets of the problems in the subprime market seems likely to be contained" (Jeremy W. Peters and Edmund L. Andrews, "Manageable Threats Seen by Fed Chief," *New York Times*, March 29, 2007.)

The credit ratings agencies also continued to maintain an implausibly upbeat outlook through the first two quarters of 2007. Only after they were the subjects of widespread mockery on the financial blogosphere, endured congressional questioning, and experienced an overall crisis of legitimacy did the agencies take serious steps to adjust MBS bond ratings to reflect the deteriorating conditions in the mortgage market. Their reasons for reticence were clear. First, they had a vested interest in hoping the situation would improve, since their reputations and a significant portion of the revenues rested on a strong market in mortgage-backed securities. Second, ratings agencies knew what downgrading ratings would mean. Moody's CEO Raymond McDaniel justified its cautious approach to downgrades, noting that "because we are an influential voice, we can create a self-fulfilling prophecy by saying that there are risks in the market ahead of those risks being revealed" ("Banks' Subprime Losses Top $500 Billion on Write Downs," Bloomberg News, August 12, 2008).

By July 2007, credit supply for nonconventional mortgages ground to a halt as demand for mortgage-backed securities based on those types of mortgages plummeted and banks became weary of the quickly weakening housing market. The volume of subprime originations declined by 90 percent between the first and second halves of 2007 (Inside Mortgage Finance 2009). The drying up of credit to fund subprime originations began hampering attempts by borrowers with adjustable-rate mortgages—even those whose houses had not yet declined in value—to refinance before their mortgage got reset to a higher rate. It also imperiled the business of large mortgage specialists like Ameriquest and Countrywide and began eating into the revenue streams of the commercial and investment banks that had come to rely on fee revenues from their vertically integrated mortgage finance franchises.

Bond defaults were initially concentrated among the lower-rated equity tranches, which were the first in line to lose in the event of revenue losses. But the rising tide of subprime delinquencies and foreclosures soon put pressure on the supposedly safe "AAA" tranches as well. Figure 2.8 shows weekly counts of negative credit actions taken by one of the big three ratings agencies against unconventional mortgage-backed securities and mortgage-related CDOs. Aside from a few small blips of activity in April and July of 2007, there were few downgrades on mortgage-backed securities, but they increased rapidly in September.

The downgrade plot's resemblance to a seismograph image is apt. Each round of mass downgrades sent tremors through the financial system. The significance of credit downgrades was that they forced leveraged banks that had taken loans to buy mortgage-backed securities either to pay off those loans or to post additional collateral with their creditors. This was because most of their loans contained covenants that required them to increase their capital investment if bond prices fell or the credit rating on the MBS collateral was downgraded. The problem, however, was that most banks were already very highly leveraged and eventually found it impossible to raise enough capital to cover their loans. This was the link between the implosion in the mortgage market and the freezing of the credit system.

The financial meltdown emerged from a novel configuration of forces, but it soon took on the relatively straightforward form of a classic banking panic. Lenders made calls on collateral, and the entities that had become highly leveraged in order to buy mortgage-backed securities suddenly found themselves in a liquidity crisis, unable to raise funds to cover debt backed by assets whose value was rapidly plummeting. This process first played out within the so-called shadow banking system of

Figure 2.8   Credit Downgrades of Mortgage-Backed Securities, by Month, 2008

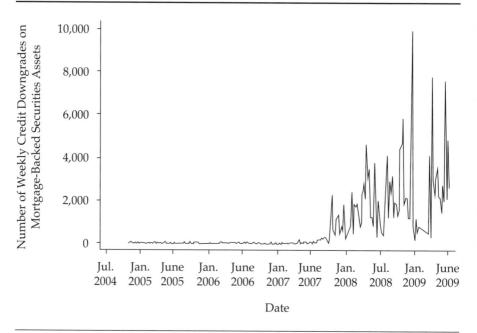

Source: Authors' tabulation, based on ratings actions reported by Bloomberg Professional Terminal.
Note: Downgrades include all negative ratings actions on private-label mortgage-backed securities and mortgage-related collateralized debt obligations by Moody's, Standard & Poor's, and Fitch.

special investment vehicles, which were usually linked to a larger institution but funded themselves through short-term debt. As the price of their mortgage-backed securities and CDO assets fell, they needed cash to post as collateral with creditors, but since the credit markets were weary of extending them emergency money, they generally had to be rescued by their parent firms and placed back on the parent's balance sheet.

Two hedge funds affiliated with Bear Stearns were the first major shadow banking institutions to fail, in July of 2007. A similar crisis soon afflicted Citigroup, which would take over $55 billion in write-downs on mortgage-related assets ("Banks' Subprime Losses Top $500 Billion on Write Downs," Bloomberg News, August 12, 2008). The problem, as Gillian Tett (2009) and others have dramatically documented, was that the elaborate system of accounting vehicles banks built to hide their leverage from regulators and the elaborate network of credit default swaps they created to hedge their risks made it impossible for the market to discern which banks were exposed to the mortgage-backed securities where the underlying mortgages were in default. The financial crisis escalated throughout the summer of 2008 in spite of efforts by the Federal Reserve to make emergency capital available.

It is useful to look at what happened to the top banks that were leaders in the mortgage securitization business circa 2005. Seven of the ten largest subprime lenders in 2005 went out of business or were absorbed by merger. Eight of the ten top subprime MBS-issuing companies in 2005 are either out of business or merged into other entities (Fligstein and Goldstein 2010). The collapse of the subprime market essentially wiped out all of the companies that had grown large on that business. The big investment banks at the core of the subprime MBS market no longer exist, with the exception of Morgan Stanley and Goldman Sachs. Citibank, Bank of America, JP Morgan Chase, and Wells Fargo have emerged as large conglomerate banks after absorbing many of the subprime losers, while both Goldman Sachs and Morgan Stanley have reorganized themselves to become commercial banks. Most of the institutions that survived only did so on account of the TARP bailout, and most took massive write-downs on MBS assets.

Summary

The preceding discussion leads us to argue that the proximate causes of the crisis can be found in two shifts in the structure of the mortgage-finance industry. First, the easy credit available to all forms of financial investors after 2000 meant that money could be made by borrowing money at a low interest rate and then turning around and buying mortgage-backed securities. This process of leveraging was the core strategy of banks and many other financial institutions. Investors worldwide who were not leveraged were also searching for higher but safe returns, and American mortgages looked good to them. These strategies brought all of the major banks aggressively into mortgage securitization and brought mortgage securitization to the center of the financial sector. It also made the financial positions of these firms especially sensitive to the credit markets, which would become negatively impacted by the core of the market, along with millions of households and the rest of the American economy.

The second cause of the crisis is as important as the first, but it is not well understood. By 2004, there were simply not enough prime or conventional mortgages left in the United States to package into mortgage-backed securities. The steep decline in mortgage originations after 2003 reflected neither weakness in the housing market nor slackening demand from the mortgage-backed securities market. Rather, a saturated prime market and an interest rate hike had led to a significant drop-off in the refinancing activity that had driven the 2003 boom. Those who had money to buy mortgage-backed securities were still looking for product, but those who were originating and packaging mortgage-backed securities didn't have enough to meet the demand. So there was a huge incentive to increase the number of mortgages; it sent loan originators looking for new mortgage markets to feed the securitization machine and led to the rapid growth of the subprime and Alt-A markets. The aggressive pursuit of those markets by banks of all kinds has led us to the current situation. The main role that regulators played was their refusal to intervene in these markets. The Federal Reserve was dominated by people who believed that in spite of this dangerous shift in the market, market actors would not take on too much risk. We now know this was wrong. The evolution of banks' strategies since the early 2000s had left them highly leveraged on assets that were largely junk.

Myths and Half-Truths

Although it is early to develop any comprehensive explanations of why the meltdown occurred, already a body of conventional wisdom has emerged that comprises a number of questionable conclusions. In this section we evaluate several oft-repeated arguments about the mortgage meltdown and show that they are inconsistent with key pieces of evidence.

Perverse Incentives and the "Hot Potato" Theory

One of the most oft-repeated morsels of conventional wisdom about the crisis is that it happened because of misaligned incentives in the securitization process. This is often known as the "originate-to-distribute hypothesis," or, more colloquially, the "hot potato" theory (Baily, Elmendorf, and Litan 2008; Purnanandam 2009). The originate-to-distribute hypothesis attributes systemic risk to perverse transactional incentives: mortgage brokers and originators had an incentive to engage in reckless and fraudulent underwriting since they were selling loans off to an MBS packager and hence had no interest in ensuring the borrower's long-term ability to repay. MBS packagers in turn had little interest in monitoring the underlying quality of the bonds because they were selling these assets off to investors (Purnanandam 2009). This incentive-based analysis of the crisis forms much of the conventional wisdom underlying current regulatory reform proposals, for instance, the provision in the 2010 Dodd-Frank Act that requires issuers of securitized assets to retain at least 5 percent of the credit risk.

Gary Gorton (2008) has argued that the originate-to-distribute model, which focuses on the securitization process as such, is overdetermined because it fails to identify the roots of the crisis in particular features of subprime mortgages. More fundamentally, our data show that most of the premises of the originate-to-distribute thesis turn out not to be true. First, the actual structure of the mortgage securitization industry differed from that presumed by the theory. The pursuit of vertical integration by the large MBS-producing firms meant that as the bubble grew, banks were increasingly originating, packaging, underwriting, and servicing mortgage-backed securities in-house rather than passing risk along a value chain of market transactions. We document this more thoroughly elsewhere (Fligstein and Goldstein 2010). Second, as shown in figure 2.3, the idea that issuers of mortgage-backed securities did not hold on to them turns out to be a myth. MBS producers aggressively marketed risky assets to investors all around the world, but they also retained a considerable portion of the assets themselves, largely because they were yielding high short-term returns (as long as borrowers made their monthly mortgage payments).

The fact that the companies most deeply involved in the production of risky mortgage-backed securities also retained such a significant portion of the securities and often went bankrupt as a result casts doubt on the notion that the crisis occurred simply because they were strategically selling the riskiest assets to unwitting investors. With the exception of Goldman Sachs and, to a lesser degree, JP Morgan, all of the large banks involved in the production of risky mortgage-backed securities continued to hold significant positions on these assets until the very end. The key players knew it was risky, but they thought they could control their risks through ploys like quasi-insurance in the form of credit default swaps (CDSs). They were making massive profits, which reinforced their views that their risks were being managed.

Another half-truth is the idea that underwriting standards were declining and investors who bought mortgage-backed securities could not know how risky the underlying loans really were. Evidence of declining underwriting standards during the 2000s is mixed. There are two sets of information about loan pools: the "hard" reported characteristics such as FICO scores and loan-to-value ratios, and "soft," "unobservable" information such as a borrower's true income in cases of stated-income loans (so-called low-documentation or "liars" loans). The soft information is often referred to as unobservable characteristics since it unknown to the securitizers who buy the mortgage, the ratings agencies, or investors. There is little evidence of systematic declines in observable characteristics within various mortgage segments (sub-prime, Alt-A, etc.)—in fact, average credit scores of subprime borrowers actually increased somewhat over the course of the bubble (Bhardwaj and Sengupta 2009b). But there is also evidence that declining underwriting standards were rendering loans riskier than the hard information would suggest (Demyanyk and Van Hemert 2009). The use of low-documentation loans expanded considerably as the bubble grew, particularly in the Alt-A segment. Studies have found that these low-documentation loans ended up defaulting at a significantly higher rate than their observable characteristics would predict (Mayer, Pence, and Sherlund 2009). This implies that low-documentation loans were indeed liars' loans. It furthermore implies that declining underwriting standards *were* making mortgage loans ever riskier as the boom grew, and that they were doing so in a way that was unobservable by investors and credit ratings agencies.

Fraud and poor underwriting standards at the point of origination clearly played a role in exacerbating default risk and allowing the housing bubble to keep growing even when there were no more qualified buyers. But pinning the causes of the crisis on misaligned incentives and resulting misbehaviors at the point of origination elides two key facts.

First, the banks that bought and packaged these mortgages were clamoring for more risky no-down-payment and interest-only loans because they could earn higher returns on such loans (Fligstein and Goldstein 2010).

Second, the observable information about loan pools itself told a very risky story. When a conduit bank wants to issue an MBS, it has to file a prospectus with the SEC that includes information on the loan collateral. These prospectuses are public information and can be accessed at the SEC's website by a few clicks of a mouse. We tried this and here briefly examine the information contained in the prospectus for GSAMP Trust 2006-NC2 (http://www.sec.gov/Archives/edgar/data/1366182/00011 2528206003776/b413822_424b.txt), a typical subprime MBS issue during the height of the bubble. There were 3,949 subprime mortgages in the trust, worth $881 million, of which 43.4 percent were used to buy a new house and the balance were to refinance existing loans. Ninety and seven tenths percent of the mortgagees were going to live in the house; 73.4 percent were single-family dwellings and the rest were condominiums; 38 percent of the homes were in California and 10.5 percent in Florida. The average borrower had a FICO score of 626; 31.4 percent had a score below 600; 51.9 percent had a score between 600 and 660, and only 16.7 percent had a score above 660. The ratio of total debt to income was 42 percent in the whole set of mortgages. About 79 percent of the bond offering was rated "AAA," the highest rating. Less than 5 percent were rated "B," which should be more typical of a subprime rating.

This information is quite detailed and it was readily available to investors. Even if mortgage fraud meant mortgage pools were often riskier than advertised, anyone who looked at the prospectus for GSAMP 2006-NC-2 would see that the reported risk profile of the mortgages was already quite high.

In our view the problem was not so much that fraudulent origination practices were surreptitiously rendering subprime loans even riskier than they appeared (though this was occurring to some extent). Rather, the real problem was that risky mortgages were becoming vastly more prevalent on account of banks' voracious appetite for raw mortgages to fuel their securitization machines. In this way high-risk loans came to constitute an ever-greater portion of financial assets.

Did Banks Underestimate the Risks?

Another overarching view of the crisis is to argue that actors underestimated the probability of rare and apparently improbable events such as a systematic drop in housing prices. This could possibly explain why supposedly risk-averse investors bought subprime mortgage-backed securities even though the underlying mortgages were clearly quite risky. We are skeptical of strong forms of this argument for a couple of reasons. First, the housing bubble looked like a bubble at the time. During the height of the boom there was a great deal of discussion in mortgage-finance trade journals about whether there was a bubble or merely local "bubbletops," as one commentator suggested. Ezra Zuckerman (2010) has conducted a content analysis that shows that the frequency of discussion about a housing bubble in the business press tracked the growth of the actual bubble. This is not a case of the blindsided herd or the "perfect storm." Moreover, the voices warning of mounting risks were not merely those of obscure contrarians. Several prominent economists, including the Federal Reserve Board governor Edward Gramlich, had been sounding numerous warnings about the subprime bubble for several years. Even more striking is that key industry actors recognized the risks. During a conference of mortgage industry executives at the height of the bubble in 2005, Countrywide's CEO Angelo Mozilo warned colleagues that they could all face an impending "catastrophe" ("Taking It Seriously," *National Mortgage News*, March 21, 2005, p. 4). Far from being beyond the realm of normal expectations, actors at the center of the bubble (who had much to lose if it burst) recognized a crash as a distinct possibility. This of course further deepens the puzzle of why, given this awareness, almost all the banks continued behaving so recklessly until it was too late. That puzzle is a central issue for future research on the crisis to investigate.

Financial Engineering and Instruments of Mass Destruction

Another explanation of the crisis focuses on the role of financial engineering innovations and the rise of exotic, highly complex financial instruments. For instance, Donald MacKenzie (2009, 10) writes, "The roots

of the crisis lie deep in the socio-technical core of the financial system."
There are several reasons why the growing complexity of financial products such as CDOs may have heightened risk or served to conceal the risk of subprime-mortgage-backed securities. Whereas standard mortgage-backed securities allowed issuers to construct predominantly AAA tranches from subprime mortgages, CDOs helped turn BBB tranches, tranches that were the first to lose in the event of default, into AAA CDO tranches. One argument is that this made CDOs especially dangerous while simultaneously making them appear less risky and more palatable (see MacKenzie 2009). Another argument is that CDOs were problematic because progressive layers of abstraction in instrument structures entailed a progressive loss of information (Gorton 2008).

We believe the data are not consistent with any strong argument that instrument complexity was a primary driving force behind the crisis (see Fligstein and Goldstein 2010). Contrary to the hypothesis that financial engineering drove ratings inflation, the most highly complex and innovative CDO instruments actually displayed greater constancy in their overall ratings composition than low-rated mortgage-backed securities. Data also show that these instruments turned out on average to be no more overrated than the underlying mortgage-backed securities on which they were built, at least as measured by the magnitude of the subsequent downgrades they experienced after the meltdown. CDOs actually tended on average to be somewhat less overrated than all of the more risky securities. This suggests that variations in overrating were related as much to the underlying quality of the mortgage debt as the complexity of the bond structure. In retrospect it is not surprising that there should be little overall difference in the performance of mortgage-backed securities and mortgage-related collateral debt obligations, since both were grounded in the same overarching housing bubble. In other words, the driving force behind the meltdown is that banks were producing trillions of dollars of mortgage-backed securities on the back of a housing bubble—not that they were doing so using ever more complex security structures.

Conclusion

In this account of the financial meltdown we challenge several conventional wisdoms that have taken hold. First, one of the "facts" that is already taken for granted by commentators of various stripes is that the banks that originated mortgages and packaged mortgage securitization never held on to the securities themselves. It is asserted that this perverse incentive made them more likely to take on larger risks since they could simply pass risk along the value chain. We show that, contrary to this view, almost every large originator and packager of mortgages held on to substantial numbers of mortgage-backed securities and that they increased their holdings dramatically after 2001. Simply put, they believed that they could control the amount of risk they held. The result is that most of these companies are either out of business, merged into larger banks, or are owned by the federal government.

Second, we present evidence contrary to the common assertion that the crisis was one that few people saw coming. We note that the presence of a housing bubble was widely discussed during the mid-2000s, and we cite several instances where bank executives and regulators at the center of the debacle expressed awareness of the risks.

Third, we argue against the idea that the increasing complexity and opacity of financial instruments, particularly CDOs, was a chief contributor to the mortgage-backed securities bubble and subsequent meltdown. We cite evidence to suggest that the most complex mortgage-related derivatives did not perform any worse on average than simpler ones backed by risky mortgages. All of these instruments were ultimately perched atop the same overarching housing bubble.

From the mid-1990s through 2007 all of the main market actors connected to mortgage securitization—the originators, the packagers, the wholesalers, the servicers, and the ratings companies—became not only larger but more concentrated. By the end, a small number of banks controlled at least 40 percent of the market in every segment of the industry, and in some market segments it was closer to 90 percent. Activity in separate product niches also increasingly condensed around the same dominant firms. As a result, the mortgage field was not an anonymous market scattered across the country but instead consisted of a few large firms.

In the end, the strategies these five dominant firms pursued created the conditions for the meltdown. Their lending strategies fueled and fed off the housing bubble, and they did so using mortgage products whose performance was premised on continued growth of that bubble. After 2004, the financial industry coalesced around high-risk mortgage lending as their primary cash cow. Subprime mortgages, which had been a relatively small business that extended credit availability to underserved borrowers, suddenly became a foundation of twenty-first-century finance capitalism. The complete collapse of the financial system and resulting recession have shown the folly of that strategy. The financial sector was saved by the government takeover of the GSEs and the bailout of the rest of the banking system. The Federal Reserve now is the largest purchaser of mortgage-backed securities.

In an ironic way, the mortgage-backed securities market has come full circle. The government created it in order to stimulate the housing market in the 1960s and 1970s. They were pleased to invent and support the market and do what it took to bring in private investment. But eventually, those banks expanded their activities into risky investments with borrowed capital. After the stock market crash of 2000, the Federal Reserve dropped interest rates dramatically. This created the conditions for a rapid expansion of the mortgage securitization market. Low interest rates gave banks access to cheap capital that they could lend to households and create mortgage-backed securities. It also effectively heightened demand for mortgage-backed securities from investors since yields on treasuries were so low. But by the end of 2003 the supply of raw mortgages had begun to run out. To fulfill secondary market demand, originator banks and conduit banks (increasingly the same people) needed to find a new mortgage market. The market they found was the subprime market, which turned out to be wildly profitable. In the end, almost all of the large players in the financial system came to own lots of mortgage-backed securities. The ones who did so by borrowing money cheaply found themselves in a liquidity crisis beginning in 2007.

Regulators and policymakers enabled this process at virtually every turn. Part of the reason they failed to understand the housing bubble was willful ignorance: they bought into the argument that the market would equilibrate itself. In particular, financial actors and regulatory officials both believed that the mortgage-backed securities markets could effectively control risk through pricing. For instance, the idea that banks could buy quasi-insurance in the form of credit default swaps was one of the arguments for allowing them to take on more leverage. If the market thought the risk of default was high, then the price of the credit default swaps would reflect that risk.

But perhaps most important of all was the fact that regulators such as Alan Greenspan failed to see how the industrial-scale infusion of credit brought on by securitization linked real estate markets together in new ways. Lenders pumped easy credit into zip codes with quickly appreciating housing prices because it satisfied the assumptions built into their mortgage products. This of course further contributed to the bubble (Mayer, Pence, and Sherlund 2009; Nadauld and Sherlund 2009; Herbert and Apgar 2010). As a result, housing prices that historically had been driven by local dynamics became linked via the lending strategies of the big firms.

It is no accident that the locus of this historic debacle was housing finance. Securitization was first developed in this area and was most mature there. Residential real estate also held special status of retaining value, allowing firms to justify risky practices as contributing to the American dream of home ownership. Perhaps most important, the MBS-fueled bubble was abetted by the ingrained myth that house prices always go up. When that idea proved to be wrong, the lives of millions of Americans were tragically shattered.

The two authors contributed equally to the ideas and research presented in this chapter. Goldstein was supported by a National Science Foundation Graduate Research Fellowship. The research was also supported in part by a grant from the Tobin Project. We would like to thank Lis Clemens, Jerry Davis, David Grusky, Paul Hirsch, and Mike Lounsbury for their comments on an earlier draft. We would also like to thank the reviewers of this volume for their comments. The opinions expressed represent those of the authors.

Notes

1. Globally linked worldwide financial markets had begun to seek out countries where various kinds of risk existed (for example, Iceland and Latvia) and sought to sell off financial assets in those countries. Some of these risks were caused by countries such as Great Britain, Ireland, and Spain emulating the U.S.-style housing bubble. Other countries, among them Greece and Hungary, were running huge current-account deficits. Finally, the slowdown in the U.S. economy had an effect on world exports, and countries such as Germany and Japan, whose economic growth depended on high exports to the United States, experienced an economic slowdown. Countries such as China and Poland, which were less exposed to any of these risks, fared better. As a result of the very different situations in different countries, these myriad effects have played themselves out in different ways in different countries.

2. The Federal National Mortgage Association (FNMA) is known as Fannie Mae, the Federal Home Loan Mortgage Corporation (FHLMC) is known as Freddie Mac, and the Government National Mortgage Association (GNMA) is known as Ginnie Mae.

References

Ashcroft, Adam, and Til Scheuermann. 2008. "Understanding the Securitization of Sub-Prime Mortgage Credit." Unpublished paper. New York Federal Reserve.

Baily, Martin, Douglas Elmendorf, and Robert Litan. 2008. "The Great Credit Squeeze: How It Happened and How to Prevent Another." Working paper. Washington, D.C.: Brookings Institution.

Barmat, Joan. 1990. "Securitization: An Overview." In *The Handbook of Asset-Backed Securities*, edited by Jess Lederman. New York: New York Institute of Finance.

Bhardwaj, Geetesh, and Rajdeep Sengupta. 2009a. "Did Prepayments Sustain the Subprime Market?" Working paper. St. Louis: Federal Reserve Bank of St. Louis.

———. 2009b. "Where's the Smoking Gun? A Study of Underwriting Standards." Working paper. St. Louis: Federal Reserve Bank of St. Louis.

Claessens, Stijn, Giovanni Dell'Ariccia, Deniz Igan, and Luc Laeven. 2010. "Global Linkages and Global Policies." *Economic Policy* 25(62): 213–18.

Davis, Gerald. 2009. *Managed by the Markets*. New York: Cambridge University Press.

Demyanyk, Yuliya, and Otto Van Hemert. 2009. "Understanding the Subprime Mortgage Crisis." *Review of Financial Studies* 24(6): 1773–81.

Federal Housing Finance Agency. (2004–2009). *Quarterly Housing Prices*. Washington: U.S. Government Printing Office.

First American CoreLogic. 2010. "New CoreLogic Data Shows Second Consecutive Quarterly Decline in Negative Equity." *Negative Equity Report*, August 26, 2010. Available at: www.corelogic.com/downloadable-docs/corelogic-q4-2010-negative-equity-report.pdf; accessed May 20, 2011.

Fligstein, Neil, and Adam Goldstein. 2010. "The Anatomy of the Mortgage Securitization Crisis." In *Markets on Trial: The Economic Sociology of the U.S. Financial Crisis*, edited by Michael Lounsbury and Paul Hirsch. London: Emerald Group Publishing.

Fligstein, Neil, and Taekjin Shin. 2007. "Shareholder Value and the Transformation of the U.S. Economy." *Sociological Forum* 22(4): 399–424.

Furlong, Fred. 2008. "Drivers of Subprime Mortgage Delinquencies and Foreclosures." Synopses of Selected Research on Housing, Mortgages, and Foreclosures. Washington: Federal Reserve.

Gorton, Gary B. 2008. "The Panic of 2007." NBER Working Paper No. 14358. Cambridge, Mass.: National Bureau of Economic Research.

Herbert, Christopher E., and William C. Apgar. 2010. *Report to Congress on the Root Causes of the Foreclosure Crisis*. Washington: U.S. Department of Housing and Urban Development.

Inside Mortgage Finance. 2009. *Mortgage Market Statistical Annual*. Bethesda, Md.: Inside Mortgage Finance Publications.

Jungman, Michael. 1996. "The Contributions of the Resolution Trust Corporation to the Securitization Process." In *A Primer on Securitization*, edited by Leon T. Kendall and Michael J. Fishman. Cambridge, Mass.: MIT Press.

Kendall, Leon T. 1996. "An Era in American Finance." In *A Primer on Securitization*, edited by Leon T. Kendall and Michael J. Fishman. Cambridge, Mass.: MIT Press.

Krippner, Greta. 2010. "The Political Economy of Financial Exuberance." In *Markets on Trial: The Economic Sociology of the U.S. Financial Crisis*, edited by Michael Lounsbury and Paul Hirsch. London: Emerald Group Publishing.

Lewis, Michael. 1989. *Liar's Poker*. New York: Penguin Press.

MacKenzie, Donald. 2009. "The Credit Crisis as a Problem in the Sociology of Knowledge." Unpublished Paper. University of Edinburgh, School of Social and Political Science. Available at: http://www.sps.ed.ac.uk/__data/assets/pdf_file/0019/36082/CrisisRevised.pdf; accessed May 20, 2011.

Mayer, Chris, Karen Pence, and Shane M. Sherlund. 2009. "The Rise in Mortgage Defaults." *Journal of Economic Perspectives* 23(1): 27–50.

Mian, Atif R., and Amir Sufi. 2010. "The Consequences of Mortgage Credit Expansion: Evidence from the 2007 Mortgage Default Crisis." NBER Working Paper No. 13936. Cambridge, Mass.: National Bureau of Economic Research.

Mortgage Bankers Association. 2010. *Mortgage Delinquency Survey*. Washington, D.C.: Mortgage Bankers Association.

Nadauld, Taylor D., and Shane M. Sherlund. 2009. "The Role of the Securitization Process in the Expansion of Subprime Credit." Finance and Economics Discussion Series No. 2009-28. Washington, D.C.: Federal Reserve Board, Divisions of Research and Statistics and Monetary Affairs.

Nocero, Joe, and Bethany McLean. 2010. *All the Devils Are Here*. New York: Portfolio.

Purnanandam, Amiyatosh K. 2009. "Originate-to-Distribute Model and the Sub-Prime Mortgage Crisis." Unpublished paper. Available at: http://www.bus .wisc.edu/finance/workshops/documents/subprime_latestversion.pdf; accessed May 20, 2011.

Quinn, Sarah. 2008. "Securitization and the State." Paper presented at the Annual Meeting of the American Sociological Association, Boston (August 1–4).

Rose, Andrew K., and Mark M. Siegel. 2010. "Cross Country Causes and Consequences of the 2008 Crisis." NBER Working Paper No. 15358. Cambridge, Mass.: National Bureau of Economic Research.

Securities Industry and Financial Markets Association. 2010. "Outstanding U.S. Bond Market Debt." Excel spreadsheet. Available at: http://www.google .com/search?hl=en&source=hp&biw=870&bih=513&q=CM-US-Bond-Market -Outstanding-SIFMA-1.xls; accessed May 20, 2011.

Sellon, Gordon H., Jr., and Deana VanNahmen. 1988. "The Securitization of Housing Finance." *Economic Review* 73(7; July–August): 3–20.

Tett, Gillian. 2009. *Fool's Gold*. London: Little, Brown.

University of Michigan. 2010. *Survey of Consumer Sentiment*. Available at: http:// www.sca.isr.umich.edu/main.php; accessed June 29, 2011.

U.S. Bureau of Labor Statistics. 2010. *Current Employment Statistics Survey*. Washington: U.S. Government Printing Office. Available at: http://www.data.bls .gov/pdq/surveyoutputservlet; accessed June 30, 2011.

U.S. Department of Housing and Urban Development. 2009. *Report to Congress on the Roots of the Foreclosure Crisis*. Available at: http://www. huduser.org; accessed May 20, 2011.

Wilcox, James. 2008. "House Price Dynamics." Synopses of Selected Research on Housing, Mortgages, and Foreclosures. Washington: Federal Reserve.

Zuckerman, Ezra. 2010. "What If We Had Been in Charge? The Sociologist as Builder of Rational Institutions." In *Markets on Trial: The Economic Sociology of the U.S. Financial Crisis*, edited by Michael Lounsbury and Paul M. Hirsch. London: Emerald Group Publishing.

PART II

Economic Effects: The Labor Market, Income and Poverty, and Wealth and Housing

Chapter 3

Job Loss and Unemployment

Michael Hout, Asaf Levanon,
and Erin Cumberworth

Americans work for their living. Having a job is an economic and moral imperative for most Americans. The wages they earn fuel the rest of the economy. Employment begets the spending that begets more employment. In good times, it is a virtuous cycle reinforcing consumer-driven capitalism. Events like the financial crisis of 2007 and 2008 reverse the cycle, spinning the economy downward with a momentum that can be hard to break. Job losses reduce spending, which kills more jobs, reducing spending even more.

Government spending can, in principle, offset the declining private spending. Paying unemployment benefits props up the spending of laid-off workers; when paychecks disappear, unemployment insurance allows unemployed workers to pay their most important bills. Government can also stimulate the economy by allocating public money to firms and institutions that can put people to work and by employing people in government jobs. In extraordinary circumstances, government can—and did in 2008 and 2009—loan money to firms that might otherwise fail. The federal government is the key player in deficit spending. Most states are constrained by laws requiring them to balance their budgets every year (Martin 2008). Without authority to borrow, states cannot spend public money to offset hard times. In fact, because state and local governments are, collectively, such large employers, public layoffs, furloughs, and hiring freezes deepen and prolong recessions. Government employment consisted of 0.9 million fewer positions in May 2011 than it did a year earlier (U.S. Bureau of Labor Statistics 2011a).

The Great Recession of 2007 to 2009 played out these general principles of recession economics in every aspect, but with an uncommon intensity. The "housing bubble" burst, Wall Street stumbled, banks stopped lending, construction workers lost their jobs, sales of building materials and appliances plummeted, truckers and dockers lost their jobs, shops and restaurants suffered, tax revenues fell, governments furloughed police and teachers, and the downward spiral spun ever lower. Federal stimulus broke the fall, but according to the latest figures available to us (U.S. Bureau of Labor Statistics 2011a), as of May 2011, 15 million people were unemployed, almost 10 percent of the labor force.

This recession was deeper and more extensive than any other since the Great Depression of the 1930s. The nation's economy lost 8.5 million jobs from the peak of 138.1 million jobs in December 2007 to the trough of 129.6 million in February 2010. The unemployment rate more than doubled in those twenty-six months, from 5.0 percent to 10.4 percent. The most recent data show modest improvement through May 2011, to 131.8 million jobs and an unemployment rate of 9.1 percent (U.S. Bureau of Labor Statistics 2011a).

Early in the Great Recession, firm failures destroyed more jobs than did layoffs at surviving firms. When a whole company goes out of business, everyone, managers and workers, loses their job. Vulnerable workers and privileged ones alike have to find new work. As the recession spread, surviving firms selectively laid off workers to balance their books. Selective layoffs affected less-educated, African American, foreign-born, and younger workers more than others. After the government took action, the recession slowed, then ceased, and some new jobs began to appear. As noted already, employment still falls far short of pre-recession levels. Although some of the unemployed have found jobs, with five job-seekers for every job opening in May 2011 (U.S. Bureau of Labor Statistics 2011b), most are left out. As employers select on the usual criteria—education, experience, and length of residence—disparities between those less and more educated, experienced and inexperienced, and immigrant and native widen.

Our goals in this chapter are to quantify these generalizations about jobs and unemployment, inject some historical and sociological perspective into the discussion, and extrapolate from what we know to what we can reasonably expect in the near future. We will show how the scale of job loss in the 2007-to-2009 recession exceeded losses in the previous five recessions; the closest historical parallel is the "double-dip" recession of 1980 to 1982 (officially two recessions). Significant job loss preceded each of the last three recessions, while employment recovered significantly more slowly than production in those recessions. Unless jobs rebound at an unprecedented pace in the next twelve months, employment will not return to its 2007 levels for two or three more years. And there remains a significant risk of a second "dip." The 2010 elections showed that voters oppose any further public stimulus, so private-sector growth will have to be strong enough to offset the layoffs that will result from the antici-pated round of public spending cuts.

Gender issues have been an important part of the public discussion about the recession. Men's unemployment has been significantly higher than women's in this recession. Men outnumber women in hard-hit in-dustries such as construction and manufacturing as well as in blue-collar occupations throughout the economy. This industry and occupation dis-parity accounts for most, but not all, of men's suffering more unemploy-ment than women during this recession.

African Americans and the less-educated are exposed to more unem-ployment than other groups, even in good times; job losses for these two groups exceeded those for others between 2007 and 2010. Immigrants are generally disadvantaged in the U.S. economy, but in this recession it was American-born workers who had higher unemployment, perhaps because some immigrants left the country when they were laid off. We explore all these economic and demographic differences in employment and unemployment in the second half of this chapter. First, however, we discuss data issues and provide a historical perspective.

Data and Measures

We use several statistics to gauge the employment situation. Each mea-sure has its characteristic strengths and weaknesses; we use them all to make as complete an assessment as possible. The familiar unemploy-ment rate, the percentage of people in the labor force who are looking for work, is the simplest measure. It comes from the Current Population Survey, a representative sample of U.S. households and the adults living there conducted by the U.S. Census Bureau on behalf of the U.S. Bureau of Labor Statistics.

In good economic times, the unemployment rate is a reliable index of how well the economy is using the available human capital. During bad times, though, many out-of-work people give up looking for work. A person has to be either employed or looking for work to be counted in the labor force; so omitting discouraged job-seekers from the count dis-torts the unemployment rate, making the economy look better than it is. Then, as the economy starts to improve and employers resume hiring, the discouraged job-seekers reenter the labor force, and that distorts the unemployment rate the other way—the economy looks worse than it is. For that reason we supplement our analyses by tracking trends in the ratio of employed people to the total population in the prime working ages of twenty-five to fifty-four years. These data also come from the Current Population Surveys.

We measure four more aspects of labor-market conditions as well. From the Current Population Survey we extract a measure of underemployment—the percentage of employed people whose employers reduced their hours at work for economic reasons—and how long unemployed people have been out of work. From a survey of employers conducted in conjunction with the Current Population Survey, we obtain estimates of the number of nonfarm jobs in the economy.[1] Combining data from the Current Population Survey and the employer survey we estimate the ratio of job-seekers to vacancies.

In combination these measures tap the major aspects of labor-force conditions. The unemployment rate, underemployment measures, and employment-to-population ratio for the prime working years each assess the degree to which the economy is making use of the productive potential of the population. The number of jobs gauges employers' behavior more than workers' behavior. The duration of unemployment spells measures the degree of hardship that underutilization imposes on the affected individuals.

Historical Context

The American economy has experienced twenty-two recessions and recoveries since 1900. Figure 3.1 plots unemployment rates throughout that whole period, annually from 1900 to 1951 and monthly—for men and women separately—from March 1947 to May 2011. We document the close correspondence between recessions and unemployment by shading recession months gray.

The two major recessions, those from 1929 to 1933 and 1936 to 1939, that constitute the Great Depression stand out as the only time when unemployment exceeded 20 percent. The unemployment rate was just 5 percent in March 1929 and 25 percent—five times higher—four years later. Almost inconceivably, unemployment exceeded 10 percent every year from 1930 to 1942 (monthly data are not available before 1947). It was, by far, the worst economic period in the twentieth century. The New Deal proclaimed by President Franklin Roosevelt at his inauguration in March 1933 was a watershed in U.S. economic history because it supplanted free-market principles with policies and institutions designed to shock the economy back to growth and to manage it with scientific principles that could prevent future collapses (Fischer and Hout 2006, 126–29).

Prior to the 1929 collapse, the economy grew and recessed in rapid succession; periods of expansion averaged less than two years (twenty-three months) from recession low point to recovery high point.[2] Since

Figure 3.1   Unemployment Rate by Year and Gender, 1900 to 2011

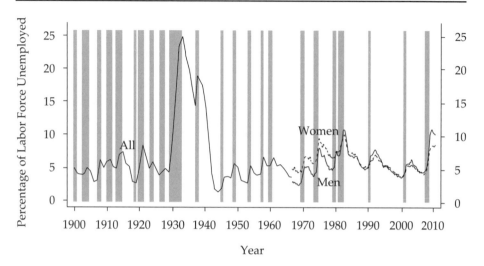

Source: Authors' compilation. Annual data for 1900 to 1930, Romer (1986); 1931 to 1947, Fischer and Hout (2006); 1947 to 1967, King et al. 2010. Monthly data since March 1967, five-month cubic moving average, shown for men and women separately (U.S. Bureau of Labor Statistics 2011c).
Notes: Vertical gray lines show recession periods, as identified by the National Bureau of Economic Research's Business Cycle Dating Committee.

1960, ups have won out over downs; periods of growth have lasted longer while the recessions have been far less frequent; the average time span from trough to peak is almost six years (seventy-one months). Macroeconomic policy, regulatory powers to carry out that policy, and the ever-greater sophistication of the scientific management tools available to the Federal Reserve Board (an institution created by New Deal reforms) tamed the boom-bust tendencies of market capitalism. During this era of macroeconomic policy, the unemployment rate rose above 10 percent only twice: from November 1982 to June 1983 (except May 1983), and then from January to March 2010.

Calling the recent recession of 2007 to 2009 "the Great Recession" attests to how exceptional it has been in both the suddenness of the economic collapse and the long duration of its employment consequences. Unemployment more than doubled, from 4.5 percent to 10.6 percent, in twenty-six months from the onset of recession in November 2007 to the peak unemployment of January 2010. In the only other period of unemployment greater than 10 percent, between November 1979 and January 1983, it took thirty-eight months for unemployment to double from 5.6 percent to 11.4 percent. A year after the peak unemployment of the recent recession, the rate was only 1.5 percentage points below the peak, whereas by January 1984 the unemployment rate was 2.6 percentage points below the peak.

The ratio of unemployed persons to job vacancies can give an indication of how quickly the labor market might rebound. If there are relatively few unemployed persons per vacancy, then unemployment is likely to decrease quickly. A high ratio of unemployed persons per vacancy is a bad sign. The most recent data available, for April 2011, show 4.6 unemployed persons per vacancy—a very bad sign. A decade ago, before the 2001 recession began, there was one unemployed person per job vacancy; during that recession, the ratio of seekers to vacancies climbed to 2.9. After an extended period of "jobless recovery," there were 1.5 unemployed persons per vacancy in the summer of 2007. There were 2.5 job-seekers per vacancy in the recession summer of 2008 and a historic 6.9 when the recession bottomed out in June 2009. Despite recovery in economic output, job creation continues to lag.

Unemployment and job-seeker data are important measures of labor market conditions, but both reflect the frustrations of active job-seekers. Out-of-work people who have given up looking are omitted from unemployment and job-seeker data. The ratio of employed persons to total population in the prime working ages between twenty-five and fifty-four years old is more comprehensive. We refer to it as the prime-age employment ratio here. In figure 3.2 we plot the trends in this indicator, separating men and women. Norms and expectations for women's work have changed so much since 1948 that the picture is just clearer if we consider men and women separately.[3]

In November 2010, 80 percent of prime-working-age men were employed, down from 88 percent before the recession. At no other time since 1948 has male prime-age employment been so low, nor has it ever fallen as much as eight percentage points during a recession before. A drop in men's prime-age employment ratio is to be expected during a recession; it has dropped during each recession in the postwar era. The surprise in figure 3.2 is in the recovery periods. Only once since 1948 did the men's prime-age employment ratio recover to pre-recession levels—and never since 1970. Each successive recession has been like a hammer driving men's employment down another notch. From its peak of 96 percent in March 1953, men's prime-age employment has fallen to 80 percent in the most recent data. Men got back to work during most recovery periods, but even during the longest growth periods, from 1983 to 1989 and from 1991 to 2001, employment did not fully recover to where it had been at the peak of the previous growth period. The American economy kept generating more jobs in each growth period, but the population grew, and women were entering the labor force in record numbers. Consequently, men's prime-age employment ratio had fallen from 96 to 88 percent before the 2007-to-2009 recession began.

Figure 3.2   Prime-Age Employment Ratio by Year and Gender, 1947 to 2011

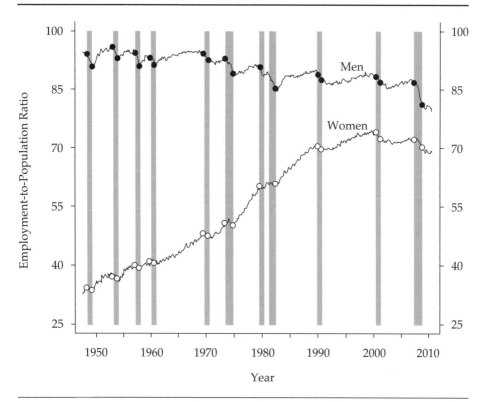

Source: Authors' calculations based on data from U.S. Bureau of Labor Statistics (2011c).
Notes: Vertical gray lines show recession periods, as identified by the National Bureau of Economic Research's Business Cycle Dating Committee.

Women's historic rise in employment throughout the postwar period halted during the first decade of the twenty-first century and fell sharply during the 2007-to-2009 recession. Women's prime-age employment ratio rose from 33 percent in 1948 to 74 percent in late 1999 and early 2000. Recessions during that half-century led to brief pauses in the upward trend, and growth periods resulted in gains beyond women's previous high points. Comparing Januaries at the beginning of each decade, we see that women's prime-age employment ratio rose six percentage points from January 1950 to January 1960, eight percentage points in the 1960s, twelve percentage points in the 1970s, nine percentage points in the 1980s, and three percentage points in the 1990s. In its first reversal in sixty years, women's prime-age employment ratio decreased four percentage points between January 2000 and January 2010.

To bring the current recession into sharper historical focus, we transform the prime-age employment ratios and time line to measure employment relative to the onset of each recession. In figure 3.3 the vertical axis arrays each month's prime-age employment ratio as a percentage of what it was when the recession started—they are all at zero the first month of the recession (month 0). The horizontal axis shows the time elapsed starting with six months before the recession (scored –6) and incrementing each month thereafter up to forty-eight months after the recession began. As in figure 3.2, we keep the men and women separate. The lines are black during the recessions and gray in other months. The aim of this figure is to show the 2007-to-2009 recession in relation to two other recessions: the 1980-to-1982 "double-dip" recession (the second worst recession since the Great Depression) and the 2001 "jobless recovery" recession (the one before the 2007-to-2009 recession).

For men the 2007-to-2009 recession combined the depth of the 1980-to-1982 recession with the jobless recovery of the 2001 recession. Men's prime-age employment ratio actually fell faster in the first "dip" of the 1980-to-1982 recession than during an equal interval of the 2007-to-2009 recession—2.4 percent in 1980 compared with 1.2 percent by August 2008. The first nine months of the 2001 and 2007-to-2009 recessions are virtually identical in this respect. But whereas the 1980 and 2001 recessions ended there, the 2007-to-2009 went into freefall. Men's prime-age employment ratio dropped from 1.2 percent below its pre-recession level to 6.9 percent below it in the second nine months of the recession.

When the 1980 recession ended in July, men's prime-age employment recovered somewhat, although it never got all the way back to the pre-recession level. When the economy took its second dip into recession a year later, in July 1981, men's prime-age employment ratio went into a dive almost as steep as in the recent recession (note how the two lines are almost parallel except for a brief break in the later line in the summer of 1982). The ratio declined from 89.2 percent to 85.4 percent (from 1.8 percent before pre-recession levels to 5.9 percent below). It continued downward until March 1983, when it began rising as rapidly as it fell. After four years of double-dip recession and recovery, men's prime-age employment ratio stood at 87.6 percent, 3.5 percent below its pre-recession level.

Today's partisan debates attribute the 1983-to-1984 recovery to the "Reagan tax cuts" of 1981. It is just as likely that the keys were the first housing bubble sparked by the deregulation of the savings and loan industry, and a recovery in manufacturing.[4] Two innovations contributed to the manufacturing recovery. The minivan, introduced by Chrysler under the names Dodge Caravan and Plymouth Voyager in 1984, was a huge commercial success for U.S. automakers. The personal computer, first on the market in the late 1970s but mass-marketed beginning in

Figure 3.3   Prime-Age Employment Ratio by Months Since Recession Began, Gender, and Recession: Selected Recessions

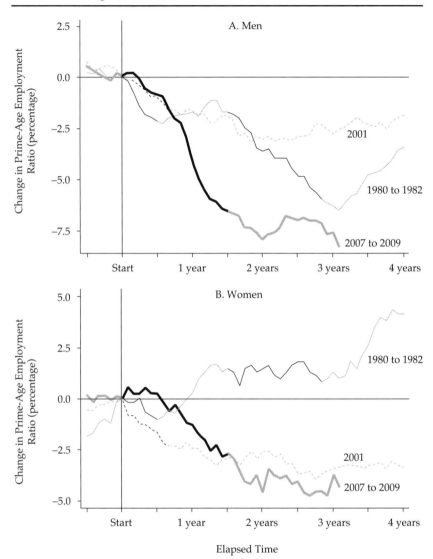

Elapsed Time

Source: Authors' calculations based on figure 3.2 using data from U.S. Bureau of Labor Statistics (2011c).
Note: The black segment of each line shows the prime-age employment during the recession; the gray segment of each line shows prime-age employment before and after the recession. Recession dates are determined by the National Bureau of Economic Research Business Cycle Dating Committee.

1981 with IBM's 5150 PC, sparked manufacturing employment as the products of dozens of companies took off in 1983. Workplace computer use expanded from 25 percent to 50 percent of workers between 1984 and 1994 (see Card and DiNardo 2007, 738, figure 1). We will return to a discussion of manufacturing employment in the next section.

In May 2011, forty-one months after the recession began, men's employment picture is quite mixed and the fear is that, for men at least, this recovery may be as "jobless" as the recovery following the 2001 recession was. Twice now, winter has brought signs of hope for men's employment. Men's prime-age employment ratio rose from its low point of 80.4 in December 2009 to 81.3 in April 2010, only to fall back to 80.5 by November 2010. It then climbed back up to 81.6 percent in February 2011 but has not changed significantly since. The private sector seems to be recovering slowly; private nonfarm employment was 1.7 million higher in May 2011 than in May 2010. But austerity in government is counteracting private gains; public employment was 0.9 million less in May 2011 than in May 2010.

The 1980-to-1982 recession barely interrupted the rise in women's prime-age employment. It declined one percentage point during the first dip in 1980, quickly recovered and superseded pre-recession levels, leveled off during the second dip, and resumed its climb in the thirty-seventh month, just as men's did. The 2001 and 2007-to-2009 recessions were very similar for the women. Following the 2001 recession, for the first time on record, women's prime-age employment ratio failed to return to pre-recession levels. In the current recession, women's prime-age employment did not start falling until the sixth month; it then fell for the rest of the recession and six months thereafter before leveling off. It is now 4.5 percent below pre-recession levels and is showing no signs of rebounding, making this the second jobless recovery in a row for women.

The gender gap noted earlier is clear in these data as well. Men's prime-age employment has hovered between 7.25 and 7.75 percent below pre-recession levels since the recovery began; women's employment has hovered between 4.0 and 4.5 percent below pre-recession levels since the recovery began.

Unemployment is persisting not only for the economy as a whole but also for individual workers. This might well be the defining difference between the Great Recession and others since World War II ended. In the four recessions between 1977 and 2001, workers were out of work an average of nine weeks at the depths of the recession—slightly less in the 1977 recession and slightly more in the 1983 recession, but the average of nine weeks is a good benchmark. In January 2010, unemployed Americans had been out of work an *average* of twenty-one weeks—five months. The consequences of long-term unemployment are far greater than those of short-term unemployment. People exhaust their savings and credit; some lose their homes. Research on past recessions by the sociologist Markus Gangl (2006) showed that the unemployed, especially those just starting their careers, bear a "scar of unemployment" that lasts for years. They fall behind while others gain experience, many desperately settle for work that requires less skill than they have, and few ever catch up, in terms of the accumulated earnings and savings, with their peers who were not unemployed. In chapter 5 (table 5.1) of this volume, Edward N. Wolff, Lindsay A. Owens, and Esra Burak estimate that, in 2009, 14 percent of Americans were behind on their mortgage and 5 percent were "delinquent." Although the data do not link these statistics to unemployment directly, the difficulties of the unemployed homeowner are manifest.

Economic Sectors and Occupations

The construction industry and the manufacturing firms that support it were ground zero for this recession—which of course makes sense, given the role of the housing bubble and subprime mortgages in the onset of the recession. People buy houses on credit; home builders borrow to build. As the defaults put pressure on the banks, lending decreased. Home builders and home buyers found loans much harder to get. Borrowing grief quickly translated to employment grief for the workers in construction. Manufacturing followed close behind as sales of durable goods to fill houses also slowed dramatically.

Evidence given in figure 3.4 bears out our expectations. Note that we "telescope" the line to highlight recent experience without giving up the perspective of past experience.[5] The construction industry has a strong seasonal component; unemployment in construction rises every winter, when bad weather slows building in most of the country. The U.S. Bureau of Labor Statistics removed these seasonal variations from the data. In good times like July 2006 to June 2007, unemployment in construction hovered around 7 percent. As the recession kicked in through the winter of 2007-to-2008, unemployment in construction was a point or two higher each month than it had been the same month a year earlier. Then through the fall of 2008, the bottom fell out of construction. November 2008 was as bad as February 2008; 19 percent of construction workers were out of work when President Barack Obama took office in January 2009. Through 2009 and 2010 unemployment in construction continued upward, to 23 percent by November 2010.

Construction work is always precarious. Unemployment in this industry ran higher than in other industries in good times and bad throughout the forty-three years shown in the figure. In early 2007, even while the rest of the economy was healthy, unemployment in construction increased from 8 to 9 percent in the twelve months before the recession.

Figure 3.4   Unemployment Rate by Year and Current or Most Recent Industry, 1967 to 2010

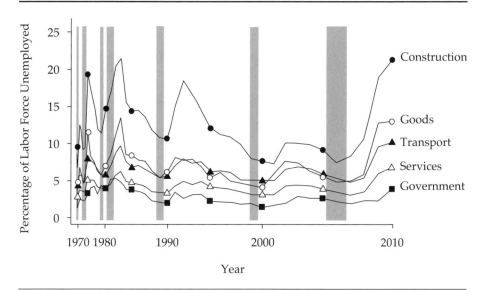

Source: Authors' calculations based on data from King et al. (2010).
Notes: Vertical gray lines show recession periods, as identified by the National Bureau of Economic Research's Business Cycle Dating Committee. Time line is number of months since March 1967, squared.

Double-digit unemployment rates among construction workers are not unprecedented. The recessions in 1973 to 1975, 1980 to 1982, and 1990 to 1991 brought construction unemployment rates over 15 percent. Reviewing those in some detail can be instructive. After cresting at 19 percent in March 1975, the last month of the 1973-to-1975 recession, unemployment in the construction industry eased somewhat, to 12 percent, by the fall of 1978. It then began rising again, even though the economy as a whole was in a growth period, and reached 14.6 percent in January 1980. Then the first dip of the 1980-to-1982 recession drove construction unemployment higher, to a peak for this time frame of 21.9 percent in February 1983. The lengthy 1980s recovery cut construction unemployment in half, but not below 10 percent. Then the next recession began in July 1990. Construction unemployment went back up to 14.5 percent during that recession and continued upward after it. Construction employment finally began to recover in the summer of 1991, embarking on a long period of improvement that ended with 7.7 percent unemployment in March 2001. Now we know that the relatively good times in construction reflected, at least partly, the false growth of the housing bubble. But it was most welcome at the time.

Manufacturing employment and unemployment are even more tightly tied to the business cycle than construction unemployment. Despite the historic decline in manufacturing employment as a fraction of total employment, it still rides the economic waves in sync with American production overall. In all but one of the recessions covered here, unemployment in the goods-producing industries began rising within a month of the onset of the recession. It also tends to decline as soon as the recession ends, but the jobless recovery of 2001 and the 2007-to-2009 recession have been exceptions. In 2001 manufacturing unemployment continued to rise until three months after the end of the recession. In 2010 it leveled off at the end of the recession, but it did not recede from the recession high until January 2011.

Unemployment in the goods-producing sector is very worrisome for the whole economy. Workers have been losing access to manufacturing jobs for almost forty years. Mechanization of production and foreign competition have put steady downward pressure on employment in U.S.-based manufacturing. When, in October 2008, candidate Obama said that most of Michigan's prime jobs were not coming back, manufacturing unemployment had risen from 4 to 7 percent. By the time he took office three months later, it was 11 percent; it crested at 13 percent in March 2009.

American industry continues to produce goods—it just uses fewer workers to do it. In 2007, during the eleven months before the recession and the first month of it, the value added by U.S. manufacturing was $1.7 trillion, an all-time high. Thirty years earlier, roughly the peak of U.S. manufacturing power, value added was $661 billion.[6] But U.S. firms produced their much bigger 2007 output with 4.8 million fewer workers than manufacturing firms employed in 1977. In other words, in 2007, American plants were producing 157 percent more with 26 percent fewer workers. Regardless of whether you call it a result of mechanization or productivity rises, it was still more output by fewer people.

Trade, transportation, and utilities workers depend on manufacturing to some extent and layoffs in those sectors echo those in manufacturing to some extent. But those who exchange and move goods can find employment moving imported goods, too. They perform a variety of other services as well, including handling used goods. Their unemployment rate plateaued at 8 percent, compared to 12 percent among those in the goods-producing industries. Workers in private and public service industries were substantially less likely to be laid off during the recession. Unemployment of government workers remained below 5 percent. Government workers are exposed to significant risk, though, as government revenues continue to lag and "deficit hawks" insist on more and more reductions in public employment.

An analysis of unemployment by occupation reinforces the impres-

Figure 3.5   Unemployment Rate by Year and Current or Most Recent Occupation, 1967 to 2010

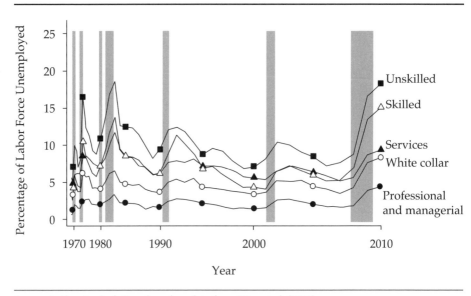

Source: Authors' calculations based on data from King et al. (2010).
Notes: Vertical gray lines show recession periods, as identified by the National Bureau of Economic Research's Business Cycle Dating Committee. Time line is number of months since March 1967, squared.

sions gleaned from examining industry differences (see figure 3.5). But whereas industry data cover everyone who works in an establishment that makes a given kind of product or provides a specific kind of service, occupation data combine people who do similar things regardless of where they do them. Thus, although a plant manager, skilled worker, and janitor at an auto factory are all in a goods-producing industry, they are classified in three different occupations. In some recessions, the rank order of unemployment rates corresponds to the socioeconomic status—the pay and credentials—of the occupations. In the 2007-to-2009 recession, the rank order of unemployment in the skilled building trades and of that in goods production reorder switched. Skilled construction and repair workers and skilled and semiskilled production workers were laid off in significantly greater proportion than were less-skilled workers in sales, clerical, and manual services such as driving, cleaning, landscaping, and personal services. Managers, professionals, and semiprofessionals experienced a rise in unemployment, from 2.5 to 5.3 percent between March 2008 and March 2010. The managerial and professional workers were largely exempt from the initial spike in unemployment at the beginning of the recession. Unemployment among high-status workers has accumulated more recently. That suggests that managers and professionals were rarely laid off. Unemployment is accumulating for these kinds of workers by a failure-to-connect problem, meaning that young people searching for first jobs and people returning to the labor force after a spell of doing something else are not finding work.

The causes and consequences of each recession leave their marks on occupations and industries that differ over time.[7] Multivariate analysis shows that the 2007-to-2009 recession more closely resembles the fundamental restructuring that accompanied the 1980-to-1983 recession than any of the others. In the 1980s, the Ronald Reagan administration and Wall Street were seeking a new economic model, a shareholder model, which would free high finance from the industrial relations model that had prevailed since the war. In the postwar industrial relations model that held from 1947 to 1979, corporate CEOs were industrial relations experts who balanced the interests of shareholders, corporate management, labor, and local communities (Fligstein 1999). The new shareholder model privileged owners of a company's stock and created a market for corporate control—actions such as hostile takeovers, leveraged buyouts, or proxy challenges that could help increase value of the company's stock—mediated by Wall Street. In chapter 2 of this volume, Neil Fligstein and Adam Goldstein detail the consequences of that shift. The comparison of unemployment across recessions indicates that the 2007-to-2009 recession is distinctive in ways that signal further restructuring of the economy and that will mean even less manufacturing than now. Depending on the outcome of political debates about regulation, it might also feature less risk taking in the credit industries that construction depends on. After all, no one builds with cash on hand. Construction depends on loans, bonds, and tax dollars. If the funds are not available, the construction industry and its skilled blue-collar jobs may go the way of the steel and automobile industries.

Human Capital

Employers strongly prefer educated workers, a point they have demonstrated over and over by paying an ever-growing premium for college graduates, seeking H-1 visas for foreign college graduates, and seizing on other tactics to locate and hire educated workers. Thus we would expect them to protect their college-educated workers from being laid off in the recession. Yet accounts of the consequences of the recession in the popular media frequently have a storyline that this recession is hurting everyone, including the college-educated. This storyline is not totally without foundation, but it is misleading and overstated, as figure 3.6 shows.

The risk of being unemployed declines sharply as education rises. As unemployment spread through the economy during 2008 and 2009, the

Figure 3.6   Unemployment Rate by Year and Education, 1967 to 2011

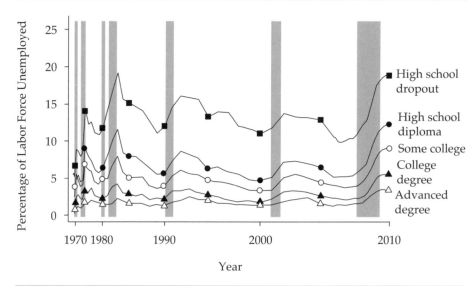

Source: Authors' calculations based on data from King et al. (2010) and U.S. Bureau of Labor Statistics (2011c).
Notes: Vertical gray lines show recession periods, as identified by the National Bureau of Economic Research's Business Cycle Dating Committee. Time line is number of months since March 1967, squared. Monthly data smoothed by locally estimated (loss) regression.

unemployment rate for each educational category rose more or less proportionally. But the baseline levels of unemployment were initially so high that the proportional increases raised unemployment most for the least-educated and least for the most-educated. So even though unemployment rose for the college-educated and even for people with master's degrees in business and other advanced degrees, high school graduates and high school dropouts bore a much greater unemployment burden. We repeated the analysis for men's and women's prime-age employment and found very similar patterns. In good times and bad, since data first became available in March 1967, prime-age employment has been significantly higher for college graduates than for people with less education.

An exception to the rule that education benefits workers showed up when we turned to the data on duration of unemployment. The published data do not include tabulations of duration of unemployment by education, so we made our own calculations from the public-use micro samples (King et al. 2010). In March 2010, unemployed college graduates had been looking for work an average of thirty-five weeks (eight and a half months), one week longer than high school graduates had been

Figure 3.7   Unemployment Rate by Year and Race and Ethnicity, 1967 to 2011

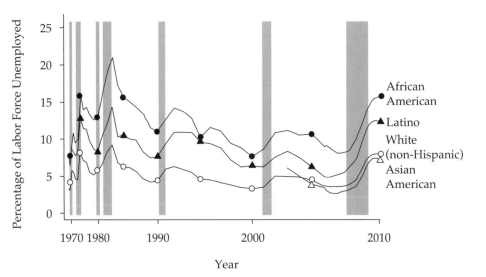

Source: Authors' calculations based on data from King et al. (2010) and U.S. Bureau of Labor Statistics (2011c).
Notes: Vertical gray lines show recession periods, as identified by the National Bureau of Economic Research's Business Cycle Dating Committee. Time line is number of months since March 1967, squared. Monthly data smoothed by locally estimated (loss) regression.

looking.[8] In March 2009, college graduates and high school graduates alike had been searching on average for twenty-two weeks.

Race, Region, and Immigration

Unemployment among African Americans was substantially higher than among other racial and ancestral groups prior to the 2007-to-2009 recession and rose to the greatest height as the recession progressed (see figure 3.7). African Americans are the only group for which unemployment continued to rise through the last quarter of 2009 and into 2010. Unemployment data omit people who do not reside in households, which is important for assessing racial and ancestry differences because these groups differ a great deal in the propensity to live somewhere other than a household. According to the sociologist Bruce Western (2006), that is especially true of the prison population. Roughly 80 percent of prisoners would be in the labor force if they were not incarcerated. African American men, in particular, are affected (Western 2006). So these data, stark as they are, understate how exceptionally high black non-employment is.

In addition, education unfortunately has substantially less return for African Americans than for other American workers. Unemployment is lower for African American college graduates than for African Americans with some college or only a high school diploma, so some return is visible. But multivariate analysis of the data indicates that a college degree gives white and Asian American workers twice the protection against unemployment (called an employment risk premium) than African Americans get.

Immigrants are an essential part of the American labor market, roughly one-sixth of America's workforce (U.S. Bureau of Labor Statistics 2011a). Immigrant workers are more likely than native-born workers to have both very high skills and low skills. Our calculations based on the American Community Survey show that nearly equal percentages of native and foreign-born workers have college degrees or higher (32 percent of natives and 30 percent of immigrants), but natives are far less likely than foreign-born workers to have no credentials (7 percent of natives and 27 percent of foreign-born).[9]

The recession hit foreign-born workers significantly sooner than native-born workers. The unemployment rate for foreign-born workers reached 10 percent exactly twelve months before it reached that milestone for native-born workers. But the gap closed during 2009; the latest data show foreign-born and native workers with the same unemployment rate. As shown in figure 3.8, the nativity difference is really limited to the least-educated. Native-born high school dropouts had the highest unemployment before and during the recession; foreign-born high school dropouts had practically the same unemployment rate as high school graduates before the recession, experienced dramatic rises in the winter of 2008 and again in the winter of 2009, and are once again unemployed at the same rate as high school graduates in the most recent data. The spike in the winter of 2009 was particularly sharp; the unemployment rate for foreign-born workers with less than a high school education rose from 7 to 16 percent between July 2008 and January 2009.

These trends reflect to some degree the industries that less-educated immigrants are concentrated in: services, construction, and agriculture. Construction and agriculture are seasonal; unemployment rises seasonally in both even during good times (note how high unemployment was for this group in January 2006 and January 2007). Another factor is probably operating too. We cannot quantify it in a single data set, but by triangulating the data in figure 3.8 with data on the size of the undocumented foreign-born population, we can make the reasonable guess that many undocumented immigrants from Mexico, and maybe from other countries, left the United States rather than stay here when they couldn't find work. The Department of Homeland Security's report of January 2010 (Hoefer, Rytina, and Baker 2011) estimated that the number of unauthorized immigrants living in the United States decreased from 11.6

Figure 3.8   Unemployment Rate of Persons with High School Education or Less by Year, Education, and Nativity, 1967 to 2011

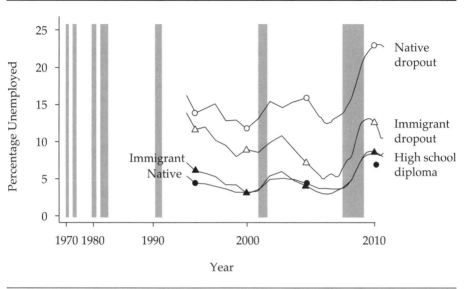

Source: Authors' calculations based on data from King et al. (2010) and U.S. Bureau of Labor Statistics (2011c).
Notes: Vertical gray lines show recession periods, as identified by the National Bureau of Economic Research's Business Cycle Dating Committee. Time line is number of months since March 1967, squared. Monthly data smoothed by locally estimated (loss) regression.

million in January 2008 to 10.8 million in January 2009. This is consistent with how undocumented immigrants behaved during previous recessions (Massey 2003). The demographer Douglas Massey argues, though, that this response is far less vigorous than it would be if the border were not so hard to cross. He argues that immigration reform could make it easier for Mexican immigrants to respond to hard times by returning to Mexico if they felt they could more easily return to the United States to work when the economy recovered. Under current immigration policy, unfortunately, they choose to scrape by on the U.S. side of the border for fear of not being able to get back into the United States. Ironically, a consequence of current policy is a larger unauthorized resident population than would be the case if the border were easier to cross legally.

Conclusions

The Great Recession of 2007 to 2009 was a jobs disaster that took unemployment to historic heights—a total of 8.5 million jobs lost, and an unemployment rate of 10.1 percent in October 2009. Any recession brings some job loss and boosts unemployment, but the number of jobs lost, the portion of the labor force unable to find work, the duration of layoffs and job search, and the ratio of job-seekers to vacancies were all at their postwar highs in the fourth quarter of 2009. In other recessions of the postwar era, job losses outnumbered job creations by a smaller margin, and laid-off workers found reemployment more quickly. The Great Recession has been a jobs disaster in large part because job creation came to a near standstill. Some observers blame this state of affairs on credit markets, lack of investor confidence, and the continuing outsourcing of jobs. Whatever the causes, two years into the recovery, the jobs outlook remained unsatisfactory.

Official definitions of recessions are pegged to broad measures of economic production; experts keep a keen watch on the gross domestic product. Meanwhile, workers worry about their jobs. Data on previous recessions imply that each additional layoff makes 2.1 additional workers nervous about their own jobs (Fischer and Hout 2006, 132–33). By that reckoning, in October 2009 nearly one-third (32.2 percent) of the American workforce was either out of work or worried about their jobs. So although economic production began to show signs of recovery in the fall of 2009, few people felt that was the end of the Great Recession.

Men were particularly hard-hit in the Great Recession, prompting some commentators to use the term "man-cession." Men were highly concentrated in the industries and occupations most affected by this crisis. When the housing bubble burst, construction halted. The promised returns to building new housing vanished and banks severely tightened credit for developers as well as buyers. Before the recession, men outnumbered women in the construction industry by 9.8 to 1 and in the building trades by 32 to 1.[10] As we have shown, unemployment was much higher in construction and the building trades than in other sectors. Manufacturing and finance, industries where men outnumber women, also took large losses.

The economic outlook is still quite mixed two years after the recovery began in the third quarter of 2009. The labor force appears to be moving in the right direction; unemployment decreased in the first quarter of 2010 and again in the first quarter of 2011, job openings rebounded in 2010, layoffs and discharges abated at the same time (U.S. Bureau of Labor Statistics 2011a). But the pace of improvement is too slow to restore security for American workers anytime soon. Between the first signs of improvement in February 2010 and the most recent data for May 2011, the recovery netted 1.80 million new jobs—roughly 120,000 new jobs per month. At that pace, it will take 73 months—until March 2016— to recover the nearly 9 million jobs lost in the recession. Nobody expects a constant rate of job creation, but this calculation indicates how inadequate the current rate of job creation is. Adding to concerns, the U.S. Bureau of Labor Statistics projects that the labor force will need to accommodate the aspirations of 12.6 million more people in 2018 than in 2008 (Toossi 2009). Baby boomers may well work longer than those projections assumed they would because the financial crisis flattened the resources they will need in order to retire—the value of their pensions and their home equity (see Wolff, Owens, and Burak, chapter 5, this volume). Factoring together slow job creation and the Bureau of Labor Statistics projection of labor-force size, we estimate that the unemployment rate will still be 7.2 percent or higher in March 2016 unless either job creation or retirements accelerate substantially.

The only other recession of this magnitude was the one from 1980 to 1982. It ended with such a strong recovery (see figure 3.3) that President Ronald Reagan's campaign ads crowed about "morning in America." Are there lessons to be gleaned from that experience that might help the nation repeat that success today? Construction and the building trades led the way out of that recession (see figures 3.4 and 3.5). The Reagan administration deregulated the savings-and-loan sector of the banking industry, allowing savings-and-loans to take on as much risk as commercial banks could. The upshot was a housing bubble, scandals involving questionable and even illegal lending, bankruptcies, a taxpayer bailout, and the incarceration of some executives. That is not the model to pursue. More sustained employment gains came from automobile and computer manufacturing. Everyone would welcome a breakthrough of that sort. But so far this recovery is relying on productivity gains—more output from fewer workers—and is thus creating too few new jobs.

The duration of the Great Recession and its differential impacts—hurting men, less-educated workers, immigrants, builders, and factory workers more than others—suggest that the American economy will have to restructure in order to make a full recovery. A major innovation in goods production along the lines of the automobile and computer innovations of 1983 and 1984 would be very welcome. No expert can say with confidence where innovation will come from—a popular new device, a bio-technology breakthrough, green energy. Noteworthy is that all of the prospects for a major job-creating innovation are very technical and likely to favor more-educated workers.

Other scenarios are, almost by definition, hard to imagine. But in thinking about it, recall that political economy played a major role in the exit from both the Great Depression and the recession of 1980 to 1982. Suppose the political conflict over regulating high finance on Wall Street or public finance in state capitols spawns a political movement. Employment restructuring in the 1980s was a continuation of the deregulation battles on Wall Street in the late 1970s and in banking and union-management relations in the Reagan era (Fligstein 1999). It would be shortsighted to count out political economy just because social science has no good predictive models of innovations in politics.

Prime-age employmentative, but it is not inevitable. Japan experienced a "lost decade" from 1991 to 2000. And the last ten years have been disappointing, too. In a sense, their economy has never fully recovered from the asset-price bubble of the 1980s (Krugman 2009).

Conjecture and speculation aside, the evidence to date suggests that it is very likely that another major restructuring of the U.S. economy will be the long-term historical significance of the Great Recession. But because the source and profile of that restructuring are not visible yet, the United States also risks sliding into its own lost decade.

Notes

1. Farm jobs are excluded for technical and historical reasons.
2. See National Bureau of Economic Research, "US Business Cycle Expansions and Contractions," http://www.nber.org/cycles/cyclesmain.html; accessed May 22, 2011.
3. The Bureau of Labor Statistics adjusted the data for seasonal fluctuations; we did no additional smoothing in this figure. We use seasonally adjusted data throughout, except in figures 3.7 and 3.8. The Bureau of Labor Statistics does not seasonally adjust data on Asians or immigrants, the subjects of those figures.
4. The bubble burst in 1988, resulting in bank failures and federal bailouts that transferred the debt to the taxpayers. Scandals involving bankers and politicians followed soon after. The economy went into recession in July 1990.
5. We accomplish the telescoping by numbering months beginning with March 1967 and then squaring that number. After squaring, the gap from one month to the next is two points bigger than the preceding gap, hence: $2^2 - 1^2 = 3; 3^2 - 2^2 = 5; 4^2 - 3^2 = 7; \ldots 30^2 - 29^2 = 59; 31^2 - 30^2 = 61 \ldots$
6. Authors' calculations from data posted on the website www.bea.gov/gdp byind data.htm, accessed January 6, 2011.
7. We present multivariate results on this online. See http://www.russellsage.org/greatrecession_onlineappendix.pdf.
8. The Current Population Survey asks this question of people who are unemployed at the time of the interview but not of discouraged workers. We limited the sample to persons twenty-five to sixty-four years old.
9. Authors' calculations from the 2005-to-2007 pooled data, persons age twenty-five and older in the labor force (King et al. 2010).
10. Authors' calculations based on the American Communities Surveys pooled data from 2005 to 2007.

References

Card, David, and John Dinardo. 2007. "Skill-Biased Technological Change and Rising Wage Inequality: Some Problems and Puzzles." *Journal of Labor Economics* 20: 733–83.

Fischer, Claude S., and Michael Hout. 2006. *Century of Difference*. New York: Russell Sage Foundation.

Fligstein, Neil. 1999. *Architecture of Markets*. Princeton: Princeton University Press.

Gangl, Markus. 2006. "Scar Effects of Unemployment: An Assessment of Institutional Complementarities." *American Sociological Review* 71: 986–1013.

Hoefer, Michael, Nancy Rytina, and Bryan C. Baker. 2011. "Estimates of the Unauthorized Immigrant Population Residing in the United States: January 2010." Washington: U.S. Office of Immigration Statistics.

King, Miriam, Steven Ruggles, J. Trent Alexander, Sarah Flood, Katie Genadek, Matthew B. Schroeder, Brandon Trampe, and Rebecca Vick. 2010. Integrated Public Use Microdata Series, Current Population Survey: Version 3.0. [Machine-readable database]. Minneapolis: University of Minnesota.

Krugman, Paul. 2009. *The Return of Depression Economics and the Downturn of 2008* (reprint edition). New York: W. W. Norton.

Martin, Isaac William. 2008. *The Permanent Tax Revolt*. Stanford: Stanford University Press.

Massey, Douglas S. 2003. *Beyond Smoke and Mirrors: Mexican Immigration in an Era of Economic Integration*. New York: Russell Sage Foundation.

Romer, Paul M. 1986. "Increasing Returns and Long-Run Growth. *Journal of Political Economy* 94(5): 1002–37.

Toossi, Mitra. 2009. "Labor Force Projections to 2018: Older Workers Stay Active Despite their Age." *Monthly Labor Review* 132(11): 30–51.

U.S. Bureau of Labor Statistics. 2011a. "The Employment Situation—November 2010." USDL-10-1662. Washington: Bureau of Labor Statistics.

——— . 2011b. "Job Openings and Labor Turnover—October 2010." News release. USDL-10-1685. Washington: Bureau of Labor Statistics.

———. 2011c. "Table A-7: Employment Status of the Civilian Population by Nativity and Sex, Not Seasonally Adjusted." Economic News Release, May 7, 2010. Washington: Bureau of Labor Statistics. Available at: http://www.bls .gov/news.release/empsit.t07.htm; accessed May 22, 2011.

Western, Bruce. 2006. *Punishment and Inequality in America*. New York: Russell Sage Foundation.

Chapter 4

Poverty and Income Inequality in the Early Stages of the Great Recession

TIMOTHY M. SMEEDING, JEFFREY P. THOMPSON,
ASAF LEVANON, AND ESRA BURAK

IN THIS CHAPTER we attempt to capture the effects of secular and cyclical forces on the incomes and economic well-being of Americans who are suffering through the Great Recession. Whenever useful and possible, we will compare this recession to earlier ones. Although our charge in this chapter is to examine how poverty and economic well-being have been affected by the Great Recession, one cannot of course understand such outcomes without looking at employment as well. We will therefore supplement some of the discussion in chapter 3, which focuses directly on the labor market and employment, with additional material that speaks to the implications of labor-market developments for poverty.

Despite the assertion of the National Bureau of Economic Research (2010) that the recession ended in mid-2009, unemployment continued to rise from 9.5 percent at the recession's "end" in July 2009 to 9.8 percent in November 2010, just a bit below the 10.1 percent peak in October 2009. The resulting increase of 5.1 percentage points in the unemployment rate since the previous peak in 2007 is by far the greatest of any recession since 1970, and the twenty-month period where unemployment is above 9 percent is also a post-Depression high. The drop in the employment-to-population ratio of 4.5 percentage points over this same period to the December 2010 level of 58.2 percent is the largest on record, almost twice as large as the decline in any other recession since 1970, and is still falling (U.S. Department of Labor, Bureau of Labor Statistics 2010b). These changes in employment have had a tremendous and continuing negative impact on the incomes and poverty rates of nonelderly Americans. Although unemployment dropped in early 2011 to 9 percent (as of January 2011), the consensus view is that unemployment will remain high over the near term.

The most recent poverty and income data we have on this phenomenon, which we draw on in this chapter, are from calendar year 2009. The full impacts of the recession will continue to deepen for working families, and we will need to await 2010, 2011, and 2012 data at the very least before a more complete evaluation can be made. Even if we are not able to capture the full impact of the recession in this chapter, our longer-term data show that this recession is liable to have a much larger negative effect on poverty and inequality than earlier recessions. Based on recent employment, poverty, and Supplemental Nutrition Assistance Program (SNAP, or Food Stamps) data, we do have some strong reasons to believe that poverty and inequality will rise in 2010 and 2011.

We begin with a discussion of emerging data on trends in the occupational employment patterns of workers that suggest both secular as well as cyclical effects on employment and on the types of jobs that will be available to low-skilled workers in the future and that therefore affect their poverty status. We then turn to the 2009 and longer-trend Census Bureau data on poverty and also poverty forecasts for 2010 through 2016. Next we move into income distribution, using the 2009 Current Population Surveys (CPSs), where we find inequality increasing in recessions and reaching all-time-high levels in 2009. This is in sync with similar trends in older but more complete data, such as that of the Congressional Budget Office. Because one cannot understand inequality in America without looking at income from capital as well as labor, we end the analytic part of the chapter with an assessment of income from labor and capital since 1989, with 2007 Survey of Consumer Finances incomes projected to 2009.

Poverty-Relevant Changes in Low-Skill Work for Men

The Great Recession is having a larger negative impact on many families than any other recession since the Great Depression because of a severe lack of jobs and employment (U.S. Department of Labor, Bureau of Labor Statistics 2010b, 2010c).[1] Long-term unemployment is at its all-time high, with 31 percent unemployed for at least a year, and 45 percent of the unemployed being in that state for more than twenty-nine weeks, according to the U.S. Department of Labor, Bureau of Labor Statistics (2010c). The current recession's impacts on overall earnings, poverty, household incomes, and their distribution are therefore likely to be stark when fully realized (Catherine Rampell, "A Growing Underclass," *New York Times*, January 14, 2010; Dynan 2010; Peck 2010).

Here, we focus on only some of the issues related to long-term unemployment and the ways it might affect poverty as related to the Great Recession. In the 1990-to-2007 period, working poverty was characterized more by low wages than by joblessness (Smeeding 2006). The picture has changed since 2007. Although low pay is still a problem, joblessness has taken the lead as the main cause of nonelderly poverty today. This is especially true among young adults under the age of thirty who are not employed or in school, including underskilled young men, women, and their children (whether living together or not). Poverty is rising among the young and least-skilled and will continue to rise in coming years. These young people not only are liable to suffer joblessness but also are more susceptible to incarceration, which has significant longer-term scarring effects on income and future employment (Western and Pettit 2010a, 2010b; Smeeding, Garfinkel, and Mincy 2011; Bell and Blanchflower 2010). Until the economy recovers enough to bring unemployment down to 5 percent or lower (which is unlikely to occur before 2014 or 2015, if then) and without some direct interventions to employ low-skilled younger workers, the young and underskilled will continue to do poorly in employment and in wages and therefore in their life chances (Peck 2010).[2] Richard Burkhauser and Jeff Larrimore (2011) also suggest that the main source of rising inequality in the current recession is male joblessness.

Youths and Undereducation

Employment reports by Kristie M. Engemann and Howard J. Wall (2010) show changes in employment for various demographic groups from the fourth quarter of 2007 through 2009. Overall employment fell by 4.7 percentage points over this period, and for men the drop was 6.4 percentage points. Employment fell most precipitously for the youngest workers (age sixteen to thirty who were not in school), while employment actually *rose* by 4.0 percent for those over age fifty-five. Employment also fell most for workers who were high school dropouts (a 7.5-percentage-point drop) and those with a high school diploma only (a 6.8-percentage-point drop) while employment for college graduates and those with higher degrees also actually ticked up by 0.4 percentage points over this period (see chapter 3, in this volume, for related results). The recession has been especially hard on young undereducated men, especially minorities. Over 15 percent of all high school dropouts are unemployed compared to 4 percent of college graduates (U.S. Department of Labor, Employment and Training Administration 2010). Nearly 40 percent of African American teens and over 30 percent of young black men age sixteen to twenty-four are unemployed, and that doesn't count those who have given up on finding work and have dropped out of the labor force (Sum et al. 2011).

By age thirty, 73 percent of undereducated men (those with a high school diploma, a GED [General Education Development] test, or less) are fathers, most of them have more than one child out of wedlock, and most of them are not living with their children. And 48 percent of all children born to the cohort that turned forty in 2004 were born to mothers with a high school degree or less (Smeeding, Garfinkel, and Mincy 2011, table 2). In addition, by age thirty, 50 percent of African American men will have been incarcerated at one time or another (Western and Pettit 2010a, 2010b) and will be forever scarred by the experience. With very limited work histories, the majority of young underskilled workers do not qualify for unemployment insurance (UI). Unemployed men under age thirty make up 39 percent of all men who are unemployed but only 20 percent of all UI recipients. Therefore, two-thirds of all young unemployed men missed out on more than $160 billion in UI aid in 2011 as the Tax Relief, Unemployment Insurance Reauthorization, and Job Creation Act of 2010 (TRUJCA) has extended UI benefits until the end of 2011 (Smeeding, Garfinkel, and Mincy 2011; U.S. Department of Labor, Bureau of Labor Statistics 2010a, 2010b; Congressional Budget Office 2011). For poor young men, the numbers look even worse. Furthermore, because they do not have custody of their children, low-income men are much less likely than poor mothers to receive income support benefits. Given this bleak picture to date, what are the chances for such men to find gainful employment and enter the middle class someday without additional education or training?[3]

Occupational Change

David Autor (2010a) has constructed a figure that we have amended to show changes in full-time annual employment from 2000 to 2005 and then from 2005 to 2009. Over this period, the labor market went from an overall 2 percent increase in full-time employment from 2000 to 2005 to a 6 percent decline from 2005 to 2009. The experiences in different occupations show wide differences, reflecting changes in labor demand as the economy changes, and many of these trends are secular, not cyclical alone. Employment rose and continues to increase for managers, financiers and businessmen, for professionals, and for education and health-care workers. Cyclical professions such as construction, transportation, sales, and office workers have shown the greatest losses mainly as a result of the recession. Cyclical losses have been high among production (manufacturing) work, but these drops are only reinforcing secular trends apparent since 2000. Personal-service workers, security workers, and cleaning workers have held their own with employment declines of less than two percentage points. Both secular and cyclical patterns of employment suggest that high-skill, high-education, and high-pay jobs are increasing—even in recessions—while production and construction jobs held by those in the middle class and the lesser-educated are falling precipitously. And the effects are much larger for men who have held jobs in contracting sectors, manufacturing, transportation, and construction than for women, who are mainly employed in expanding sectors such as health care and education, and whose schooling increasingly outstrips that of men of the same age (Nancy Folbre, "The Declining Demand for Men," *New York Times*, December 13, 2010).

Construction jobs may come back, though not for a long time. The building boom of the early 2000s has produced a surplus of housing and office space, and, despite tax breaks for new buyers that stimulated housing temporarily in 2009 and 2010, there are few younger families who are qualified to purchase a home (Edward L. Glaeser, "Children Moving Back Home and the Construction Industry," *New York Times*, February 16, 2010). A limited number of new construction jobs were created by the American Recovery and Reinvestment Act (ARRA), but most workers with these jobs are older and are just hanging on until retirement (Burtless 2009; Autor and Dorn 2009a). Lower-skill manufacturing is likely to decline even more in future years along with related clerical and office work, as manufacturing productivity and the use of technology requiring skilled workers continue to grow. Retail sales jobs may tick upward, but the long-term trend is down as Internet shopping continues to grow (Autor 2010b, figure 1). There is already some steadying, and likely some significant future increase, in the low-skill, low-education, "nonroutine" service sector as we emerge from the recession (Autor and Dorn 2009a, 2009b). But these jobs are unlikely to pay enough to support a family with children in a middle-class lifestyle ($40,000 to $80,000 annual income), even if both low-skill adults work full-time (see U.S. Department of Commerce, Economics and Statistics Administration 2010a).

Summary

In short, there appears to be a hollowing out of the middle in occupations, as growth occurs in the high- and lower-skill segments of the labor market. This hollowing out has been accelerated by the recession. Autor

Figure 4.1   Percent Change in U.S. Full-Time Employment, by Occupation, 2000 to 2005 Compared with 2005 to 2009

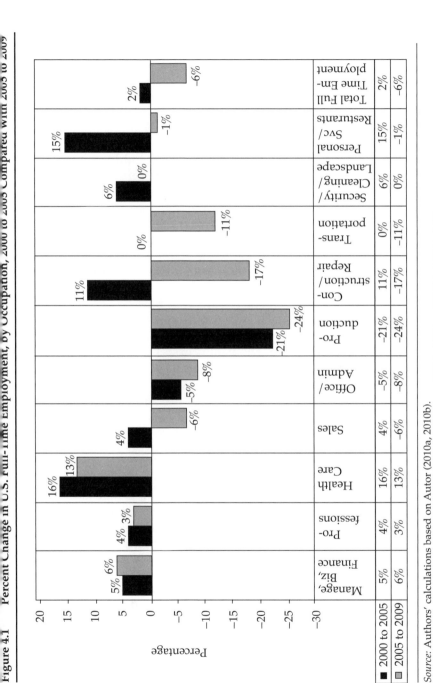

	Manage, Biz, Finance	Pro- fessions	Health Care	Sales	Office/ Admin	Pro- duction	Con- struction/ Repair	Trans- portation	Security/ Cleaning/ Landscape	Personal Svc/ Resturants	Total Full Time Em- ployment
2000 to 2005	5%	4%	16%	4%	-5%	-21%	11%	0%	6%	15%	2%
2005 to 2009	6%	3%	13%	-6%	-8%	-24%	-17%	-11%	0%	-1%	-6%

Source: Authors' calculations based on Autor (2010a, 2010b).
Note: The correlation between employment share changes from 2000 to 2005 and 2005 to 2009 is 0.67.
Manage=management; Biz=business; Admin=administrative; Svc=services

(2010b) and Autor and David Dorn (2009b) show strong evidence that aggregate employment demand has shifted over the last several years and surely over the last decade against low- and middle-skill, routine, task-intensive work (jobs disproportionately held by older workers) and toward the tails of the occupational skill distribution. They argue that both tails of the distribution are made up of service-sector jobs, such as retail clerks, administrative assistants, and registered nurses, which they describe as "nonroutine" and therefore not easily mechanized or exported. But these service jobs differ greatly in the skills needed to do them, the chances for job advancement, and pay and benefits. Others (notably Holzer and Lerman 2007 and Holzer 2010) argue that good middle-skill jobs (for instance, in welding and plumbing) will emerge as the economy gradually moves out of the recession over the next several years. If so, these jobs will be found in the service sectors on the bottom of figure 4.1. But in any case, the longer-term trends described in detail by Autor (2010b) are worrying because the traditional routes out of poverty and into the middle class for those with less education and skill are closing with the decline in manufacturing, construction, retail sales, and even in public-sector jobs.

With the huge spike in longer-term unemployment and the record number of unemployed who have been out of work twenty-seven weeks or longer (U.S. Department of Labor, Bureau of Labor Statistics 2010a), some experts are talking about the creation of a new "jobless underclass." These unemployment trends are likely to most greatly affect young workers with low skills (Sum et al. 2011; Smeeding, Garfinkel, and Mincy 2011; Peck 2010). Further, there is convincing evidence that the young, especially young men, are particularly susceptible to the negative effects of spells of unemployment and low wages well after their initial experience of joblessness (see Van Wachter 2010 for a summary of earlier studies). Economists calculate that we need 11 million to 12 million more jobs over the next five years to both reemploy the jobless and absorb labor-force growth. And we have barely turned the corner on the largest number of job losses since the Great Depression, with employment gains lagging and even flat for the last six months of 2010 (David Leonhardt, "Comparing Recoveries: Job Changes," *New York Times*, January 7, 2011).

We now turn to an assessment of the effects of these labor-market changes on poverty and income inequality during this recession with the recognition that the data on the full impact of the recession on earnings and household incomes are not yet fully visible. One thing that is clear is that the rise in poverty witnessed in 2009 is liable to be large again in 2010, even with the favorable impact of the temporary extension of unemployment benefits originally in the 2009 ARRA (Monea and Sawhill 2010; Sherman 2010).

Officially Defined Poverty

We begin with a review of the longest-running U.S. poverty measure, the official poverty series, through the periods of growth and recession from 1967 to 2009. Next we assess which groups suffer the most from the increase in poverty resulting from the Great Recession. Will poverty be experienced evenly across all regions of the United States? Will it soar mainly for disadvantaged groups, such as children, elderly people, and female-headed households? Or will the brunt of the income declines be experienced by every group in the Great Recession? Then we briefly shift to a discussion of poverty rates that takes into account noncash antipoverty programs that have expanded during this recession, especially refundable tax credits, Food Stamps, and other programs. These changes are in line with measuring resources according to the 1995 National Academy of Sciences (NAS)-type measures (see Citro and Michael 1995) as deployed in the U.S. Census Bureau's "Poverty: Experimental Measures" series, running from 2000 to 2009 (U.S. Census Bureau 2011; Short 2010).[4] We then examine the effects of taxes and benefits, including the 2009 ARRA, on poverty in 2009. Finally, we close the section with forecasts about how poverty is likely to change in 2010 and beyond.

Definitions of Poverty

The official definition of poverty takes money income before taxes and adds in cash transfers but does not subtract taxes or add in refundable tax credit or noncash incomes (figure 4.2). The attraction of the official series is to provide a longtime series where income and poverty are consistently measured. The poverty line is adjusted annually only for prices, so in 1960 it was just below half of median income, but by 1977 had fallen to 33 percent of the poverty line, and by 2000 to 27 percent of median income, where it was the same in 2007. It has risen slightly since then because of the recession's effects, which depressed earnings and jobs (Smeeding 2006 and authors' calculations). Despite the long-term falling level of the poverty line compared to national median and overall income growth, poverty has not been eliminated. Indeed, it looks as though poverty rates mirror the changes in the ratio of the poverty line to median income except in the late 1990s. The 11.3 percent poverty rate in 2000 was just about the same as the 1973 low point of 11.1 percent. But the poverty rate has risen almost continuously since 2000.

Moreover, these two lines begin to diverge in the early 1980s, when wage and earnings inequality begin rising, and have grown further apart in recessions and in booms since then. Rebecca M. Blank et al. (1993) suggested that poverty rates through the early 1990s were closely related to both employment and wage distributions, and our figure sug-

Figure 4.2   Official Poverty Rates and Ratio of Poverty Line to Median Income Across Recessions, 1960 to 2009

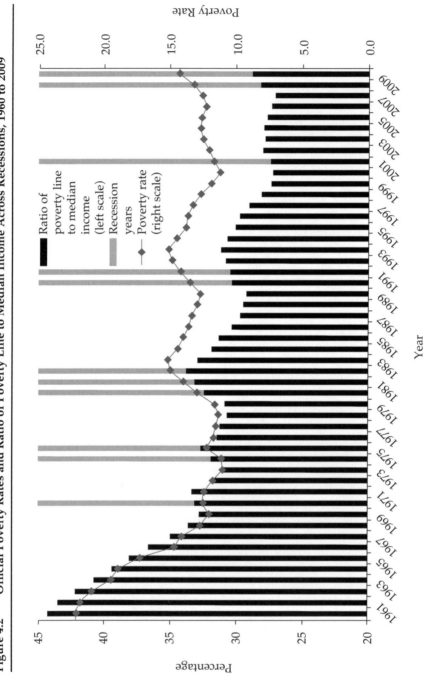

Source: Authors' calculations, based on DeNavas-Walt, Proctor, and Smith (2010), Smeeding (2006), and U.S. Census Bureau (2011).

gests that these differences, driven by the same factors, have been further strengthened since then, once again lending credence to the importance of the labor market and low-skill employment.

Poverty rates have spiked in every recession since 1967 and continued for one year or longer after the recession ended at the beginning stages of each of the last four decades (in 1970, 1973 to 1975, 1981 to 1982, 1990 to 1992, and to a lesser extent in 2001 to 2002). This recession appears to be similar to but longer and deeper than earlier recessions. By these measures the poverty rate was greatest in the early 1980s and 1990s so far, but these rates could easily be surpassed by the ongoing recession, should current poverty trends and predictions prove to be accurate. Labor-market trends, especially unemployment rates, wage growth, and patterns of wage inequality, are usually the main force behind changes in levels of poverty (Blank et al. 1993). The dramatic increase in unemployment during the Great Recession can therefore be expected to lead to increased poverty, just as with other past recessions.

Poverty Trends Among Regions, Ages, and Groups

Following the employment trends and especially the decline in manufacturing, transportation, and construction employment shown in figure 4.1, poverty rates increased most in the Midwest (from 11.1 percent in 2007 to 13.3 percent in 2009) and in the West (from 12.0 percent in 2007 to 14.8 percent in 2009). All regions experienced higher poverty rates in 2008 than in earlier years. Indeed, poverty has risen relentlessly in the Midwest, increasing from 9.0 percent in 2000 to 13.3 percent in 2009, reflecting the continual decline in well-paid manufacturing work (especially in automobile manufacturing, transportation, and related industries) shown in figure 4.1. Declining jobs in construction have been mostly experienced by the western states.

The recession does not seem to have increased the poverty rates proportionally among all vulnerable groups. Census Bureau data (DeNavas-Walt, Proctor, and Smith 2010) show that upward trends in poverty since 2007 were experienced by prime-working-age adults in all racial groups and by female-headed families and all other families with children. Children under age eighteen have been especially affected; their poverty rates rose from 18 percent in 2007 to 20.7 percent in 2009, while poverty rates have risen to 23.8 percent for children under age six, most likely owing to the poor employment and wage performance of their younger parents. Poverty rates increased most substantially for those without employment, those with less than full-time employment, and those who were unable to work at all. There was little or no change in poverty for families with at least one full-time, full-year worker

Figure 4.3   Poverty Rates Using Official Measure, by Education Level and Age

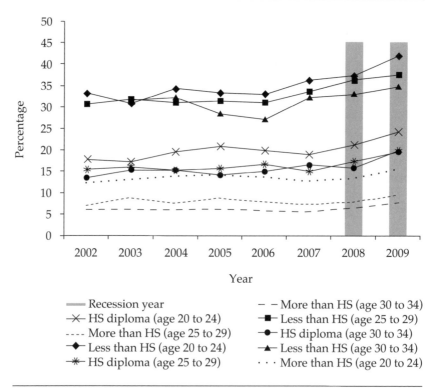

Recession year
—✕— HS diploma (age 20 to 24)
---- More than HS (age 25 to 29)
—◆— Less than HS (age 20 to 24)
—✳— HS diploma (age 25 to 29)

— — More than HS (age 30 to 34)
—■— Less than HS (age 25 to 29)
—●— HS diploma (age 30 to 34)
—▲— Less than HS (age 30 to 34)
· · · More than HS (age 20 to 24)

Source: Authors' calculations, based on U.S. Census Bureau (2011). Series not available before 2002.
Note: HS=high school.

(DeNavas-Walt, Proctor, and Smith 2010, table 4). And official poverty rates continued to fall among the elderly, reaching a fifty-year low of 8.9 percent in 2009. Numerous factors led to this result, including (but not limited to) indexation of Social Security benefits and higher employment levels among older workers.

Poverty Among Younger Adults

Most especially, poverty rates among young, single males increased during the recession, whereas rates for their female counterparts slightly decreased (DeNavas-Walt, Proctor, and Smith 2010). This trend closely corresponds with the unemployment and joblessness trends for men versus women in this recession. The increases were greatest among those who were not high school graduates, reflecting the joblessness figures and the drop in employment noted in the first section of this chapter. Indeed, when poverty rates are sorted by age and education level (see figure 4.3), clear patterns emerge. At the very top of the graph, poverty rates rise most steeply for those with less than a high school diploma, and twenty- to twenty-four-year-olds have higher poverty rates than the older groups. Clearly, high school dropouts do worse, no matter what their age, as all such persons age thirty-four and under are recording poverty rates of 35 to 43 percent. The poverty figures also exclude about 2 million incarcerated men, most of whom would be poor if they were not imprisoned. There are over 7 million adults in the United States in prison, on probation, or on parole, most with very poor labor-market prospects (Western and Pettit 2010a, 2010b). In addition, younger high school graduates (including those with GEDs) with poverty rates between 20 and 25 percent in 2009 also experienced rising poverty, as shown in the middle block of lines in figure 4.3. Those with more than a high school diploma had the lowest poverty rates (under 10 percent) other than the twenty- to twenty-four-year-old age group, many of whom are still in college and thus have low earnings.

And all of this increase in poverty took place despite the fact that there was an increase of 8.4 percent in young adults (ages twenty-four to thirty-five) living with their parents as well as an 11.6 percent increase in families who moved in with relatives in large part to avoid poverty. If these two groups instead lived alone, their poverty rates based on their own income would be 43 percent (Johnson 2010). And so it is the current and future job status of the less-educated and underskilled younger workers, parents and nonparents, whose poverty we are most concerned about, both in this recession and as we begin to move out of it.

How to Better Measure Poverty

Many experts feel that official cash income–only definitions and measures of poverty used in the official definition (figures 4.2 and 4.3) do not convey an accurate picture of poverty in the United States. They feel that the official definition of poverty overcounts people in poverty. While the official measure gives us a long-term perspective on poverty across recessions, it does not include the effect of several noncash and refundable tax credit programs that have greatly improved the situation of the poor in recent years. Other experts counter that the official poverty line is not adjusted for changing consumption patterns among lower- and middle-income households. A better definition of poverty that measures government efforts to fight poverty in this recession would also make consumption adjustments based on low-income expenditure patterns and account for taxes and near-cash benefits. The experimental poverty measures in figure 4.4 do both.

**Figure 4.4   Official and National Academy of Sciences Experimental
Poverty Rate Series, 1999 to 2009**

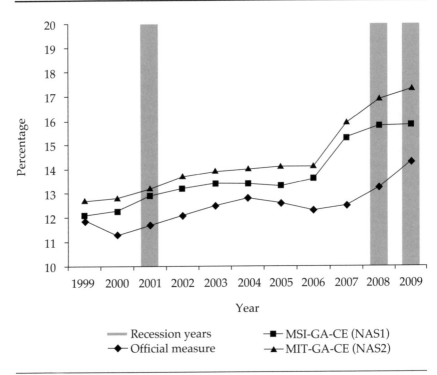

Source: Authors' calculations based on data from the U.S. Census Bureau (2011).
Notes: Medical care expenses subtracted from income (MSI) and medical care expenses in
the poverty threshold (MIT) include medical out-of-pocket expenses; NM (no medical)
does not. GA (geographically adjusted) includes geographic housing-price differences. All
experimental rates are based on incomes that are after-tax and noncash benefits and include the American Recovery and Reinvestment Act economic stimulus and recovery payments such as the "Making Work Pay" tax credits. They are based on thresholds that
change according to the consumer expenses of low-income households for the base
FCUM-CE (includes spending for food, clothing, shelter, utilities, and medical expenses
based on Consumer Expenditure survey definitions) poverty line used in the two National
Academy of Sciences poverty measures. This series is consistently defined only from 1999
to 2009 (see http://www.census.gov/hhes/povmeas/data/nas/web_tab5_povertythres
2009.xls). For glossary of abbreviations used see the appendix, "Definitions of Income
Measures."

In 1995 the NAS published a report, "Measuring Poverty," which argued for both a more up-to-date poverty line and an expanded income
definition that included noncash benefits and refundable tax credits. Following the NAS report, the Census Bureau provided a consistent series
of "experimental" poverty rates from 1999 to 2009 that followed these
guidelines.[5] The experimental rates, which cover only the current and

2001 recessions, include the expanded income definition and a 10 to 12 percent higher poverty line (compared to the official line) that increases with general population income growth but does not rise as fast as median income (and in fact fell with median income in 2009; see U.S. Census Bureau 2011). Adjustments in these poverty rates are also made for geographical cost-of-living differences, for medical out-of-pocket costs, for work-related costs including child care, and for transportation.

Figure 4.4 presents two series of these estimates with different medical-care adjustments. These measures either subtract actual out-of-pocket medical expenses (MSI) or build an allowance for expected expenses into the poverty threshold (MIT). Both of these estimates include geographic housing price adjustments to reflect cost-of-living differences across regions and states (GA). Both of the alternative series include a poverty line that changes with consumer expenditures by lower-income Americans (CE). We add the official poverty measure as well, for contrast. And we shade in the 2001 and 2007-to-2009 recessions for comparisons.

It is immediately clear that both of the NAS poverty measures are unambiguously above the official poverty measure. Using the NAS measures, poverty rates in 2009 were between 15.7 and 17.3 percent. Adjustments for out-of-pocket medical costs, whether included in the threshold (MIT—medical included in threshold) or subtracted from income (MSI—medical subtracted from income), produce poverty rates above the official rate.[6] The differences between the official and experimental rates grew steadily until 2009, when one series (the MSI estimates) of the NAS poverty measures remained flat from 2008 to 2009. This may reflect the reduction of the poverty line between 2008 and 2009, as 2009 consumption budgets tightened and fell in the midst of the recession and as medical expenses in the MSI measure were reduced due to falling incomes or forgoing care. Both sets of NAS estimates reflect the antipoverty effect of the ARRA.

A shorter consistent experimental series on children's poverty (2007 to 2009, but not shown here) is also available from the U.S. Census Bureau (2011) and suggests that the near-cash, cash, and tax income support system already in place plus the new ARRA efforts also helped reduce the rise in child poverty rates during the recession. Official child poverty rates increased from 18.0 to 20.7 percent from 2007 to 2009, but the experimental child poverty rates using the same methods as in figure 4.4 found a somewhat smaller increase in child poverty, from 19.1 percent in 2007 to 19.8 percent in 2009. This is encouraging news, yet child poverty still remains around 19 to 21 percent, whether the official or the experimental poverty measure is used. While it is not clear that the new Supplemental Poverty Measure will produce these same results, using improved experimental measures that reflect recent public antipoverty policy policies to boost benefits, and that reflect low-

Figure 4.5   Official Poverty Rate (1968 to 2009) and Poverty Rate After Taxes and Transfers, Using the Official Poverty Line Measure (1979 to 2009)

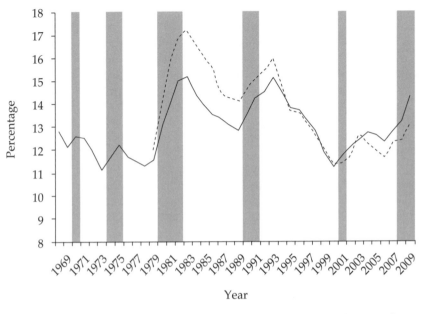

Year

―― Recession years   ―― Official poverty rate (cash income)

---- Net poverty rate (net income including taxes, Food Stamps, Earned Income Tax Credit)

Source: Authors' calculations based on data from Meyer and Wallace (2009, figure 2.1, 45) 1968 to 2006, and U.S. Census Bureau (2011).

income Americans' consumption expenses and the cost of earning incomes, will produce a more accurate and policy-relevant picture of poverty than does the official poverty measure.

The Longer-Term Effect of Taxes and Transfers on Poverty

Over the past thirty years, governments have reduced income taxes on the poor and have increased negative taxes like the Earned Income Tax Credit (EITC) and benefits such as Food Stamps. But low-income workers also pay payroll taxes. The census after-tax and near-cash benefit data did not begin until 1979 and, following the lead of Daniel R. Meyer and Geoffrey L. Wallace (2009), we have shown in figure 4.5 the effects of these taxes and benefits alone on poverty using the current poverty line (not the NAS-like experimental poverty line in figure 4.4). The results shown here are not adjusted for medical expenses or for work-related costs (child care and transportation). These estimates thus provide a longer-term picture of poverty changes and policy effects, which is useful but does not reflect any of the other changes recommended by the NAS, as explained earlier.[7]

From 1980 to 1992, the poverty rates including taxes and near-cash benefits (public housing and SNAP) were above the official measure because low-income people paid both federal income and payroll taxes, SNAP beneficiaries were fewer, and the EITC was far smaller than it is now. From the mid-1990s onward, the poverty rate after taxes and SNAP parallels the official poverty rate, driven mainly by economic cycles. And finally, after 2003, these benefits show slightly lower "net poverty rates" than the official measure, reducing poverty from the official level of 14.3 percent in 2009 to just over 13.0 percent.

Comparing the last two figures over recessions, it is clear that introducing a consumption-based poverty line that includes the cost of working (child-care and transportation costs), medical-care costs, and refundable credits and near-cash benefits makes a larger difference in overall poverty (figure 4.4) than one that counts tax credits and SNAP benefits only using the official poverty line (figure 4.5). The poverty rates for the experimental series show poverty rates above the official measure; the net poverty rates show rates below the official measure; but all types of poverty measures, with one exception, show increases during recessions. The unofficial measures also reveal how near-cash benefits and refundable taxes help reduce the recession's impact on the poor, a topic we now examine in some detail.

Effects of Automatic Stabilizers and Antipoverty Policy During the Recession

As suggested, the effects of the recession on poverty would have been much worse were it not for existing federal cash and near-cash income support programs and federal policy changes that boosted and stabilized incomes during the recession. For instance, the 2009 ARRA boosted UI outlays, leading to over $100 billion being paid out in total state and federal UI benefits in 2008 and nearly $160 billion in 2010 (Congressional Budget Office 2011, figure 3-2). UI benefits have also been continued for another fifty-two weeks, through the end of 2011, by TRUJCA.

SNAP benefits were increased by 14 percent on April 1, 2009, and are now as close to a universal safety net as we have ever come in this nation. In order to be eligible for Food Stamps, unit income has to be less than 130 percent of the official poverty line, and in the recession more than half of all states do not have liquid-assets-eligibility tests. We also know that SNAP rolls shot up by 24 percent from 2008 to 2009 and another 20 percent during 2010, so that 42 million Americans benefited from SNAP in October 2010. About one in eight adults and one in four children benefit from food and nutrition assistance (Jason DeParle and Robert Gebeloff, "Food Stamp Use Soars, and Stigma Fades," *New York Times,* November 28, 2009; Isaacs 2010a). In 2008, we spent $35 billion for SNAP, but outlays for SNAP were $70 billion by 2010, and they are forecast to reach $77.0 billion in 2011 (Congressional Budget Office 2011).[8] In contrast, the Temporary Assistance for Needy Families (TANF) program has been much less responsive in the recession and may actually decrease between now and 2012 (Bitler and Hoynes 2010; Congressional Budget Office 2011).

Refundable tax credits, including the EITC and increases in child credits, totaled $77.0 billion in 2010, but will decrease in 2011 and beyond (Congressional Budget Office 2011, 65). The effects of the 2010 TRUJCA will not be felt until 2011 and will exclude the making-work-pay tax credits, which had a substantial effect on poverty in 2009 (Sherman 2010, 2011), but the effects of the 2008 ARRA on poverty in 2009, including these one-time tax credits, can already be estimated. For instance, consider cash safety net transfer from the ARRA. The Census Bureau estimates that UI (existing program plus ARRA subsidies) kept 2.3 million adults age eighteen to sixty-four from being poor in 2009 compared to only 600,000 in 2008. Without extended UI and with no other changes in behavior, we would have witnessed a doubling of the 2.5 million person increase in official poverty observed in 2009 (DeNavas-Walt, Proctor, and Smith 2010, 15; Johnson 2010).

But an even larger antipoverty effect of the safety net, including the ARRA enhancements in 2009, came from SNAP and refundable tax credits, including the EITC and the working family tax credits, and the one-time making-work-pay credits, all of which also helped reduce the increase in poverty from 2007 through 2009 as gauged by the experimental measures shown in figure 4.4. Arloc Sherman (2010, 2011) finds that these programs reduced poverty by 4.2 million people, or by about 10 percent, using an NAS-type poverty definition.[9] The Census Bureau has made very similar estimates (Johnson 2010). A 10 percent antipoverty effect means that without these ARRA benefits poverty would have increased by about 1.4 percentage points, using either the official rates or the NAS experimental rate calculation.

Poverty Forecasts for 2010 and Beyond

We know that unemployment skyrocketed in 2009, leading to severe drops in employment, especially for young unskilled workers in most

Figure 4.6   Simulated Poverty Rate for All Persons, 2010 through 2016

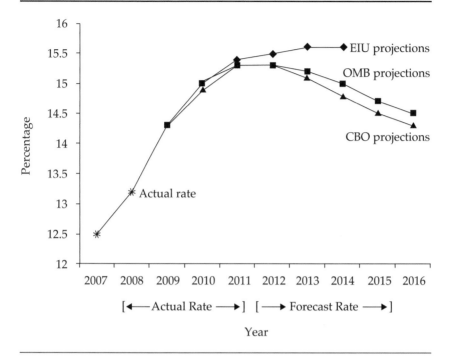

Source: Authors' calculations based on data from Monea and Sawhill (2010).
Note: EIU = Economist Intelligence Unit
OMB = Office of Management and Budget
CBO = Congressional Budget Office

states and double-digit unemployment in thirty-six of the fifty states at the end of 2009. These effects led to a substantial increase in poverty in 2009. There is widespread agreement that the official poverty rate will rise in 2010 and, we expect, again in 2011. But by how much will it rise?

Emily Monea and Isabel Sawhill (2010), using a methodology developed by Rebecca Blank (2009), forecast official poverty rates by looking at recent and projected unemployment rates in conjunction with economic and unemployment forecasts by the Congressional Budget Office, the Office of Management and Budget, and the Economist Intelligence Unit. Using this methodology, they were able to forecast official poverty rates from 2010 to 2016 based on actual 2009 and earlier rates (see figure 4.6). The projection is that the official poverty rate for 2010 in this model will be 15 percent (compared to the actual 14.3· percent rate in 2009) and poverty will continue to rise in 2011 and 2012, peaking at about 15.5 percent.

Julia Isaacs (2010a, 2010b) uses trends in SNAP enrollments to forecast poverty for children. Fifteen and a half million children (20.7 percent of all children under age eighteen) were poor in 2009, according to the official poverty measure. An additional 3.2 million children were receiving SNAP in 2010 compared to 2009.[10] If all of the 3.2 million will be otherwise poor in 2010, child poverty will increase by over 21 percent. Even if just two-thirds of the new beneficiaries are poor, the child poverty rate will go up by 12 percent, to almost 22.8 percent of all children. Monea and Sawhill's estimates for the increase in poverty among children beyond 2010 (not shown) are even more dramatic. Monea and Sawhill (2010, figure b) estimate that the number of poor children could increase by at least 6 million, or by 38 percent over the next several years, with the child poverty rate rising from 20.7 percent in 2009 to 22.8 percent in 2010 (just about the same rate predicted by Isaacs 2010b), and then to the 24 to 25 percent range in 2012 to 2013.

In summary, despite the helpful impacts of income stabilizers and new initiatives to maintain many ARRA benefits in the 2010 TRUJCA, it appears that the country is headed for even higher official poverty rates as this recession works its way out. We guess that the official poverty rate will be in the neighborhood of 15 percent in 2010, and higher still in 2011. NAS-like measures such as the experimental poverty series in figure 4.4, which reflect all of the ARRA efforts, have higher poverty rates than do the official series and will likely show smaller increases in poverty in 2010 and 2011 while also offering the opportunity for measuring the effects of policy, including the antipoverty effects of the ARRA and TRUJCA in this recession.

Income Inequality: The Census and the Congressional Budget Office Data Views

With the exception of the Great Depression of the 1930s, past recessions tended to hurt people at the bottom of the income distribution more than people in the middle or at the top. These effects are usually tempered by social insurance and the safety net and are driven by the loss of jobs and labor-market earnings, which recover when employment recovers. In terms of job loss and employment, the return to pre-recession peaks has taken an increasingly longer time frame for each recession since 1982, none of which were as deep as the Great Recession in employment terms (David Leonhardt, "Comparing Recoveries: Job Changes," *New York Times*, January 7, 2011). However, a major aspect of the current recession has been the concomitant drop in property income, the value of financial assets, interest rates on savings, and home prices, as well as employment losses at both higher and lower earning levels. In 2009, stocks and bonds began to recover from their 2008 nadir and continue to do so as of December 2010. Housing values continued to fall through 2010 and have declined nationwide by 30 percent from their late 2006 peak, with little sign of rising as of October 2010 (Calculated Risk 2010). Will this "financial" recession lead to greater income losses at the top of the income distribution than at the bottom, thus reducing inequality; or, will this "financial" recession lead to an expansion in income inequality in the United States if the rich lose less than the poor?

For the first time, the Census Bureau has provided estimates of household-size-adjusted cash incomes from 1967 to 2009 (DeNavas-Walt, Proctor, and Smith 2010, table A-3). Data adjusted for changes in household size are preferable to those that are not, for two reasons: first, because they capture economies of scale in household expenses in any given time period, and second, because they capture changes in household size and structure when deployed over long time periods (see, for instance, Brandolini and Smeeding 2009; Burkhauser 2011; Burkhauser and Larrimore 2011).

Figures 4.7 and 4.8 show that income inequality generally increases in recessions, whether we consider the Gini coefficient (figure 4.7) or the aggregate shares of income received (figure 4.8). Figure 4.9, which uses these same data, shows changes in income quintiles' shares from 1967 to 2009 in a different way, using these same Census-adjusted data on quintiles' shares but anchored at 100 percent in 1967. All of the increases in inequality began in about 1979. The bottom quintile share was 5.2 percent in 1967 and 1979 but fell to 3.6 percent in 2008 and to an all-time low of 3.4 percent in 2009, a drop from start to finish of about 45 percent (figure 4.9). The second quintile has also lost income share, falling 20 percent, from 11.9 to 9.2 percent of total income in 2009, again an all-time low. The precipitous declines in income share at the bottom of the income distribution in this recession are fully consistent with the effects of long-term joblessness on low-income workers' poverty, as discussed in the previous section and in Burkhauser and Larrimore (2011). Even the middle quintile experienced a 10 percent drop in share over this recession, while the fourth quintile shows little change, ranging between 22 and 24 percent of total income, albeit with a larger rise in the 1980s and a smaller decline since 1993. In contrast, the top quintile's income share has risen from 42.5 to 49.4 percent of total income in 2009, an all-time high, reached also in 2006.

These estimates also suggest that since 1983, income inequality changes have been driven almost exclusively by increases in the top quintile income share (see also Jencks et al. 2010, figure 3a; Burkhauser et al. 2009; Burkhauser 2011). However, a recent paper by Burkhauser and Larrimore (2011) using the same data as in figures 4.7, 4.8, and 4.9 also suggests that the main reason for greater rising inequality in this recession compared to earlier ones was a big increase in joblessness at the

Figure 4.7   Equivalence-Adjusted Household Money Income, 1967 to 2009, Using Gini Index of Income Inequality

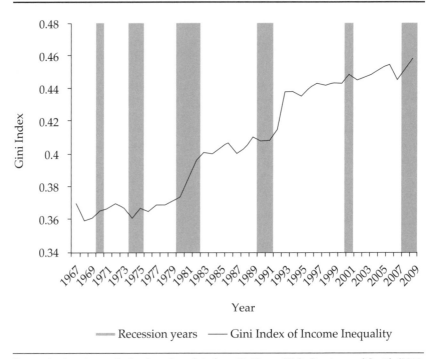

Year

——— Recession years   ——— Gini Index of Income Inequality

Source: Authors' compilation based on data from DeNavas-Walt, Proctor, and Smith (2010, table A-3, 45–48).
Note: The Gini Index varies from perfect equality (0.00) to perfect inequality (1.00).

bottom of the income distribution, only partially offset by increased income transfers, especially UI.

The losses in the bottom three income quintiles in this recession are of great concern and, compared to the rise in the top income share, suggest a hollowing out of the money income distribution. By any of these measures, inequality has increased in this recession. The top income share has risen, driven mostly by the highest income centiles; the bottom shares are dropping as a result of joblessness.[11]

Other more inclusive time series for income inequality, for example the Congressional Budget Office (CBO; 2010) series, allow us to trace the effects of past recessions but are available only up to 2007 and thus do not show the effect of the current recession. Like the broader income definition used in the new census poverty measures, the CBO series in figure 4.10 help confirm the trends shown in figure 4.9, while at the same time capturing much more of all types of cash and noncash income, em-

Figure 4.8   Equivalence-Adjusted Household Money Income, 1967-to-2009 Quintile Share Ratios

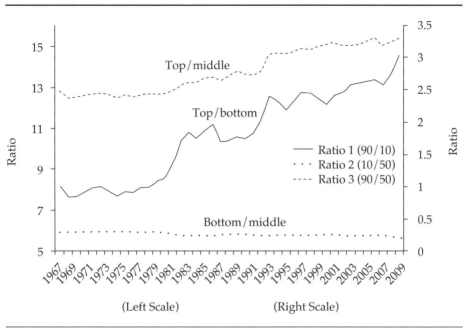

(Left Scale)   (Right Scale)

Source: Authors' compilation based on data from DeNavas-Walt, Proctor, and Smith (2010, table A-3, 45–48).
Note: Estimates are for ratios of quintile shares for the top, middle, and bottom quintiles. The 90th, 50th, and 10th percentiles are the medians of each quintile.

ployee benefits, realized capital gains, and the burden of all taxes, including tax rebates. When the census data are statistically matched to Internal Revenue Service (IRS) tax return data, they show much more realized property income than does the Census Bureau series mentioned earlier. Moreover, they show an even larger rise in inequality up to 2007 than the Census Bureau series, especially driven by changes in incomes at the very top of the distribution. The full definition of CBO household enriched income is found in the appendix "Definitions of Income Measures."

The CBO data show that inequality contracted in the 1990-to-1993 and 2001-to-2002 recessions but exploded after 2002. The top quintile's share is 52.5 percent of after-tax net income in 2007, according to the CBO series, compared to 49.4 percent in the census money income inequality series employed earlier (compare figure 4.9 to figure 4.10). The trend toward inequality is driven by the top 1 percent share (which rises by 228 percent, from 7.5 percent in 1979 to 17.1 percent in 2007) but also by a

Figure 4.9   **Percentile Shares of Adjusted Household Income by Quintile Share of Income of Each Quintile Relative to Share in 1967 and Actual Share in 2009**

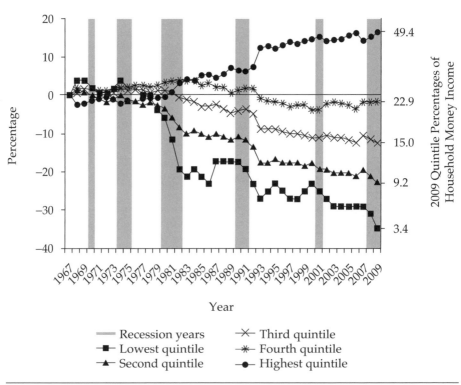

Source: Authors' calculations based on data from DeNavas-Walt, Proctor, and Smith (2010, table A-2, 40–43).

15.2 percent increase in the share of the next 4 percent of household units, with no change in the share of the next 10 to 15 percent. Hence, inequality in the CBO data since 1993 and through 2007 is driven almost exclusively by gains in the income of the 95th and higher percentiles of households. We also note that the CBO share of net income in the bottom quintile is 4.9 percent by their measure in 2007, compared to 3.7 percent in the 2007 census income data used in figure 4.9. And so the poor have a slightly larger share of the pie using the CBO's more comprehensive data, but the trends in both series are the same, with the CBO showing declining income shares for *all* of the bottom four quintiles since 2002, though especially for the bottom two quintiles.[12]

However, even these enriched CBO data exclude the vast majority of capital income that is not realized in a given year, including imputed

Figure 4.10   Percent Change in Congressional Budget Office Household After-Tax Comprehensive Income Inequality, 1979 to 2007

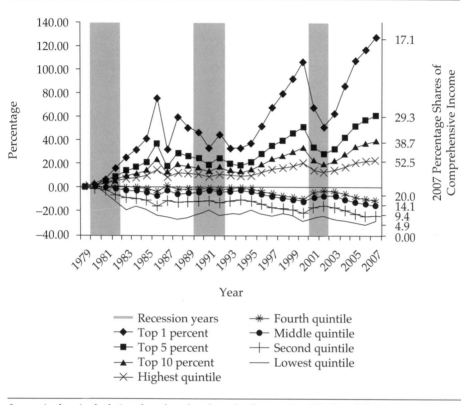

Recession years

—◆— Top 1 percent
—■— Top 5 percent
—▲— Top 10 percent
—✕— Highest quintile

—✳— Fourth quintile
—●— Middle quintile
—+— Second quintile
—— Lowest quintile

Source: Authors' calculations based on data from the Congressional Budget Office (2010).

rent on owner-occupied homes as well as accumulated financial and business wealth and changes in such incomes over the 2007-to-2009 recession and earlier recessions. These are the issues we turn to next.

Income from Wealth and Income from Labor: Stocks, Flows, and More Complete Measures of Well-Being

Most of the recent income gains have gone to the richest 1 percent to 5 percent of households, especially since 2002 (see figure 4.10). These income measures have included earnings, taxes, transfers, and other benefits but use only cash property actually received in the form of interest, rent, and dividends (as well as realized capital gains in the CBO data). It is generally agreed that property incomes drop in a recession, especially the 2007-to-2009 recession. But how have recessions since 1989 impacted the income distributions when a full measure of property income is employed? In a recent paper, Timothy M. Smeeding and Jeff E. Thompson (2011) addressed these issues using the Survey of Consumer Finances (SCF) from 1988-to-1989 to 2006-to-2007 and simulations to adjust for property and employment income losses in 2008 and property income recovery in 2009. This section of the chapter summarizes and extends their findings.

Over the past several years, the income distribution as normally measured by the Census Bureau has shown almost no significant change in incomes below the 90th percentile (DeNavas-Walt, Proctor, and Smith 2010) and a declining cash median income for nonelderly households. The CBO data (see figure 4.10) suggest that the gains in shares accrued to the top 1 and next 4 percent of households.

Emmanuel Saez (2010), using IRS data, finds that the top 1 percent share of total taxable income, which peaked in 2007, had declined by less than 9 percent from 2007 to 2008, owing mainly to lower realized capital gains in the recession. Others, such as Jonathan Parker and Annette Vissing-Jorgenson (2010), in contrast, argue that the most volatile elements in the top income brackets are due to changes in labor income. Labor economists also point to the growing inequality in the U.S. earnings distribution, also at the very top, and to conventional household micro data showing earned incomes as more or less 70 to 75 percent of total income in most years (see, for example, Krueger et al. 2010; Parker and Vissing-Jorgenson 2010). Earnings are the key, though not the only, determinant of changes in the distribution of income, according to these sources.

In contrast to this, we argue that although earnings are indeed important at all levels of the income distribution, these studies all ignore a major source of growing income inequality in America: accumulated wealth. Wealth is more permanent and more durable than traditionally measured annual cash income, with or without capital gains. It offers a buffer against income downturns and provides a source of consumption, private security, and power, especially among top wealth and income holders. At the same time that micro-oriented labor economists suggest labor income from employment is the major determinant of household incomes and concentrate on its effect on inequality, macroeconomists and national income accountants find that labor income in the form of wages and salaries and employee benefits has now declined to 63 percent of national income, a fifty-year low (Glyn 2009). Macroanalysts point to the rising share of corporate profits in national income, now at 12 to 13 percent of total national income (see table 4.1). Adding up labor income (including supplements for employee benefits) and corporate profits still misses more than a fifth of the nation's economic pie. Other uncounted components such as net interest, proprietor's income,

Table 4.1   Relation of Gross Domestic Product, Gross National Product, and National Income, Including Those Accounted for in this Chapter, in Billions of Dollars (Quarters Seasonally Adjusted at Annual Rates)

	2006-III	Share	2009-IV	Share
National income	12,093.0		12,465.6	
Compensation of employees	7,484.1	61.9%	7,773.1	62.4%
Wage and salary accruals	6,075.4	50.2%	6,266.3	50.3%
Supplements to wages and salaries	1,408.7	11.6%	1,506.8	12.1%
Proprietors' income with inventory valuation and capital consumption adjustments	1,131.2	9.4%	1,060.3	8.5%
Rental income of persons with capital consumption adjustment	140.3	1.2%	286.7	2.3%
Corporate profits with inventory valuation and capital consumption adjustments	1,655.1	13.7%	1,467.6	11.8%
Net interest and miscellaneous payments	661.6	5.5%	782.6	6.3%
Taxes on production and imports less subsidies	991.6	8.2%	1,034.1	8.3%
Business current transfer payments	83.6	0.7%	128.2	1.0%
Current surplus of government enterprises	–4.7	0.0%	–6.5	–0.1%

Source: Authors' calculations based on data from U.S. Department of Commerce, Bureau of Economic Analysis (2009).
Note: We account for supplements to wages and salaries only insofar as they appear as part of defined contribution pension plans. Health care and other employer subsidies are not counted as labor income (Smeeding and Thompson 2011).

and imputed rents for owner-occupiers are largely missing from census, IRS, CBO, and other income distribution calculations (table 4.1). Even these streams of capital income, however, only represent a portion of the accrued gains, since most assets are not sold in a given year. A more thorough accounting of income from wealth—whether realized or not—is an important part of understanding the full distribution of economic resources, particularly in understanding the dynamics at the very top of the income distribution in this recession and in earlier recessions.

Methods

We employ the 1989-to-2007 SCF to develop new estimates of "more complete income" (MCI), meaning income accrued from the ownership of wealth (whether realized or not) as well as actual labor and other (net transfer) income. Many decades ago, Robert M. Haig (1921) and Henry Simons (1938) defined "income" as one's ability to consume without drawing down one's stock of wealth. In the spirit of Haig-Simons, MCI combines actual earnings and transfer income with imputed earnings for assets. These imputed flows are based on different asset classes in the SCF and historic rates of return to those assets so that we can trace out changes in MCI across recessions and recoveries. Our method is to first subtract out reported property income from the SCF, then systematically add back the returns on financial wealth, retirement assets, housing, other investments (including real estate), and finally business income for owners and proprietors over the 1988-to-1989 to 2006-to-2007 period. We apply long-term average rates of return from 1977 to 2007 to make these calculations.

Our long-run average rates of return are shown in table 4.2. The assumption is a 7 percent real return for stocks (roughly the same rate as assumed by the Social Security Administration), a 6 percent return for housing (which includes imputed rent), and a 5 percent return for bonds.

The SCF measures wealth at the point of the interview in the latest year and incomes for the year before. Hence, 2006 incomes and 2007 property values are combined to give 2006-to-2007 MCI. To update measures, and to reflect the major upheavals in the housing and financial markets, we calculate MCI measures for 2008 and 2009 based on projected values for income and asset classes in the SCF. NIPA (National Income and Product Accounts), Flow of Funds, and CPS data are used to project all of the income and asset amounts used in calculating MCI at its 2008-to-2009 level.[13]

Financial and Housing Recession Background

In a financial recession like the 2008 collapse, wealth values for housing and financial instruments, especially stocks, did significantly recede (as shown in table 4.3). The negative effects of the recession differentially affected some groups compared to others and compared to past recessions. Homes are the major asset of the middle class, and their value has declined 30 percent from 2006-to-2007 to the end of 2010 (Calculated Risk 2010). Retirement accounts have been mildly affected by declines in pension wealth, but they are recovering in 2009 and 2010 just as our income flow figures for pension wealth demonstrate. Alicia Munnell and Jean-Pierre Aubry (2010) find that those with balanced portfolios may have recovered fully. The elderly who were already retired in 2008 lost some home value but were generally invested in relatively safe portfolios, which protected their assets and income flows during the recession,

Table 4.2   Adjustments Made to SCF Income and Asset Categories for 2009 Projection

Income	Matching Source Table (Row Number)	Source Detail	Percentage Change 2007 Q3/4 to 2009 Q3/4 Change
Interest	NIPA. 2.1(14)		−5.8%
Dividends	NIPA. 2.1(15)		−28.6%
Non-taxable investment income	NIPA. 2.1(14)	SCF detail refers to bonds*	−5.8%
Other Business/investment/rent/trust	NIPA.1.12 (9, 39)	Combined rental and proprietor	5.7%
Earnings	Analysis of CPS ORG, Jan. to Nov.		Varies by industry, education
Proprietor's income	NIPA. 2.1(9)		−4.4%
Capital gains	CBO Jan. 2009 Budget Outlook	Anticipated tax revenue decline of 40 percent	−40.0%
Public transfers (excluding Social Security)	NIPA. 2.1(17 less 18)		36.2%
Retirement income (including Social Security)	NIPA. 2.1(18)		15.3%
Assets			
Certificates of deposit	FOF. B.100(12)	Time and savings deposits	4.9%
Stocks	FOF. B.100(24)	Corporate equities	−21.6%
Stock mutual funds	FOF. B.100(25)	Mutual fund shares	−12.6%
Bonds	FOF. B.100(18)	Treasury securities	404.2%
Other bond mutual funds	FOF. B.100(21)	Corporate and foreign bonds	21.9%
Savings bonds	FOF. B.100(17)	Savings bonds	−2.5%
Government bond mutual funds	FOF. B.100(19)	Agency and GSE-backed securities	−83.7%
Tax-free bond mutual funds	FOF. B.100(20)	Municipal securities	9.2%
Combination and other mutual funds	FOF. B.100(25)	Mutual fund shares	−12.6%
Other (trusts, annuities, and so forth)	FOF. B.100(30)	Miscellaneous	10.8%

(Table continues on p. 110)

Table 4.2 *(Continued)*

Income	Matching Source Table (Row Number)	Source Detail	Percentage Change 2007 Q3/4 to 2009 Q3/4 Change
Home equity	FOF. B.100(49)	Owner's equity in household real estate	–41.0%
Quasi-liquid retirement	Urban Institute Analysis of FOF	www.urban.org/retirement_policy/url.cfm?ID=411976	–14.0%
Transaction accounts	FOF. B.100(11)	Checkable deposits	140.1%
Life insurance	FOF. B.100(27)	Life insurance reserves asset	3.8%
Nonresidential real estate	FOF. B.100(49)	Owner's equity in household real estate	–41.0%
Other residential real estate	FOF. B.100(4)	Modify in same way as residential real estate	–21.4%
Debt for other residential property	FOF. B.100(33)	Home mortgages	–1.3%
Other financial assets	FOF. B.100(30)	Miscellaneous assets	10.8%
Other nonfinancial assets	FOF. B.100(7) and (30) combined	Consumer durables or miscellaneous assets	9.8%
Business with active or nonactive household interest	FOF. B.100(29)	Equity in non-corporate business	–23.6%
Vehicles	FOF. B.100(7)	Consumer durables or miscellaneous assets	9.6%
Total debt	FOF. B.100(31)	Total liabilities	–1.4%
Mortgages and home equity loans	FOF. B.100(33)	Home mortgages	–1.3%
Home equity lines of credit	FOF. B.100(33)	Home mortgages	–1.3%

Source: Authors' compilation based on data from Smeeding and Thompson (2011).
Note: NIPA = National Income and Product Accounts; FOF = Flow of funds; SCF = Survey of Consumer Finances; CBO = Congressional Budget Office; GSE = government-sponsored entreprise; CPS ORG = Current Population Survey, Original Data
*The SCF equivalant of the MIPA category Nontaxable Interest is captured by Bonds in our measure.

Table 4.3   **Short-Run (Three-Year Average) and Long-Run (1988 to 2007) Rates of Return (Percents)**

	Housing Index (HI)	Stock Indices (SI)	Bond Indices (BI)	Inflation (Consumer Price Index)
A. "Short-Run"				
1989	6.0%	14.7%	8.6%	4.3%
1992	2.3	7.0	7.8	4.0
1995	2.5	15.2	6.5	2.6
1998	4.1	21.0	6.0	2.1
2001	6.4	4.4	5.5	2.5
2004	7.4	3.6	4.3	2.6
2007	7.0	7.3	4.5	3.5
B. "Long-Run"	6.0%	7.0%	5.0%	3.0%

Source: Authors' calculations based on Smeeding and Thompson (2011).
Note: Rates used in simulation for all years in this chapter.

though relatively low returns in interest income have reduced this realized income flow (Gustman, Steinmeier, and Tabatabai 2010).

On the basis of these and other studies, we feel that the assumptions behind the MCI estimates are reasonable and that our measures are more durable and permanent than those of others based on annual "high-income" measures, or on annuitized wealth distributions, which also turn stock values into flows but tend to overvalue flows to older households owing to a shorter remaining lifetime. Our estimates reflect the effects of past recessions as well as the drop in wealth in 2008 and partial recovery in 2009 and the full flow value of assets including the ongoing housing crisis during the Great Recession.

Results

We compare the 2006-to-2007 estimates to other periods and note that imputing income flows to assets increased the real incomes of almost all households, and most by a substantial amount: a 31 percent increase at the mean and 16 percent at the median in 2006-to-2007. Of course, the top percentiles of the MCI distribution saw larger income from wealth gains of 32 percent to 41 percent at the 90th percentile and 95th percentile (see table 4.4). But by 2009 these increases had shrunk to 27 percent at the mean and 15 percent at the median. In 2008-to-2009, our simulated MCI at higher percentiles also fell because of asset declines in 2008, but still they increased incomes by 26 percent at the 90th percentile and by 32 percent at the 95th percentile. Because of the declines in asset values in 2008, all of the changes in MCI in 2008-to-2009 are smaller than were

Table 4.4 Increases in Income Using MCI Compared to After-Tax SCF Income, in 2009 Real Dollars

	Mean		Median		P10		P90		P95	
	Dollar Change	Percent Change	Dollar Change	Percent Change	Dollar Change	Percent Change	Dollar Change	Percent Change	Dollar Change	Percent Change
2003 to 2004	$21,639	30.6	$6,937	16.1	$1,059	9.4	$37,170	28.7	$65,823	35.6
2006 to 2007	$26,003	30.9	$7,709	16.3	$2,057	16.7	$45,005	31.9	$84,133	40.7
2008 to 2009	$22,005	26.7	$7,072	15.3	$1,284	9.5	$36,179	26.1	$66,451	32.3

Source: Authors' calculations based on data from Smeeding and Thompson (2011).
Note: For abbreviations, see income definitions appendix.

Figure 4.11   Gini Index with After-Tax Survey of Consumer Finances Income and More Complete Income

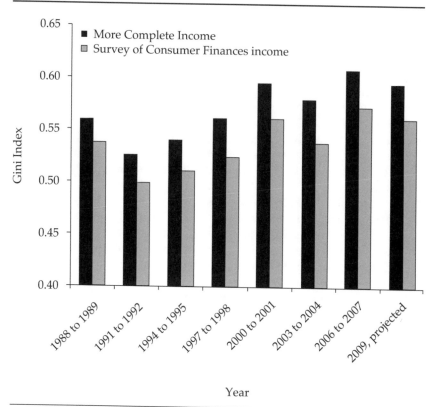

Year

Source: Authors' calculations based on data from Smeeding and Thompson (2011). See text and appendix income definitions for More Complete Income (MCI) and Survey of Consumer Finances (SCF) income.

the gains in MCI in 2006-to-2007, just as was the case in the 1991-to-1992 recession and the aftermath of the 2001 recession reflected by MCI inequality in 2003-to-2004, also shown in figure 4.11. All results are measured in 2009 real dollars as holdings in cash (demand deposits) and reflect a loss due to long-run average inflation for holding cash.

The major source of income from wealth gains at the median is homeownership. Of course, homeowners suffered major losses in 2008 and 2009 (and especially compared to the 2001 recession, where housing values continued to rise), reducing the flow value of their housing equity (or imputed rent) on average by at least 10 percent in 2008 alone (Case and Shiller 2010; Carson and Dastrup 2009). Ownership of financial assets, other investments, and the value of businesses all increased income from wealth for the top income groups relative to the median as reflected by the 2003-to-2004 to 2006-to-2007 rise in stock markets and home values. But these same sources led to the 2008-to-2009 declines in wealth values and income from that wealth, just as occurred in the recessions in the early 1990s and in 2001.

The summary chart, figure 4.11, shows the trend in both MCI and after-federal tax, post-transfer cash income inequality (SCF income, including realized capital gains) as conventionally measured by the SCF across the most recent three recessions. The trend in Gini coefficients from 1988-to-1989 to 2008-to-2009 suggests increasing inequality in both measures, with inequality highest in 2006-to-2007, but with 2008-to-2009 higher than 2003-to-2004 using either income measure. MCI inequality declines in recessions but bounces back even more strongly as recoveries take hold.

Standard after-tax SCF income inequality peaked in 2006-to-2007 but by 2009 had receded very slightly to 2000-to-2001 inequality levels, owing mainly to recession-driven realized capital losses in 2008 (which are not included in the census inequality measures). Inequality using MCI declined in the recessions of the early 1990s and in 2008 but rose faster between 1992 and 2007 than it did using SCF income. Hence 2008-to-2009 MCI inequality has receded from the 2006-to-2007 peak but is still above 2000-to-2001 and 2003-to-2004 levels. We sum up these trends by noting that inequality of both SCF income and MCI fell slightly in 2009, consistent with earlier recessions. But the overall trend in both measures since 1988-to-1989 is toward increased inequality.[14]

Now in early 2011 we are already seeing that income declines at the top of the distribution are quickly recovering and, based on historic experience, they should rise again in the recovery, moving beyond their previous peak, as observed in the periods immediately after past recessions (Atkinson 2009; Saez 2010). However, housing values are now 30 percent below their late 2006 peak (Case and Shiller 2010), suggesting that asset returns to middle-class households in the form of imputed rent are still falling, even as we come out of the recession.

Political Economy: Labor and Capital Shares

We also assess the level and trend in the functional distribution of income between capital and labor as we have defined it in figure 4.10 across the same time span and the same recessionary and boom periods (see figure 4.12). We find very much the same results, a steadily rising share of income accruing to capital or wealth. While the 1991-to-1992 recession depressed capital's share from that in 1988-to-1989, the 2001 recession had little effect on shares from 1991-to-1992 to 2006-to-2007.

Figure 4.12   Labor and Capital Shares Using MCI

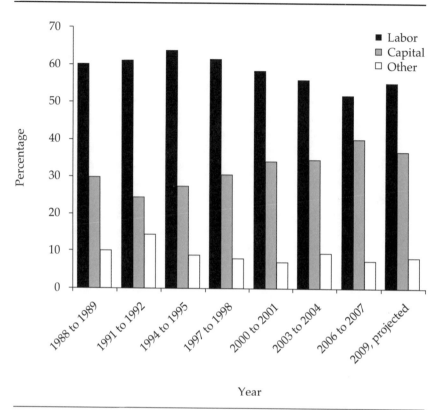

Year

Source: Authors' compilation based on data from Smeeding and Thompson (2011).
Notes: For definitions of capital income and labor income see entries for Survey of Consumer Finances and labor income in the appendix, "Definitions of Income Measures." Self-employment income is broken into labor income (70 percent) and capital income (30 percent), following Bureau of Economic Analysis income definition rules. Other income is net public income transfers after subtracting direct taxes.

Our 2008-to-2009 predictions are for a modest decline in the capital share. Hence in 2008-to-2009, the labor share surged higher compared to 2006-to-2007, as the capital share receded, but only to levels slightly above the 2003-to-2004 level. Even in 2008-to-2009, income from capital was 38 percent of total income and the labor share was less than 58 percent.

The capital share is concentrated among near-retirees, retirees, and the richest segments of the population: financiers, lawyers, athletes, and celebrities (Kaplan and Rauh 2010). A recent article by Tyler Cowen (2011) explains why workers in the financial sector make risky bets that are insured by policies such as the Troubled Asset Relief Act (TARF) of 2008 and how financiers continue to benefit from these risks. These financiers share "overlapping social networks" (David Brooks, "The Goldman Drama," *New York Times*, April 26, 2010, p. A23) and therefore make their voices heard in Washington. Powerful interests in the medical-care and pharmaceutical industries (where employment has increased substantially, see figure 4.1) have increasingly exerted their influence—witness, for instance, the generous treatment of pharmaceuticals and prescription drugs in the 2010 Affordable Care Act.

But these "capitalists" who watch stock markets more than labor markets go far beyond households in the top 5 percent of income brackets. They also include much larger and more important groups of voters such as the baby boomers and the elderly, for whom capital income (in pension wealth and housing wealth) is increasingly more important than is labor income. Unlike in Europe, where there is a strong labor party in most nations, labor in the United States has become relatively powerless (Levy and Temin 2007).

Since the financial collapse in 2007, there has been considerable scrutiny of CEO, or "executive," pay, but much less attention has been paid to stock options or other nonsalary elements of corporate remuneration (see Parker and Vissing-Jorgenson 2010 for an exception), despite large differences in tax rates between these two forms of income.[15] In the current era of recovering capital markets, stock options and unrealized capital gains have consequently become even more valuable, as reflected in our measures of MCI.

Chapter Summary

In this chapter we suggest that income poverty as officially measured will rise with high and continuing joblessness (especially for the less-skilled) and that home values, the main asset of the middle class, have been substantially depressed and will continue to fall. Income stabilization policies like ARRA have, however, helped lessen the increase in poverty during the Great Recession. Still, the bottom 80 percent of the income distribution is losing income share in the recovery as of 2009, continuing a trend evident since the early 1990s, but accelerating for the lowest income quintiles in this recession. And inequality continues to rise in and after recessions regardless of the income series we use.

We also argue that one cannot fully understand the distribution of income, and the way it affects key social and economic institutions, without also understanding how income from wealth affects income distribution, living standards, and well-being more generally across recessions. Indeed, we believe that despite recent crises in the financial sector, the twenty-first century is already on its way to becoming the century of wealth and that such a development will further exacerbate future inequality.

This trend of income from wealth is in strong contrast to the difficulties that lower-skilled workers are having in finding access to steady employment. Rising poverty, especially among young jobless adults and families, is permanently scarring the futures of millions of unemployed younger (under age thirty) unskilled workers and their children, a full 48 percent of whom are growing up in households headed by a mother with a high school education or less. Unless short-term action is taken to improve employment prospects for these particular workers, and to support the incomes of their children as we come out of the recession, poverty will remain high among this group.

Over the longer term, traditional upward routes to the middle class, in manufacturing and construction jobs, will continue to disappear. And it will take five years or longer for employment to rise to levels where low-skilled workers can find jobs. These individuals need more productive skills than they have at this time, given their current levels of education and human capital, and we ought to continue to emphasize skill-building measures over the next five years.

Among policy pundits, everyone suggests that we increase our stock of human capital (as suggested by Goldin and Katz 2008). But we have not yet been very effective at reaching this goal (consistent with the polarization in jobs by occupation as seen in figure 4.1). Graduation rates from high school are now below 1980s rates, unless GED degrees are included, and then they become flat since 1980. College completion rates by males, especially those from the most disadvantaged backgrounds, are abysmally low (Haveman and Smeeding 2006). The 2010 education bill will help increase postsecondary enrollment and completion (including two-year technical colleges). Larger future increases in human capital are therefore anticipated and will be necessary to increase employment and incomes for more Americans.

Poverty can be alleviated through tax and transfer policy, as shown by the ARRA. But the solution to permanent poverty reduction is a steady well-paying job for otherwise poor people. Unfortunately these jobs are not currently on the horizon for low-skilled workers, and especially not for low-skilled men.

The authors wish to thank several sponsors for their support (we hold all of these organizations harmless regarding the conclusions and analyses presented in this chapter): the Stanford Center for the Study of Poverty and Inequality; the Tobin Group; the Institute for Research on Poverty at the University of Wisconsin, Madison; and the Political Economy Research Institute at the University of Massachusetts, Amherst. Special thanks are given to two anonymous referees; to Bob Plotnick, Sandy Jencks, and Chris Wimer for helpful suggestions; and to David Autor for sharing some of his recent work. David Chancellor, Dawn Duren, and Deb Johnson helped prepare the manuscript. We assume full responsibility for any errors of omission and commission.

Appendix: Definitions of Income Measures

Equivalence-Adjusted Household Money Income. Traditional census money income adjusted for differences in household size allows one to go back to 1967 to assess differences in inequality for households. Income is defined as income received on a regular basis (exclusive of certain money receipts such as capital gains) before payments for personal income taxes, Social Security, union dues, Medicare deductions, and other items. The figures here are further adjusted for differences in household size using an equivalence scale. It is also the sum of money income received in the previous calendar year by all household members fifteen years old and over, including household members not related to the householder, people living alone, and others in nonfamily households. See http://www.census.gov/prod/2010pubs/p60-238.pdf, table A-3.

Survey of Consumer Finances (SCF) Income. This is a measure used by the Federal Reserve Board that defines household income for the previous calendar year as the following: wages, self-employment and business income, taxable and tax-exempt interest, dividends, realized capital gains, Food Stamps and other support programs provided by the government, pension income and withdrawals from retirement accounts, Social Security income, alimony and other support payments, and miscellaneous sources of income. The disposable personal income (SCF-DPI) measure we calculate estimates federal taxes using the National Bureau of Economic Research (NBER) tax simulator. See Smeeding and Thompson (2011) for more on this measure.

MCI Income. This is SCF income as defined above, minus income from wealth (interest, dividends, rent, royalties, and income from trusts and nontaxable investments, including bonds, as well as some self-employment income) plus imputed flows to stocks, bonds, annuities, and trusts plus imputed flows to quasi-liquid retirement accounts—such as 401(k)s, IRAs, and so forth—plus imputed flow to primary residence plus imputed flow to other residences and investment real estate, transaction accounts, CDs and whole life insurance plus imputed flow to other assets and businesses plus imputed flow to vehicle wealth minus imputed interest flow for remaining debt (after adjusting for negative incomes). See Smeeding and Thompson (2011) for more on this measure.

Comprehensive CBO Household Income. This equals pretax cash income plus income from other sources. Pretax cash income is the sum of wages, salaries, self-employment income, rents, taxable and nontaxable interest, dividends, realized capital gains, cash transfer payments, and retirement benefits plus taxes paid by businesses (corporate income taxes and the employer's share of Social Security, Medicare, and federal unemployment insurance payroll taxes) and employees' contributions to 401(k) retirement plans. Other sources of income include all in-kind benefits (Medicare, Medicaid, employer-paid health insurance premiums, Food Stamps, school lunches and breakfasts, housing assistance, and energy assistance).

Income categories are defined by ranking all people by their comprehensive household income adjusted for household size—that is, divided by the square root of the household's size. (A household consists of the people who share a housing unit, regardless of their relationships.) Quintiles, or fifths, contain equal numbers of people. Households with negative income (business or investment losses larger than other income) are excluded from the lowest income category but are included in totals.

Individual income taxes are attributed directly to households paying those taxes. Social insurance, or payroll, taxes are attributed to households paying those taxes directly or paying them indirectly through their employers. Corporate income taxes are attributed to households according to their share of capital income. Federal excise taxes are attributed to them according to their consumption of the taxed good or service. For more information, see http://www.cbo.gov/publications/col lections/collections.cfm?collect=13 and http://www.cbo.gov/publica tions/collections/tax/2009/after-tax_income_shares.pdf.

Labor income is income from employment in the form of wages, salaries, and sometimes employer-subsidized benefits like health care and pensions. In the CBO definition, benefits are included. In the others (Census cash income and MCI) benefits are not included.

Notes

1. A more detailed and in-depth review of employment can be found in chapter 3 of this volume, by Michael Hout, Asaf Levanon, and Erin Cumberworth.
2. Our labor-market analyses of low-skill employment are mostly focused on the issue of employment changes and job loss (job gain) and not just unemployment. We focus on employment because unemployment is affected by

discouraged workers, by those dropping out of or entering into the labor force, and by other changes for experienced workers (such as continuing to register as unemployed as a condition of receiving extended Unemployment Insurance [UI] benefits).

3. The broad middle class is defined here as being between $20,000 and $100,000 in annual income, including all types of households and compared to a median income of about $50,000. A more precise definition would require knowledge about who the definition applies to. For example, a definition of middle class for families with one or, at most, two children would be more narrow, as in $40,000 to $80,000 annual household income

4. Because the Department of Commerce has proposed a new Supplemental Poverty Measure (SPM) that will use a different but still NAS-like methodology from 2010 going forward, we do not dwell on these measures except that they give us data since 1999 that include the effects of tax rebates and near-cash benefits on poverty.

5. The Census Bureau has also begun to make this series into an agreed upon alternative measure to be released in fall 2011 (U.S. Department of Commerce, Economics and Statistics Administration 2010b; Short 2010). The findings for the 2008 income year are very close to the MSI-GA-CE (medical care expenses subtracted from income, geographically adjusted, consumer expenditure data) estimate of 15.7 percent in figure 4.4. However, because the similarity of estimates might well be due to coincidence, given the differences between the experimental poverty series in figure 4.4 and the new SPM measure, and because the SPM is limited to one year only so far, we do not mention it beyond this note.

6. These estimate large increases in elder poverty when medical expenses are taken into account, in contrast to the official cash-only figures cited earlier, where elder poverty has fallen.

7. Recent work by Robert D. Plotnick (2010) compares poverty series before and after taxes and transfers and shows very similar effects. Deteriorating labor market conditions in all recessions, combined with widening earnings inequality and a shrinking safety net (until 2009 at least), have combined to produce little change in poverty since 1980 by this metric as well.

8. See also the "SNAP Annual Summary" at http://www.fns.usda.gov/pd/SNAPsummary.htm; accessed May 23, 2011.

9. Recent work by Arloc Sherman (2011) at the Center on Budget and Policy Priorities confirms the fact that the ARRA and other safety net provisions kept poverty from increasing in terms of the NAS MSI income and poverty definitions used in figure 4.4.

10. And the Congressional Budget Office (2011, 65) reports that SNAP will rise another 10 percent in 2011.

11. This decrease in bottom share takes place despite the 10 to 15 percent increase in the number of family units that are extended families during this recession reported earlier (Johnson 2010). Were the members of these extended families able to live apart from their relatives in separate households, inequality would have increased and income share would have dropped by even more at the bottom of the income distribution during the course of this recession. These findings are also consistent with those of

Dirk Krueger and colleagues (2010) and Jonathan Heathcote, Fabrizio Perri, and Giovanni Violante (2010), who also find income inequality rising secularly and in almost all rich countries in recent recessions, including this one.

12.   Richard Burkhauser and colleagues (2009), using non-top-coded census income data, also find that most of the change in income inequality over the past fifteen years has been among the rich in the top 1 percent (as do Jencks et al. 2010, figure 4). Jonathan Parker and Annette Vissing-Jorgenson (2010) suggest that top incomes and income shares are more volatile than other incomes during the recession and therefore business cycles can lower and raise top shares. Such a pattern is evident in the Congressional Budget Office data provided in figure 4.10. Parker and Vissing-Jorgenson argue that these changes are driven mainly by earned income and not stock markets or wealth changes alone. But we disagree, basing our conclusions on the methods used in the next section of the chapter.

13.   Details behind these imputations, including details on the rates of return, asset classes, and our method for projecting SCF income and assets to 2009 levels, are in tables 4.1 to 4.4 and also in Smeeding and Thompson (2011, "Technical Appendix").

14.   These trends are also fully consistent with the long-run trends in "high incomes" produced by Anthony Atkinson, Thomas Piketty, and Emmanuel Saez (2009); Piketty and Saez (2006); Saez (2010); and Atkinson (2009) and as shown in Smeeding and Thompson (2011).

15.   This is something of a mystery, as longer-term (one-year or more) stock option gains are taxed at only 15 percent when realized, and CEO pay, which is both highly public and increasingly under pressure for reduction, is taxed at 40 percent. Many private financiers and private equity fund managers make great use of such options to minimize tax burdens (Cowen 2011). There is considerable elasticity in substituting one form of pay for the other, and the incentive to do so is high when tax rates differ by twenty-five percentage points or more (Gruber and Saez 2002; Kaplan and Rauh 2010).

References

Atkinson, Anthony B. 2009. "Income Inequality in Historical and Comparative Perspective: A Graphic Overview." Presentation to the Conference on Inequality in a Time of Contraction. Stanford University (November 13).

Atkinson, Anthony B., Thomas Piketty, and Emmanuel Saez. 2009. "Top Incomes in the Long Run of History." NBER Working Paper No. 15408. Cambridge, Mass.: National Bureau of Economic Research.

Autor, David H. 2010a. "Low-Skill Work in High-Skill Countries: Poverty and Policy Implications." Paper presented at the Institute for Research on Poverty, University of Wisconsin, Madison (January 28). Reorganization of Social Policy in a Recession Seminar Series. Available at http://www.irp.wisc.edu/newsevents/seminars/Presentations/2009-2010/Autor-IRP-Wisc-Jan-2010-final.pdf; accessed May 23, 2011.

———. 2010b. "The Polarization of Job Opportunities in the U.S. Labor Market: Implications for Employment and Earnings." Paper jointly released by the

Center for American Progress and the Hamilton Project. Available at http://www.americanprogress.org/issues/2010/04/job_polarization.html; accessed May 23, 2011.

Autor, David H., and David Dorn. 2009a. "'This Job Is Getting Old': Measuring Changes in Job Opportunities Using Occupational Age Structure." *American Economic Review* 99(2): 45–51.

———. 2009b. "Inequality and Specialization: The Growth of Low-Skill Service Jobs in the United States." NBER Working Paper No. 15150. Cambridge, Mass.: National Bureau of Economic Research. Available at: http://www.nber.org/papers/w15150.pdf; accessed December 17, 2010.

Bell, David, and David G. Blanchflower. 2010. "Youth Unemployment: Déjà vu?" IZA DP No. 4705. Bonn: Institute for the Study of Labor, January. Available at: http://ftp.iza.org/dp4705.pdf; accessed May 23, 2011.

Bitler, Marianne, and Hilary W. Hoynes. 2010. "The State of the Safety Net in the Post-Welfare Reform Era." NBER Working Paper No. 16504. Cambridge, Mass.: National Bureau of Economic Research.

Blank, Rebecca M. 2009. "Economic Change and the Structure of Opportunity for Less-Skilled Workers." In *Changing Poverty, Changing Policies*, edited by Maria Cancian and Sheldon H. Danziger. New York: Russell Sage Foundation.

Blank, Rebecca M., David Card, Frank Levy, and James L. Medoff. 1993. "Poverty, Income Distribution, and Growth: Are They Still Connected?" *Brookings Papers on Economic Activity* 1993(2): 285–339.

Brandolini, Andrea, and Timothy M. Smeeding. 2009. "Income Inequality in Richer and OECD Countries." In *Oxford Handbook of Economic Inequality*, edited by Wiemer Salverda, Brian Nolan, and Timothy M. Smeeding. Oxford: Oxford University Press.

Burkhauser, Richard V. 2011. "Evaluating the Questions that Alternative Policy Success Measures Answer." Presidential address, Association for Public Policy Analysis and Management, Boston, Mass. (November 5). *Journal of Policy Analysis and Management* 30(2): 205–15.

Burkhauser, Richard V., Shuaizhang Feng, Stephen Jenkins, and Jeff Larrimore. 2009. "Recent Trends in Top Income Shares in the USA: Reconciling Estimates from March CPS and IRS Tax Return Data." *Review of Economics and Statistics*. Forthcoming.

Burkhauser, Richard V., and Jeff Larrimore. 2011. "Median Income and Income Inequality During Economic Declines: Why the First Two Years of the Great Recession (2007–2009) Are Different." Unpublished paper. Cornell University.

Burtless, Gary. 2009. "The 'Great Recession' and Redistribution: Federal Antipoverty Policies." *Fast Focus* No. 4-2009, December. Published by the Institute for Research on Poverty, University of Wisconsin. Available at: http://www.irp.wisc.edu/publications/fastfocus/pdfs/FF4-2009.pdf; accessed May 23, 2011.

Calculated Risk. 2010. "Case-Shiller House Prices: Which Cities Will Hit Post-Bubble Lows Next?" Calculated Risk Finance & Economics (website), December 29, 2010. Available at: http://www.calculatedriskblog.com/2010/12/case-shiller-house-prices-which-cities.html; accessed May 23, 2011.

Carson, Richard, and Samuel Dastrup. 2009. "After the Fall: An Ex Post Characterization of Housing Price Declines Across Metropolitan Areas." Working Paper. University of California, San Diego.

Citro, Constance F., and Robert T. Michael. 1995. *Measuring Poverty: A New Approach*. Washington, D.C.: National Academy Press.

Congressional Budget Office. 2010. "Average Federal Tax Rates for All Households, Comprehensive Household Income Quartile, 1979–2007." Available at: http://www.cbo.gov/publications/collections/tax/2010/average_rates.pdf; accessed May 23, 2011.

———. 2011. *The Budget and Economic Outlook; Fiscal Years 2011 to 2021*. Washington: CBO, January. Available at: http://www.cbo.gov/ftpdocs/120xx/doc12039/01-26_FY2011Outlook.pdf; accessed July 12, 2011.

Cowen, Tyler. 2011. "The Inequality That Matters." *The American Interest Magazine*, January–February. Available at: http://www.the-american-interest.com/article-bd.cfm?piece=907; accessed May 23, 2011.

DeNavas-Walt, Carmen, Bernadette D. Proctor, and Jessica C. Smith. 2010. *Income, Poverty, and Health Insurance Coverage in the United States, 2009*. Current Population Reports, P60-238. Washington: U.S. Census Bureau.

Dynan, Karen. 2010. "The Income Rollercoaster: Rising Income Volatility and Its Implications." Washington, D.C.: Brookings Institution, April. Available at: http://www.brookings.edu/articles/2010/0401_income_volatility_dynan.aspx; accessed May 23, 2011.

Engemann, Kristie M., and Howard J. Wall. 2010. "The Effects of Recessions Across Demographic Groups." *Federal Reserve Bank of St. Louis Review* 92(1): 1–26.

Glyn, Andrew. 2009. "Functional Distribution and Inequality." In *Oxford Handbook of Economic Inequality*, edited by William Salverda, Brian Nolan, and Timothy Smeeding. Oxford: Oxford University Press.

Goldin, Claudia, and Larry Katz. 2008. *The Race Between Education and Technology*. Cambridge, Mass.: Harvard University Press.

Gruber, Jon, and Emmanuel Saez. 2002. "The Elasticity of Taxable Income: Evidence and Implications." *Journal of Public Economics* 84(1): 1–32.

Gustman, Alan, Thomas Steinmeier, and Nahid Tabatabai. 2010. "What the Stock Market Decline Means for the Financial Security and Retirement Choices of the Near-Retirement Population." *Journal of Economic Perspectives* 24(1): 181–82.

Haig, Robert M. 1921. "The Concept of Income—Economic and Legal Aspects." In *The Federal Income Tax*. New York: Columbia University Press.

Haveman, Robert, and Timothy M. Smeeding. 2006. "The Role of Higher Education in Social Mobility." *Future of Children* 16(2): 125–50.

Heathcote, Jonathan, Fabrizio Perri, and Giovanni L. Violante. 2010 . "Inequality in Times of Crisis: Lessons from the Past and a First Look at the Current Recession." VoxEU.org, February 2. Available at: http://www.voxeu.org/index.php?q=node/4548; accessed May 23, 2011.

Holzer, Harry. 2010. "Is the Middle of the Job Distribution Really Disappearing?" Center for American Progress. May. Available at: http://www.nationalskillscoalition.org/homepage-archive/documents/cap_holzer_2010-05.pdf; accessed May 23, 2011.

Holzer, Harry, and R. Lerman. 2007. "America's Forgotten Middle-Skill Jobs: Education and Training Requirements in the Next Decade and Beyond." Skill 2Compete. Available at http://www.urban.org/UploadedPDF/411633_for gottenjobs.pdf; accessed May 23, 2011.

Isaacs, Julia B. 2010a. "The Effects of the Recession on Child Poverty: Poverty Statistics for 2008 and Growth in Need During 2009." Washington, D.C.: Brookings Institution, January. Available at: http://www.brookings.edu/ papers/2010/0104_child_poverty_isaacs.aspx; accessed May 23, 2011.

————. 2010b. "Predicting Child Poverty Rates During the Great Recession." *First Focus Report*. Washington, D.C.: Brookings Institution. December. Available at http://www.brookings.edu/papers/2010/1209_child_poverty_isaacs.aspx; accessed May 23, 2011.

Jencks, Christopher, Ann Owens, Tracey Shollenberger, and Queenie Zhu. 2010. "How Has Rising Economic Inequality Affected Children's Economic Outcomes?" Paper presented at the Kennedy School of Government. Harvard University, August 14.

Johnson, David S. 2010 "Income, Poverty, and Health Insurance: 2009." Webinar. Prepared for the U.S. Census Bureau, Housing and Household Economic Statistics Division. Available at: www.census.gov/newsroom/releases/pdf/ 09-16-10_slides.pdf; accessed on May 23, 2011.

Kaplan, Steven N., and Joshua D. Rauh. 2010. "Wall Street and Main Street: What Contributes to the Rise in the Highest Incomes?" *Review of Financial Studies* 23(3): 1004–50.

Krueger, Dirk, Fabrizio Perri, Luigi Pistaferri, and Giovanni L. Violante. 2010. "Cross-Sectional Facts for Macroeconomists." *Review of Economic Dynamics* 13(1): 1–14.

Levy, Frank, and Peter Temin. 2007. "Inequality and Institutions in 20th Century America." NBER Working Paper No. 13106. Cambridge, Mass.: National Bureau of Economic Research.

Meyer, Daniel R., and Geoffrey L. Wallace. 2009. "Poverty Levels and Trends in Comparative Perspective." In *Changing Poverty, Changing Policies*, edited by Maria Cancian and Sheldon Danziger. New York: Russell Sage Foundation.

Monea, Emily, and Isabel Sawhill. 2010. "An Update to 'Simulating the Effect of the "Great Recession" on Poverty.' " Washington, D.C.: Brookings Institution, Center on Children and Families. Available at: http://www.brookings.edu/ papers/2010/0916_poverty_monea_sawhill.aspx; accessed May 23, 2011.

Munnell, Alicia H., and Jean-Pierre Aubry. 2010. "Returns on 401(k) Assets by Cohort." Publication Number 10-6. Chestnut Hill, Mass.: Boston College, Center for Retirement Research.

National Bureau of Economic Research. 2010. "US Business Cycle Expansions and Contractions." Available at http://www.nber.org/cycles.html; accessed May 23, 2011.

Parker, Jonathan A., and Annette Vissing-Jorgensen. 2010. "The Increase in Income Cyclicity of High Income Households and Its Relation to the Rise in Top Income Shares." NBER Working Paper No. 16577. Cambridge, Mass.: National Bureau of Economic Research.

Peck, Don. 2010. "How a New Jobless Era Will Transform America." *Atlantic Monthly*, 305(2): 42–44, 46–48, 50–56.

Piketty, Thomas, and Emmanuel Saez. 2006. "The Evolution of Top Incomes: A

Historical and International Perspective." *American Economic Review: Papers and Proceedings* 96(2; May): 200–205.

Plotnick, Robert D. 2010 "The Alleviation of Poverty: How Far Have We Come?" Unpublished paper. Prepared for Oxford Handbook of the Economics of Poverty, edited by Philip N. Jefferson. Oxford: Forthcoming.

Saez, Emmanuel. 2010. "Striking It Richer: The Evolution of Top Incomes in the United States (Updated with 2008 Estimates)." Available at http://www.econ .berkeley.edu/~saez/saez-UStopincomes-2008.pdf; accessed May 23, 2011.

Sherman, Arloc. 2010. "Projecting the Anti-Poverty Effect of Key Provisions of the 2009 Recovery Act." Paper presented at the APPAM Fall Conference, Boston (November 10). Available at: http://www.irp.wisc.edu/research/ povmeas/Sherman%20ArraAntipovertyEffects%20Appam2010_r11-3-10.pdf; accessed May 23, 2011.

——. 2011. "Despite Deep Recession and High Unemployment, Government Efforts—Including the Recovery Act—Prevented Poverty from Rising in 2009, New Census Data Show." Report. Washington, D.C.: Center on Budget and Policy Priorities, January 5.

Short, Kathleen. 2010. "Who Is Poor? A New Look with the Supplemental Poverty Measure." Paper prepared for the 2011 Conference of the Allied Social Science Associations, Society of Government Economists. SEHSD Working Paper No. 2010-15. Washington: U.S. Census Bureau, December 20. Available at: http://www.census.gov/hhes/povmeas/methodology/supplemental/re search/SGE_Short.pdf; accessed May 23, 2011.

Simons, Henry. 1938. *Personal Income Taxation: The Definition of Income as a Problem of Fiscal Policy*. Chicago: University of Chicago Press.

Smeeding, Timothy M. 2006. "Poor People in Rich Nations: The United States in Comparative Perspective." *Journal of Economic Perspectives* 20(1): 69–90.

Smeeding, Timothy M., Irwin Garfinkel, and Ronald Mincy. 2011. "Introduction to Young Disadvantaged Men: Fathers, Families, Poverty, and Policy." *Annals of the American Academy of Political and Social Science* 635(May): forthcoming.

Smeeding, Timothy M., and Jeff E. Thompson. 2011. "Recent Trends in Income from Wealth and Income from Labor: Stocks, Flows and More Complete Measures of Well Being." *Research in Labor Economics*. Forthcoming.

Sum, Andrew, Ishwar Khatiwada, Joseph McLaughlin, and Sheila Palma. 2011. "No Country for Young Men." *Annals of the American Academy of Political and Social Science* 635(May): forthcoming.

U.S. Census Bureau. 2011. "Poverty: Experimental Measures." Annual Tables. Available at: http://www.census.gov/hhes/povmeas/data/nas/tables/index .html; accessed May 23, 2011.

U.S. Department of Commerce, Bureau of Economic Analysis. 2009. "U.S. Economic Accounts—National." Available at: http://www.bea.gov/national/ index.htm#personal; accessed July 11, 2011.

U.S. Department of Commerce, Economics and Statistics Administration. 2010a. "Middle Class in America." Report. Prepared for the Office of the Vice President of the United States Middle Class Task Force. Washington, D.C.: January. Available at: http://www.esa.doc.gov/sites/default/files/reports/docu ments/middleclassreport.pdf; accessed May 23, 2011.

——. 2010b. "Observations from the Interagency Technical Working Group on Developing a Supplemental Poverty Measure." Available at: http://www.cen

sus.gov/hhes/www/povmeas/SPM_TWGObservations.pdf; accessed May 23, 2011.

U.S. Department of Labor, Bureau of Labor Statistics. 2010a. "Overview of BLS Statistics on Unemployment." Available at: http://www.bls.gov/bls/unem ployment.htm; accessed May 23, 2011.

———. 2010b. "Sizing up the 2007–09 Recession: Comparing Two Labor Market Indicators with Earlier Downturns." *Issues in Labor Statistics*. Summary 10-11, December. Available at: http://www.bls.gov/opub/ils/pdf/opbils88.pdf; accessed May 23, 2011.

———. 2010c. "Ranks of Those Unemployed for a Year or More." *Issues in Labor Statistics*. Summary 10-10, October. Available at: http://www.bls.gov/opub/ils/pdf/opbils87.pdf; accessed May 23, 2011.

U.S. Department of Labor, Employment and Training Administration. 2010. "Characteristics of the Insured Unemployed." Available at: http://work forcesecurity.doleta.gov/unemploy/chariu.asp; accessed May 23, 2011.

Van Wachter, Till. 2010. "Avoiding a Lost Generation: How to Minimize the Impact of the Great Recession on Young Workers." Testimony before the Joint Economic Committee of the U.S. Congress. May 26. Available at: http://jec .senate.gov/public/?a=Files.Serve&File_id=c868a8d3-3837-4585-9074-48181c 5320e6; accessed May 23, 2011.

Western, Bruce, and Becky Pettit. 2010a. *Collateral Costs: Incarceration's Effect on Economic Mobility*. Washington, D.C.: Pew Charitable Trusts, Pew Economic Mobility Project. Available at: http://www.economicmobility.org/assets/pdfs/EMP_Incarceration.pdf; accessed May 23, 2011.

———. 2010b. "Incarceration and Social Inequality."*Daedalus*, Summer, 8–19.

Chapter 5

How Much Wealth Was Destroyed in the Great Recession?

EDWARD N. WOLFF, LINDSAY A. OWENS, AND ESRA BURAK

T HE UNITED STATES has now undergone the worst recession since the Great Depression of the 1930s. The Great Recession has clearly taken a toll on people's income and employment. While adequate levels of income are vital to everyday lives of Americans, the current recession is particularly notable for its enormous destruction of wealth. This wealth destruction may have long-term economic effects that persist well after employment rebounds. In addition, the recession's roots lie in the housing market, which is where its long-term consequences might also be most felt. How are housing and wealth changing through the Great Recession? And how is this pain being spread across the population?

In this chapter we investigate which groups have borne the brunt of the Great Recession in terms of household wealth. In particular, we are interested in the effects of the recent recession on the poor, the very rich, and those in the middle class. Regarding the poor and the middle class, we are particularly interested in what has happened to their housing wealth: How many households have faced foreclosure? How many are, or will soon be, delinquent on their mortgages? How many have suffered personal bankruptcies? How many households are "underwater" in terms of net home equity? What has happened to credit card debt during the Great Recession? We are also interested in what has happened to their retirement wealth and their resulting retirement prospects. At the rich end, what has happened to the wealth holdings of the superrich? Have they also suffered declines in their net worth? Have these been as great in relative terms as those of the lower-income and middle-class Americans?

For the very top end of the wealth distribution, we use several data sources. The first is the Forbes 400, listing the estimated net worth of the richest 400 Americans. Our results indicate a severe drop-off in the average net worth of the richest 20 Americans from 2008 to 2009. Similar trends are evident for the top 50, top 100, top 200, and top 400. The second is the Capgemini and Merrill Lynch World Wealth Report, 2000 to 2010. It also shows a decline in the number of persons that they classify as "ultra and high net worth persons" in North America and the United States between 2007 and 2008. The third is the 2007 Survey of Consumer Finances (SCF; Board of Governors of the Federal Reserve 2007), the latest year currently available. On the basis of asset price changes, we can simulate the change in net worth of the richest 1 percent from 2007 through the end of 2009. Our results also show a sharp decline in the wealth of the top 1 percent.

To look at home ownership trends and track price changes through 2010, we make use of data from the National Association of Realtors, published by the U.S. Department of Housing and Urban Development, on the median prices of existing homes. Once again, using the 2007 SCF we can simulate the effects of the price decline of houses from 2007 to 2009 on the percentage of households whose net home equity is negative (so-called "underwater" households). We find that the proportion of underwater households increased substantially between 2007 and 2009. Another source is the Panel Study of Income Dynamics (PSID) for 2009, which has a special supplement on home foreclosures and "distressed" mortgages. Our analysis reveals a high concentration of homeowners with delinquent mortgages, particularly among minority households and young households. Data provided by RealtyTrac also indicate an explosion of foreclosures between 2006 and 2009.

We also examine trends in bankruptcy, drawing primarily from data collected by the U.S. courts and as reported in the media. There is already evidence of a surge in bankruptcies in 2009, up by 32 percent over 2008 (Mike Barber, "Bankruptcies Surge 32 Percent in 2009," Associated Press, January 4, 2010).

Finally, we examine the effects of the Great Recession on those nearing retirement. Drawing on data from research at the Center for Retirement Research at Boston College, a survey undertaken by the Bank of America, and our own calculations from the SCF, we show that persons nearing retirement lost, on average, one-third the value of their retirement accounts between 2007 and 2010. Although the rebound in the markets has alleviated some of this decline, the average retirement account value is still about 15 percent below its peak. Further, many individuals are now considering delaying their retirements.

The chapter is organized as follows: First we look at changes in the wealth of the rich and the superrich. Then we consider what has happened to housing wealth, particularly of the middle class. The following section carries on the topic of housing by focusing on the explosion in foreclosures. Then we shift our focus to credit card debt and delinquencies. After that we look at the effects of the Great Recession on rates of bankruptcies. In the penultimate section we look at the effects of the current recession on the pension wealth of older Americans and how it affects their retirement plans. We offer some concluding remarks in the final section.

Wealth Losses of the Ultrarich and the Rich

Turmoil in the stock market led to a great destruction in wealth at the very top of the income distribution. Those with the most money invested in the markets had the most to lose when the stock market crashed in late 2007. Data from Forbes 400 (figure 5.1) show the impact of the recession on the 400 Americans with the highest net worth, usually at least a billion dollars worth of property and assets per person.[1] From August 2007 to August 2008, the wealth of the richest Americans was still increasing, albeit more slowly than in previous years, following a long trend of increasing wealth. However, from August 2008 to September 2009, a substantial decrease in wealth occurred among the very richest. In 2008 the total net worth of the ten richest Americans was $285.1 billion; this figure fell to $245.9 billion by September of 2009, resulting in an average of $3.9 billion in wealth destruction per person. (Compare this figure of $3.9 billion to the median net worth of all households in 2007: $102,500.)

Although wealth destruction was greatest for the richest of the rich in terms of absolute billions of dollars, this was not the case when we look at percentage of net worth lost. Although the very richest of the rich have had much more to lose to begin with, they fared better than most in terms of the percentage of their net worth they lost. Among the richest 400 Americans, the richest ten Americans lost, on average, 13.7 percent of their net worth. Meanwhile those at the lower ranks were the harder hit: the top 50, which includes the top 10, lost on average 17 percent of their total net worth; the top 100 lost 18.2 percent; the top 200 lost 18.7 percent; and the top 400 lost 19.4 percent. This inequity, smaller losses for higher incomes, may be due to the fact that the wealthiest had a

Figure 5.1   Mean Net Worth for Americans with Highest Net Worth, 2003 to 2010

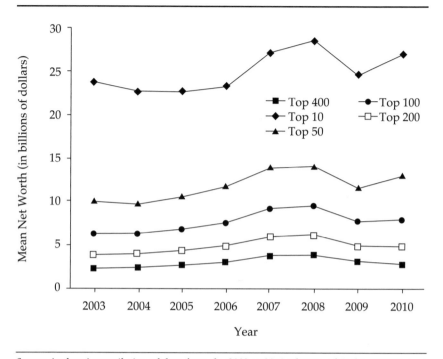

Source: Authors' compilation of data from the 2003 to 2010 editions of *Forbes* "400 Richest Americans" list (*Forbes,* various years).

smaller percentage of their net worth invested in the market, or that their market assets did better, on average, than those of their slightly less wealthy peers. Furthermore, the figure shows that the very richest are also recovering more quickly than those who are less well off. The average wealth of the richest ten Americans gained 9.8 percent from 2009 to 2010 and that of the top 50 grew by 11.4 percent; in contrast, the average wealth of the top 200 and that of the top 400 actually went down.

Data from the World Wealth Report (figure 5.2) also show that the number of ultrarich individuals, defined as those who hold at least $30 million in investable assets—excluding primary residence, collectibles, consumables, and consumer durables—fell dramatically between 2007 and 2008. In 2007 there were 41,200 ultrarich individuals in North America. In 2008, that number dropped to 30,600, a 26 percent decrease. Similarly, the number of high-net-worth individuals, defined as individuals with at least $1 million in investable assets, excluding primary residence, collectibles, consumables, and consumer durables, fell sharply between

Figure 5.2   **Ultra-High- and High-Net-Worth Individuals (HNWIs) in North America, 2003 to 2009**

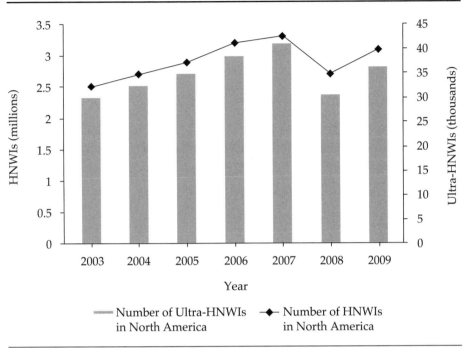

Source: Authors' compilation of data from World Wealth Reports (Merrill Lynch and Capgemini 2000–2010).

2007 and 2008. There were 3.3 million high-net-worth individuals in 2007 and only 2.7 million in 2008, an 18 percent decline.[2]

So how much wealth did these groups lose in just one year? The answer, from the Capgemini and Merrill Lynch World Wealth Reports, is a stunning $2.6 trillion! Our own estimates of the fortunes of the rich are derived from the 2007 SCF. We first update asset values to the end of 2009 (December 31, 2009, to be exact) on the basis of asset price changes. All figures are in 2007 dollars on the basis of the change in the Consumer Price Index (CPI), which increased by 4.2 percent from mid-2007 to the end of 2009.[3] We use the National Association of Realtors (NAR) series on the median sales price of existing homes to gauge the change in housing prices.[4] The average price decline in real terms for housing over this period for the nation as a whole was 26.3 percent.[5] All other price changes are derived from the Federal Reserve Board's Flow of Funds.[6] By our calculations, the value of non-home real estate plunged by 42.0 percent, that of equities (corporate stock) by 24.5 percent, unincorporated business equity by 30.1 percent, and financial securities by 13.8 percent. These asset price changes by themselves would have led to a 37.1 percent drop in the average holdings of the top 1 percent of households, or $5 million, from $18.5 million to $13.5 million.

Thus, the Great Recession is notable particularly for its great destruction of wealth at the very top, though there was some recovery from 2009 to 2010. Few, however, are losing much sleep worrying about the fortunes of the Forbes 400 or our collection of high-net-worth individuals (though this does have implications for our overall economic well-being and our nation's global competitiveness). What about the rest of the population? What is happening to the assets of people on Main Street? To answer this question, we must take a closer look at the housing market, which is where the assets of most people who hold wealth are.

Housing

It is perhaps no surprise that the housing sector took an especially large hit—the prime culprits in this crisis were the mortgage industry and the creation of faulty financial instruments by the financial sector that were tied to the fate of the housing market. The housing bubble in the early part of this decade, which artificially inflated home prices to unprecedented levels, certainly set the stage for a major market "correction." Indeed, on the basis of the Case-Schiller Home Value Index, as of spring 2011, home values now stand at their 2003 level. Given that housing makes up 30 percent of total assets for all Americans and 65 percent of total assets for middle-class Americans (Wolff 2010), any economic downturn that affects the housing market will naturally hurt the wealth of the middle class. Of course the housing market also impacts the health of housing-related industries, such as the construction industry, which has seen a precipitous decline in housing starts, from over 2.1 million units of new construction annually in the mid-2000s to just over 500,000 by the end of 2010.[7]

Using median sales prices for existing homes in the United States, figure 5.3 tells the story of declining home values. In November 2009, the median sales price for existing homes in the United States was $50,000 less than it was near the height of the housing bubble in 2006. The biggest change occurred in the West, where November 2009 prices stood $135,000 below what they were in 2006. This represented a real decline in housing prices, after accounting for inflation, of 39.4 percent. Price declines were more moderate in other regions—19.4 percent in the Northeast, 21.7 percent in the Midwest, and 19.9 percent in the South.[8] Home sales prices are not expected to recover their 2008 values for some

Figure 5.3   Median Sales Prices for Existing Homes, 1980 to 2010

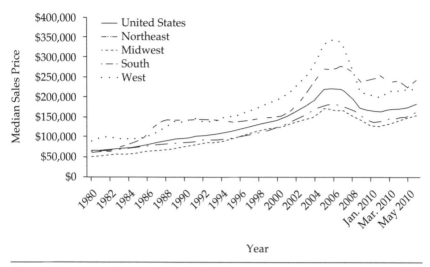

Source: Authors' compilation of data from U.S. Department of Housing and Urban Development (2010b).
Note: Data include prices of existing single-family homes before 1989. After 1989, prices of existing condominiums and cooperatives are also included.

time.[9] The trends clearly show that home values greatly depreciated after the Great Recession, particularly in the West, where a sharper pre-recession housing bubble resulted in a more dramatic collapse. However, it appears that the housing market may have bottomed out in January 2010. The median sales price was up by 11.4 percent nationwide between January and June 2010, and it advanced in all regions of the country except the Northeast (where declines had been less dramatic). The collapse in home values has led to a huge uptick in the number of families "underwater," with negative home equity. Table 5.1 shows the percentage of homeowners with negative home equity by household type. In 2007, only 1.8 percent of homeowners reported that their net home equity was negative on the basis of the 2007 SCF. By the end of 2009, however, we estimate that 16.4 percent of homeowners were "underwater." An even more recent estimate puts the figure at 20 percent (see David Streitfeld, "U.S. Plans Big Expansion of Aid to Homeowners," *New York Times,* March 26, 2010, p. A1).

We might expect that the poorest households have the greatest incidence of being underwater, but this is not always the case. Although minorities had a much higher incidence of negative home equity than (non-Hispanic) whites—28 percent for African American homeowners

Table 5.1   **Share of Homeowners Who Have Negative Home Equity and Are Delinquent on Their Mortgages, by Household Characteristic (Percentages)**

	Projected Share of Homeowners with Negative Home Equity, 2009	Decline In Average Value of Home Equity by Group, 2007 to 2009	Share of Home-Owners Delinquent on Their Mortgage, 2009	Share of Home-Owners Likely Behind on Their Mortgage, 2009
All households	16.4	39.1	5.1	14.1
Race or ethnicity[a]				
Non-Hispanic white	14.5	36.9	3.4	9.9
African American	27.9	48.0	11.0	21.2
Hispanic	23.2	44.6	15.4	44.4
Family type				
Married couples	17.4	39.2	4.6	13.6
Single males	16.7	37.8	3.7	12.9
Single females	12.9	34.2	7.8	16.5
Education[b]				
Less than twelve years of schooling	7.0	33.4	11.8	25.5
Twelve years of schooling	16.5	38.8	6.0	14.8
Thirteen to fifteen years of schooling	18.8	40.3	5.0	12.0
Sixteen or more years of schooling	17.7	38.0	1.6	7.1
Age group[c]				
Under thirty-five	49.9	68.3	4.6	13.2
Thirty-five to forty-four	25.5	49.7	6.5	17.3
Forty-five to fifty-four	11.7	40.1	5.6	15.6
Fifty-five to sixty-four	7.2	35.4	4.7	13.0
Sixty-five to seventy-four	6.5	30.9	1.0	4.1
Seventy-five and over	0.9	27.5	3.9	12.2
Income class				
Under $15,000	5.3	31.1	7.7	22.6
$15,000 to $24,999	8.6	31.2	5.5	21.4
$25,000 to $49,999	18.0	36.6	8.4	20.9
$50,000 to $74,999	22.8	42.2	6.4	14.0
$75,000 to $99,999	20.6	42.4	4.2	11.7
$100,000 to $249,999	15.3	40.6	2.7	10.6
$250,000 and over	7.2	34.4	0.4	2.7

Source: Columns 1 and 2 authors' calculations based on data from the Survey of Consumer Finances (Board of Governors of the Federal Reserve System 2007).
Columns 3 and 4: Authors' calculations, based on data from the Panel Study of Income Dynamics (2009).
[a.] Asian and other races are excluded from the table because of small sample sizes.
[b.] Households are classified by the schooling level of the head of household.
[c.] Households are classified by the age of the head of household.

and 23 percent for Hispanics compared to "only" 15 percent for whites—somewhat surprisingly, single females, the poorest of the three family types, had the lowest incidence of negative home equity among homeowners of this type, 13 percent, compared to 17 percent of married couples and single males. The reason for this is likely the lower mortgage debt of single females (that is, they had less expensive houses to begin with). Also, again somewhat surprisingly, homeowners in the lowest educational group, those with less than twelve years of schooling, had the smallest incidence of negative home equity, only 7 percent. In contrast, the incidence ranged from 17 percent to 19 percent among high school graduates, those with some college, and college graduates.

The age pattern is more consistent with our expectations. Homeowners in the youngest age group, under age thirty-five, have by far the highest incidence of negative home equity, almost 50 percent. The incidence of negative home equity declines almost directly with age, reaching just 1 percent for the oldest age group, seventy-five years and older. This reflects the fact that mortgages are generally paid off as people age. Moreover, the overall ratio of debt to net worth also declines directly with age.[10]

However, the pattern by income class is again unexpected. The overall pattern is U-shaped, with the lowest incidence of negative home equity in the lowest class of annual income (under $15,000) and the highest income class ($250,000 or more). The incidence of negative home equity among homeowners peaks in the $50,000 to $75,000 income class. Thus, the middle class was hit hardest by the collapse in housing prices. The reason is that they took on much higher mortgage debt, through refinancing, secondary mortgages, and home equity lines of credit, relative to their home values than either the poor or the rich (Wolff 2010).

Thus, even though non-Hispanic whites, married people, people with greater levels of education, older people (particularly ages sixty-five to seventy-four), and people with higher income have the highest rate of home ownership, the groups with the highest ownership rates do not necessarily have the highest share of homeowners with negative home equity. According to our projections, at the end of 2009, homeowners expected to have the highest percentages with negative home equity were African Americans, married individuals, those with greater than a high school education, younger people, and people with incomes between $50,000 and $100,000. Young homeowners under the age of thirty-five, of whom 49.9 percent have negative home equity, are projected to be the hardest hit by the recession.[11]

The PSID added a special supplement to its 2009 wealth survey on distressed mortgages. In particular, families were asked new questions about mortgage distress, foreclosure activity, falling behind in payments, mortgage modification, and expectations about mortgage payment difficulties in the coming twelve months. Results of this survey on the share of home owners who were delinquent on their mortgages in 2009 are shown in the third column of table 5.1 and results of the responses to the question "How likely is it that you will fall behind on your mortgage or remain behind on your mortgage in the next 12 months?" are reported in the fourth column of table 5.1.

The interesting feature of these results is that they do not automatically line up with the share of underwater households. That is, the mere fact that a family has negative home equity in its home does not necessarily mean that the family will walk away from its home by stopping mortgage payments. In fact, low-income groups tend to have the highest delinquency rate, which seems to imply that affordability is the main determinant of mortgage delinquency. This is consistent with reports from the Federal Housing Finance Agency that suggest that the top five reasons for default are "trigger events" such as income loss (36 percent), excessive obligations such as supporting dependents or paying high amounts of debt (19 percent), unemployment (8 percent), illness and associated medical costs or loss of income (6 percent), and marital breakup (3 percent; Federal Housing Finance Agency 2009). Individuals who are least able to handle unexpected financial hardships are the most likely to default, regardless of their home equity levels. However, a lack of home equity may make these individuals even more vulnerable to foreclosure if they are unable to refinance or sell their homes.

The overall delinquency rate among homeowners in 2009 was 5.1 percent, and the percentage of American homeowners that will likely continue to be behind or fall behind soon was a startling 14.1 percent. Indeed, among all of the demographic features of the heads of households, the percentage of individuals who will likely fall behind or remain behind on their mortgage payments is approximately three times the percentage of individuals who are currently behind, suggesting that rates of default and foreclosure are showing no signs of slowing. Among white households, the percentage was only 3.4 percent but among blacks it was 11.0 percent and among Hispanics, a somewhat startling 15.4 percent (in contrast, the share of blacks who were underwater was greater than for Hispanics). Single females were further behind on mortgage payments (a 7.8 percent delinquency rate) than single males or couples, even though single females had the smallest share of underwater mortgages and experienced the smallest decline in home equity values.

There is a negative linear relationship between delinquency rate and educational attainment. The lowest education group had a 11.8 percent delinquency rate, compared to 6.0 percent for high school graduates, 5.0 percent for those with some college, and a mere 1.6 percent for college graduates. This trend mimics the trend in homeowners who will likely fall behind on their mortgage. Perhaps the most frightening result of the current wave of the PSID is that over one-quarter (25.5 percent) of homeowners with less than a high school education report that they will likely be behind or will remain behind on their mortgage payments in the next twelve months.

Mortgage delinquency rates do seem to line up fairly well with the percentage of homeowners with negative home equity. The highest incidence occurs among the non-elderly, among whom delinquency rates range from 4.7 to 6.5 percent. In contrast, among those age sixty-five to seventy-four the delinquency rate was only 1.0 percent. Delinquency rates also tend to line up well with income class: the lowest income groups have the highest delinquency rates. The bottom income class, less than $15,000 in annual household income, had a delinquency rate of 7.7 percent; the income class $25,000 to $50,000 a rate of 8.4 percent; and the income class $50,000 to $75,000 a rate of 6.4 percent, compared to 2.7 percent for the second highest class, $100,000 to $249,999, and only 0.4 percent for the highest income class, over $250,000.

A report from the Office of the Comptroller of the Currency (David Streitfeld, "Households Facing Foreclosure Rose in 4th Quarter," *New York Times*, March 26, 2010, p. B6) indicates a surge in the delinquency rate between June 30, 2008, and December 31, 2009. The report uses as the variable of interest first-lien mortgages at least ninety days past due. According to their calculations, the number more than tripled over this period, from just under 0.5 million to over 1.5 million.[12] Even more recent data from the Mortgage Bankers Association (David Streitfeld, "Mortgage Data Leaves Bankers Uncertain of Trend," *New York Times*, May 20, 2010, p. B3) indicate that the mortgage delinquency rate rose in the first quarter of 2010 to 9.38 percent of all outstanding loans, up from 8.22 percent in the same period of 2009. It was also reported (Associated Press, "Mortgage Delinquencies, Foreclosures Break Records," May 19, 2010, online) that more than 10 percent of homeowners with a mortgage had missed at least one payment between January and March 2010. This figure, up from 9.1 percent a year ago, is a record high. But homeowner mortgage delinquencies may finally be beginning to turn around: according to even more recent figures released by the Mortgage Bankers Association (David Streitfeld, "Fewer Fall Delinquent in Paying Mortgages," *New York Times*, November 19, 2010, pp. B1–B2), the share of homeowners behind on their mortgage payments fell from 14.42 percent in the second quarter of 2010 to 13.52 percent in the third quarter. It was the lowest delinquency rate since the beginning of 2009.

The Foreclosure Explosion

Delinquency rates may translate into foreclosures, though not necessarily. Figure 5.4 shows that the number of foreclosures increased dra-

Figure 5.4   Number of Foreclosure Filings and Percentage of U.S. Housing Units in Foreclosure, 2006 to 2010

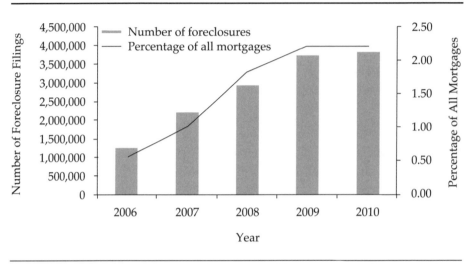

Source: Authors' compilation based on RealtyTrac Year-End foreclosure reports (various years).

matically since the beginning of the recession, affecting more and more households. The figure shows the numbers and percentages of households experiencing foreclosure proceedings in a certain year. Between 2006 and 2010, the number of foreclosure filings increased by a factor of 4, and the share of households in the midst of foreclosure proceedings rose from 0.5 percent to over 2.0 percent. In 2010, close to 4 million households, or one in forty-five, were affected. More recent data from RealtyTrac indicate that foreclosure rates are at their highest point in thirty years. Payments on 5 percent of loans nationwide are ninety days in arrears or more, and 2.9 million loans were foreclosed in 2010. Not surprisingly, an increasing percentage of housing sales (more than 30 percent, compared to less than 5 percent in 2006) are distressed properties—real estate owned (REOs) properties and short sales—rather than new homes. (REOs are properties owned by lenders, usually banks. Short sales refer to properties sold for less than the outstanding mortgage balance. The lender agrees to these properties being sold at a loss.)

According to data from RealtyTrac (see Renae Merle, "Foreclosure[s] Continue to Rise as Banks Work on Backlogs," *Washington Post*, May 14, 2010, online), the number of homes repossessed nationwide was 94,432 in April 2010. This was up only 1 percent from March but represented a jump of 45 percent from April 2009. Using the same data source, the *Los Angeles*

Figure 5.5   **Percentage of Loans in Foreclosure by Market Segment, 1998 to 2009**

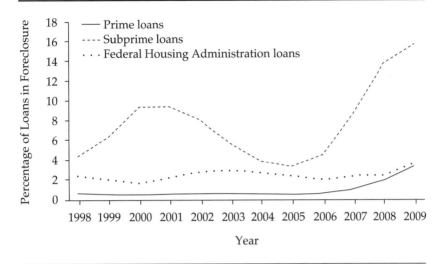

Source: Authors' compilation of data from U.S. Department of Housing and Urban Development, Office of Policy Development and Research (2010a, figures 5.6, 7).
Note: Yearly data based on quarterly averages.

Times (Alejandro Lazo, "US Home Foreclosures Reach Record High in Second Quarter," *Los Angeles Times*, July 15, 2010, online) indicated that the number of U.S. homes taken back by banks through foreclosure hit a record high in the second quarter of 2010. U.S. bank repossessions increased 38 percent between the second quarter of 2009 and of 2010.

Not all types of loans are equally likely to be foreclosed. The Mortgage Bankers Association (MBA), in their national Delinquency Survey, began distinguishing between prime and subprime loans in 1998.[13] Between 1998 and 2009, the rate of foreclosure filings in subprime loans was many multiples of the rate of prime loans (see figure 5.5). Beginning in 2006, however, the increase in foreclosure filing among subprime loans began rising dramatically. By the close of 2009, the rate of foreclosures for subprime loans was 15.6 percent of all filings, while that for prime mortgages was 3.3 percent.

The increase in the rate of subprime loans in default is partly driven by the increase in subprime loans' market share. Between 1998 and 2001, subprime loans only accounted for about 2.4 percent of all mortgages. By 2006, this share had increased to 13.5 percent. The percentage of loans in foreclosure was actually quite similar for prime (about 860,000) and subprime (about 900,000) loans in 2008 (U.S. Department of Housing and Urban Development 2010a).

Another strong predictor of delinquency and foreclosure is adjustable-rate mortgages (ARMs).[14] ARMs account for a disproportionate amount of prime and subprime loans that are in foreclosure. Although ARMs account for only 18 percent of prime loans and 48 percent of subprime loans, they make up 52 percent of prime foreclosure starts and 73 percent of subprime foreclosure starts (U.S. Department of Housing and Urban Development 2010a). Taken together subprime loans and subprime ARMs are far more likely to be delinquent and even more likely to be ninety days delinquent than prime loans or loans guaranteed by the U.S. Department of Veterans Affairs or the Federal Housing Administration. By the first quarter of 2010, 29 percent of subprime ARMs and 26 percent of subprime loans were thirty days delinquent, whereas the delinquency rate for all loans was only 10 percent (Mortgage Bankers Association of America 1998–2009).[15]

There has been a change in the geographical locus of housing market woes over the past three decades. Much attention has been paid recently to the high rates of foreclosure and default in the so-called sand states—California, Florida, Arizona, and Nevada. In the 1980s recessions, however, the oil states, Texas and Oklahoma, were most affected, and in the 2000s recession, states in the Midwest and the South were most affected. In 2006, Indiana, Ohio, and Michigan had the highest rates of foreclosure starts, which was due to existing weaknesses in their local economies. Then, with the beginning of the current Great Recession, levels of foreclosure starts began to spike nationwide. In 2008, forty-six states' foreclosure start rates were at least 0.5 percent of all mortgages.[16]

In the Great Recession the sand states do reveal unprecedented rates of foreclosure starts. The average rate of foreclosure starts in the sand states (1.76 percent) is more than twice the national average. This is likely due to a combination of steep drops in home values after the run-up in prices before the crisis, high rates of subprime lending, and particularly high rates of unemployment in these states (see chapter 3, on unemployment, in this volume).

Finally, we looked at the sociodemographic dispersion of pain in the housing market using data from the U.S. Department of Housing and Urban Development (HUD) on foreclosure starts and data from the 2000 census on the percentage of individuals who are African American or living in poverty in a given census tract.[17] Wall Street bankers are largely to blame for the housing crisis, yet it is the poorer and more heavily minority areas where homes are being foreclosed upon. Foreclosure rates are highest in high-poverty areas and in areas with a large percentage of African Americans. Even after controlling for the levels of poverty in an area, the link between foreclosure rates and African American neighborhoods remains.[18]

In the popular imagination, the causes and the consequences of the

Great Recession are largely defined in relation to the housing market. And this is a valid perception. As we have shown, the high rates of foreclosure, almost 3 million in 2009 alone, are certainly in line with this sentiment. Additionally, foreclosures were unevenly distributed across homeowners: low-income and minority individuals, who were most likely to get subprime loans, were the most likely to have their loans foreclosed, as were those individuals who already experienced another consequence of the Great Recession, unemployment. Housing debt, however, was not the only type of debt that characterized this period. In the next section we examine credit during the Great Recession.

Credit Card Debt Exposure and Delinquencies

The effects of the recession have not been confined to the housing market. The flip side of assets is debt, and another potential casualty of the current recession is an upsurge of delinquencies on credit card debt. However, somewhat surprisingly, a report issued by TransUnion, an organization that specializes in monitoring credit card debt, on February 22, 2010, did not reach this conclusion (Dave Blumberg and Clifton M. O'Neal, "Average Credit Card Delinquency Rates Rise in Fourth Quarter, Debt Goes Down—According to TransUnion," *Marketwire*, February 22, 2010, online). TransUnion's quarterly analysis of trends in the credit card industry found that the national rate on credit card balances (defined as the ratio of bankcard borrowers at least ninety days delinquent on one or more of their credit card balances) increased to 1.21 percent in the fourth quarter of 2009, up 10 percent over the previous quarter.[19] Year over year, however, from 2008 to 2009 credit card delinquencies remained flat.[20] The *New York Times* (Eric Dash, "Investors Ease Strain on FDIC," May 20, 2010, p. B1, and Floyd Norris, "The Growing Resilience of Plastic," July 31, 2010, p. B3) reported a decline in both the credit card delinquency rate and the credit card default rate between 2009 and the second quarter of 2010 on the basis of data from the Federal Deposit Insurance Corporation.

The report also found that the incidence of credit card delinquency was highest in Nevada (2.00 percent), followed closely by Florida (1.75 percent) and Arizona (1.62 percent). These are also among the states with highest foreclosure rates. The lowest credit card delinquency rates were found in Alaska (0.67 percent), North Dakota (0.69 percent), and South Dakota (0.74 percent), and seven states experienced a drop in their credit card delinquency rates.

Delinquencies aside, in 2009, average credit card debt fell nationally by 3.18 percent, to $5,434, from the previous quarter's $5,612, and down 5.15 percent from that in the fourth quarter of 2008 ($5,729). The state with the highest average credit card debt was Alaska, at $7,328, followed by Tennessee, at $6,823, and Alabama, at $6,332. Iowa had the lowest average credit card debt ($4,139), followed by North Dakota ($4,318) and West Virginia ($4,448). No state showed an increase in average credit card debt from the prior quarter. The authors of the report suggest (though the evidence appears rather limited) that the decline in credit card balances in the fourth quarter was due in part to the efforts of consumers to pay down their credit card balances in response to continued financial uncertainty and to provide a credit cushion for hard times.

Interestingly, the national trends in credit card delinquencies over the course of the current recession were not that closely correlated with the unemployment rate. In contrast, in the relatively mild recession of 2001, in which unemployment rates were much lower than those during the current recession, credit card delinquencies rose almost 25 percent. Over the course of this recession, credit card delinquency rates have not moved past the 1.36 percent level of the fourth quarter of 2007, which marked the beginning of the economic downturn. The authors of the TransUnion report argue that this is due to a large extent to the fact that falling home values have motivated consumers with negative equity to walk away from their mortgage debt obligations in order to remain current on their credit card payments. However, this may be purely speculation on the part of the report's authors. If true, it would represent a fundamental shift in consumer behavior from that during the 2001 recession.

Further fallout from the Great Recession is the contraction in consumer credit. From 1983 to 2007 there was an enormous upsurge of consumer debt, such that in 2007 the total outstanding amount, more than $2.577 trillion, was more than five times the 1983 amount (see figure 5.6).[21] However, a retrenchment of consumer debt began around the first quarter of 2008, and by the first quarter of 2010 outstanding credit had fallen by about 10 percent from its peak in the first quarter of 2008. Interestingly, this contraction occurred in both revolving and nonrevolving credit accounts but more so for the former. According to Federal Reserve figures, total credit card balances declined from $957.3 billion in December of 2008 to $886 billion in December of 2009; that's $91.3 billion, 9.54 percent.

We might speculate that both supply and demand factors are at work in this contraction of outstanding consumer credit. Households are cutting back on their debt because of reduced incomes and increased uncertainty about the future. Another factor is that the household debt service ratio—the ratio of annual repayments of household debt to household income—rose from a low of 10.73 percent in the fourth quarter of 1993 to a high of 13.91 percent in the first quarter of 2008 before declining a bit to 12.85 percent in the fourth quarter of 2009. However, equally important for the contraction of consumer debt is that banks and other financial

Figure 5.6   Total Consumer Credit Outstanding, 1943 to 2010

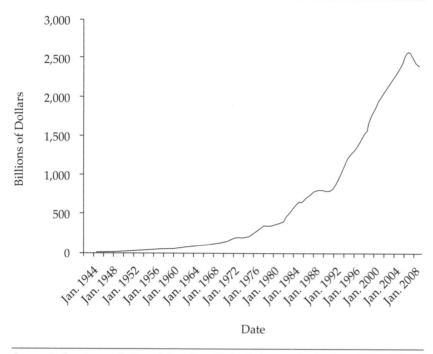

Source: Authors' compilation of data from Federal Reserve Bank of St. Louis (various years).

institutions have cut back on credit cards issued and lines of credit and lowered credit limits (exact figures on this are difficult to come by).

Bankruptcy

With the recession hammering away at Americans' economic outlook, it stands to reason that personal bankruptcies might be on the rise. And despite new laws in 2005 making bankruptcy much harder to claim, that is exactly what we are seeing. It is first of interest to see what the figures from the SCF show. According to our calculations and our projections to 2009, the share of households with negative net worth rose from 15.5 percent in 1983 to 17.7 percent in 2001 and then increased moderately to 18.6 percent in 2007. After that, as a result of the stock market and housing market collapses, by the end of 2009 the share of households with negative net worth had skyrocketed to 24.8 percent. This likely set the stage for the rash of bankruptcies that have occurred.

There has been a striking rise in the number of total filings since the 1980s.[22] Figure 5.7 shows the number of total bankruptcy filings in the

Figure 5.7   Total Bankruptcy Filings, 1980 to 2009

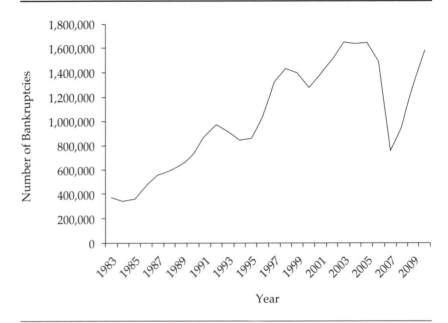

Year

Source: Authors' compilation based on data from United States Courts (various years).

U.S. since 1980. Bankruptcies surged to a bit over 2 million in 2005 as individuals hurried to file for bankruptcy before the new bankruptcy law took effect, and then fell to about 600,000 in 2006. Since then the number of bankruptcies has been steadily climbing; in 2009 it reached 1.3 million and in 2010, 1.6 million. The number of bankruptcies in 2010 became the fourth highest on record, behind 2003, 2004, and 2005.[23]

There have also been a host of stories in the media documenting the surge in bankruptcies in 2008 and 2009. Mike Barber ("Bankruptcies Surge 32 Percent in 2009," Associated Press, January 4, 2010) reported that bankruptcies increased 32 percent between 2008 and 2009 on the basis of data collected by the Associated Press from the country's ninety bankruptcy districts. The Associated Press calculated that there were 1.43 million bankruptcy filings in 2009 and 116,000 recorded bankruptcies in December 2009, which was an increase of 22 percent over December 2008. As we suggested earlier, part of the increase is due to families adapting to the new bankruptcy law introduced in 2005. However, the evidence still points to a correlation between the increase in bankruptcies and areas hit hard by the recession. For example, western states saw the fastest increase, with Arizona reporting the largest percentage increase of bankruptcy filings between 2008 and 2009 (77 percent), followed by Wyoming (60 percent), Nevada (59 percent), and California (58 percent). More recent data (Duff Wilson, "Sharp Increase in March Personal Bankruptcies," *New York Times*, April 2, 2010, p. B3), indicate that federal court bankruptcy filings surged by 35 percent from February to March 2010 and were up 19 percent over March 2009.

Older Workers and Pensions

The sharp decline in the stock market in 2008 put many Americans nearing retirement in a difficult financial situation. Although the market had rebounded to some degree as of March 2010, after hitting a low point in March 2009, important losses have occurred. The Urban Institute and Center for Retirement Research at Boston College have both been involved in efforts to try to predict the effects of the stock market crash on the retirement readiness of older Americans.

Figure 5.8, derived from Barbara A. Butrica and Philip Issa (2010), shows the impact of the recession on retirement accounts (contribution plans and Individual Retirement Accounts, or IRAs) in the United States. They used data from the Federal Reserve Board's Flow of Funds to do the updating. From the third quarter of 2007 to the first quarter of 2009, the value of retirement accounts declined from a peak of $8.6 trillion to $5.9 trillion, a loss of $2.8 trillion or 31.4 percent of their value in nominal terms. In real terms—that is, after accounting for inflation—the loss was even greater—33.7 percent.[24] However, the value of these accounts has recovered considerably, and by the fourth quarter of 2009, their value was $7.6 trillion, 14.6 percent below their peak value. Although retirement account assets are still below their peak values in 2007, in real terms their value is now back to where it was in the first quarter of 2006.

According to a study done by Steven A. Sass, Courtney Monk, and Kelly Haverstick (2010) at the Center for Retirement Research at Boston College, the stock market crash of 2008 significantly dimmed the retirement prospects of many workers who were approaching retirement. These workers are in general heavily dependent on 401(k) plans for their retirement income, as opposed to traditional defined benefit pensions. During the economic downturn, these plans lost about one-third of their value. Even before the crash, many older workers lacked the assets needed to enjoy a comfortable retirement. We perform similar calculations on the loss of value on defined contribution retirement accounts such as 401(k)s. As we noted, by our calculations, the price of equities (corporate stock) fell by 24.5 percent and that of financial securities by 13.8 percent between mid-2007 and the end of December 2009. We also calculated that 43.6 percent of pension accounts were held in the form of corporate equities. Using data from the 2007 SCF, we calculated

Figure 5.8   Accumulations in Retirement Accounts, 2005 to 2009

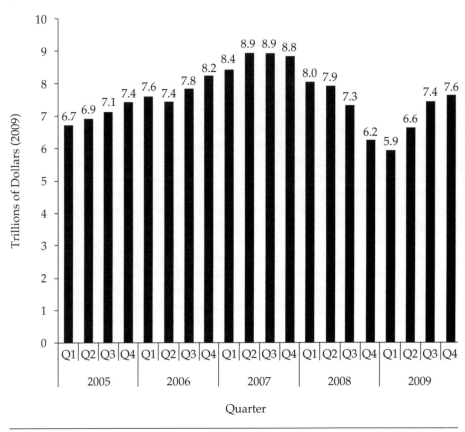

Source: Authors' tabulation based on Butrica and Issa (2010).

an average loss of 22.4 percent on the value of retirement accounts. The rational response to a sharp decline in retirement wealth is to save more, work longer, and consume less in retirement. The extent to which workers are absorbing a portion of the loss by saving more and working longer is thus critical for assessing their economic prospects at retirement.

To examine these issues, in the summer of 2009 the Center for Retirement Research (CRR) surveyed a nationally representative sample of 1,317 workers age forty-five to fifty-nine and thus approaching retirement on changes in their retirement saving and expected retirement ages. The investigators' major findings were that two-thirds of working people in this age group said that they now have less retirement savings than they did before the recession, 40 percent expected to retire on average four years later than they had earlier planned, and many reported experiencing a level of distress equal to or even greater than that caused by the terrorist attacks on September 11, 2001. However, in contrast to 60 percent of the workers who reported having changed their spending levels, two-thirds of the workers in their sample reported not having changed their saving behavior for their 401(k)s, IRAs, and other retirement accounts. The main conclusion of the CRR study is that there was a significant increase in expected retirement age but not much change in saving for retirement. The study found no differences in saving behavior by race or sex.

A survey done by Bank of America (2010) also found that people are not saving more. The survey results showed that a growing number of Americans were concerned that the economic crisis was threatening to leave them further behind on their retirement plans. The article reported that six in ten Americans were spending less than they had been three months previously as a result of the economic climate. However, even with this decreased spending, 51 percent of the general public and 40 percent of affluent Americans were also saving less than they had been three months previously, and approximately one in five stated that they were saving "much less." Like the CRR's research, the findings of this survey also underscored how deeply troubled Americans were about their retirement savings and financial well-being, with about 23 percent of respondents indicating that the impact of economic turbulence on their retirement savings was the financial issue that concerns them most.

Yet these reports of savings behavior may be out of date. Recent data from the Bureau of Economic Analysis's National Income and Product Accounts indicate an uptick in the personal savings rate from 2.4 percent in January of 2008 to 5.7 percent in October of 2010.[25]

The Bank of America (2010) survey shows that many Americans (43 percent) believed they now face more years in the workforce than they expected one year before as a result of recent economic turbulence. This will clearly affect baby boomers the most, especially those approaching retirement who may not have time to recover the financial losses incurred during recent months. For this reason, it is not surprising that 36 percent of affluent respondents said that current economic conditions have led them to defer their expected retirement age. Rich Morin (2009) of the Pew Research Center reached similar conclusions as a result of a survey of a nationally representative sample of 2,969 adults from February 23 through March 23, 2009. During the current recession, which has taken a heavy toll on household wealth, just over 50 percent of all working adults age fifty to sixty-four said that they might delay their retirement and another 16 percent said that they never expect to stop working. Overall, 37 percent of full-time employed adults of all ages said that they had thought in the past year about postponing their eventual retirement. This proportion increased to 52 percent among full-time workers

fifty to sixty-four years of age—whom Pew calls the "Threshold Generation" because they are perpetually on the threshold of exiting the workforce. Sixteen percent of them said they never planned to retire, twice as
many as younger workers (8 percent). Moreover, those in the Threshold
Generation who did plan to retire someday said that they planned to
keep working, on average, until they were age sixty-six—which would
make them four years older than the average age at which current retirees age sixty-five or older reported that they stopped working.

Investment losses and the size of the losses appeared to play an important role in the decision of when to retire. Among the Threshold Generation and other age groups, higher-income earners were only slightly
less likely than lower-income adults to have considered postponing retirement. But regardless of income or age, those who lost 40 percent or
more of their retirement account were roughly twice as likely as those
who had not lost money in the market meltdown to say they had thought
about delaying their eventual retirement from the workforce. The rising
inclination to delay retirement is driven in part by the current recession,
but it is also in conformity with longer-term labor-market trends. Morin
(2009) reported that the labor-force participation rate of those ages sixty-
five and older had already increased from 12.9 percent in 2000 to 16.8
percent in 2008.

Demographic factors also play a role in people's decisions about
when to retire. Among all age groups, 46 percent of all full-time employed women said that they had thought about delaying retirement in
the past year, compared with 31 percent (less than a third) of all working
men. Also, 40 percent of whites thought about extending their working
lives, compared with 32 percent of blacks and 34 percent of Hispanics.
Income differences mattered less for retirement decisions. Among those
with family incomes of less than $30,000, 44 percent thought about post-
poning their retirement, compared with 37 percent of those earning
$100,000 or more. Similarly, 36 percent of those making $30,000 to $50,000
and 38 percent of those making $50,000 to $100,000 considered working
longer as the recession settled in during the past year.

Fifty-two percent of adults age fifty to sixty-four who were employed
full-time said that they had thought about delaying retirement, and
women once again were more likely to say this than men. Sixty percent
of women working full-time in this age group said they had reconsid-
ered when they will retire, compared with slightly less than half of all
men. This gender gap is consistent with other research that has shown
that older women approaching retirement have fewer economic resources to draw on than do men, which could be driving their decisions
to stay in the workforce longer. There was little difference by income
among these late-middle-aged adults regarding their retirement deci-

sion: those with family incomes of $75,000 or more were as likely as those earning less to say that they had considered delaying retirement. Working adults who were closer to age sixty-five, the traditional retirement age, were even more likely than younger members of the Threshold Generation to have considered delaying their retirement. Over two-thirds of those age fifty-seven to sixty-four said they had thought about delaying retirement, compared with 44 percent of those age fifty to fifty-six.

Working members of the Threshold Generation were the least confident of any age group that they would have enough money to last through their retirement years. Barely 21 percent of those fifty to sixty-four said that they were "very confident" that they had enough income and assets to tide them over, compared with 37 percent of full-time workers under thirty and 40 percent of those age sixty-five and older. Most Americans, young or old, said that the recession made it harder to take care of their financial needs in retirement. However, more working adults in the Threshold Generation than in any other age group feel this way. Among those age fifty to sixty-four with full-time jobs, 78 percent said that the recession made it more difficult to take care of their financial needs in retirement, compared with 66 percent of those under fifty. Income differences played little role in fueling the recession-driven financial worries of the Threshold Generation. Sixty-nine percent of those with family incomes under $30,000 and 76 percent of those with incomes of $100,000 or more said that the recession would make it harder to take care of their financial needs when they retired. Similarly, there was little difference by gender, by level of education, or by race.

It is also the case that among all adults, the Threshold Generation saw the value of their investments shrink the most. About three-quarters of adults ages fifty to sixty-four said that they lost money in mutual funds, individual stocks, or retirement accounts such as a 401(k)s, compared with barely half of those under fifty. Working members of the Threshold Generation who lost money on investments were also more likely than those who did not suffer losses to say that they considered delaying retirement (54 versus 45 percent), and they were more likely to have considered taking this step than were adults under fifty who lost money in the market (54 versus 34 percent). Investment losses also affected financial confidence. More than 80 percent of working members of the Threshold Generation who had lost money in the previous year said that the recession will make it harder for them to meet their financial needs in retirement, compared with 66 percent of those ages eighteen to forty-nine. The Bank of America (2010) survey results suggest that many Americans were not fully able to save what is needed to retire as they had planned, and some were tapping into their nest eggs to meet more immediate financial needs. Although 68 percent of respondents with at least one retirement account said that they did not withdraw assets from their accounts prematurely, more recent economic conditions caused nearly one in five to withdraw assets prematurely. The leading reasons for these early withdrawals were near-term financial obligations, such as credit card debt (26 percent) and mortgage payments (22 percent), with an additional 22 percent citing recent job loss. The article argued that if the economy continues to worsen, these numbers may increase significantly. The possibility of many more Americans dipping into their retirement savings could have profound implications for the country's future economic well-being.

Alan L. Gustman, Thomas L. Steinmeier, and Nahid Tabatabai (2009) offer a much more sanguine view of the effects of the stock market crash on retirement preparedness. Their findings indicate that although the consequences of the stock market downturn of 2008 to 2009 are serious for those approaching retirement, the average person approaching retirement age was not likely to suffer a life-changing financial loss from the downturn. Likewise, the likely effects of the stock market downturn on retirement resources have been greatly exaggerated. If there is any postponement of retirement due to stock market losses, on average it will be a matter of a few months rather than years. When layoffs are counted, retirements may be accelerated rather than reduced.

Concluding Remarks and Some Policy Recommendations

The fallout from the current recession has taken many forms and has struck broadly among the American population but has hit some groups harder than others. It has impacted the wealth at both the top and the bottom of the income distribution. For those at the top, on the basis of the Forbes 400 we calculated that the average net worth of the top 50 Americans fell by 17 percent between 2008 and 2009, although there was some recovery from 2009 to 2010. There was also a falloff in the average net worth of the top 100 and top 400, but there was no recovery from 2009 to 2010 for these groups. Data from the World Wealth Report indicate that the number of ultrarich individuals in North America, defined as individuals who hold at least $30 million in investable assets, fell by 18 percent between 2007 and 2008. Our own calculations from the SCF suggest a 37 percent reduction in the average holdings of the wealthiest 1 percent of households.

Many families have seen the value of their main nest egg, their home, shrink. Data from the National Association of Realtors series on the median price of existing homes indicate a 26 percent drop in home prices from 2007 through 2009, though home prices bottomed out in January 2010 and have since recovered somewhat. Still, many of those homeowners have also seen the value of their home equity become negative. On the basis of the 2007 SCF, we estimate that 16.4 percent of homeowners were "underwater" by the end of 2009. An even more recent estimate puts the figure at 20 percent. On the basis of data from the 2009 PSID, we found that the overall delinquency rate among homeowners in 2009 was 5 percent and the percentage of American homeowners that will likely continue to be behind on their mortgage payments or will fall behind soon was a startling 14 percent.

Particularly hard hit have been young families, minorities, and, surprisingly, middle-class households (with annual incomes of $50,000 to $75,000). Many such families have become delinquent in paying off their mortgages and have been forced into foreclosure of their mortgages. This has been particularly true for low-income and less educated families and those families that reside in the West, which has been particularly hard hit by the steep decline in housing prices.

According to RealtyTrac data, between 2006 and 2009 the number of foreclosures annually increased by a factor of 4, and the share of households experiencing a foreclosure rose from 0.5 percent to over 2.0 percent. In 2009, close to 2 percent of households in the United States were affected. More recent data from RealtyTrac indicate that foreclosure filings increased by 15 percent between 2009 and 2010.

Though we have not witnessed a surge in credit card delinquencies as we did in the 2001-to-2002 recession, this recession has been particularly characterized by a contraction of consumer credit. There was an enormous upsurge of consumer debt from 1983 to 2007, in which period the total outstanding amount jumped by more than 500 percent. However, a retrenchment of consumer debt began some time around the first quarter of 2008, and by the first quarter of 2010, outstanding debt fell by about 10 percent from its peak in first quarter 2008. Whether this trend is a good thing or a bad thing is debatable, but it probably means that there will continue to be a decline in consumption.

In extreme cases, household debt has led many families to declare bankruptcy. Indeed, there has been a surge in personal bankruptcies despite a change in the bankruptcy law in 2005 that imposes more stringent conditions on declaring bankruptcy. The number of bankruptcies surged to over 2 million in 2005 as individuals hurried to declare bankruptcy before the new law took effect and then fell to about 600,000 in 2006. Since then, the number of bankruptcies has been steadily climbing; in 2010 it reached 1.6 million.

Older workers nearing retirement and even retirees have been adversely affected by severe declines in their pension wealth, particularly their 401(k)s. Data from the Flow of Funds indicate that from the third quarter of 2007 to the first quarter of 2009, retirement accounts in total declined by 34 percent in real terms. Although the value of these accounts has rebounded somewhat, by the fourth quarter of 2009 their value was still 15 percent below that at their peak. Our own calculations on the basis of the 2007 SCF indicate that from mid-2007 to the end of December 2009 there was an average loss of 22 percent of the value of retirement accounts. As a result, many older Americans have cut back on their consumption. Others, according the Center for Retirement Research, have now decided to postpone the date of their retirement.

We can already see that some major institutional changes are in order to respond effectively to the financial fallout of the Great Recession. Because there are opportunities for intervention in this domain that are readily seized, it makes sense to focus this chapter, more so than some of the others in this book, on policy changes that may result from the Great Recession. We conclude by laying out some opportunities for new policies regarding foreclosures, predatory lending, and retirement readiness.

Predatory Lending and Home Foreclosures

The creation of a Consumer Financial Protection Agency may curb abuses associated with subprime mortgages and "teaser rates." Further, the Barack Obama administration has enacted several programs designed both to keep homeowners in their homes and to facilitate short sales among homeowners. The purpose of the Home Affordable Modification Program (HAMP), established in February of 2009, was to facilitate loan modifications by incentivizing lenders to modify loans by reducing or fixing the interest rate, extending the terms of the loan, or reducing the principal balance. However, this program, which was initially hoped to help 3 million to 4 million homeowners by 2012, is widely considered to be a failure and has helped only a few hundred thousand. The failure of the program has largely been attributed to a lack of cooperation on the part of the lenders. More recently, as of April 2010, the Home Affordable Foreclosure Alternatives Program (HAFA) began offering incentives for homeowners ($3,000) and lenders to facilitate short sales. However, this program is again conditional on the lender's approval, which to this point has not been particularly easy to get.

The creation of a Consumer Financial Protection Agency may help to reduce or even eliminate predatory lending, hidden fees, and other credit card abuses. The drying up of consumer credit may prove to be more difficult to reverse. However, as the economy improves, one would expect that credit card companies will once again expand their lines of credit.

Pension Security

Defined contribution (DC) pensions, like (401)k plans, are a ticking time bomb because the value of such accounts is subject to the vagaries of the stock market and is therefore at risk. There should be four major goals in reforming the present DC system: (1) increase participation rates; (2) increase the amount contributed into the system by current workers and their employers; (3) increase the returns on retirement accounts; (4) stabilize the returns on these accounts and reduce the risk associated with them.

Another problem is that a lot of low-income workers and young workers simply cannot afford a 401(k) or even an IRA. To deal with this problem, tax incentives need to be changed. Under existing law, high-income employees receive the largest tax subsidy for payments into their pension plans, and low-income employees receive the lowest. Thus, replacing the current system whereby a tax deduction is given for retirement plan contributions with a system of tax credits would still provide everyone with a tax incentive but would shift the benefit down the income ladder. This would presumably increase the savings of low-income workers. The system would make the amount of tax credit dependent on family income and would turn the tax credit into a refundable tax credit in the case of low-income families. Thus, the government would subsidize low-income workers for putting part of their savings in a retirement account. Moreover, an additional special tax credit might be provided to young families in order to boost the number of them who establish retirement accounts.

Another recommendation is that the Obama administration push for comprehensive retirement coverage. Less than half of employees have a retirement plan at work. The so-called universal IRA, which would provide all workers with an individual retirement account, an idea advanced by Obama during the presidential campaign, would help make a retirement account available to all workers.

Another problem is with the return on the investments in retirement accounts. One possible measure to prevent wide variations in payouts from retirement plans at the time of retirement would be to develop a saving plan in which the federal government shared the risk. This could be implemented by providing a guarantee that returns would not fall below a certain level. A similar proposal has been advanced by Teresa Ghilarducci (2007, 2008), and she calls it a Guaranteed Retirement Account (GRA). In her proposal, participation in the program is mandatory except for workers participating in an equivalent or better employer defined-benefits plan. Contributions are set equal to 5 percent of earnings, to be paid equally by the employer and the employee. Participants are guaranteed a minimum 3 percent annual rate of return on their account, adjusted for inflation. The guarantee is provided by the federal government.

We support such an approach. One possibility is to offer federal bonds with fixed yields. Such bonds actually already exist as Treasury Inflation-Protected Securities (TIPS), though the yields have historically been quite low. Another possibility is to have the federal government or the employer make up the difference between the actual yield on a retirement account such as a 401(k) and some pre-set minimum. (Such a plan requires some further refinement.)

We would propose an even stronger measure: universal, guaranteed employer pension coverage (much like the proposal for guaranteed health insurance). The first step is to make participation universal within a company, so that all workers are covered. Second, it should not be necessary to require employee contributions in order to have funds provided (or matched) by the employer. Third, employer contributions should be mandatory. A certain minimum contribution should be required from each employer (in much the same way as minimum standards should be drawn up for an employer-provided health policy). Fourth, employee contributions should be voluntary.

The "Great Recession" has ravaged Americans' wealth, from stocks to housing to retirement accounts. Though we are now seeing some recovery, the scarring and pain dealt to Americans' portfolios is likely to be long-lasting. With careful consideration of some of the policy recommendations offered here, such scarring and pain may be mitigated somewhat.

Notes

1. *Forbes* obtains data on property and assets as well as debt using a large variety of sources, from newspapers to court records. The value of privately held companies is estimated through comparisons to similar publicly owned companies.

2. These data and those on ultrarich individuals were collected and aggregated from annual Merrill Lynch and Capgemini World Wealth Reports from 2001 to 2010. The report in a given year (say, 2009) presents statistics from the preceding year (2008) and revises any figures from earlier years (2000 to 2007). World Wealth Reports are produced and published by Merrill Lynch and Capgemini. Capgemini/Merrill Lynch use national statistics from the International Monetary Fund and the World Bank.

3. "Table B-60: Consumer Price Indexes for Major Expenditure Classes." In *Economic Report of the President, 2010*, http://www.gpoaccess.gov/eop/2010/B60.xls; accessed May 26, 2011.

4. National Association of Realtors, "Existing Home Sales," http://www.realtor.org/research/research/ehsdata; accessed May 26, 2011.

5. The National Association of Realtors data also include price changes on the regional level. Unfortunately, the 2007 SCF does not have a variable indicat-

ing region of residence, so we were forced to use the national price index in our calculations in table 5.1.

6. Board of Governors of the Federal Reserve System, "Flow of Funds Accounts of the United States, Flows and Outstandings, Fourth Quarter 2009," Federal Reserve Statistical Release, March 21, 2010.

7. Federal Reserve Bank of St. Louis, FRED Statistics Online Database, "Housing Starts: Total: New Privately Owned Housing Units Started (HOUST)," http://research.stlouisfed.org/fred2/series/HOUST/downloaddata?cid =97; accessed December 13, 2010.

8. National Association of Realtors, "Existing Home Sales," http://www .realtor.org/research/research/ehsdata; accessed May 26, 2011. The data come from the National Association of Realtors (NAR), which collects monthly data on home sales prices from local associations and multiple listing services (MLS) nationwide; the NAR captures 30 to 40 percent of all monthly existing-home sale transactions in the United States. Comparisons done by NAR using the American Housing Survey show that these data are representative of prices in each corresponding region.

9. For example, a home purchased for $500,000 in California in 2008 was worth $365,000 in spring 2011. If values increase at an optimistic rate of 3.5 percent (the historical rate of appreciation for housing) per year, it will take about ten years for the home to recover its lost value.

10. On the basis of the 2007 SCF, the overall ratio of debt to net worth fell from 93 percent for those under thirty-five to 2 percent for those seventy-five and over.

11. We also show the percentage decline in the average value of home equity from mid-2007 to December 31, 2009, for all households: 39.1 percent. The pattern by demographic group tends to mirror that of the first column of table 5.1, the share of households that are underwater. African American households appear to have suffered the largest decline, 48 percent, followed by Hispanics, 45 percent, and then whites, 37 percent. Single female–headed households experienced a somewhat smaller decline than single male–headed households or married couples. The least-educated households suffered a smaller decline than the more-educated (33 percent versus about 39 percent). There is tremendous age variation, with older households more immune to the housing price collapse. The youngest age group experienced a 68 percent fall in the equity of their homes while the oldest age group had "only" a 28 percent decline. Middle-class households (defined by household income) suffered the highest depreciation in home equity, around 42 percent, while the two lowest income classes had only a 31 percent decrease and the highest income class a 34 percent decline.

12. The report's figures are based on about two-thirds of first-lien mortgages, so the actual national numbers are likely to be higher.

13. There is no standard definition for subprime loans, but generally subprime loans are those offered to individuals with imperfect credit or a high debt-to-income ratio (their FICO score is often below 640).

14. Adjustable-rate mortgages (ARMs), as opposed to fixed-rate mortgages, are loans whose interest rate changes at reset time points, typically three to five years after the origination, in accordance with the interest rate of a given index such as the LIBOR (London Interbank Offered Rate), CMT (Constant

Maturity Treasury), or COFI (11th District Cost of Funds Index), among others. The rates at origination are generally lower "teaser" rates.

15. U.S. Department of Housing and Urban Development, http://www .huduser.org/portal/Publications/PDF/Foreclosure_09.pdf (page 8); accessed May 26, 2011.

16. Note that 0.5 percent is considered an indicator of distress. See Mortgage Bankers Association, "National Delinquency Survey," http://www.mbaa .org/ResearchandForecasts/ProductsandSurveys/NationalDelinquency Survey.htm; accessed May 26, 2011.

17. Data for analyses of foreclosure rates and minority populations at the census tract level are from the U.S. Department of Housing and Urban Development Neighborhood Stabilization Project (2008) and the 2000 decennial census planning database (U.S. Census Bureau 2000). To compensate for the dearth of available foreclosure data HUD analysts estimated foreclosure rates at the census tract level for 2007 and the first half of 2008 using Federal Reserves Home Mortgage Disclosure Act data on high cost loans, Office of Federal Housing and Enterprise Oversight Data on home prices, and Bureau of Labor Statistics data on unemployment rates. Predicted foreclosure rates are estimated by the following model:

$$Yi = -2.211 - (0.131*\text{PriceDrop}) + (0.152*\text{HighCostLoan}) + (0.392*\text{Unemployed}),$$

where Yi is the predicted foreclosure start rate, PriceDrop is the percentage change in the Office of Federal Housing Enterprise Oversight and Metropolitan Statistical Area (MSA OFHEO) current price relative to the maximum price in the past eight years, HighCostLoan is the percentage of total loans made between 2004 and 2006 that are high cost, and Unemployed is the percentage unemployed in a tract in June 2008. Estimates were checked against Equifax delinquency data from credit reports and the intercounty correlation was 0.835 (higher for larger counties). For additional sensitivity analyses see the Neighborhood Stabilization Program methodology report at http://www.huduser.org/DATASETS/nsp.html.

18. On the basis of ordinary least squares regression analyses controlling for poverty rates at the tract level, we found the associations between foreclosure start rates and the percentage of African Americans in a tract to be robust.

19. A credit card account is declared delinquent if the minimum payment is not made by the account holder.

20. This information was based on approximately 27 million anonymous, randomly sampled, individual credit files representing approximately 10 percent of credit-active U.S. consumers.

21. See Federal Reserve Bank of St. Louis, "Total Consumer Credit Outstanding." Data retrieved July 8, 2011, from http://research.stlouisfed.org/ fred2/series/TOTALSL.

22. These data are aggregated from annual bankruptcy statistics published by the administrative office of the U.S. Courts and can be found at uscourts. gov. The number of total bankruptcy filings may overcount individuals

who file, drop the case, and file again a later date. In order to capture the greatest number of years for our historical trends, a year begins on July 1 and ends June 30.

23. The 2005 bankruptcy act made bankruptcy filings more cumbersome, a move that followed concerns of lenders that some families were abusing the system to wipe out their debts. The new bankruptcy law, officially named the Bankruptcy Abuse Prevention and Consumer Protection Act (BAPCPA), was signed by President George W. Bush on April 20, 2005.

24. The total value of retirement accounts was converted to 2009 dollars on the basis of an inflation calculator provided at http://www.measuringworth .com/ppowerus/.

25. See "Table 2.6. Personal Income and Its Disposition Monthly" (U.S. Bureau of Economic Analysis 2010).

References

Bank of America. 2010. "Bank of America Survey Finds Despite Tightening Their Wallets, Americans Are Further from Achieving Their Retirement Goals Amidst Weakening Economy." Press release. Available at: http://newsroom .bankofamerica.com/index.php?s=43&item=8308; accessed May 26, 2011.

Board of Governors of the Federal Reserve System. 2007. *Survey of Consumer Finances.* Available at: http://www.federalreserve.gov/pubs/oss/oss2/scf index.html; accessed July 8, 2011.

Butrica, Barbara A., and Philip Issa. 2010. "Retirement Account Balances (Updated 4/11)." Urban Institute Fact Sheet. Washington, D.C.: Urban Institute. Available at: http://www.urban.org/publications/411976.html; accessed May 26, 2011.

Federal Housing Finance Agency. 2009. *Foreclosure Prevention Report, First Quarter 2009.* Available at: http://www.fhfa.gov/webfiles/2976/1Q09_Fore closure_Prevention_Report_Final_06-23-09.pdf; accessed May 26, 2011.

Federal Reserve Bank of St. Louis. various years. "Total Consumer Credit Outstanding." Available at: http://research.stlouisfed.org/fred2/series/TO TALSL; accessed July 7, 2011.

Forbes. various years. "Forbes 400 Richest Americans List." Most recent list available at: http://www.forbes.com/wealth/forbes-400; accessed July 8, 2011.

Ghilarducci, Teresa. 2007. "Guaranteed Retirement Accounts: Toward Retirement Income Security." EPI Briefing Paper No. 204. Washington, D.C.: Economic Policy Institute. Available at: http://www.sharedprosperity.org/bp204 .html; accessed May 26, 2011.

———. 2008. *When I'm Sixty-four: The Plot Against Pensions and the Plan to Save Them.* Princeton, N.J.: Princeton University Press.

Gustman, Alan L., Thomas L. Steinmeier, and Nahid Tabatabai. 2009. "How Do Pension Changes Affect Retirement Preparedness? The Trend to Defined Contribution Plans and the Vulnerability of the Retirement Age Population to the Stock Market Decline of 2008–2009." Michigan Retirement Research Center Working Paper 2009-206. Ann Arbor: University of Michigan, October.

Merrill Lynch and Capgemini. 2000–2010. *World Wealth Reports.* New York: Cap-

gemini and Merrill Lynch. Most recent edition available at: http://www
.us.capgemini.com/services-and-solutions/by-industry/financial-services/
solutions/wealth/worldwealthreport/?f_site=www; accessed July 8, 2011.

Morin, Rich. 2009. "Most Middle-Aged Adults Are Rethinking Retirement Plans:
The Threshold Generation." Pew Research Center Publication No. 1234, May
28. Washington, D.C.: Pew Research Center. Available at: http://pewresearch
.org/pubs/1234; accessed May 26, 2011.

Mortgage Bankers Association of America. 1998–2009. "MBA Mortgage Originations Estimates, National Delinquency Survey." Washington, D.C.: Mortgage
Bankers Association. Available at: http://www.mortgagebankers.org; accessed July 7, 2011.

Panel Study of Income Dynamics. 2009. *Panel Study of Income Dynamics* [public
use dataset]. Produced and distributed by the Institute for Social Research,
Survey Research Center, University of Michigan, Ann Arbor, Mich. Available
at: http://psidonline.isr.umich.edu; accessed July 11, 2011.

RealtyTrac. various years. "Year-End Foreclosure Report." 2007 data available at:
http://www.realtytrac.com/content/press-releases/us-foreclosure-activity
-increases-75-percent-in-2007-3604?accnt=64847; accessed July 7, 2011.

Sass, Steven A., Courtney Monk, and Kelly Haverstick. 2010. "Workers' Response to the Market Crash: Save More, Work More?" CRR Working Paper
Number 2010-3. Boston: Boston College, Center for Retirement Research at
Boston. Available at: http://crr.bc.edu/briefs/workers_response_to_the
_market_crash_save_more_work_more_.html; accessed May 26, 2011.

United States Courts. n.d. "Bankruptcy Cases Commenced, Terminated and
Pending During the 12-Month Periods Ending June 1983–2009." Available
at: http://www.uscourts.gov/uscourts/Statistics/BankruptcyStatistics/Bank
ruptcyFilings/1983-2003_Filings_Ending_June.pdf; accessed July 7, 2011.

U.S. Bureau of Economic Analysis. 2010. "National Income and Product Accounts, Table 2.9: Personal Income and Its Disposition by Households and by
Nonprofit Institutions Serving Households." Available at: http://www.bea
.gov/iTable/iTable.cfm?ReqID=9&step=1; accessed August 30, 2011.

U.S. Census Bureau. 2000. *Census 2000 Planning Database*. Available at: http://
2010.census.gov/partners/xls/Tract_Level_PDB_Version2.xls; accessed July
8, 2011.

U.S. Department of Housing and Urban Development, Office of Policy Development and Research. 2008. "Neighborhood Stabilization Project." Available at:
http://www.huduser.org/datasets/nsp.html; accessed July 7, 2011.

———. 2010a. "Interim Report to Congress on the Root Causes of the Foreclosure Crisis." Washington, D.C.: HUD. Available at: http://www.huduser
.org/Publications/PDF/int_foreclosure_rpt_congress.pdf; accessed May 26,
2011.

———. 2010b. "Historical Data: Exhibit 7. Existing Home Sales, 1969–present."
Available at: http://www.huduser.org/portal/periodicals/ushmc/summer10/
hist_data.pdf; accessed June 7, 2011.

Wolff, Edward N. 2010. "Recent Trends in Household Wealth in the United
States: Rising Debt and the Middle-Class Squeeze—An Update to 2007."
Working Paper No. 589. Annandale-on-Hudson, N.Y.: Levy Economics Insti-
tute.

PART III

SOCIAL EFFECTS: CONSUMPTION, ATTITUDES, AND FAMILY

Chapter 6

An Analysis of Trends, Perceptions, and Distributional Effects in Consumption

IVAYLO D. PETEV, LUIGI PISTAFERRI, AND
ITAY SAPORTA-EKSTEN

C ONSUMPTION DECISIONS ARE crucial determinants of business cycles and growth. As a share of U.S. gross domestic product (GDP)
personal consumer expenditure has grown steadily since the
early 1970s to reach, by 2008, 70 percent of GDP. The particularity of severe downturns is that consumer spending is likely not only to decline
but also to undermine the prospects for recovery. In this chapter we review the evidence on changes in consumer spending during the so-
called Great Recession, which began officially in December 2007 and
ended June 2009. The objective is to explore the distinctive consumption
aspects of this recession: How are the various components of household
consumption affected? How is the impact of the recession distributed
across sociodemographic groups? How does this recession compare to
previous recessions in respect to consumption? For the purposes of our
analysis, we rely on the most recent available national accounts data at
the time of writing (April 2011) provided by the Bureau of Economic
Analysis (BEA), and micro-level data from the Consumer Expenditure
Survey (CEX) and the University of Michigan Surveys of Consumers
(see Curtin 2010).

There are three distinctive features of the Great Recession. First, it was deep. Consumption per capita fell monotonically from the last quarter of 2007 (the official starting date of the recession) throughout the first half of 2009—a decline greater than 3 percent from peak to trough. The decline was stronger for durables (including vehicles), but spending on nondurables and services also fell significantly compared to previous recessions. Interestingly, consumption was more volatile than disposable income, partly as a result of an increase in government transfers to households (particularly, unemployment insurance claims). Second, the recession was long. In fact, it was the longest recession to date since the Great Depression, with consumption still trailing 2 percent below pre-recession levels after twelve quarters from the starting date and five quarters after the recession had officially ended. Finally, the varying impact the recession has had across age, race, education and wealth groups resulted in a decline in consumption inequality.

We single out four explanations for the observed change in consumption during the Great Recession and for its unequal impact on sociodemographic groups. One is the "wealth effect," that is, the response of consumers to the destruction of wealth that followed from the burst of the housing bubble and the stock market collapse of 2008. A second is an increase in uncertainty, a decline in consumer confidence that may have reduced spending through accumulation of precautionary savings (or reduction of debt) as well as deferment of spending, most notably on durables. Third, changes in relative prices, especially gasoline, may have reverberated on the consumption both of gasoline as well as of its complementary goods such as cars and transportation services. Finally, the credit crunch that followed the financial crisis may have prevented some households from purchasing goods that are typically acquired through borrowing, such as cars or other big-ticket items.

In the subsequent analysis, which is descriptive in nature, we provide suggestive empirical evidence for each of these four factors, whose interaction and contribution to the recession we leave for future research to disentangle with the benefit of more complete data and a better vantage point. We start with a discussion of the macroeconomic picture, followed by an analysis of trends in consumer confidence, and end with a study of the redistributive effects of the recession using micro-level data on consumer spending. We conclude with a general summary of our results.

The Macroeconomic Picture

Here we review the evolution of personal consumption expenditure and disposable income at the aggregate level. Unless noted otherwise, we use National Income and Product Accounts (NIPA) data provided by the U.S. BEA.

Figure 6.1   Consumption and Disposable Income

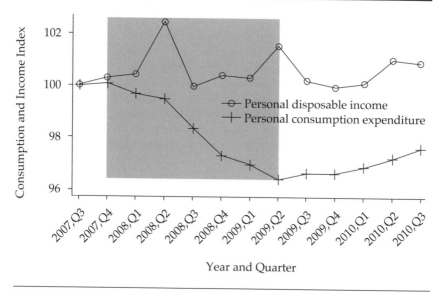

Source: Authors' calculations based on U.S. Department of Commerce, Bureau of Economic Analysis (2011; tables 2.1, 2.3.4, 2.3.5).
Note: Gray area represents period of recession.

Personal Consumption and Personal Disposable Income

We start by asking whether trends in consumption spending during the Great Recession are similar to trends in personal disposable income.[1] Economic theory predicts that the link between income shocks and consumption is strongest in the case of permanent or unpredictable income shocks. Hence, consumption may fall as a direct consequence of a fall in income induced by job loss, reduced hours or productivity, and negative returns from assets—even more so if these are long-term changes to a household's economic resources.

In figure 6.1 we plot trends in per capita personal consumption expenditure and personal disposable income over the Great Recession period. Unless noted otherwise, all data are expressed in per capita terms, deflated using the CPI (Consumer Price Index), and deseasonalized.[2] Both the consumption and income series are set equal to 100 in the quarter immediately preceding the start of the 2007 recession. What is remarkable about this graph is that although per capita consumption declines monotonically until the middle of 2009, disposable income is relatively stable.[3] The breakdown of disposable income into its three components (transfers, wages, and financial income) reveals that the stability in per capita disposable income is explained entirely by a strong increase in government transfers to households (+18.8 percent from the last quarter of 2007 to the last quarter of 2009), while both wages (–6.6 percent) and particularly financial income (–15.1 percent) fell as expected from the nature of the recession. The increase in government transfers was attributable partly to an increase in the take-up rates of unemployment insurance and Food Stamps[4] and partly to an increase in the generosity of means-tested programs put forward by the Barack Obama administration—extension of time limits for unemployment insurance,[5] tax cuts to households and businesses, and increase in Food Stamps benefits and emergency Temporary Assistance for Needy Families cash assistance (see Burtless 2009).[6]

Of course, government transfers benefit primarily households on the lower end of the income distribution under the assumption that the others can use accumulated savings to buffer themselves against income shocks. However, the sharp decline in financial income during this recession has weakened the accumulated buffer stock of wealthy households, who in the absence of access to government transfers are likely to have lowered their consumption significantly. As we shall see in the analysis of microeconomic data, this wealth effect explains a considerable portion of the fall in consumption.

Total Consumption and Its Components

In figure 6.2 we zoom out of the Great Recession period and look at the macro picture for consumption components over the first decade of the twenty-first century. In particular, we plot the quarterly growth of the three components of personal consumption expenditure—durables, nondurables, and services—over the 2000-to-2010 period. The period includes two recessions, identified in the graph by the shaded gray areas.

Three points are worth noting. First, the graph shows the well-known fact that spending on durables is much more volatile than spending on nondurables or services, with wide upward swings at the onset of booms and downward swings at the onset of recessions.

Second, the last two recessions differ dramatically in terms of their impact on consumption. The 2001 recession, induced by the deflating of the dot-com bubble and probably prolonged by the 9/11 terrorist attacks, was very shallow. In fact, only durables declined in real terms during this recession, and only by a negligible amount. Actually, in 2001 the growth in overall consumer spending only slowed down relative to the previous years. The availability of easy credit and the low unemployment rates very likely provided the favorable climate for the resilience, during that recession, of Americans' consumer spending and for its subsequent growth. In stark contrast to the 2001 recession, the Great Reces-

Figure 6.2   Growth Rate of Consumption Components

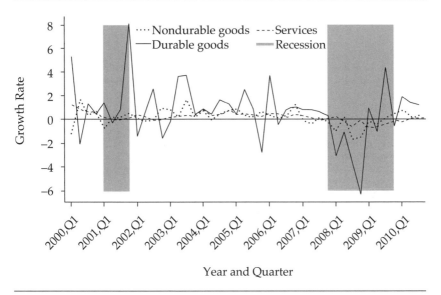

Source: Authors' calculations based on U.S. Department of Commerce, Bureau of Economic Analysis (2011; tables 2.1, 2.3.4, 2.3.5).

sion, which began with the burst of the housing bubble and the global financial crisis that ensued, is characterized by a decline in real terms in all consumption components. Throughout 2008 the fall is substantial for expenditures on nondurables and precipitous for durables. To be sure, consumption growth recovered in the second half of 2009, but the recovery is likely due in no small part to government intervention. The growth in spending on durable goods coincides with the July and August government stimulus policy for car purchases, or "cash for clunkers"; growth in spending on nondurables and services may be due partly to the effects of the Obama stimulus (the American Recovery and Reinvestment Act of 2009, or ARRA) and partly to rising consumer confidence (itself probably induced by the recovery in the stock market).

Third, the Great Recession is substantially longer than its predecessor. In fact, it is one of the longest on record. To put this in perspective and to appreciate the popular reference to this recession as the "Great Recession," we plot in figure 6.3 the Great Recession next to all the U.S. recessions that have occurred since the early 1970s. We first illustrate changes in terms of quarterly growth rates of per capita personal consumption expenditure (top left graph) and repeat the comparison for the three main consumption components, durables (top right), nondurables (bot-

Figure 6.3   Consumption During Great Recession Versus Previous Recessions, by Quarter from Start of Great Recession

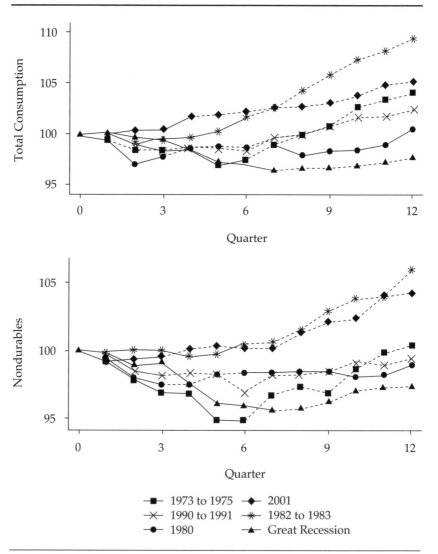

Source: Authors' calculations based on U.S. Department of Commerce, Bureau of Economic Analysis (2011; tables 2.1, 2.3.4, 2.3.5).
Note: Figures track twelve quarters from onset of given recession, normalized to be 100 in the quarter immediately preceding the start of each recession.

tom left), and services (bottom right). In each graph, consumption is plotted over twelve quarters from the onset of the recession (normalized to be 100 in the quarter immediately preceding the start of each recession). We also present the post-recession data in a dashed pattern.[7]

Figure 6.3   (*continued*)

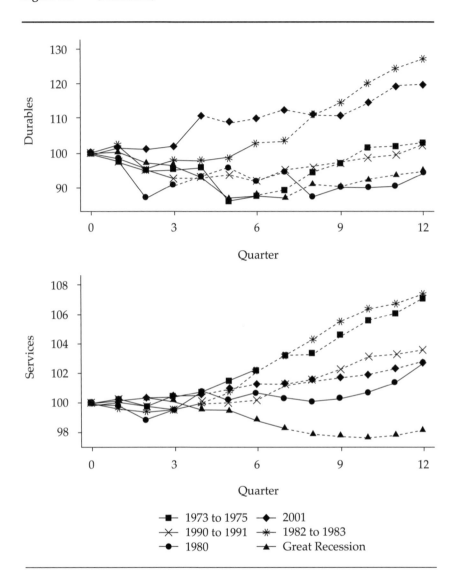

Since the early 1970s, the U.S. economy has experienced six recessions: the 1973-to-1975 recession (related to the 1973 oil shock and remembered as the stagflation recession), the 1980 recession (induced by money supply restrictions), the 1982-to-1983 recession (which resulted from the combination of the energy crisis and the tight monetary policy of the Federal Reserve), the 1990-to-1991 recession (the "Bush recession," which resulted from the combination of the 1990 oil price shock, the debt accumulation of the 1980s, new banking regulations, and a fall in consumer confidence), and the two most recent recessions discussed earlier.

A number of facts emerge from looking at the top left panel of figure 6.3. First, unlike the 1980 or 1973-to-1975 busts—when consumption fell quite dramatically right at the start of the recession—during the Great Recession the fall in consumption was initially more muted.[8] Second, a defining feature of the Great Recession is its much longer duration. Moreover, consumption remains below the pre-recession levels for a longer period than any other recessions represented in the graph. The historical comparison illustrates that an economic bust is defined not only by the extent of the fall in the components of GDP (in this respect, in the 1980 recession the U.S. economy experienced a more dramatic one-quarter fall in consumer spending) but also by the time it takes to fully recover. For example, after twelve quarters from the onset of the Great Recession, consumption is still about 2 percent below pre-recession levels. For comparison, if we exclude the 1980-to-1983 period, which had two consecutive recessions, the slowest-recovery recession (the 1990-to-1991 one) was, after twelve quarters from the onset, displaying a level of consumption 2.4 percent above the pre-recession levels.

Trends in total consumption mask considerable heterogeneity in the behavior of its three components. Spending on durables falls substantially, the fall in nondurable spending is more moderate, while spending on services falls monotonically but at a substantially lower rate. Interestingly, it is the rapid and significant recovery in services spending that helps the recovery of total consumption in previous recessions (see the bottom right panel of figure 6.3). In the Great Recession, however, spending on services declines monotonically, which stands out as a further peculiar feature of this recessionary episode.

The Behavior of Durables, Nondurables, and Services Components of Consumption

A detailed look at the composite categories of durables, nondurables, and services spending reveals additional aspects of the Great Recession. For instance, breaking down durable spending into its main components—motor vehicles and parts; furniture and equipment; and recreational goods and vehicles—we find that the bulk of the decline in per capita spending is attributable to purchases of cars (a 25 percent decline by the end of 2008) and partly of furniture (a 9 percent decline), while spending on recreational goods (such as LCD TV sets, iPhones, game consoles, and so on) is stable and even increases during the first year of the recession (perhaps because of more available free time resulting from job losses or reduced working hours). All goods display some recovery in the second half of 2009 and early 2010, although spending on cars remains substantially below pre-recession levels.[9] Part of the decline in durables may be explained by increased uncertainty leading to the postponement of the purchase of goods with large adjustment costs. In the case of cars, the higher price of its main complementary good, gasoline, may underlie the decline in spending, further evidence for which we provide later. Moreover, the financial crisis may have restricted available credit lines for the purchase of durable and semidurable products such as cars and appliances. Finally, there is evidence suggesting that consumer incentive programs were responsible for the temporary increase in durables spending on vehicles in the second half of 2009. Note that aggregate data do not allow us to make the distinction between extensive margins (how many people buy the goods) and intensive margins (how much buyers spend on the goods that they purchase) in order to disentangle the effect of the incentive programs from other confounding factors. Only the analysis of micro-level data permits this, and such data have yet to be made available (see U.S. Department of Transportation 2009 for an analysis of the effectiveness of the Consumer Assistance to Recycle and Save [CARS] program using customized aggregate survey data).

We next break down nondurable spending into its main categories—food at home; apparel; and gasoline. The decline in spending on apparel continues well into 2009, while food expenditures recover slightly following a significant drop in the summer and fall of 2008.[10] Gasoline consumption, however, appears to follow closely the sharp oscillation of oil prices—evidence of the contribution of change in relative prices to amplifying the recession effect on nondurables spending. In particular, the price of gasoline increased dramatically during the early stages of the recession (50 percent from the beginning of 2007 to the third quarter of 2008), went down very steeply in the last few months of 2008, and then kept rising slowly for the rest of 2009. James D. Hamilton (2009) attributes the rise in oil prices to a bottleneck effect: a strong increase in demand at the international level not being met by a proportional increase in supply. According to his analysis, the effect of rising oil prices contributed to the recession by lowering demand for the popular but extremely fuel-inefficient sports-utility vehicles (SUVs). The claim is corroborated by the decline in the price of vehicles for that same period, presumably reflecting a lower demand due to both lower income and higher oil price.

The unusual decline in food spending—a fundamental subsistence consumer category and a solid indicator of living standards—raises concerns about the extent and depth of the strain households are undergoing in the Great Recession. Note that earlier research by Mark Aguiar and Erik Hurst (2005) shows that a decline in food spending is not necessarily associated with a decline in nutritional content if consumers switch to home production or devote more time to shopping for better deals. Even though their research focused primarily on individuals who face a sudden decrease in earnings and more free time as they enter retirement, the logic of the argument could be extended to individuals who expect involuntary job loss or reduced work hours during the recession. Data from the American Time Use Survey (ATUS) allow us to test whether the decline in food spending in fact corresponds to a parallel increase in time spent on food preparation at home and on researching purchases.[11] We find no clear evidence in support of the hypothesis, most likely due to the fact that the increase in leisure came as a shock to most individuals. Time spent on preparing food at home remains stable (about 30 minutes per day on average), both throughout the 2003-to-2008 period of available data and particularly in 2008, when we observe food spending decline. We do record nonetheless a minor fall in the amount of time per day spent shopping (from 24 to 22 minutes) and a very slight increase in the amount of time spent on researching purchases (from an average of 0.06 in 2003-to-2007 to 0.10 minutes in 2008).

The last component of consumption that we study is services. The behavior of its subcategories—transportation; recreation; housing and utilities; finance and insurance; food services; and health care—is very heterogeneous. Spending on health services increases, is stable for housing and utilities, but declines substantially for services related to transportation (closely linked to swings in gasoline consumption and prices) and food and recreation (both of which represent relative consumption luxuries).[12] In regard to leisure and recreation services, our analysis of data from the ATUS shows evidence of a recession-related substitution: we find a strong increase in time devoted to home-based leisure activities such as watching TV and playing games and a decline in social activities requiring the expenditure of money, such as hosting parties or going to sports or cultural events. In sum, the overall stability of services masks declines in non-necessity spending that are offset by spending on commitments that are difficult to change even during recessions, of which rent and utilities are clear examples (see Chetty and Szeidl 2007).

Great Recession: Great Uncertainty

In addition to concrete changes in the economic environment, recessions are associated with a widening sense of uncertainty. Economic theory predicts that prudent households will respond to increased uncertainty by delaying purchases of durable goods and by saving for precautionary reasons (Bertola, Guiso, and Pistaferri 2005; Carroll and Samwick 1997).[13] Recent research has also pointed to the effect that "uncertainty shocks" may have on economic recessions (Bloom 2009). Indeed, one possible reason for the decline in consumption during recessions is the sense of increased insecurity about the future. Individual perceptions about one's prospects for employment, income, and human capital investments acquire during recessions a societal dimension, which runs the risk of turning perceptions into self-fulfilling prophecies and exacerbating an economy's downward plunge. For this reason the uncertain prospects of the economy warrant a closer look at consumer confidence.

Consumer Confidence

We use consumer confidence data to explore the influence of uncertainty on consumer behavior during the Great Recession. We measure consumer confidence with the University of Michigan's Index of Consumer Sentiment (ICS; see Curtin 2008). The ICS is a widely used indicator that is based on nationally representative surveys with a monthly sample of at least five hundred households, recruited on a rotating-panel basis. The index reflects responses to five general questions about respondents' perception of their current and future financial situation, of current and future business conditions, and of favorability of conditions for durable purchases.[14] The index ranges from 0 to 200.[15]

One fundamental aspect of the consumer confidence data is that in the case of the U.S. economy, growth in personal spending is trailed closely by consumer confidence, as illustrated by the historical trends in the top left panel of figure 6.4.[16] During the Great Recession the ICS declines dramatically. The depth of the decline is rivaled only by the low levels of consumer confidence reached during the recessions of the mid-1970s and of 1980. In other words, similar to its impact on actual consumption, the recession marks a complete turnaround in consumer confidence after several decades of relative optimism, which peaked in the late 1990s.

A noteworthy aspect of the current dip in consumer confidence is its duration. Consumer skepticism about the state of the economy lingered on for a year around exceptionally low levels, between the second quarter of 2008 (ICS of 60) and the first quarter of 2009 (ICS of 58). Slower than the increase in actual consumer spending, the recovery of confidence has been compromised by another decline in the third quarter of 2010 (our last data point at the time of writing).

Aggregate indices are likely to conceal potential differences in perceptions among sociodemographic groups. In times of economic growth, consumer confidence is predictably lower among respondents who are poorer, older, and of Hispanic or African American origin, whereas recessions tend to narrow between-group differences. The Great Recession is unexceptional in this regard: witness the near-complete evaporation of between-group differences in consumer confidence. By this measure, the Great Recession stands out, along with the recession of 1980, with its characteristic widespread feeling of uncertainty.

Figure 6.4   Consumption Growth, Consumer Confidence, and Heterogeneity

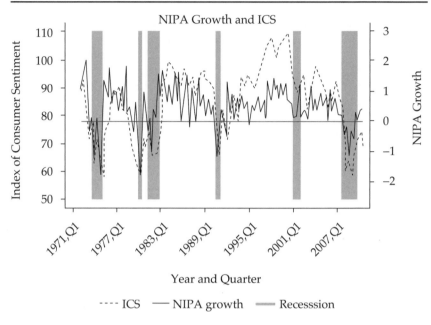

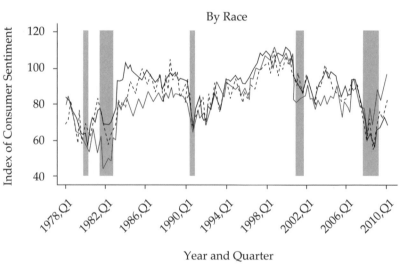

Source: Authors' calculations based on data from U.S. Department of Commerce, Bureau of Economic Analysis (2011, table 2.3.1) and Michigan Consumer Sentiment Survey (Souleles 2004).
Note: ICS = Index of Consumer Sentiment; NIPA = National Income and Product Acounts

Figure 6.4   *(continued)*

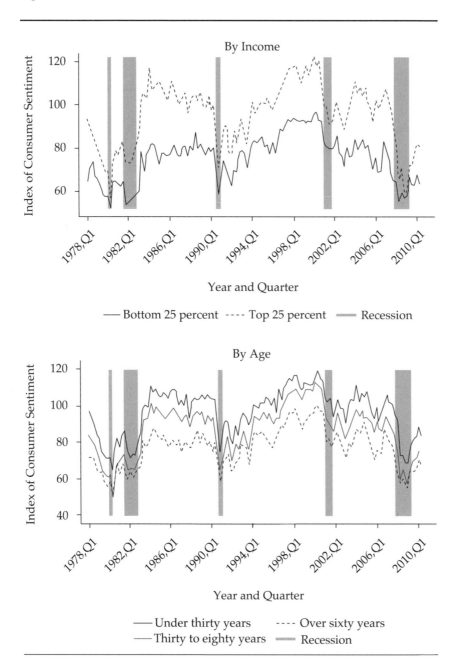

By Income

Bottom 25 percent ---- Top 25 percent ▬ Recession

By Age

——Under thirty years   ---- Over sixty years
——Thirty to eighty years   ▬ Recession

The gap between the reported confidence level of respondents from the bottom and from the top income quartiles declined in almost every recession between 1978 and 2010, the period for which data on sociodemographic variables are available for the ICS. The gap narrows as a result of the higher rate of decline in consumer confidence of high-income respondents. As the top right panel of figure 6.4 shows, the decline is most abrupt for the Great Recession, in which the confidence of respondents from the top income quartile decreased fifty points between the first quarter of 2007 and the last quarter of 2008. For comparison, the level of consumer confidence for respondents from the bottom income quartile dropped by approximately twenty points in the same period. The gap closed almost completely at the end of 2008, when respondents from both the top and the bottom income quartiles reported historically low confidence levels of fifty-nine and fifty-seven points, respectively. Similarly, as illustrated by the lower two panels of figure 6.4, the dispersion in reported consumer confidence across race or age groups declines during the recession.

But if skepticism about economic prospects is widespread at the onset of recessions, it develops unequally afterward. Consider, for instance, the trend among respondents from the top income quartile, whose consumer confidence decline in 2007 and 2008 is as sharp as its relative recovery in 2009 and in the first half of 2010 (at the time of writing data are available only until the second quarter of 2010). By contrast, the sense of uncertainty among respondents from the bottom income quartile is more robust and the recovery of confidence, hesitant. The divergence in the trends of consumer confidence highlights differences in the perception and, as this and the other chapters of the book amply document, in the concrete experience of the recession by sociodemographic groups. In the next section we explore this issue further as we look at the reasons respondents give to explain their perception and experience of this most recent recession.

Finally, it is worth noting the peculiar trend in consumer confidence among black respondents during the Great Recession. Their confidence level increased at a remarkable rate compared to that of white and Hispanic respondents. The effect is robust for differences in income, age, and education. Its timing, from the second quarter of 2008 onward, may reflect a complex mixture of economic concerns and political hopes associated with the 2008 presidential election. This relative optimism resulting from the apparent "Obama effect" overshadows, without necessarily improving, the concrete economic consequences of the recession.

Perceptions of Personal Financial Perspectives

Underlying the decline in consumer confidence is a deterioration in concrete aspects of individuals' financial situations. Sixty percent of the in-

Figure 6.5   Perceptions of Worsening of Financial Situation

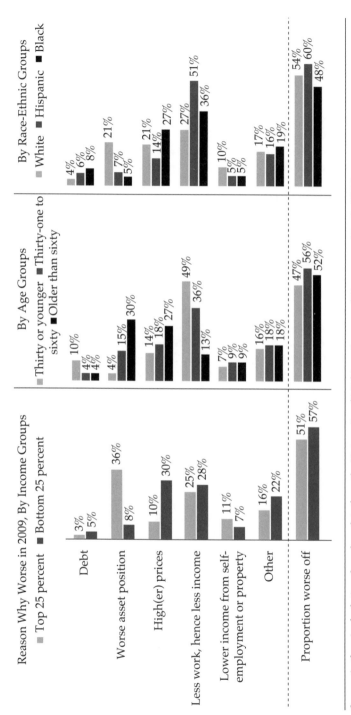

Source: Authors' calculations based on data from the University of Michigan Surveys of Consumers (Curtin 2010).

dividuals in our sample report that their financial situation in 2009 is worse than in 2008. Just 30 percent had that opinion in 2006. In figure 6.5 we stratify our sample by income (top and bottom quartile), age (under thirty; thirty-one to sixty; over sixty), and race (white; Hispanics; African American). At the bottom of each panel we plot the portion of each group that reports that their situation has worsened and, conditioning on reporting a worse financial situation, we display statistics on the reasons respondents provide.

The answers illustrate people's very tangible sense of the recession and its immediate consequences: devaluation of financial assets, tight labor market, limited business opportunities, and tough debt reimbursement. The mention of the pressure of higher prices suggests a misunderstanding of the behavior of prices during the recession. With the exception of the fluctuating gasoline prices noted earlier, most prices have changed only modestly during the Great Recession. But the persistence with which concerns over purchasing power are voiced should not be dismissed as it most likely expresses a general sense of financial vulnerability.

The differences in the reasons provided by specific sociodemographic groups paint a coherent picture of the wide impact the recession has had on Americans, or at least on their perceptions of its impact. No group is spared, though groups are affected in different ways. The relatively sheltered segments of the population—whites, the middle-aged and elderly, and high-income respondents generally—perceive the recession distinctively as a threat to their wealth, in terms of either their financial assets or, to a lesser extent, lower income from self-employment and property. "A worse asset position" is the primary reason given for the negative impact of the recession on their financial position by 36 percent of the top income quartile, by 30 percent of respondents above sixty years of age, and by 21 percent of whites. A non-negligible portion of these groups cite the loss in purchasing power, although this is the primary concern for the poor and the young, as well as for members of minority groups traditionally overrepresented in precarious jobs, like the African American and Hispanic populations. Almost half of Hispanics and of young respondents cite the job market as a reason for their worse financial situation in 2009. Higher prices take precedence among one third of African Americans and of respondents from the bottom income quartile. In addition, though to a far lesser extent, these two groups are most concerned by worsening debt.

In conclusion, the wide scope and intensity of the sense of uncertainty Americans report and the close match between the perceived reasons and the underlying socioeconomic realities raise a fundamental question about the implications of these observations: What are the immediate prospects for consumer spending's bouncing back to pre-recession levels? If consumer confidence were a reliable predictor of the likelihood of consumers favoring spending over saving, it would be a good predictor of business cycles. By this token, the considerable rise in savings since the beginning of the recession is an accurate reflection of the very low confidence of consumers. Their skepticism has lingered on in spite of the increase in consumer spending in 2010. Whether this attitude expresses a long-lasting rather than a temporary transformation of consumer behavior is open to speculation. It is worth noting that consumer confidence is relatively inaccurate for predicting both the timing and the amplitude of a business cycle because of the unequal effects of a recovery across sociodemographic groups (Souleles 2004)—a point amply underpinned by the data here presented.

The Microeconomic Picture

Having shown in the preceding section evidence of differences in the perception of the Great Recession, we now examine how actual consumer behavior varies across sociodemographic groups. To do this we use data from the CEX, which provides the only micro-level data available for the years of the Great Recession (as we write, the data include monthly information up to February 2010).[17] Given the complexity of the data, several technical explanations are in order before we move to the discussion of our findings.

Consumer Expenditure Survey

The CEX, conducted by the Bureau of Labor Statistics, is used to help in the construction of the CPI for certain items not covered by NIPA. The survey contains a comprehensive measure of consumption, although research has pointed out problems of comparability and coverage with NIPA (see Attanasio, Battistin, and Leicester 2006). (We refer the interested reader to the appendix, "CEX Versus NIPA," for more details on the comparison between CEX and NIPA data.) The subsequent analyses are based on the comprehensive interview sample of the survey, from which we extract data on households' consumer expenditures, sociodemographic variables, and income and wealth.[18]

In the analysis of the redistributive effects of the recession on consumption, we compare annual growth rates of group-specific average consumption from 2007 to 2009. Given that we condition on only a few demographic characteristics at a time, this analysis is meant to be primarily descriptive.[19]

The last expansion period (2003 to 2006) serves as a reference period for the comparison of consumption growth during the recession. To control for differences in family size and to make meaningful comparisons across years, we transform household expenditures into adult equivalents[20] and deflate them by the relevant price deflation.[21]

Redistributive Effects

Figure 6.6 summarizes the main results on the redistributive effects of the recession. The first two panels on the top left stratify the sample by the age (thirty or younger; thirty-one to sixty-four; sixty-five and older) and education (high school or less; some college) of the household head. Middle-aged, high school or less education, and college-educated individuals are the ones experiencing the largest decline in consumption over the Great Recession, regardless of education (–3.9 to –4.4 percent). Older individuals' consumption is decreasing by 2.1 to 2.4 percent on average. Interestingly, when looking at medians, the older group is the only group not experiencing any decrease in consumption but rather a slight increase (the results for medians are not reported for brevity).[22] A simple life-cycle model would predict that young, college-educated households, who have low current income but high permanent income, finance their consumption by borrowing against their future human capital. Since the recession was characterized by an increase in the incidence of borrowing constraints, the consumption of young, college-educated households may have declined as a consequence of the credit restrictions they faced. Further, Edward Wolff (2010) predicts that the fraction of homeowners with negative home equity for 2009 is highest among individuals under thirty-five and those with more than high school education. Hence, consumption for young, college-educated households may have declined in response to this wealth shock as well. One reason that the middle-aged college-educated group experienced a large negative growth in consumption is that this group is holding a large share of the financial assets in the economy, making it more vulnerable to the effect of wealth destruction, which is well correlated with negative consumption growth, as we shall show.[23] For the middle-aged, high school–educated individuals, the explanation is more complex, and it may involve uncertainty about employment and earnings prospects.

In the top right panel of figure 6.6 we stratify the sample by race. The largest decline (–4.9 percent) as well as the largest drop in growth is associated with the Hispanic population (the same finding holds true when looking at medians, –2.3 percent).

What might explain these differences? We suggest two possible explanations. First, the difference observed between the growth rates of the different groups may reflect occupation or industry composition effects. As of 2008, for example, Hispanics accounted for 14 percent of total employment in the economy but 24.6 percent of employment in the construction industry, which has been severely hit by the recession. Indeed, unemployment rates grew more for the Hispanic population between the second half of 2007 and the second half of 2008 (from 5.7 to 8.3 percent) than for the white population (4.1 to 5.6 percent).[24] Second, there

Figure 6.6   Means of Total Consumption Growth, by Group

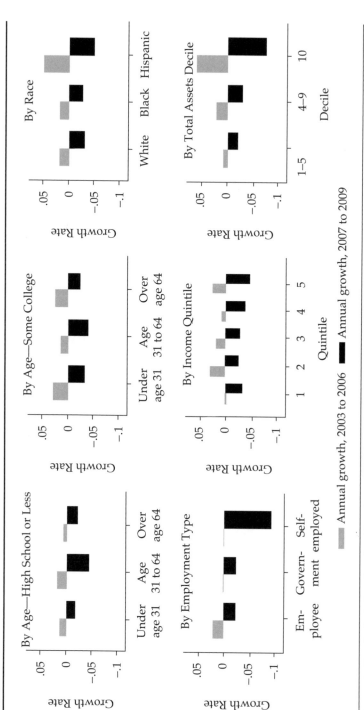

Source: Authors' calculations based on data from the Consumer Expenditure Survey (U.S. Department of Labor, Bureau of Labor Statistics, various years).

may be an association between negative home equity and negative consumption growth. As shown in table 5.1 in chapter 5, there is a higher projected proportion of homeowners with negative home equity among Hispanics (23.2 percent) than among whites (14.7 percent). Thus it is possible that the decline in housing values induced by the housing bubble's bursting may have pushed most subprime borrowers (who are overrepresented among non-whites; see Calem, Gillen, and Wachter 2004) into negative equity territory and hence induced a fall in their consumption spending.

Next we examine the impact of the recession on consumption by occupation, distinguishing between private employees, public employees, and the self-employed. The recession has an extremely negative effect for the self-employed (a 9.1 percent decline in total consumption), who in addition experience the largest change relative to the pre-recession period. It is possible that reports of "self-employment" are masking effective unemployment, and hence the decline in consumption captures the fall in income experienced by the unemployed or underemployed, despite the role of the safety net. Given that the self-employed have more volatile income than public or private employees, it is possible that this also reflects the effect of uncertainty, which suggests a more cautious consumer spending attitude. Both private and public employees have stable consumption patterns, although there is a significant slowdown relative to the pre-recession period.

Lastly, the two bottom right graphs of figure 6.6 stratify the sample by measures of economic well-being, income (quintiles) and total assets (decile groups). The measure of income is defined as total after-tax income from all sources including salaries, income from business and farm, Social Security, unemployment benefits, workers' compensation, welfare and Food Stamps, income from assets, pensions, rent, alimony, and child support. The measure of total assets represents the gross asset holdings of the household, including the household's holdings in checking and savings accounts, bonds, securities, money owed to the household, and the value of the house and other real estate.[25] As with consumption, we deflate and transform the assets and income variables into adult-equivalent measures.

The middle bottom panel of figure 6.6 shows that the fall in consumption is higher at higher levels of income, even though differences across income groups are not significant.[26] Moving on to the last panel of figure 6.6, we look at consumption growth for three groups: the first to fifth deciles of the wealth distribution, sixth to ninth deciles, and those in the tenth decile. This grouping is justified by the extremely high concentration of wealth; indeed, individuals in the first five deciles have very little wealth, whereas those in the top decile own about 50 percent of total wealth and 90 percent of financial wealth (total assets excluding housing) in our sample.[27] One remarkable finding is that respondents in the top decile of the wealth distribution are the ones who decrease spending during the Great Recession (–7.5 percent).[28] This finding holds also when looking at spending on nondurables and services, although the negative growth rates are slightly smaller (–7.1 percent for the top wealth deciles). The fall is smaller when looking at medians (–3.3 percent for total consumption and –3.9 percent for nondurables plus services).[29] The larger negative growth measured by means compared to medians is the result of the consumption distribution becoming less skewed for the households in the top decile of wealth.[30]

This finding may appear puzzling at first—indeed, wealthy individuals are expected to have better tools to smooth their consumption during rough periods. However in the context of the Great Recession, another effect might dominate the consumption behavior of wealthy individuals. As shown in chapter 5, the recession was characterized by large wealth destruction suffered by rich individuals. This suggests that they lost a large fraction of their "buffer" wealth, which was supposed to be used exactly for the purpose of smoothing their consumption during the "rainy days" of the recession. To restore their "buffer stock" these individuals may have needed to save more, which would have decreased their consumption growth.

The response of consumption to wealth shocks is known in the literature as the "wealth effect" (see Poterba 2000). Since shocks to wealth are presumably transitory, the theory predicts that consumers should respond very little to them. The evidence on the actual response of consumption to wealth shocks is mixed at best, but most studies do indeed obtain small estimates of wealth effects. The evidence regarding the differential response to shocks to housing wealth and shocks to corporate equity is also mixed.[31]

We will not try to resolve this debate. Instead we take some representative lower- and upper-bound estimates of the wealth effect from the literature. A simple back-of-the-envelope calculation shows that the typical estimates of the wealth effect for stocks found in the literature can explain a significant fraction of the decline in consumption by the wealthy when one takes into account their initial high wealth-to-consumption ratio. Table 6.1 details the calculation. For example, over the 2007-to-2009 period, households in the top decile of the wealth distribution lost on average about $209,000 of their assets (in 2007 dollars), corresponding to a 29 percent decline (see panel A). Using the window of estimates from the wealth effect literature (1 to 7 cents decline in consumption per dollar of wealth destroyed), we predict that annualized consumption growth could have been anything between –1.5 and –10.5 percent. The actual negative consumption growth experienced by the wealthy was 7.3 percent, which shows that estimates of the wealth effect

Table 6.1   **The Wealth Effect for the Top Decile of Financial Assets**

Panel A: Weighted means	(1)	(2)	(3)
Estimate of the wealth effect from the literature	0.01	0.04	0.07
Average annual consumption 2009		$59,528	
Average annual consumption 2007		$69,718	
Average total wealth 2009		$717,349	
Average total wealth 2007		$926,280	
Predicted annualized consumption growth	−1.50%	−5.99%	−10.49%
Actual annualized consumption growth		−7.30%	

Panel B: Medians	(1)	(2)	(3)
Estimate of the wealth effect from the literature	0.01	0.03	0.07
Median annual consumption 2009		$48,814	
Median annual consumption 2007		$52,243	
Median total wealth 2009		$517,082	
Median total wealth 2007		$673,439	
Predicted annualized consumption growth	−1.49%	−5.98%	−10.48%
Actual annualized consumption growth		−3.30%	

Source: Authors' calculations based on data from the Consumer Expenditure Survey (U.S. Department of Labor, Bureau of Labor Statistics, various years).

might explain the actual decline in consumption experienced by the wealthy. Panel B repeats the exercise for medians and confirms qualitatively these findings. We also find qualitatively similar results if we consider a measure of wealth that excludes housing.

Although individuals in the bottom part of the consumption distribution were less likely to be affected by the wealth effect, another potential explanation for the moderate negative consumption growth of the bottom decile of the wealth distribution during the Great Recession is the large increase in transfer payments that took place during the recession. Since transfer payments are more likely to be channeled to the poor, the increase in transfer payments during this recession might have helped individuals with less wealth to smooth consumption to a larger extent than individuals with more wealth. To address this point, we compare inequality trends between the Great Recession and the 1990-to-1991 recession, in which there was a milder increase in transfer payments. We find that in the 1990-to-1991 recession, the top and bottom deciles of the wealth distribution were moving together, both showing large declines in consumption between the second half of 1989 and the first half of 1991. Although we cannot establish a causal relation between the increase in transfer payments and the stability of consumption at the bottom decile of the wealth distribution in the Great Recession, the findings from the comparison with the 1990-to-1991 recession appear to be consistent with this idea.

Consumption Inequality and Consumption Mobility

As we have shown in the previous section, there is evidence that the consumption distribution became less skewed to the right between 2007 and 2009. The direct implication of this evidence is a decline in consumption inequality. In this section we take a closer look at the consumption distribution and particularly at consumption inequality and consumption mobility related to the Great Recession. Jonathan Heathcote, Fabrizio Perri, and Gianluca Violante (2010) document that although disposable income inequality slightly increased in 2008 compared to 2007, inequality in consumption of nondurable goods decreased. They show that this decline in inequality is due to a large decline in the 90th percentile of nondurable consumption combined with a mild decline at the 50th percentile and a slight increase at the 10th percentile. Figure 6.7 shows the 10th, 50th, and 90th percentiles as well as the variance of semiannual consumption, controlling for household size.[32] The percentile series are normalized to 100 in the first half of 2006. The figure shows that their findings hold also for our measure of total consumption and that consumption inequality starts going back up during the second half of 2009, right after the end of the recession.

Two points are worth noting. First, changes in the variance of log consumption are primarily driven by changes in the consumption of the 90th percentile, at least since 2007. This finding is even more evident when looking at quarterly series (not reported here): the correlation between the quarterly variance of log total consumption and the 90th percentile of log total consumption is 0.8, whereas the correlation of the variance with the 10th percentile is only –0.53. Therefore we can conclude that at least around the Great Recession, the decline in consumption inequality is driven by a decline in consumption in the upper parts of the distribution. Second, in the period just before the recession the top and bottom deciles move up at somewhat similar rates. However, during the recession, the top decile goes down significantly, while the bottom decile remains relatively stable. The two trends, taken together, imply a reduction in consumption inequality during the Great Recession. Once more, this is in accordance with some of the group-specific trends in consumption growth analyzed previously, namely the proportionally greater decrease in consumption among the wealthy (who are presumably also at the top of the consumption distribution) than among the poor. Whether this is part of a more general trend or an episodic

Figure 6.7   Measuring Inequality Using Log (Total Consumption)

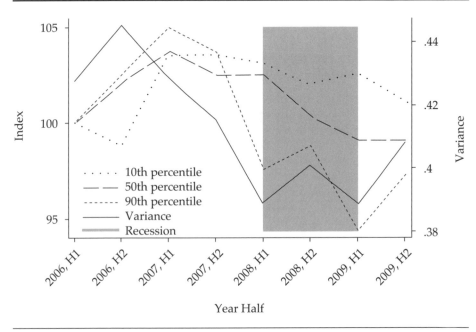

Year Half

Source: Authors' calculations based on the Consumer Expenditure Survey (U.S. Department of Labor, Bureau of Labor Statistics, various years).

event linked to the recession is hard to determine with our limited data, and hence we leave it to further inquiry with better and more extended microdata.

Another aspect of redistribution one can look at is mobility. The distinction between consumption inequality and consumption mobility is, in effect, a distinction between static and dynamic features of a distribution. Inequality refers to the dispersion of consumption at a point in time. Mobility describes movements within the consumption distribution over time. A direct implication for welfare analysis is that stability in consumption inequality may mask a great deal of mobility in the distribution.

The first step of our analysis is to construct an empirical transition matrix of consumption. This requires panel data. The CEX is a quarterly rotating panel, and hence it can be used to construct a measure of mobility. Our preferred measure is the Shorrocks index.[33] This is an approximate measures of the fraction of individuals moving across the distribution; a higher value of the index (which ranges from 0 to 1) is associated with a higher degree of mobility from one year to the next. In figure 6.8

Figure 6.8   Consumption Mobility

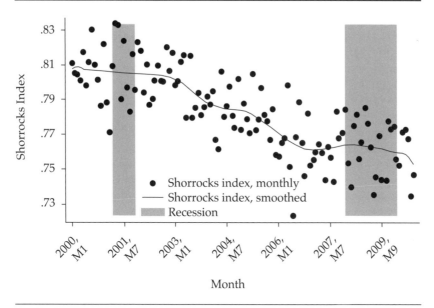

Month

Source: Authors' calculations based on data from the Consumer Expenditure Survey (U.S. Department of Labor, Bureau of Labor Statistics, various years).

we plot the monthly Shorrocks indexes as well as the local regression smoothed version (the solid line). Overall, there seems to be a general declining trend in the amount of mobility in consumption. What can explain this trend?

Tullio Jappelli and Luigi Pistaferri (2004) argue that under full consumption insurance (that is, in an economic environment in which households can purchase insurance against all possible shocks they face), individual consumption growth is independent of idiosyncratic shocks, and it varies only in response to aggregate consumption growth. It follows that the cross-sectional distribution of consumption of any group of households is constant over time. Of course aggregate consumption can increase or decrease, so that the growth of consumption for any household can be positive or negative, but the relative position of each household in the cross-sectional distribution of consumption does not change over time. Hence, consumption insurance implies absence of consumption mobility between any two time periods, regardless of the nature of the individual income shocks and the time frame considered. To be sure, this framework is clearly unrealistic in its pure formulation, but the idea behind it is not. An improvement in the amount and nature of insurance available to households (such as through a process of financial market liberalization that makes credit more easily available and more widespread, as happened during the 1990s and part of the 2000s) may well have contributed to a reduction in the amount of mobility by attenuating the response of consumption to shocks. The idea that credit market development in the United States has helped households in smoothing shocks more efficiently is also advanced by Dirk Krueger and Fabrizio Perri (2006).

An important question we may ask is whether the Great Recession reverts this declining trend. The effect of the recession on consumption mobility may have worked through the tightening of the credit markets. When credit is easily available, people can smooth uninsurable shocks by borrowing, and so their consumption will not fluctuate much from one year to the next. Hence, with well-functioning credit markets there is less scope for consumption mobility. The tightening of credit that occurred during the Great Recession may have exposed more households to uninsurable shocks and thus increased consumption mobility. To check whether the data support this view, we regress the Shorrocks index on a linear time trend, a dummy for the period covered by the Great Recession (December 2007 to February 2009), and the interaction of the linear time trend with the Great Recession dummy. We find that, as expected, there is a statistically significant general downward trend in the data. The trend appears to have reverted or slowed down during the Great Recession (the coefficient on the interaction is positive, as the previous discussion would suggest); however, too few months are covered by the recession to make this statement unambiguously statistically precise.

Conclusions

In this chapter we have analyzed the behavior of consumption during the Great Recession. Three basic facts emerge from the analysis. First, the recession was long. It set the record of being the longest recession since the Great Depression. Second, the recession was deep. Consumption fell significantly in 2008 and in the first half of 2009, before recovering slightly in the second half of 2009. However, the level of consumption in the third quarter of 2010 was still about 2 percent below the pre-recession level. The fall in consumption has been particularly strong among durables, but consumption of nondurables and of services has also fallen. Finally, we find important redistributive effects of the recession, in particular a decline in consumption inequality and a slowing down in the decline in mobility that had characterized the consumption distribution during the expansion years of the 2000s.

Our reading of the available evidence is that the Great Recession was not consumption driven. The fall in consumption occurred after the financial crisis and the deflation of the housing bubble, not before. Of course, once the consumption decline was in full swing, it acted to prolong the recession. There is the broader and perhaps deeper issue of whether the ultimate explanation for the financial crisis was an increase in the demand for credit induced by an increase in consumer demand not matched by a concurrent increase in permanent income. However, Atif Mian and Amir Sufi (2009), using U.S. county data, conclude that the subprime crisis was primarily driven by shifts in credit supply induced by greater risk diversification (such as mortgage securitization) or simply greater assumption of moral hazards on the part of lenders, rather than shifts in demand.

It is also interesting to notice the differences between the consumption response in the Great Recession and the consumption response in the 2000-to-2001 recession. In the 2000-to-2001 recession consumption hardly fell—in fact, one can argue that the rapid recovery was due to consumers keeping their spending high despite the recession. In hindsight, we know that the high level of spending was sustained by unsustainable debt. In the Great Recession there is instead ample evidence for household deleveraging.

At the beginning of this chapter we mentioned a number of possible explanations for consumption behavior during the recession. The first is the wealth effect. Given that the Great Recession was characterized by a large destruction of wealth, especially wealth embodied in housing and equity, this explanation is potentially important. We indeed find that the consumption of the wealthy fell more than that of the less wealthy during the recession. Using the typical estimates of the "wealth effect" available in the literature, we show that this factor can explain a significant fraction of the fall in consumption experienced by the wealthy. This is not surprising. In response to the large negative shock to their wealth, rich households may have responded by increasing their savings in the attempt to restore their buffer stock. Nevertheless, the wealth-effect explanation is unlikely to make much headway in explaining the changes in the consumption of the less wealthy. It is possible, however, that the decline in housing values may have pushed some "subprime borrowers" (who are overrepresented among minorities) into negative equity territory and induced a decline in their consumption. A similar effect may have been at work among young, college-educated households.

A second explanation for the peculiarity of the Great Recession that we advanced at the beginning of the chapter was the increase in uncertainty. The financial breakdown of 2007 led to historically low levels of confidence among Americans. Three years after the official start of the recession and almost a year and a half after its official end, consumer confidence has yet to recover to pre-recession levels. Furthermore, the steeper decline in confidence among high-income households is in line with our findings on the greater decline in the spending of that group. However, the slower rate of recovery in the consumer confidence of lower-income households reflects most likely not only their greater uncertainty but the permanent consequences that this recession has had on the stability and the future prospects of their employment.

Third, there were significant concomitant price effects. The rollercoaster behavior of the price of gasoline (and all complements to it) appears important enough to explain not only the decline in the purchase of gasoline itself but also that of cars and transportation services. These changes in relative prices may have had a large impact on poorer families' budgets. Finally, one of the main outcomes of the financial crisis was the credit crunch. Financial intermediaries became extremely reluctant to lend, even to otherwise safe borrowers. This may have prevented some consumers from purchasing big-ticket items that are traditionally purchased on credit, such as cars and appliances.

Since the available data are still incomplete, we believe it is still too early to reach a definite consensus on the causes of the trends in consumer spending over the Great Recession and of its timing. We have attempted in this chapter to suggest possible interpretations, present some suggestive evidence, and raise a number of important questions that we leave for future explorations.

We wish to thank the anonymous reviewers of this chapter and Tullio Jappelli, Fabrizio Perri, and participants at the Recession Task Force Conference in Stanford, February 2010, for their comments.

Appendix: CEX Versus NIPA

To justify our choice of using the CEX microdata when investigating the response of personal consumption in the Great Recession, we first check to what extent population estimates obtained using the CEX mirror aggregate data from the NIPA time series generated by the BEA.[34] In its officially distributed tables, the Bureau of Labor Statistics provides only annual series of aggregated CEX measures. Since we prefer to use quarterly and semiannual data to analyze the effect of the recession, we construct these measures directly from the CEX microdata. There are several issues that need to be addressed when mapping CEX to NIPA. First, CEX consumer expenditures are collected by matching household expenditures to classification codes (for example, food consumed at home, food consumed away from home, and so forth). To be able to compare CEX aggregate measures to NIPA data, we need to take a stand on how these classification codes are mapped into broader categories, such as food. We adopt the NIPA categorization (as in Harris and Sabelhaus 2000).[35] Second, the CEX data need to be seasonally adjusted for comparability with NIPA series.[36] Third, NIPA series are available either in total or per capita form. We obtain the per capita equivalent in the CEX by dividing average consumption across all consumer units by average family size. We find that CEX quarterly nondurable consumption tracks the NIPA equivalent rather well: the two series have a 0.78 correlation since the year 2000. The equivalent series for total consumption show a lower correlation, 0.45. Both CEX series capture the decrease in consumption in the Great Recession, though the CEX total expenditure series is more volatile than the NIPA series. The high correlation between CEX and NIPA consumption series, together with the finding that the CEX captures the drop in consumption during the Great Recession, suggests that the CEX is a suitable tool to use for assessing the consumption response in this recession.

Notes

1. In the BEA definition, personal disposable income is the sum of "compensation of employees, received" (wages and employers' contribution to Social Security), "proprietors' income with inventory valuation and capital consumption adjustments" (business income), "rental income of persons with capital consumption adjustment" and "personal income receipts on assets" (income from assets), "personal current transfer receipts" (transfers from the government and businesses), net of taxes paid (U.S. Department of Commerce, various years.

2. On average, durables account for about 10 percent of the total and nondurables for about 25 percent, and the remaining 65 percent is accounted for by services.

3. In previous recessions, disposable income fell more than consumption, with the exception perhaps of the 1973 recession.

4. The take-up rate is defined as the ratio of beneficiaries to eligible individuals (for unemployment insurance) or households (for Food Stamps).

5. The remarkable extension of unemployment insurance benefits to twenty-two months (from the conventional six months duration in most states) may have contributed to an increase in long-term unemployment rates by creating disincentives to search for active employment.

6. From the onset of the recession in 2007, fourth quarter, to 2009, fourth quarter, spending on unemployment insurance soared by a staggering 293 percent. There was also a significant reduction in tax receipts (−29.9 percent) and an increase in veterans' benefits (+22 percent), most likely associated with the impact of the Iraq and Afghanistan wars.

7. The line for the 1980 recession has a solid-dash-solid pattern because it overlaps with the 1982-to-1983 recession.

8. The fact that consumption falls only late in the cycle suggests that it is not

the engine of the economic bust. However, its late fall may also have contributed to the length of the bust itself. Note, however, that the attenuated response of consumption at the start of the recession could be explained by the effect of the 2008 tax rebate, which families received in the first and second quarters of 2008. According to Christian Broda and Jonathan Parker (2008), consumption in the second and third quarters of 2008 was boosted by the receipt of the rebate, with most families spending it on food, mass merchandise, and drugs.

9. The reversal of the decline in spending on durables raises the question of whether the sharp decline in 2008 reflected tighter budgeting by consumers or simply a more cautious withdrawal from the market in the anticipation of impending lower prices. Indeed, by the first quarter of 2009, surveys were registering an upturn in consumers' perceptions that the time was right for purchasing durable goods. Not only were the richest Americans particularly likely to find early 2009 a favorable time to make major purchases; when it came to potential investments in a new home or vehicle, all income groups appeared more likely to be making major purchases.

10. The usage of Food Stamps has also spiked dramatically (see Mabli et al. 2010).

11. ATUS is a time-use survey conducted by the Bureau of Labor Statistics, designed to measures how people allocate their available time to activities such as paid work, child care, volunteering, and socializing.

12. Health spending has been growing almost monotonically since the early 1970s. In fact, growth rates slowed down during the early 2000s and were basically flat during the Great Recession period.

13. There was indeed a strong increase in savings during the Great Recession. In fact, it was the first time in more than twenty-five years that savings increased consistently for two years in a row. At the same time there was a process of household deleveraging. The debt-service ratio, having increased from 11 percent in 1993 to almost 14 percent at the outset of the Great Recession in 2007, fell to about 12.5 percent in just the following two years.

14. The five questions are as follows:

    1. We are interested in how people are getting along financially these days. Would you say that you (and your family living there) are better off or worse off financially than you were a year ago?

    2. Now looking ahead, do you think that a year from now you (and your family living here) will be better off financially, or worse off, or just about the same as now?

    3. Now turning to business conditions in the country as a whole, do you think that during the next twelve months we'll have good times financially, or bad times, or what?

    4. Looking ahead, which would you say is more likely, that in the country as a whole we'll have continuous good times during the next five years or so, or that we will have periods of widespread unemployment or depression, or what?

    5. About the big things people buy for their homes, such as furniture, a

refrigerator, stove, television, and things like that. Generally speaking, do you think now is a good or bad time for people to buy major household items?

15. The index's computation involves the sum of the relative scores (X1, X2, X3, X4, X5) on each of the five questions in the previous note (that is, percentage of favorable responses minus percentage of unfavorable responses, plus 100), divided by a 1966 base period total, plus a constant (which corrects for sample design changes from surveys in 1950s): ICS = 2.0 + (X1 + X2 + X3 + X4 + X5)/6.7558.

16. This is of course not a statement about causality. People's lack of confidence may reflect information about the current state of the economy, rather than a prediction of future consumption behavior. Indeed, Sidney Ludvigson (2004) concludes that the forecasting power of consumer confidence indexes for consumer spending is very modest at best.

17. In the United States, the only three general-purpose surveys with some information on consumption are the Health and Retirement Study, the Panel Study of Income Dynamics, and the CEX. Unlike the CEX, however, the Health and Retirement Study and the Panel Study of Income Dynamics surveys are conducted biannually and their last available waves refer to years prior to the current recession.

18. The CEX consists of two samples: a diary sample and an interview sample. The diary is designed to provide detailed expenditures data on small and frequently purchased items, recorded over the period of two consecutive weeks. The interview sample surveys the whole range of expenditures of households for a maximum of five quarters. Expenditures are reported at every interview for the quarter preceding the month of the interview, and income is reported only in the second and fifth interviews for a period of twelve months prior to the month of the interview. Information on assets is reported only in the fifth interview and refers to the amounts held as of the last month before the interview. In addition to stocks of wealth, households also report the change in wealth in the twelve months prior to the fifth interview, which allow researchers also to construct the initial wealth of the households at the time it enters the survey (namely, the stock of wealth just before the first interview).

19. The CEX sample for 2007 to 2009 consists of 270,487 monthly observations, corresponding to 27,876 households. We drop observations that have incomplete income data; observations from those living in rural areas; observations for which consumption is reported for the month of the interview; observations of individuals living in student housing, multiple household units, and households with less than three reports per quarter (in this case we drop only the interview with the missing reports and not the entire household); and observations of armed forces personnel. The final sample consists of 188,958 monthly observations, corresponding to 22,183 households.

20. The normalized measure is consumption/(number of family members)$^{0.5}$.

21. We deflate using the Bureau of Labor Statistics's all-urban CPI. Since the

Bureau of Labor Statistics does not provide a deflator for the sum of nondurables and services, whenever this measure is used we use the services index to deflate this sum. This choice is driven by the much larger budget share of services; on average, the services budget share is 70.6 percent whereas that of nondurables is 24.7 percent in the 2007-to-2009 sample.

22. Most of these patterns are replicated when we examine other measures of consumption, such as nondurables or nondurables plus services, with the main difference that for nondurables the most negative consumption growth (–6 percent) is recorded for the young college-educated group.

23. Middle-aged college-educated are 41.4 percent of our sample at 2007, but they are 58.4 percent of the individuals in the top financial assets decile for this year.

24. Authors' calculation of data from Current Population Survey, 2007 and 2008 (U.S. Department of Labor, Bureau of Labor Statistics 2011).

25. The allocation of individuals to income quintiles is done using the income data collected in the second and fifth interviews. The allocation to asset deciles is done using the asset holdings data reported in the fifth interview. This implies that for income we are left with 91,091 observations for 2007 to 2009. For assets we are left with 46,055 observations for 2007 to 2009.

26. Johnathan Parker and Annette Vissing-Jorgensen (2009) report somewhat similar findings, showing that high-consumption households report larger responses to aggregate consumption shocks than households with low levels of initial consumption.

27. Wolff (2010) reports a somewhat similar percentage for financial wealth (81 percent) using data from the 2004 Survey of Consumer Finances, a data set on the wealth of American households that is much richer than the CEX.

28. To obtain this figure, we compare average monthly consumption in 2007 for individuals who in that period were in the top 10 percent of the total asset distribution with average monthly consumption in 2008 for individuals who were in the top 10 percent of the total asset distribution in that period and repeat this exercise for 2008 and 2009. Ideally, one would like to have panel data and compare the consumption of the two periods for individuals who were in the top decile of the total asset distribution at baseline. Unfortunately, the structure of the CEX is such that this ideal comparison is not feasible. However, given that we have two observations on assets for most families, we have verified that there is very little mobility out of the top and bottom deciles of assets over a twelve-month period.

29. We also calculated the growth of means and medians for financial wealth (total wealth excluding housing and real estate). When we look at means of total consumption, the tenth decile still shows the most negative consumption drop. When looking at medians, the tenth decile shows the least negative growth.

30. The ratio of consumption of the 90th percentile to the median consumption in the top wealth decile is 2.2 for 2007 and 1.96 in 2009.

31. For example, a survey by the Congressional Budget Office (2007) states that "a $1,000 increase in the price of a home this year will generate $20 to $70 of extra spending this year and in each subsequent year" (7), while James M. Poterba (2000) writes that "the long-run impact of a $1 increase in stock

market wealth is a consumption increase of 4.2 cents, while an increase in non-equity wealth raises consumer spending by 6.1 cents" (105). In contrast, F. Thomas Juster et al. (2006) report that their estimates "suggest that a one-dollar capital gain in corporate equities increases spending in a five-year interval by as much as 19 cents" (20) and that their analysis robustly shows that "the spending response to capital gains in corporate equities is larger than to capital gains in other assets, including housing" (20).

32. The definition of consumption is as in the previous section.

33. The index is defined as $(q - 1)^{-1}(q - \Sigma_{i=1}^{q} p_{ii})$, where q is the number of quintiles into which the distribution has been divided and p_{ii} is the proportion of individuals who remain in quintile i for two successive periods. In our analysis, we work with deciles ($q = 10$).

34. When comparing with NIPA, we use a less restrictive sample, dropping only observations for which consumption is reported for the month of interview. However, we also trim the top percentile of the distribution for each consumption category, to remove outliers.

35. We update the mapping to account for changes that have occurred in the CEX after 1998, the last year for which they have constructed the mapping.

36. We perform the seasonal adjustment using the Census Bureau X-12-ARIMA software (note that for the microdata analysis the data are not seasonally adjusted).

References

Aguiar, Mark and Erik Hurst. 2005. "Consumption vs. Expenditure." *Journal of Political Economy* 113(5): 919–48.

Attanasio, Orazio, Eric Battistin, and Andrew Leicester. 2006. "From Micro to Macro, from Poor to Rich: Consumption and Income in the UK and the US." Unpublished manuscript. National Poverty Center, University of Michigan.

Bertola, Giuseppe, Luigi Guiso, and Luigi Pistaferri. 2005. "Uncertainty and Consumer Durables Adjustment." *Review of Economic Studies* 72(4): 973–1007.

Bloom, Nicholas. 2009. "The Impact of Uncertainty Shocks." *Econometrica* 77(3): 623–85.

Broda, Christian, and Jonathan Parker. 2008. "The Impact of the 2008 Tax Rebates on Consumer Spending: Preliminary Evidence." Unpublished manuscript. Kellogg School of Management, Evanston, Ill.

Burtless, Gary. 2009. "The Social Protection for the Economic Crisis: The U.S. Experience." Washington, D.C.: Brookings Institution.

Calem, Paul, Kevin Gillen, and Susan Wachter. 2004. "The Neighborhood Distribution of Subprime Mortgage Lending." *Journal of Real Estate Finance and Economics* 29(4): 393–410.

Carroll, Christopher D., and Andrew A. Samwick. 1997. "The Nature of Precautionary Wealth." *Journal of Monetary Economics* 40(1): 41–71.

Chetty, Raj, and Adam Szeidl. 2007. "Consumption Commitments and Risk Preferences." *Quarterly Journal of Economics* 122(2): 831–877.

Congressional Budget Office. 2007. "Housing Wealth and Consumer Spending." Washington: U.S. Government Printing Office.

Curtin, Richard. 2008. "Consumer Sentiment Index." In *Encyclopedia of Survey Research Methods*, edited by Paul J. Lavrakas. Thousand Oaks, Calif.: Sage Publications.

――――. 2010. "Surveys of Consumers." Ann Arbor: University of Michigan.

Hamilton, James D. 2009. "Causes and Consequences of the Oil Shock of 2007–08." *Brookings Papers on Economic Activity*, Spring 2009: 215–59.

Harris, Ed, and John Sabelhaus. 2000. "Consumer Expenditure Survey. Family Level Extracts 1980:1–1998:2." Unpublished manuscript. Cambridge, Mass.: National Bureau of Economic Research.

Heathcote, Jonathan, Fabrizio Perri, and Gianluca Violante. 2010. "Inequality in Times of Crisis: Lessons from the Past and a First Look at the Current Recession." VoxEU.org, February 2. Available at: http://www.voxeu.org/index.php?q=node/4548; accessed May 26, 2011.

Jappelli, Tullio, and Luigi Pistaferri. 2004. "Intertemporal Choice and Consumption Mobility." *Journal of the European Economic Association* 4(1): 75–115.

Juster, F. Thomas, Joseph P. Lupton, James P. Smith, and Frank Stafford. 2006. "The Decline in Household Savings and the Wealth Effect." *Review of Economics and Statistics* 88(1): 20–27.

Krueger, Dirk, and Fabrizio Perri. 2006. "Does Income Inequality Lead to Consumption Inequality? Evidence and Theory." *Review of Economic Studies* 73(1): 163–93.

Ludvigson, Sidney. 2004. "Consumer Confidence and Consumer Spending." *Journal of Economic Perspectives* 18(2): 29–50.

Mabli, James, Rhoda Cohen, Frank Potter, and Zhanyun Zhao. 2010. "Hunger in America 2010." Cambridge, Mass.: Mathematica Policy Research.

Mian, Atif, and Amir Sufi. 2009. "The Consequences of Mortgage Credit Expansion: Evidence from the U.S. Mortgage Default Crisis." *Quarterly Journal of Economics* 124(4): 1449–96.

Parker, Jonathan A., and Annette Vissing-Jorgensen. 2009. "Who Bears Aggregate Fluctuations and How?" *American Economic Review* 99(2): 399–405.

Poterba, James M. 2000. "Stock Market Wealth and Consumption." *Journal of Economic Perspectives* 14(2): 99–118.

Souleles, Nicholas. 2004. "Expectations, Heterogeneous Forecast Errors, and Consumption: Micro Evidence from the Michigan Consumer Sentiment Surveys." *Journal of Money, Credit, and Banking* 36(1): 39–72.

U.S. Department of Commerce, Bureau of Economic Analysis. 2011. "GDP and the National Income and Product Account (NIPA) Historical Tables." Available at: http://www.bea.gov/iTable/index_nipa.cfm; accessed July 12, 2011.

U.S. Department of Labor, Bureau of Labor Statistics. Various years. "Consumer Expenditure Survey." Public Use Microdata. Available at: http://www.bls.gov/cex/; accessed July 12, 2011.

――――. 2011. "Current Population Survey: Monthly Table: Employment Status by Race and Hispanic Ethnicity, Table A.4." Available at: http://www.bls.gov/cps/demographics.htm#race; accessed July 12, 2011.

U.S. Department of Transportation. 2009. "Consumer Assistance to Recycle and Save Act of 2009." Report to the House Committee on Energy and Commerce, the Senate Committee on Commerce, Science, and Transportation, and the

House and Senate Committees on Appropriations. Washington: U.S. Government Printing Office.

Wolff, Edward. 2010. "Recent Trends in Household Wealth in the United States: Rising Debt and the Middle-Class Squeeze." Working Paper No. 583. New York: Levy Economics Institute of Bard College.

Chapter 7

The Surprisingly Weak Effect of Recessions on Public Opinion

LANE KENWORTHY AND LINDSAY A. OWENS

H AS THE GREAT Recession altered Americans' views about business, finance, government, opportunity, inequality, and fairness? Has it changed the public's preferences about the appropriate role of government in regulating the economy and helping the less fortunate? Has it shifted political orientations or party allegiances?

Public opinion surveys suggest that in some respects Americans' attitudes *have* shifted in reaction to the Great Recession. But that isn't especially surprising. Nor are changes in public opinion as important in a social or moral sense as loss of jobs, income, and wealth. More interesting and consequential is the question of whether changes in public attitudes induced by the Great Recession will last. Will they endure, or will the public's views return to prior positions once the economy gets back on its feet?

The Great Depression of the 1930s did produce lasting shifts in public attitudes, particularly toward the role of government and the Democratic and Republican parties. But the Great Depression was much larger in magnitude and duration than other economic downturns, including the Great Recession. Surprisingly, we know relatively little about the medium- or long-term impact on public opinion of other recessions.

Good public opinion data are available on a variety of interesting issues since the early 1970s. In this chapter we use these data to examine changes in public opinion in response to the past five economic recessions, including the Great Recession. Our focus is on the effects of the Great Recession, but examining trends in public opinion in prior recessions will assist us in understanding the possible long-term effects of the Great Recession. This general analysis of recession effects poses six questions: Do Americans notice and feel adversely affected by economic downturns? Do attitudes toward business and finance sour? Do attitudes toward government sour? Do people perceive less fairness and opportunity and more inequality? What do Americans think government can and should do to alleviate hardship? Do party allegiances and political orientations shift?

One possibility is that the impact of economic conditions on public opinion is symmetric across phases of the business cycle. Downturns have an impact, but the changes they produce are offset by shifts in the opposite direction during growth periods, so recessions have no long-term effect on public attitudes.

A second possibility is that recessions have a scarring impact that persists, but only on people in their formative years of life—say, age eighteen to twenty-four. The attitudes created by a recession endure for this group, producing significant differences in opinions across cohorts. In a recent study, Paola Giuliano and Antonio Spilimbergo (2009, 1) find that "individuals experiencing recessions during the formative years believe that luck rather than effort is the most important driver of individual success, support more government redistribution, and have less confidence in institutions." But in the absence of large differences in cohort size or a steady increase in the frequency or magnitude of economic downturns, this scarring effect will yield no noteworthy shift for the population as a whole.

A third possibility is that the impact of recession periods and growth periods is asymmetric: the effect of declining economic fortunes on public opinion is stronger or longer lasting than the effect of economic growth. This was true of the Great Depression. Even if change generated by recessions is not as strong as change during depressions, if recession-induced changes ratchet up over time they can cumulate into significant shifts.

Our principal data sources are the General Social Survey (GSS), conducted by the National Opinion Research Center, and the Trends in Political Values and Core Attitudes surveys conducted by the Pew Research Center (Pew). These are nationally representative surveys. The GSS has been conducted annually or biannually since 1972, with the most recent survey in 2010 (National Opinion Research Center 2010). The Pew surveys have been conducted at irregular intervals since 1987 (Pew Research Center for the People and the Press 2009). The Pew data thus do not include the early-1970s and early-1980s recessions, but Pew has a larger number of relevant questions, and some Pew questions have been asked at multiple points during the same year.

So as not to overwhelm the reader, we show the over-time patterns for only some of the public opinion questions for which data are available. We discuss others and show them in charts available in the online appendix at http://www.russellsage.org/greatrecession_onlineappendix.pdf.

Our chief conclusion is that recent economic recessions have had real but mostly temporary effects on American attitudes on key economic, political, and social issues. The lone exception is political views and party identification; the recessions of the mid- and late 1970s may have contributed to disenchantment with liberalism and the Democratic Party. This suggests that the ultimate impact of the Great Recession on public opinion hinges on whether its economic magnitude, and that of the ensuing recovery, turns out to be closer to that of other recent recessions or to that of the Great Depression. As of this writing (February 2011), it is still too soon to tell.

Do Americans Notice and Feel Adversely Affected by Economic Downturns?

Recessions are significant economic downturns. They reduce employment, incomes, and assets for a substantial number of people. That is why we expect to see an impact of recessions on public opinion. But it is important to examine the extent to which Americans perceive their economic situation as deteriorating during downturns. To what degree does economic suffering show up in survey questions that ask about people's impression of their economic circumstances? We look at trends in responses to six GSS and Pew questions.

The over-time pattern for one of these six questions is displayed in figure 7.1a.[1] (The others are shown in the online appendix.) In this figure and all subsequent ones, recession periods are shaded. Those periods, as determined by the National Bureau of Economic Research, are November 1973 to March 1975, January 1980 to July 1980 and July 1981 to November 1982 (we treat this as a single recession), July 1990 to March 1991, March 2001 to November 2001, and December 2007 to June 2009.

Our interest is in changes in public opinion, rather than in the level of agreement or disagreement with the particular statement. In the graphs we therefore use a common range of values on the vertical axes of forty percentage points. This enables comparison of the magnitude of (absolute) change across figures.

Americans do notice economic downturns. In figure 7.1a we see that

Figure 7.1a   Do Americans Notice and Feel Adversely Affected by Economic Downturns?

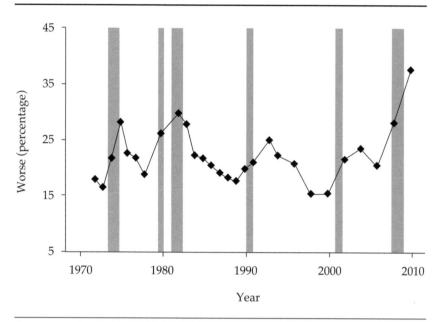

Source: Authors' compilation based on data from General Social Surveys (National Opinion Research Center 2010).
Note: Response: "My financial situation has been getting worse during the last few years." Other response options: "Better"; "Stayed the same." Gray bars represent recession periods.

the share of Americans agreeing that their financial situation has worsened increased by five to ten percentage points in each of the previous four recessions. The rise spurred by the Great Recession is about twice that size. A Pew item on satisfaction with how things are going for the respondent financially also suggests that the increase in financial dissatisfaction has been larger than in prior downturns (online appendix figure 7A.3).

Figure 7.1b summarizes the impact of recessions on all six survey questions. For each question, it shows the average change in public opinion given an increase of one percentage point in the unemployment rate. For instance, the "estimated change" for the item "my financial situation has been getting worse" is approximately 2.5. This means that as unemployment rose by 5 percentage points during the Great Recession (from 4.7 percent in late 2007 to 9.7 percent in early 2010), we would expect the share of Americans saying their financial situation has been get-

Figure 7.1b   Do Americans Notice and Feel Adversely Affected by Economic Downturns?

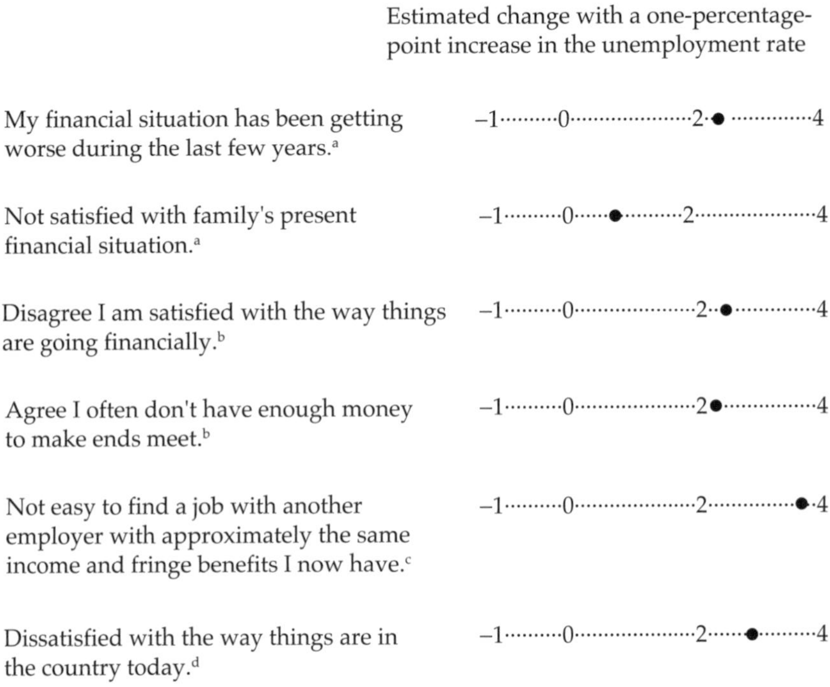

Estimated change with a one-percentage-point increase in the unemployment rate

My financial situation has been getting worse during the last few years.[a]

−1·········0····················2·●·············4

Not satisfied with family's present financial situation.[a]

−1·········0····●··········2····················4

Disagree I am satisfied with the way things are going financially.[b]

−1·········0····················2··●·············4

Agree I often don't have enough money to make ends meet.[b]

−1·········0····················2●················4

Not easy to find a job with another employer with approximately the same income and fringe benefits I now have.[c]

−1·········0····················2·············●·4

Dissatisfied with the way things are in the country today.[d]

−1·········0····················2······●·········4

Source: Authors' compilation based on General Social Surveys (National Opinion Research Center 2010) and Pew Research Center for the People and the Press (2009).
Note: Estimated change is from a regression of the survey response on the unemployment rate and a time variable; the data are monthly. For more details, see the online appendix.
[a.] GSS, 1972 to 2010, 28 data points
[b.] Pew, 1987 to 2009, 14 data points.
[c.] GSS, 1977 to 2010, 20 data points.
[d.] Pew, 1988 to 2010, 96 data points.

ting worse to have increased by about 12.5 percentage points. In this chart and analogous ones in subsequent sections, we show the response—"Agree," "Disagree," "Satisfied," "Dissatisfied," and so forth—whose incidence we expect to increase as the unemployment rate goes up during a recession.

For five of the six survey items we observe that recessions definitely affect Americans' perceptions of their financial well-being and the state of the country. Americans clearly do notice the impact of recessions.

Note that a large "estimated change" in public opinion in response to unemployment does not indicate a change that lasts. In fact, it often suggests the reverse: public attitudes shift when the unemployment rises during a recession, but then they shift back when the unemployment rate goes down during the growth phase of the business cycle. The pattern of responses to the GSS item "My financial situation has been getting worse," shown in figure 7.1a, is illustrative; public opinion moves up and down in sync with the unemployment rate.

A small (or negative) "estimated change" in public opinion in response to unemployment can indicate one of two things: that public opinion is relatively unaffected by recessions, or that public opinion does respond to recessions and the change then persists during the subsequent economic upturn. To figure out which is the case, we need to look at the over-time patterns displayed graphically. The charts shown here and the full set in the online appendix allow us to do that.

Are there differences across sociodemographic groups? Not surprisingly, Americans with less education are more likely to report deterioration in their financial situation during recessions. In the 1970s and 1980s that was also true of African Americans, but the racial difference has diminished substantially since then. In the Great Recession, we observe for the first time a pronounced gender difference; the rise in financial dissatisfaction is much larger among men than among women. This may reflect disparities in unemployment between men and women during this period (see chapter 3, this volume).

Do Attitudes Toward Business and Finance Sour?

When bad things happen, we often look for someone to blame. In economic downturns, likely scapegoats include large firms and financial institutions. The GSS and Pew have six relevant questions.

As figure 7.2a suggests, the data offer mixed support for the hypothesis that Americans sour on big business during economic downturns. For two of the six survey items, a GSS question asking how much confidence people have in banks and financial institutions and a Pew question that asks whether Americans think corporations fairly balance profits with serving the public interest, we see a sizable responsiveness to the unemployment rate. For the other four items, public attitudes have not tended to track the unemployment rate particularly closely.

Figure 7.2b offers a closer look at two of the six items. The share of Americans saying they have hardly any confidence in major companies jumped by more than ten percentage points in the early-1970s recession but less in the early-1990s and early-2000s downturns and not at all in the early 1980s. The increase sparked by the Great Recession is similar to that in the early 1970s, on the order of ten percentage points.

Figure 7.2b also shows the share of Americans expressing hardly any confidence in banks and financial institutions. Here, too, we observe rel-

Figure 7.2a   Do Attitudes Toward Business and Finance Sour?

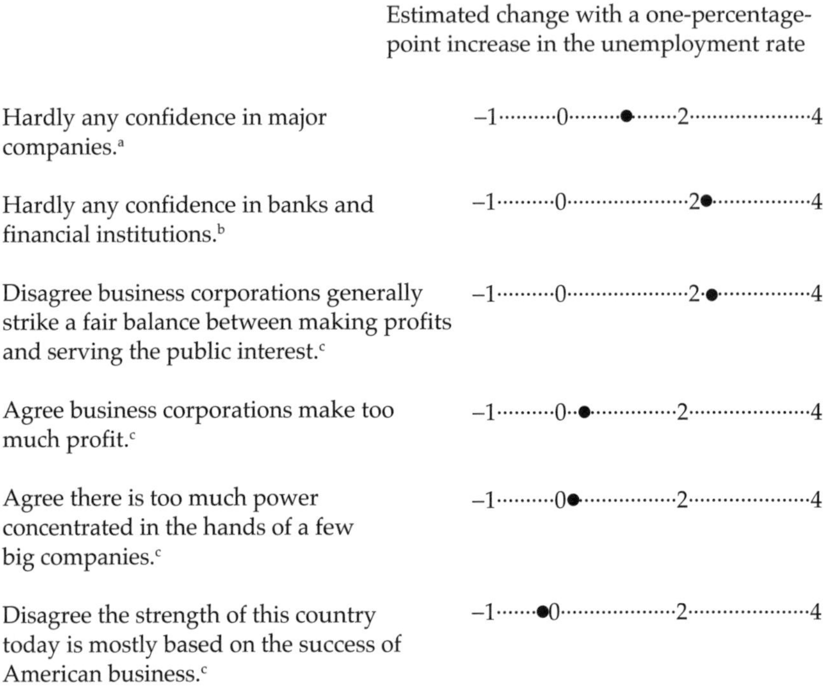

	Estimated change with a one-percentage-point increase in the unemployment rate
Hardly any confidence in major companies.[a]	−1·········0········●·······2·····················4
Hardly any confidence in banks and financial institutions.[b]	−1·········0·····················2●··············4
Disagree business corporations generally strike a fair balance between making profits and serving the public interest.[c]	−1·········0·····················2·●··············4
Agree business corporations make too much profit.[c]	−1·········0··●···············2·····················4
Agree there is too much power concentrated in the hands of a few big companies.[c]	−1·········0●················2·····················4
Disagree the strength of this country today is mostly based on the success of American business.[c]	−1·······●0·····················2·····················4

Source: Authors' compilation based on General Social Surveys (National Opinion Research Center 2010) and Pew Research Center for the People and the Press (2009).
Note: Estimated change is from a regression of the survey response on the unemployment rate and a time variable; the data are monthly. For more details, see the online appendix.
[a] GSS, 1973 to 2010, 26 data points.
[b] GSS, 1975 to 2010, 24 data points.
[c] Pew, 1987 to 2009, 14 data points.

atively modest increases during most economic downturns—with two major exceptions. One is the early-1990s recession, when the share jumped nearly fifteen percentage points. That was likely a product of the savings and loan crisis, which had already caused a significant rise in hardly-any-confidence responses even before the recession. The other exception, not surprisingly, is the Great Recession. The share expressing hardly any confidence in banks and financial institutions rose seven percentage points between 2006 and early 2008. The financial crisis hit in the fall of 2008, and by 2010 the hardly-any-confidence share had risen by an additional twenty percentage points.

Pew asks four questions about corporations' fairness and power. For

Figure 7.2b   Do Attitudes Toward Business and Finance Sour?

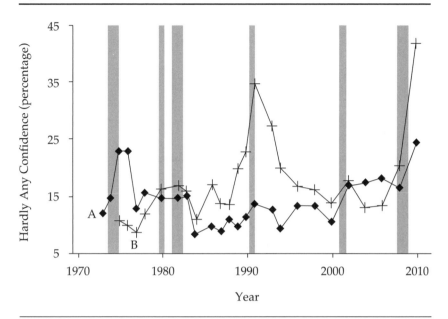

Source: Authors' compilation, based on General Social Survey (National Opinion Research Center 2010).
Note: A: "Hardly any confidence in major companies." Other response options: "A great deal"; "Only some."
B: "Hardly any confidence in banks and financial institutions." Other response options: "A great deal"; "Only some."
Gray bars represent recession periods.

three of the four, we observe little or no impact of economic recessions (figure 7.2a and online appendix figures 7A.9 to 7A.12). The one for which shifts are apparent asks for responses to the statement "Business corporations generally strike a fair balance between profits and the public." Here we see a sizable increase in disagreement during and after the early-1990s and early-2000s downturns. As of April 2009, however, the same was not true of the Great Recession. The particular characteristics and media portrayal of recessions are likely to have mattered here. The early-2000s recession, for instance, was identified with the collapse of the dot-com bubble and was followed by the Enron scandal. The Great Recession, by contrast, has been blamed primarily on large financial companies.

If public opinion toward business and finance has correlated only modestly with changes in unemployment (see figure 7.2a), is that because public opinion has shifted during recessions and then endured?

No. It is because of inconsistent or small shifts in public attitudes produced by recessions themselves. Figure 7.2b shows this for attitudes toward major companies and financial institutions, and figures in the online appendix show the same to be true for the Pew questions.

Changes in attitudes toward business and finance during recessions have varied somewhat across sociodemographic groups. Particularly notable is a strong increase during the Great Recession in lack of confidence in banks and financial institutions among white men, including those with higher education. This is a new development.

Do Attitudes Toward Government Sour?

In addition to or instead of big corporations and finance, Americans might blame government for the country's economic plight during downturns. Alternatively, they may look more favorably upon government if they believe (or hope) it to be helpful in reversing the downturn. We examine changes in attitudes toward government using eight questions from the GSS and Pew surveys. These are listed, and their responsiveness to shifts in the unemployment rate depicted, in figure 7.3a.

Economic downturns, including the Great Recession, have had surprisingly little impact on Americans' views of government, even in the short run. We can point to a few instances of apparent support for the notion that views sour when the economy turns bad. For instance, as figure 7.3b shows, the share of Americans saying they have hardly any confidence in the president or in Congress increased in a few recessions (see also online appendix figure 7A.15). But in the early-1970s recession this may have been a product of Watergate rather than the economy, and in the early-1980s recession it reversed well before the downturn had ended. The Great Recession seems to have had limited impact, though that could be because lack of confidence in both the president and Congress had already risen sharply in the years leading up to the economic crisis.

Pew has five questions designed to elicit views about government's responsiveness to the citizenry. Here too we find little indication of a consistent or meaningful effect of economic downturns (figure 7.3a and online appendix figures 7A.16 to 7A.20). In the recessions of the early 1990s and early 2000s, as well as in the Great Recession, the levels move only slightly and in inconsistent directions, if they move at all.

There are no noteworthy differences across sociodemographic groups. One exception is that in the 2007-to-2009 period the share of black Americans disagreeing with the statement "The government is run for the benefit of all people" dropped sharply, but that is surely due to the election of the first African American president rather than to the economic downturn.

Figure 7.3a   Do Attitudes Toward Government Sour?

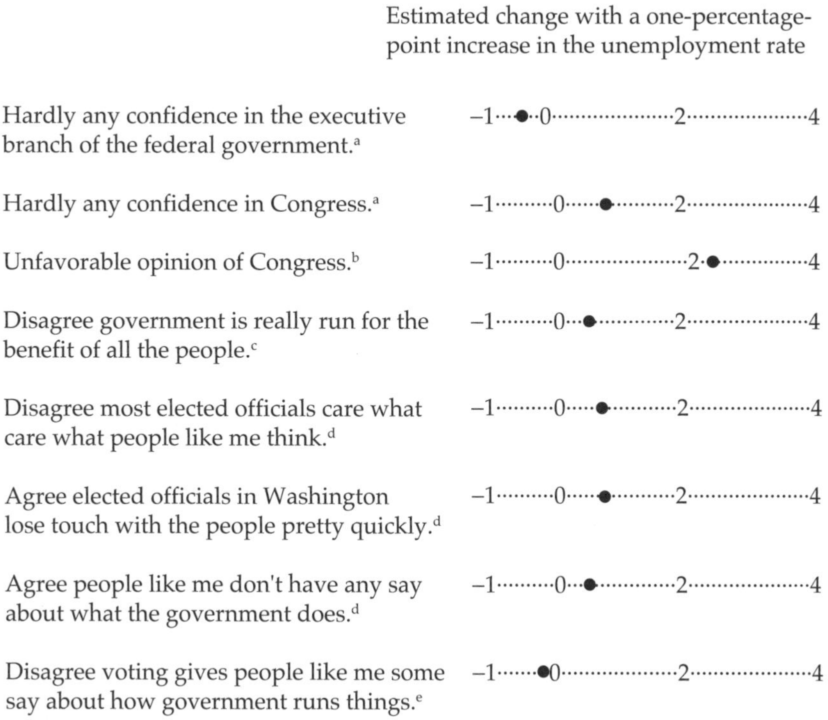

Estimated change with a one-percentage-point increase in the unemployment rate

Hardly any confidence in the executive branch of the federal government.[a]	−1···•·0·····················2·····················4
Hardly any confidence in Congress.[a]	−1··········0·····•··········2·····················4
Unfavorable opinion of Congress.[b]	−1··········0·····················2·•··············4
Disagree government is really run for the benefit of all the people.[c]	−1··········0···•··············2·····················4
Disagree most elected officials care what care what people like me think.[d]	−1··········0·····•··········2·····················4
Agree elected officials in Washington lose touch with the people pretty quickly.[d]	−1··········0·····•··········2·····················4
Agree people like me don't have any say about what the government does.[d]	−1··········0···•··············2·····················4
Disagree voting gives people like me some say about how government runs things.[e]	−1········•0·····················2·····················4

Source: Authors' compilation based on General Social Surveys (National Opinion Research Center 2010) and Pew Research Center for the People and the Press (2009).
Note: Estimated change is from a regression of the survey response on the unemployment rate and a time variable; the data are monthly. For more details, see the online appendix.
[a] GSS, 1973 to 2010, 26 data points
[b] Pew, 1985 to 2010, 50 data points.
[c] Pew, 1987 to 2009, 13 data points.
[d] Pew, 1987 to 2009, 14 data points.
[e] Pew, 1987 to 2009, 12 data points.

Do People Perceive Less Fairness, Less Opportunity, More Inequality?

Recessions bring poverty, inequality, opportunity, and justice into stark relief. Mass layoffs, empty store fronts, and stories in the media of lines at food banks are among the consequences of recessions that might heighten Americans' perception of economic suffering. The GSS and Pew surveys have six items that help us to gauge shifts in attitudes about fairness, opportunity, and inequality.

Figure 7.3b   Do Attitudes Toward Government Sour?

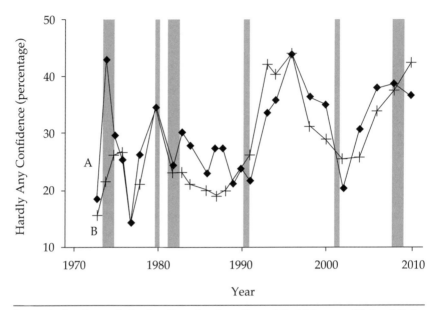

Source: Authors' compilation based on data from General Social Surveys (National Opinion Research Center 2010).
Note: A: Hardly any confidence in the executive branch of the federal government. Other response options: "A great deal"; "Only some."
B: Hardly any confidence in Congress. Other response options: "A great deal"; "Only some."
Gray bars represent recession periods.

Figure 7.4a reveals nontrivial responsiveness to recessions on three of the four items that ask about beliefs concerning fairness and opportunity. When the economy turns bad, more Americans tend to view hard work as a weak guarantee of success, to believe that success is determined by forces beyond our control, and to be pessimistic about their family's likelihood of improving its living standards. However, the two questions on inequality offer a mixed story. The share of Americans thinking the rich are getting richer and the poor, poorer seems to have been affected by recessions, whereas the share believing the country is more and more divided between the haves and the have-nots doesn't.

Figure 7.4b offers a closer look at the trends for three of these survey items. It shows that in each of the five downturns since the early 1970s there has been an increase in the share of GSS respondents saying that people get ahead as a result of lucky breaks or help from others rather than from hard work. However, this rise is always small—five percent-

Figure 7.4a   Do People Perceive Less Fairness, Less Opportunity, More Inequality?

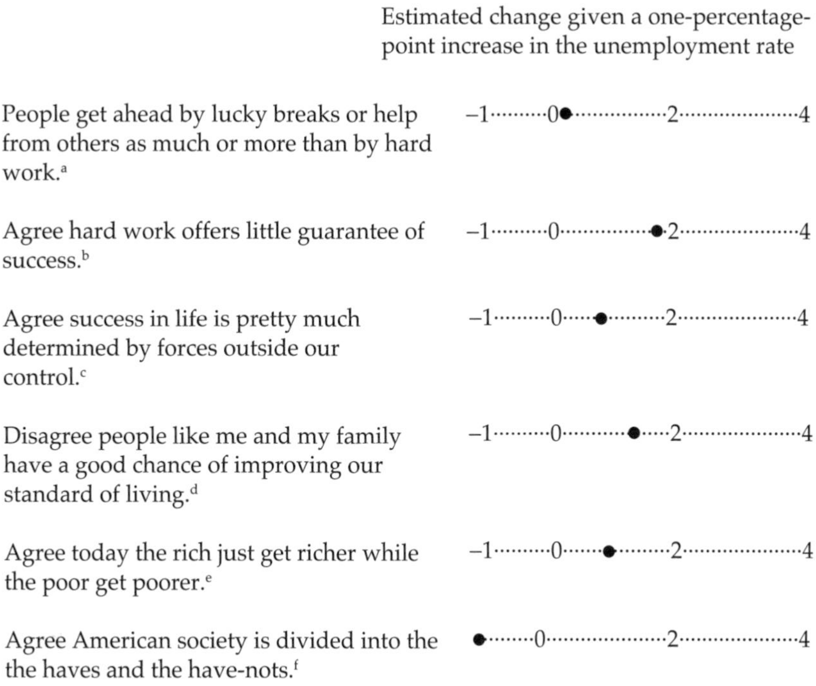

Estimated change given a one-percentage-point increase in the unemployment rate

People get ahead by lucky breaks or help from others as much or more than by hard work.[a]

−1·········0●················2·····················4

Agree hard work offers little guarantee of success.[b]

−1·········0···············●·2·····················4

Agree success in life is pretty much determined by forces outside our control.[c]

−1·········0····●··········2·····················4

Disagree people like me and my family have a good chance of improving our standard of living.[d]

−1·········0···········●····2·····················4

Agree today the rich just get richer while the poor get poorer.[e]

−1·········0······●·········2·····················4

Agree American society is divided into the the haves and the have-nots.[f]

●·······0·····················2·····················4

Source: Authors' compilation based on General Social Surveys (National Opinion Research Center 2010) and Pew Research Center for the People and the Press (2009).
Note: Estimated change is from a regression of the survey response on the unemployment rate and a time variable; the data are monthly. For more details, see the online appendix.
[a] GSS, 1973 to 2010, 23 data points
[b] Pew, 1987 to 2009, 13 data points.
[c] Pew, 1987 to 2009, 12 data points.
[d] GSS, 1987 to 2010, 10 data points.
[e] Pew, 1987 to 2009, 14 data points.
[f] Pew, 1987 to 2009, 13 data points.

age points or less. A GSS question included semiregularly since the late 1980s more directly addresses people's perceptions of economic opportunity, asking whether the respondent believes the statement "People like me and my family have a good chance of improving our standard of living." This too is included in figure 7.4b. Here we do observe shifts during or shortly after each of the past three recessions, with the share disagreeing rising by five to ten percentage points. Following the early-1990s and early-2000s recessions, however, the share returned to essentially the pre-recession level.

Figure 7.4b   Do People Perceive Less Fairness, Less Opportunity, More Inequality?

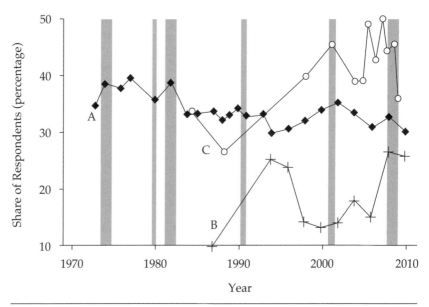

Source: Authors' compilation based on General Social Surveys (National Opinion Research Center 2010) and Pew Research Center for the People and the Press (2009).
Note: A: GSS: "People get ahead by lucky breaks or help from other people." Other response option: "Hard work."
B: GSS: "Disagree [that] people like me and my family have a good chance of improving our standard of living." Other response option "Disagree."
C: Pew: "Agree American society is divided into the haves and the have-nots." Other response option: "Disagree."
Gray bars represent recession periods.

Between September 2007 (just before the Great Recession) and April 2009 the share of respondents agreeing with the statement "American society is divided into the haves and the have-nots" fell by nearly fifteen percentage points (see figure 7.4b). This is surprising, given that both the media and policymakers have put a sizable portion of blame for the economic crisis on overpaid bankers and financial players. Perhaps Americans feel that the sharp declines in stock and home values have had a leveling effect.

What the survey data suggest, then, is that Americans have tended to view recessions as curtailing economic opportunity, but only temporarily, and as having no enduring impact on economic justice or inequality.

There also are no significant differences across sociodemographic groups in reactions on these issues.

What Do Americans Think Government Can Do and Should Do?

One hypothesis concerning the expected role of government is that sentiment in favor of government activism, particularly to help the less fortunate, will increase during economic recessions (Erikson, MacKuen, and Stimson 2002; Blekesaune and Quadagno 2003; Blekesaune 2007). A second hypothesis is that even if this occurs, its impact will be outweighed by self-interested reactions of middle- and upper-class taxpayers, who see their own bank accounts shrinking and therefore are less willing than usual to support government redistribution to the needy (Durr 1993; Friedman 2005). Another possibility is that neither hypothesis is correct, or that both are correct but they cancel each other out (Kam and Nam 2008).

We examine thirteen GSS and Pew items in figure 7.5a. The first four of these questions are about government regulation, government intervention in daily life, the appropriate balance between local and federal government, and whether government management is efficient. Figure 7.5b displays the trends for two of these questions. On each of the two items shown and on the two items not shown here but included in the online appendix, we observe an increase in support, typically of around five percentage points, for government activism in the early-2000s downturn and in the Great Recession. But in the early-1990s recession there was no such increase.

The remaining nine questions are about attitudes toward government's role in helping the less fortunate. None of the responses to these items suggest a significant shift in public opinion during or shortly after recessions. We observe increases in a few of these items during recessions, but those increases are consistently small, and they are balanced by an equal number of small decreases. Overall, the story is one of no noteworthy change. Figure 7.5c displays the trends for two of these items.

What should we make of these two contradictory patterns—on the one hand rising support for government regulation in the early- and late-2000s recessions but not in the early-1990s downturn, and on the other hand no change in attitudes toward government help for the less fortunate? One explanation might be the shifting nature of job loss during recessions. The early-2000s downturn was the first in which middle-class, white-collar employees were just as likely as less-skilled and lower-paid workers to experience job loss. That downturn and the Great Recession also were characterized by massive drops in stock values and, in the Great Recession, drops in home values too. In short, these two most recent recessions have hit middle-class Americans fairly hard. Persons with lower incomes are more likely to support government activism during nonreces-

Figure 7.5a   What Do Americans Think Government Can and Should Do?

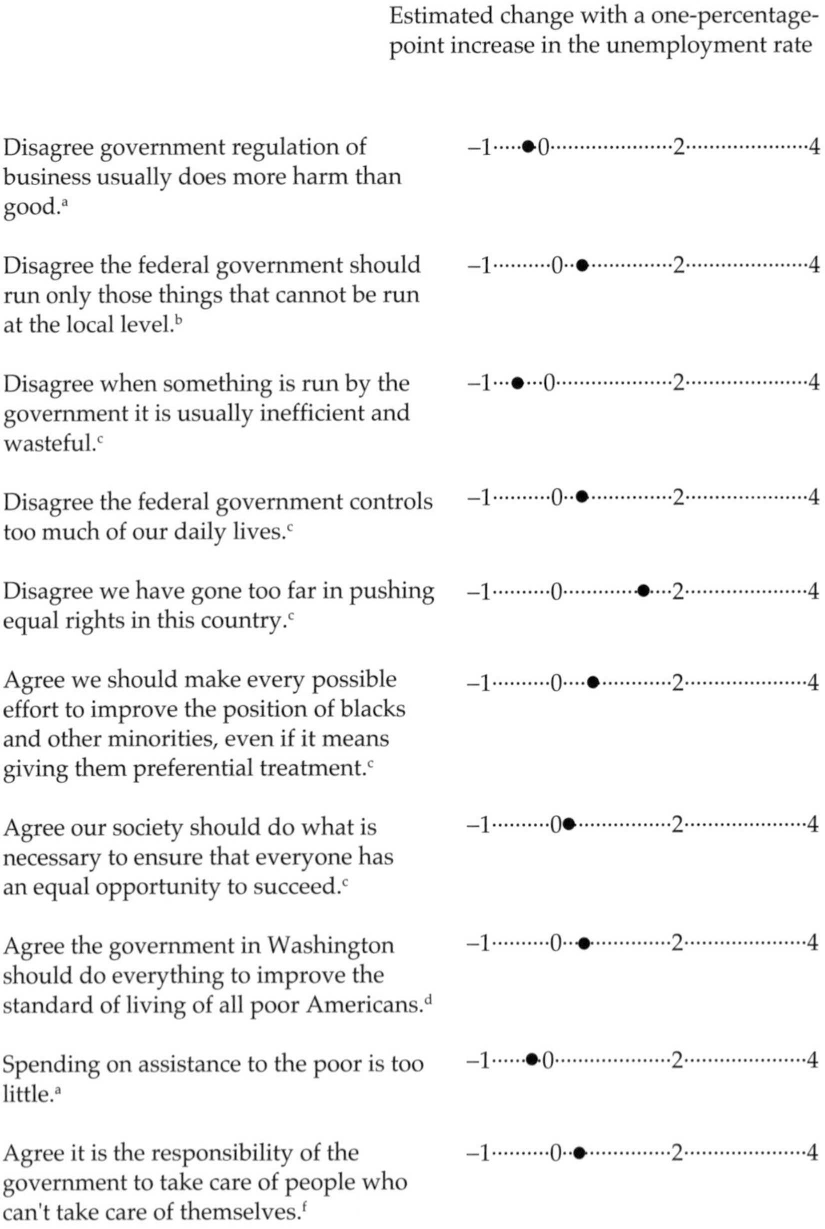

Estimated change with a one-percentage-point increase in the unemployment rate

Disagree government regulation of business usually does more harm than good.[a]

−1·····●·0·····················2····················4

Disagree the federal government should run only those things that cannot be run at the local level.[b]

−1··········0··●·············2····················4

Disagree when something is run by the government it is usually inefficient and wasteful.[c]

−1···●··0·····················2····················4

Disagree the federal government controls too much of our daily lives.[c]

−1··········0··●·············2····················4

Disagree we have gone too far in pushing equal rights in this country.[c]

−1··········0············●···2····················4

Agree we should make every possible effort to improve the position of blacks and other minorities, even if it means giving them preferential treatment.[c]

−1··········0···●············2····················4

Agree our society should do what is necessary to ensure that everyone has an equal opportunity to succeed.[c]

−1··········0●················2····················4

Agree the government in Washington should do everything to improve the standard of living of all poor Americans.[d]

−1··········0··●·············2····················4

Spending on assistance to the poor is too little.[a]

−1·····●·0·····················2····················4

Agree it is the responsibility of the government to take care of people who can't take care of themselves.[f]

−1··········0··●·············2····················4

Figure 7.5a   *(continued)*

Estimated change with a one-percentage-
point increase in the unemployment rate

Agree the government should help more   −1·······●0·····················2·····················4
needy people even if it means going
deeper in debt.[g]

Agree the government should guarantee   −1·········0●·················2·····················4
every citizen enough to eat and a place to
sleep.[g]

Agree the government in Washington   −1·······●0·····················2·····················4
ought to reduce the income differences
between the rich and the poor.[h]

Source: Authors' compilation based on General Social Surveys (National Opinion Research Center 2010) and Pew Research Center for the People and the Press (2009).
Note: Estimated change is from a regression of the survey response on the unemployment rate and a time variable; the data are monthly. For more details, see the online appendix.
[a.] Pew, 1987 to 2009, 11 data points
[b.] Pew, 1987 to 2009, 9 data points.
[c.] Pew, 1987 to 2009, 14 data points.
[d.] GSS, 1975 to 2010, 19 data points.
[e.] GSS, 1984 to 2010, 18 data points.
[f.] Pew, 1987 to 2009, 12 data points.
[g.] Pew, 1987 to 2009, 13 data points.
[h.] GSS, 1978 to 2010, 20 data points.

sion periods; hence recessions are not likely to have much impact on attitudes among this group. A downturn that hits the middle class may well produce a shift in its attitudes, since during normal times this group tends to be less supportive of government regulation and management. Even while increasing their support for government intervention, though, middle-class victims of recessions may be no more inclined than usual to support enhanced help for the disadvantaged.

Another (not incompatible) possibility is that welfare reform in 1996 and perhaps the economic boom in the second half of the 1990s altered the way Americans think about what is needed from government in bad economic times. Whereas formerly the default policy response was assistance for the less fortunate, it may now have shifted to (temporary) government activism aimed at righting the economic ship.

Once again we observe few noteworthy differences across socio-demographic groups. One exception is that during the Great Recession

Figure 7.5b   What Do Americans Think Government Can and Should Do?

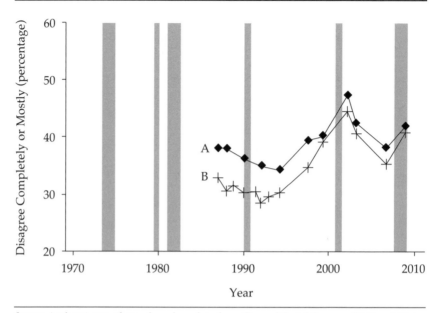

Source: Authors' compilation based on data from General Social Surveys (National Opinion Research Center 2010).
Note: A: "Disagree government regulation of business usually does more harm than good." Other response options: "Agree completely"; "Agree mostly."
B: "Disagree when something is run by the government it is usually inefficient and wasteful." Other response options: "Agree completely"; "Agree mostly."
Gray bars represent recession periods.

the share of African Americans favoring government action to reduce income differences has increased much more than among whites. This too may be an Obama effect rather than a product of the economic downturn.

Do Party Allegiances and Political Orientations Shift?

Economic recessions should tend to reduce support for the party in power and increase support for the other party. Whether such changes will endure is less obvious. The same considerations hold for the political views of conservatism and liberalism, though any shifts in these deeper-seated orientations are likely to be smaller than for party allegiances. We examine standard survey measures of party identification and political orientation in the GSS and Pew surveys (see figure 7.6a).

Figure 7.5c   **What Do Americans Think Government Can and Should Do?**

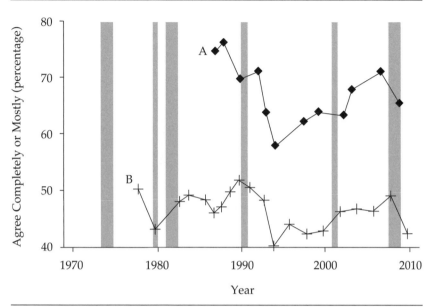

Year

Source: Authors' compilation based on General Social Surveys (National Opinion Research Center 2010) and Pew Research Center for the People and the Press (2009).
Note: A: Pew: "Agree it is the responsibility of government to take care of the people who can't take care of themselves." Other response options: "Agree completely"; "Agree mostly."
B: GSS: "Agree the government ought to reduce the income differences between the rich and the poor."
Response options on a scale from 1 to 7. Gray bars represent recession periods.

In measuring party identification, both surveys offer seven choices to respondents. Those who respond "independent" are allowed to reclassify themselves, if they wish, as "weak" identifiers with one of the two parties or as "leaning" toward one of them. We count the weak and leaning identifiers as Democrat or Republican, rather than as independent (Keith et al. 1992; Sides 2009).

The over-time patterns for party identification and political orientation are shown in figures 7.6b and 7.6c, respectively. In figure 7.6b we combine the GSS and Pew data, using the GSS through early 2008 and Pew since then.

Whereas recent recessions seem to have had little impact on individual-issue attitudes we have examined up to now, a case can be made that some recent recessions have had a lasting impact on both political views and party identification. Figures 7.6b and 7.6c show that there were sig-

Figure 7.6a   Do Party Allegiances and Political Orientations Shift?

Estimated change with a one-percentage-point increase in the unemployment rate

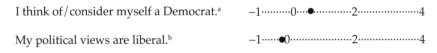

I think of / consider myself a Democrat.[a]   –1·········0···●·············2·····················4

My political views are liberal.[b]   –1······●0·····················2·····················4

Source: Authors' compilation based on General Social Surveys (National Opinion Research Center 2010) and Pew Research Center for the People and the Press (2009).
Note: Estimated change is from a regression of the survey response on the unemployment rate and a time variable; the data are monthly. For more details, see the online appendix.
[a] GSS and Pew, 1972 to 2010, 51 data points.
[b] GSS, 1974 to 2010, 26 data points.

Figure 7.6b   Do Party Allegiances Shift?

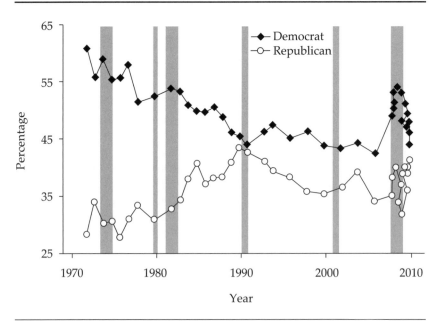

Sources: Authors' compilation based on General Social Survey (National Opinion Research Center 2010) 1972 to 2010; Pew Research Center for the People and the Press (2009) 2008 to 2010.
Note: On a seven-point scale ranging from "strong Democrat" to "strong Republican." Gray bars represent recession periods.

Figure 7.6c   Do Political Orientations Shift?

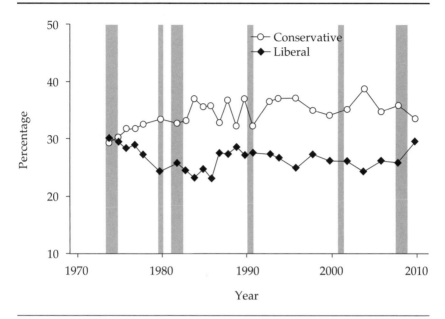

Source: Authors' compilation based on data from General Social Surveys (National Opinion Research Center 2010).
Note: On a seven-point scale ranging from "extremely liberal" to "extremely conservative." Gray bars represent recession periods.

nificant shifts from Democratic identification to Republican and from liberal to conservative following the early-1970s and early-1980s recessions. Arguably these movements were causally connected (Kenworthy et al. 2007). The recession of the early 1970s, coupled with the ensuing period of stagflation, contributed to growing disenchantment with the Democratic Party, which had dominated American politics since the 1930s. Republicans argued that the Democrats had overreached and that liberal policies had gone too far. Ronald Reagan pressed this argument as a presidential candidate in 1979 and 1980, and as president he attributed the early-1980s recession to the same cause. These shifts in party identification and political orientations surely were products of a number of factors, but the recessions very likely contributed.

Conversely, the early-1990s downturn, occurring after more than a decade of Republican occupation of the White House, may have contributed to ending the rise in Republican identification. Around the same time there were two important foreign policy successes under Republican presidents that should have boosted their popularity: the collapse of the

Soviet Bloc beginning in 1989 and the successful prosecution of the first Gulf War. These successes strengthen the idea that the recessions played a sizable role in the reduction in voters' identifying as Republicans. No similar change, however, is observable for political orientations.

Given the magnitude of the Great Recession and the fact that Republicans held the presidency and both houses of Congress for much of the preceding eight years, we would expect the Democrats to have benefited from this downturn. But as figure 7.6b indicates, thus far that has not been the case. Democratic identification began to rise in the mid-2000s and continued through 2008, the first year of the Great Recession. But in 2009 and 2010 that gain was reversed.

The one sociodemographic difference of note has to do with education. Typically in recessions those with less education are a little more likely than those with more education to shift toward liberal views or to identify as a Democrat. In the Great Recession the reverse has been true, although the difference is not large.

Conclusions

We have examined data from the GSS and the Pew Research Center's Trends in Political Values and Core Attitudes surveys to assess the effect of the five economic recessions since 1970, including the Great Recession, on American public opinion. We conclude by summarizing the answers to our six questions and by considering what our findings imply for the long-term impact of the Great Recession on public attitudes.

Do Americans notice and feel adversely affected by economic downturns? Yes, they do. The magnitude of changes typically has been on the order of five to ten percentage points, larger in the Great Recession. These effects have tended to disappear as the economy moves out of recession, though the lag was noticeably longer following the early-1990s and early-2000s recessions than it had been in the previous two. This is consistent with trends in the unemployment rate, which remained high for sustained periods following the downturns of the early 1990s and early 2000s.

Do attitudes toward business and finance sour? Yes, but perhaps not as much as we might expect. Only during the early-1970s and early-2000s (Enron) recessions and the Great Recession do we observe a sharp rise in the share of Americans expressing hardly any confidence in major companies, and only in the early-1990s recession (savings-and-loans crisis) and the Great Recession do they express that view of banks and financial institutions. On three of four Pew questions as to whether businesses are fair or whether they are too powerful, recessions have produced no apparent change of attitude.

Do attitudes toward government sour? Economic downturns, including the current one, appear to have had little impact on Americans' views of government, even in the short run.

Do people perceive less fairness and opportunity and more inequality? Recessions do reduce Americans' perception of their own economic opportunity, but only temporarily. They appear to have less of an impact, if any, on perceptions of justice and inequality.

What do Americans think government can do and should do to alleviate hardship? Here most of the relevant survey data are available for only the three most recent recessions. The story they tell is mixed. On the one hand, in the two most recent downturns, those of the early and late 2000s, we observe a rise in approval of general government activism. On the other hand, there is no indication of any increase in support for policies that enhance opportunity, support for the poor, or support for redistribution.

Do party allegiances and political views shift? The recessions of the early 1970s and the early 1980s, coupled with the stagflation of the late 1970s, arguably contributed to a significant shift in party identification and political orientation. A growing number of Americans came to consider themselves conservative rather than liberal, and there was an even larger switch from Democratic Party identification to Republican. The downturn of the early 1990s may have contributed to a reversal of that pro-Republican trend in party identification.

Why have economic recessions produced so little enduring change in the attitudes of the American public on specific issues? One possibility is that public opinion has a strong tendency to stay locked into place and nothing shifts it, including recessions. Though there may be some truth in this, we can spot lasting changes in public opinion on a few of the issues we have considered here, such as income inequality (see figure 7.4b). The same is true for some other issues we have not examined, such as government spending on education and attitudes toward race and sexual orientation (see Loftus 2001; Erikson, MacKuen, and Stimson 2002; McCall and Kenworthy 2009).

Instead, the lack of enduring changes in public opinion in response to recessions suggests that the shifts economic downturns do produce tend to be small and that they tend to be either period effects or cohort effects. Period effects are offset by contrasting shifts in attitudes during periods of economic health. Cohort effects persist among those who were in their formative years during the recession, but they are offset for the full population by different attitudes held by nonrecession cohorts. For the most part, recessions have not produced lasting changes—scarring effects—in attitudes throughout the full population.

The story is different for party identification and political orientation. Here the recessions of the 1970s, 1980s, and 1990s do seem to have had a lasting impact, particularly on party allegiances. In some respects this is not surprising. Even if Americans' attitudes on particular issues remain relatively constant, they may change their minds about which party is better able to deliver what they want, including a healthy economy. Moreover, although both the early-1970s and early-1980s recessions occurred under Republican presidents, the Democrats had dominated American politics for a generation and were in power during the years of stagflation that connected those two recessions. This allowed Republicans to blame the Democrats for what amounted to a decade of hard economic times.

What do our findings imply for the long-run effect of the Great Recession on Americans' views about fairness, opportunity, business, finance, and government activism? If the economy returns to normalcy in the near future, the pattern of responses to the four prior downturns suggests that its impact may be limited. But the Great Recession could be different (Bivens and Shierholz 2010; Peter S. Goodman, "Millions of Unemployed Face Years Without Jobs," *New York Times*, February 21, 2010; Peck 2010). Employment fell more rapidly and by a larger amount than in any downturn since the Depression. And, as noted earlier, the pace of job expansion has been slower in each succeeding recession since the early 1980s. Given the depth of the Great Recession and the pattern of slow job growth following the two prior downturns, it may be quite a long while before the labor market recovers. As of early 2011, a year and a half after economic growth had resumed, the share of Americans unemployed for more than six months was more than double that of the previous high, in the early-1980s downturn.

If the recovery does turn out to be slow or feeble, the lessons of recent recessions may not hold. In the early years of the Great Depression it was not clear that large changes in Americans' attitudes toward politics, fairness, and government activism were under way (Newman and Jacobs 2010). But in the end the Depression did contribute to enduring shifts. The same may yet prove true of the Great Recession.

Note

1. In the figures and the figure source notes, "GSS" refers to the General Social Survey conducted by the National Opinion Research Center (2010). "Pew" refers to the Trends in Political Values and Core Attitudes surveys conducted by the Pew Research Center for the People and the Press (2009).

References

Bivens, Josh, and Heidi Shierholz. 2010. "For Job Seekers, No Recovery in Sight." Briefing Paper 259. Washington, D.C.: Economic Policy Institute. Available at: http://epi.3cdn.net/aecff0c1614f632f15_epm6ibkcy.pdf; accessed May 31, 2011.

Blekesaune, Morten. 2007. "Economic Conditions and Public Attitudes to Welfare Policies." *European Sociological Review* 23(3): 393–403.

Blekesaune, Morten, and Jill Quadagno. 2003. "Public Attitudes Toward Welfare State Policies: A Comparative Analysis of 24 Nations." *European Sociological Review* 19(5): 415–27.

Durr, Robert H. 1993. "What Moves Policy Sentiment?" *American Political Science Review* 87(1): 158–70.

Erikson, Robert S., Michael B. MacKuen, and James A. Stimson. 2002. *The Macro Polity*. Cambridge: Cambridge University Press.

Friedman, Benjamin. 2005. *The Moral Consequences of Economic Growth*. New York: Knopf.

Giuliano, Paola, and Antonio Spilimbergo. 2009. "Growing Up in a Recession: Beliefs and the Macroeconomy." IZA Discussion Paper No. 4365. Bonn, Germany: Institute for the Study of Labor.

Kam, Cindy D., and Junju Nam. 2008. "Reaching Out or Pulling Back: Macroeconomic Conditions and Public Support for Social Welfare Spending." *Political Behavior* 30(2): 223–58.

Keith, Bruce E., David B. Magleby, Candice J. Nelson, Elizabeth Orr, Mark C. Westlye, and Raymond E. Wolfinger. 1992. *The Myth of the Independent Voter*. Berkeley: University of California Press.

Kenworthy, Lane, Sondra Barringer, Daniel Duerr, and Garrett Andrew Schneider. 2007. "The Democrats and Working-Class Whites." Unpublished paper. University of Arizona. Available at http://u.arizona.edu/~lkenwor/thedemocratsandworkingclasswhites.pdf; accessed May 31, 2011.

Loftus, Jeni. 2001. "America's Liberalization in Attitudes Toward Homosexuality, 1973 to 1998." *American Sociological Review* 66(5): 762–68.

McCall, Leslie, and Lane Kenworthy. 2009. "Americans' Social Policy Preferences in the Era of Rising Inequality." *Perspectives on Politics* 7(3): 459–84.

National Opinon Research Center. 2010. *General Social Survey (GSS)*. Chicago, Ill. Available at: http://www.norc.org/GSS+Website/About+GSS; accessed February 1, 2011 (see further links).

Newman, Katherine S., and Elizabeth Jacobs. 2010. *Who Cares? Public Ambivalence and Government Activism from the New Deal to the Second Gilded Age*. Princeton: Princeton University Press.

Peck, Jon. 2010. "How a New Jobless Era Will Transform America." *The Atlantic*, March: 42–56.

Pew Research Center for the People and the Press. 2009. "Trends in Political Values and Core Attitudes, 1987 to 2009." News release, May 21. Washington, D.C.

Sides, John. 2009. "Three Myths About Political Independents." Available at: http://themonkeycage.org/blog/2009/12/17/three_myths_about_political_in; accessed May 31, 2011.

Chapter 8

The Great Recession's Influence on Fertility, Marriage, Divorce, and Cohabitation

S. PHILIP MORGAN, ERIN CUMBERWORTH,
AND CHRISTOPHER WIMER

THE EXPERIENCE OF the Great Recession is not confined to the spheres of jobs, earnings, and wealth. Amid the turmoil and economic upheaval in the wider economy, individuals and families go about their lives, planning marriages, suffering through breakups and divorces, planning families, and sorting out their living arrangements. The recession could conceivably have major effects on all of these family processes. Weddings and babies, after all, can be expensive endeavors. At the same time, partnering can create economies of scale that make meeting daily expenses easier. Financial strains can lead to strained relationships. And hardships can also bring families together. Stated differently, people not only "feel" the recession in their families, they also respond to it, not only as individuals but as members of families. Studies of how recent recessions impact the family are rare (for an exception, see Moen 1979); more research is available on the Great Depression (for example, Elder 1974).

In this chapter, we examine the recession's effects on fertility and family planning use; unions—marriage, divorce, cohabitation; and living arrangements of those not in unions. Is the recession altering the fabric of the American family? Or are families functioning pretty much as usual? Did the Great Recession have disproportionate impacts on identifiable population subgroups? Bringing together data from the National Vital Statistics System and the Current Population Survey, this chapter attempts to examine such questions. Though questions of establishing causal processes generally remain outside the scope of this chapter, we provide a wide range of evidence as to how American families are changing in the face of one of the biggest economic calamities since the Great Depression.

Fertility

Fertility rates in the United States have varied dramatically over the past century, plummeting during the Great Depression, skyrocketing during the post–World War II baby boom, declining again in the baby bust of the 1970s. The total fertility rate (TFR), the most commonly used fertility measure, is defined as the number of births a woman would have if she experienced over her lifetime the age-specific rates of a given period. The major changes in the TFR occurred during periods of massive social transformation, such as the Great Depression in the 1920s and 1930s and the postwar baby boom and bust of the 1950s and 1960s. Since then, the United States has experienced an extended period of striking stability, with Americans averaging close to two children per woman. For several decades prior to the Great Recession the U.S. TFR hovered around 2.1, or near the "replacement rate"—the level necessary for replenishing the population (net any immigration and the effects of existing age structure). But even small changes in the TFR translate to large and substantial changes in the absolute number of children born each year—more than 4 million babies were born each year in the period from 2000 to 2008, so even a modest decline (say, 5 percent) means several hundred thousand fewer births (200,000). Moreover, the relative stability of the TFR in recent decades masks other important changes such as a dramatic increase in nonmarital fertility and a two-decade-long increase in ages of a woman's first birth. The Great Recession could impact these aspects of fertility as well as the overall rates and absolute numbers.

So how might the experience of the 2008-to-2009 Great Recession affect fertility? Over three decades ago, the demographers William P. Butz and Michael P. Ward (1979) argued that a "counter-cycle" fertility response was emerging. Specifically, because more women were in the workforce they might use periods of unemployment and weak employer demands as an opportune time to have children. In other words, the opportunity costs of children would be less during economic downturns.

Further, with greater gender equality child care provided by the un- or underemployed spouse (mother or father) would lower the primary cost of childbearing in terms of lost wages and income.

No doubt such calculations influence some women and couples, but past evidence from the United States and other developed countries suggests that the dominant effects of economic downturns reduce fertility (Sobotka, Skirbekk, and Philpov 2010). Why? Making the decision of when to have a child is one of the most important decisions people can make because of its dramatic short-term costs and long-term implications. For most couples, having a child is a decision best made when they can arrange to take care of a baby and when they are sufficiently economically secure in their jobs and their future to make such a long-term commitment. Thus, in times of recession, when uncertainty and insecurity about the future runs rampant, we might expect that persons would postpone having children and fertility rates would drop (Bongaarts and Feeney 1998). To this dominant narrative, one must note its inconsistency with important "facts on the ground" in the United States: over 38 percent of births are to unmarried women (Martin et al. 2009), and 49 percent of all pregnancies are unintended (Finer and Henshaw 2006). Thus, many of the decisions about pregnancy and birth are not made by married couples, and many decisions about childbearing are made after an unintended pregnancy occurs. Most evidence suggests that less certain times would reduce the likelihood of births among the unmarried, too, and might lead some to abort unplanned pregnancies that they might have carried to term in more secure economic circumstances.

How married and unmarried women respond differently and whether the resolution of unintended pregnancies is changing are both crucial questions, though not ones that can be directly answered at this time. The data needed to address these questions will not be available for several more years (from important and detailed data like those available in the National Survey of Family Growth, or NSFG). But we can examine overall fertility trends using monthly data published by the National Vital Statistics Service (see figure 8.1). In addition to the TFR (left axis), we show on the right axis the number of births per thousand women of "childbearing years," defined here as those age fifteen to forty-four (this is referred to as the General Fertility Rate, or GFR). The GFR is a less refined measure than the TFR. We use it later in this chapter when the TFR is not available. We find that fertility does appear to be changing course in the current recession, using either fertility measure.

Let us begin with the most recent experience. The TFR and GFR show a clear reversal in 2008 after rising steadily from 2003. The fertility rates dropped even further in 2009. Given that the recession began in December 2007 (when the economy was officially declared to be in recession),

Figure 8.1   The First Drop in Fertility Rate Since 2003

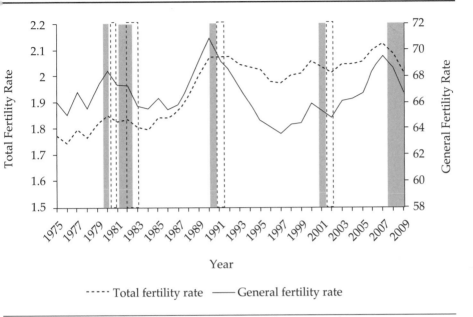

Year

----- Total fertility rate   ——— General fertility rate

Source: Authors' compilation based on data from the National Center for Health Statistics (Martin et al. 2010; Hamilton, Martin, and Ventura 2010a, 2010b).
Note: The vertical bars shaded gray show recession periods. The vertical bars outlined by dotted border show a nine-month lag to the recession period.

the timing of this reversal is generally consistent with the hypothesis that people are responding to the recession by curtailing or postponing births.[1]

Moving to earlier periods, figure 8.1 shows the effects of previous recessions on fertility. As in other chapters we show recession periods by shaded rectangles where the width of the rectangle indexes each recession's duration. Using the TFR as the key fertility measure to assess the effects of these prior recessions, note that the TFR consistently responds to recessions by downward deflections of the fertility trend (that is, by reversing an upward trend or, as in the case of the 1990, halting the increase).

But note that the TFR change is modest in response to both recessions and most other factors in the post-1975 period. The TFR has varied in a relatively narrow range, from about 1.75 to 2.1. The lower TFR rates prior to 1990 reflect pervasive postponement of childbearing that is less dramatic in recent years; controlling for this pervasive postponement would raise fertility to replacement levels (a TFR of approximately 2.1) across

Figure 8.2   Trends in Fertility and Unemployment

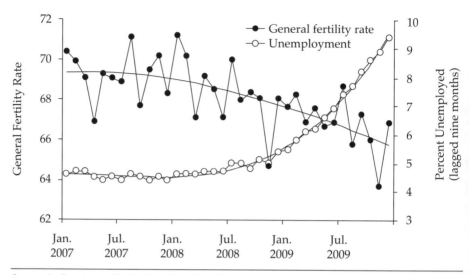

Source: Authors' compilation based on data from U.S. Bureau of Labor Statistics (2011a) and the National Center for Health Statistics (Martin et al. 2010; Hamilton, Martin, and Ventura 2010a, 2010b).
Note: Figure shows the general fertility rate published by the National Center for Health Statistics in their monthly National Vital Statistics Report and the official unemployment rate from the Bureau of Labor Statistics (lagged nine months).

almost all of the 1975-to-2006 period (see Bongaarts and Feeney 1998). Compared to the dramatic shifts earlier in the century, the changes associated with recent recessions (shown in figure 8.1) are modest. For example, the TFR changed by over one birth in response to the Great Depression (decline), the baby boom (increase), and the baby bust (decline; see Morgan 1996 for data). In comparison the TFR only declined by about 0.1 in response to the most recent recessions (about 5 percent). The 2001 recession was associated with a 2 percent decline in the TFR. Taken all together the evidence consistently points to a modest 2 to 5 percent decline in fertility associated with the initial stages of the Great Recession.

Of course, it is difficult to conclude that a simple 2008 reversal in fertility rates is truly a response to the recession, no matter how suggestive the timing. We must look for other ways to test whether the observed declines are sensitive to changes in economic conditions (or perceptions thereof). Figure 8.2 provides the first piece of evidence—a focus on monthly levels of the GFR compared to the unemployment rate nine months earlier. Changes in these indicators show a clear inverse association; increases in unemployment (a near doubling from roughly 4.5 to 9 percent) are associated with fertility declines of approximately 5 percent

(GFR declines from approximately 69 to 65 births per 1000 women aged fifteen to forty-nine). The upturn in unemployment is matched closely by a fertility downturn roughly nine months later.

A related question is whether states particularly hard hit by the recession are showing steeper fertility declines. To examine this question, we first simply examined fertility trends for states with the largest jumps in unemployment between December 2007 and December 2009 and states with the smallest jumps in unemployment in the same time period (December 2009 being the last month with available data prior to this analysis). In fact, both the least and worst hit states showed similar declines since the start of the recession.[2] Thus initially we found no evidence that the hardest hit states had the greatest declines in fertility.

But other evidence does suggest that the nationwide declines in fertility may be driven by concerns about the economy. In a recent survey of women conducted by the Guttmacher Institute, many women reported that they wanted to reduce or delay their childbearing because of the economy. In total, over 40 percent of surveyed women answered affirmatively to having such concerns, and over 50 percent of low-income women and women who reported being financially worse off than they were in the prior year, 2008, reported such concerns (Guttmacher Institute 2009b). If these women's concerns translate into actual behavior, then the recent declines in fertility may indeed be a reaction to the anxiety and uncertainty caused by the Great Recession.

Another survey by the Guttmacher Institute suggests that women's concerns are indeed translating into action. Based on a 2009 survey of sixty family planning centers, the Guttmacher Institute reports that two-thirds of centers were serving increasing numbers of clients overall, while an even higher percentage of centers reported serving more low-income and uninsured clients. Nearly two-thirds reported declines in clients paying full fees, suggesting that for many centers, the recession was straining their abilities to meet women's reproductive needs. This strain is mirrored by reports of various service delivery challenges experienced by these family planning centers. Nearly half of surveyed centers reported staff layoffs or hiring freezes in early 2009, and about a third reported cutting back certain types of treatments or services to clients (Guttmacher Institute 2009a). A quarter of family planning centers reported longer wait times in their offices. We should note that this evidence springs from one point-in-time survey, and more conclusive longitudinal evidence would be necessary to firmly establish that these family planning centers are seeing a rise in economically motivated fertility decisions. Nevertheless, the available evidence does suggest that women's increasing demand for family planning services is stressing family planning providers. Family planning centers' difficulty in meeting service demands makes it also seem likely that the percentage of unplanned pregnancies could be increasing. These service shortages may have the effect of attenuating the overall Great Recession fertility decline, if women cannot get the services they need to help them curtail their fertility.

This evidence prompted us to examine the state-level differences more closely for evidence of greater fertility declines in states hardest hit by unemployment. Figure 8.3 helps demonstrate our strategy. Figure 8.1 compared the TFR and GFR birth rates for twelve-month calendar-year periods. Panel A in figure 8.3 shows that 2008 births (January through December 2008) are produced by conceptions concentrated nine months earlier, between mid-2007 and mid-2008. This "conception period" overlaps somewhat but does not correspond closely to the beginning of the recession. In fact, half of the conceptions producing 2008 births likely occurred before the recession officially began. Thus panel A shows that the contrast of the 2008 and 2007 calendar years provides a weak contrast of periods with and without recession. In addition, in December 2007 (the date we identify as the beginning of the recession) there was some disagreement regarding whether the United States was heading into a recession, and certainly the extent of the economic downturn was unanticipated by many in December 2007. Thus, a strong behavioral response in these early months of the recession is unlikely. In short, upon closer examination the contrast between the 2008 and the 2007 calendar years provides a weak test of Great Recession effects on fertility.[3]

Panel B of figure 8.3 provides a stronger test: a comparison of births in the first third of each year from 2007 to 2009. We also show "conception periods" (dashed lines) beginning nine months earlier, when most pregnancies leading to these births began. These three conception periods provide sharp contrasts: the one in 2007 is well before the recession, the one in 2008 is a few months prior to the onset of the recession, and the one in 2009 was when the recession was approaching the crisis period of late 2008 and early 2009. Recent data from the National Center for Health Statistics (NCHS; 2009) provide a count of births from January to April by state and year. We use these data to see if fertility declines from 2007 to 2009 were greater in states where the recession was more severe.

Either outcome—that declines were or, alternatively, were not greater in states hardest hit by the recession—is plausible. A finding of greater declines in harder-hit states could reflect the individual behaviors of those who feel the economic downturn most intensely—those who lose jobs, for instance. More persons affected would translate to more people altering their behavior. Individual responses to the felt consequences of the downturn would cumulate to produce measurable aggregate-level effects. Alternatively, persons might feel the recession as intensely if many in their neighborhoods, communities, and state are being negatively affected by the recession—if, for instance, they know of someone or have heard about neighbors losing their jobs. Thus, the effects might

Figure 8.3   Timing of Births, Pregnancies, and the 2008-to-2009 Recession

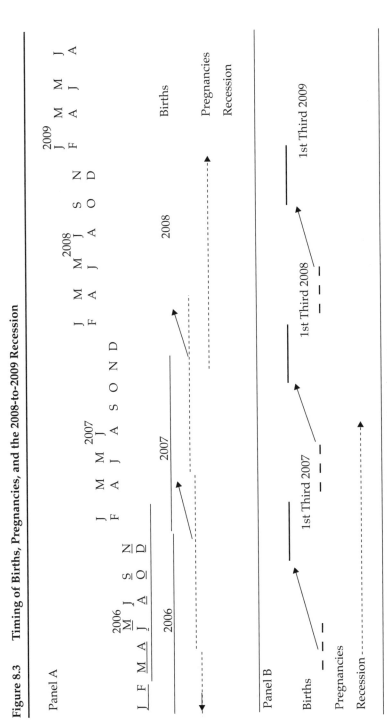

Source: Authors' schematic of appropriate months to estimate effects of recession.

be felt at a community (state) level and influence most people in the state, whether they personally felt the effects of the downturn or not. A final possibility is that people's sense of the crisis might driven by a national media that makes events in Detroit or Jackson, Mississippi, feel as immediate as if they were happening in Denver and Raleigh, North Carolina. The interrelatedness of the national economy and the pervasiveness of national news coverage may make all events local in their effects. Thus, there are plausible scenarios for both larger effects in hardest-hit areas and for pervasive effects across all states.

Using the fifty states, we estimate a "difference-in-difference" model, that is, we regress changes in the January-to-December birth rate (2009/2007 or 2009/2008) on changes in unemployment.[4] The ratio of the birth rate in 2009 to the 2007 rate is an estimate of the percent change associated with the Great Recession. Panel B of figure 8.3 shows the timing of the fertility measurement. The contrast in the unemployment rates is calculated as the difference in the state unemployment rate from June 2009 to June 2007. The timing of this measurement is aimed at capturing the hardest-hit states; this measurement is a contrast between unemployment at the recession's peak and pre-recession unemployment.

Figure 8.4 shows a simple scatter plot of these differences-in-differences; an association is clearly visible between unemployment changes and fertility changes. The simple correlation between the birth rate and unemployment changes is –0.38. If we treat these observations as a simple random sample, then we could easily reject the null hypothesis (that is, no association) at conventional levels ($p = 0.02$). More important, the association reflected by a simple linear association is substantively important. A doubling of the unemployment rate (say from 4 to 8 percent, an increase in factor change from 1 to 2) reduces fertility by 2.5 percent. At the national level (if we agree that the recession doubled the unemployment rate), these results imply that the recession would reduce the number of 2009 births relative to 2007 by about 100,000 ($0.025 \times$ approximately 4 million births).[5]

Interestingly, these results remain virtually unchanged if we substitute the 2009/2008 change for the 2009/2007 change just analyzed. This result confirms that the timing of the fertility response is clearly visible in the period roughly twelve months after the onset of the recession. Analysis of subsequent data will allow us to document the longer-term effects.[6]

These results suggest the question: Is there heterogeneity in state responses to the recession? The scatter plot in figure 8.4 certainly suggests that this could be the case; the linear description of the association only accounts for 11 percent of the state variation. We address several interesting hypotheses linked to the striking fertility differences between "red" and "blue" states. Specifically, Ron J. Lesthaeghe and Lisa Neidert

Figure 8.4   **Greatest Falls in Fertility in States with Biggest Unemployment Increases**

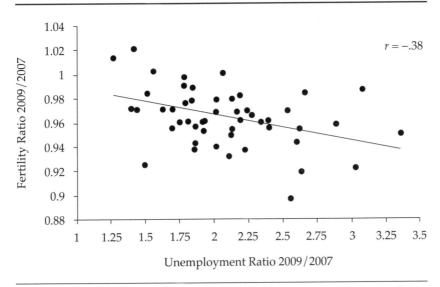

Source: Authors' compilation based on data from the U.S. Bureau of Labor Statistics (2011a) and the National Center for Health Statistics (Martin et al. 2010; Hamilton, Martin, and Ventura 2010a, 2010b).
Note: The fertility ratio is the ratio of the general fertility rates for 2009 and 2007, as reported by the National Center for Health Statistics. Values less that 1.00 indicate lower fertility in 2009, and values greater than 1.00 indicate higher fertility in 2009. The unemployment ratio is the ratio of the unemployment rates from June of 2009 and 2007, as calculated from the Current Population Survey. Values greater than 1.00 indicate higher unemployment in 2009 than in 2007.

(2006, 2009) show strong associations between state-level measures of the TFR and the percentage of citizens who voted for Democratic versus Republican presidential candidates. For instance, using data for 2000, the state-level correlation of the TFR and the percentage voting for Bush in 2000 was +0.78 (Lesthaeghe and Neidert 2006, figure 8.8); fertility is substantially higher in red states. So, do red and blue states vary in their response to the Great Recession? This question has broad and important implications. For example, is the behavioral response to a recession caused or perpetuated by a set of material circumstances or by a perceptual frame that interprets these material conditions as problematic or threatening? The most reasonable answer is that these two factors interact to produce a response to the Great Recession (see Sewell 1992, 2005). A community of individuals, through a process of interaction and communication, mutually construct a recession from material conditions and shared perceptual frames. We know that economic downturns occur periodically; our observations, experiences, media accounts, and official declarations lead us to acknowledge the current one as quite serious. But do perceptions of the Great Recession's seriousness vary systematically, and does such variation affect childbearing?

Let us now develop two competing processes whereby interpretative frames would play a crucial role. First, Lesthaeghe and Neidert (2006) interpret the blue-versus-red-state difference as reflecting more and less movement, respectively, toward features of the "second demographic transition," a term that refers to increased cohabitation, postponed marriage and childbearing, and small families.[7] This transition in turn is fueled by schemas stressing secular individualism and self-actualization. In the context of the Great Recession, this second demographic transition might be curtailed in red states because timely family formation—marriage and childbearing—carries a greater importance in red states than in blue states. The higher fertility in red states suggests greater pronatalism in the face of globalizing forces that have pushed fertility well below the replacement level in most economically developed countries. So net of objective economic conditions, this scenario suggests less responsiveness (smaller fertility declines) in the less secular, red, states.

A second hypothesis can be developed around inferred differences in the perception of the recession as a crisis and its long-term impacts. The blue-versus-red difference corresponds to a partisan "MSNBC-versus–Fox News" viewing pattern. The optimism that Barack Obama's election generated, especially in blue states, may have dampened blue-state residents' concern about the recession or increased optimism that it would end quickly and well—with a robust recovery. This hypothesis stresses, in addition to the objective real-time circumstances, the influence that partisan perceptions regarding the severity and long-term impact of the Great Recession could have on fertility-related decisions.

We explore this hypothesis by calculating for each of the fifty states a simple blue-red indicator—the ratio of the percentage voting for Obama rather than John McCain in November 2008. A value of 1.0 is a fifty-fifty split (as in North Carolina); Wyoming and Vermont set the observed range among the fifty states, with values of .50 and 2.2, respectively. We use the difference-in-difference approach again and regress state fertility change on state unemployment change, but this time we include the blue-red factor.[8] Our hypothesis is that the unemployment change might have different effects, depending on this blue-red contrast.

This substantive argument implies an interactive effect described formally in the online appendix. Its substantive implication can be seen in table 8.1, where we show expected state values, given their increase in unemployment and their blue-red voting pattern. Our estimates suggest that the more "blue" the state, the weaker the negative effect of the recession. Stated differently, the recession was felt or perceived as more se-

Table 8.1   Recession Effects by State Voting Pattern (Blue Versus Red)

Selected State	Observed Voting Pattern	Predicted Recession Effect
Wyoming	0.50	–0.05
Arkansas	0.75	–0.04
North Carolina	1.00	–0.03
Minnesota	1.25	–0.02
California	1.50	–0.01
Vermont	2.20	0.01

Source: See online appendix 8A.1 for source details.
Note: The observed voting pattern is the proportion voting for Barack Obama divided by the proportion voting for John McCain in the November 2008 presidential election. The predicted recession effect is the percent change in fertility that results from a doubling of the unemployment rate. See online appendix 8A.1 (http://www.russellsage.org/great recession_onlineppendix.pdf for full details of analysis.

vere in red states. In figure 8.4 we show that across all states a doubling of the unemployment rate lowers fertility by an average of .025 (or 2.5%). In comparison, the reddest state, Wyoming, has an effect approximately 50 percent larger. This model predicts that the bluest state, Vermont, will have no fertility decline. These precise predictions (expected values for particular cases) are only meant to be illustrative; the broader conclusion is that partisan perceptions seem to condition the effects of the recession on fertility, at least in the recession's earliest stages. To repeat our substantive conclusion: the fertility of those in blue states was less affected by a given severity of the recession; we suggest that this is because of their populations' greater optimism regarding the recession: that it would be of modest duration and severity and the recovery would be robust.

This narrative is consistent with these data, and so are many other stories that we or others could develop.[9] Why believe this one? S. Philip Morgan's collaborators can attest that Morgan predicted this scenario prior to looking at the data, drawing on personal experiences of Republican versus Democratic responses to the Great Recession at—yes—a family event! The perceptual biases reflected in the coverage of contemporary events by MSNBC and Fox News are striking. So this hypothesis, though arising partly from personal experience, is a "real test" based on full national data and is not a post-hoc rationalization.

Recent survey data also provide evidence that supports these claims (Gallup 2010). Specifically, survey data show a blue-red difference in perceptions of the Great Recession. We found these survey results following the tests just described, and they provide powerful evidence of partisan perceptions regarding both the intensity and likely duration of the Great Recession. Figure 8.5 shows responses from Democrats, independents, and Republicans to the question "Right now do you feel your standard of living is getting better or worse?" One would expect the proportion saying "better" to decline during the recession, and it does; but the differential changes of the partisan groups show that their interpretation of the underlying material conditions are quite different. With the inauguration of the Obama administration the Republicans on average have adopted a more pessimistic view of their standard of living while the Democrats on average have adopted a more optimistic one. Consistent evidence comes from questions about how long the Great Recession will last or whether a recovery will begin next year. Responses to both questions show strong partisan patterns: Republicans predict a longer recession and a lower likelihood of recovery next year than Democrats. The conclusions of a Gallup report from March 2009 (Gallup 2010) mirror the argument we are making here:

> Life evaluation trends among all Americans have followed a roller-coaster route over the course of the economic downturn. Throughout the past two years, however, two factors—income and politics—were consistently related to respondents' optimism about their lives. . . . Democrats at all income levels have developed a more upbeat view of economic conditions since Obama's election, whereas Republicans have generally soured on the economy. These findings offer a stark demonstration of how politics influences our perceptions not only of how we view the world around us, but also how we view our own lives. (para. 14)

We continue to monitor these trends. The political landscape has changed dramatically, as indicated by the 2010 midterm election. Repeating the analysis for subsequent quarters of 2009 shows a weakening of this partisan effect over time. But this may well reflect that the Obama-Bush voting differential no longer captures the partisan environments of late 2009. More detailed analysis is required to document these subsequent dynamics (see Morgan, Cumberworth, and Wimer 2011).

Pursuing this strategy of examining heterogeneous effects further is hampered by inadequate data availability at this time. The monthly vital statistics reports, the source for the data used in the previous analysis, disaggregate counts by state only. With more detailed data, the social demographic strategy of decomposition would provide many other clues, such as to which groups show larger and smaller fertility changes to the Great Recession. In time we will know if planned versus unplanned, marital versus nonmarital, teen versus older, and Hispanic versus non-Hispanic pregnancies and other fertility factors were responsive to this recession.[10] The empirical patterns examined here provide the broad contours of the richer narrative that will eventually be told.

Figure 8.5   **Partisan Responses to Question "Right Now, Do You Feel Your Standard of Living is Getting Better or Getting Worse ?" from January 2008 to December 2009**

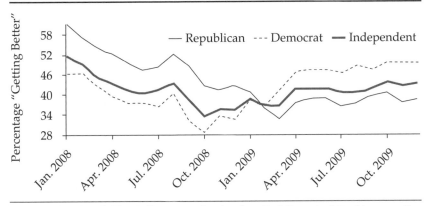

Source: Gallup (2010). This is direct reproduction from 2nd figure in: http://www.gallup .com/poll/124928/republicans-life-ratings-drop-democrats-improve.aspx.

Marriage, Divorce, and Cohabitation

The recession might also influence people's likelihoods of getting married. One could imagine either greater or fewer numbers of couples deciding to tie the knot. On the one hand, marriages can be costly affairs, such that couples may defer getting married if they plan on having a relatively costly wedding. Also, if financial strains disrupt relationships and cause more tension and fighting in relationships, couples might also defer marriages. Research shows that one of the most consistent and robust predictors of marriage is men's employment and economic potential (Smock and Manning 1997; Sweeney 2002; Xie et al. 2003; Sobotka, Skirbekk, and Philpov 2010). In many samples covering many time periods, those who are employed and who demonstrate greater economic potential have been shown to be more likely to enter into marriage. Thus, in times of economic uncertainty such as a recession, we might expect the number of marriages entered into to decline. On the flip side, getting married confers some tax benefits to couples and also allows couples to create so-called "economies of scale," for two can live together more cheaply than each alone. So entering into marriages might increase during recessions.

What do the data show? Figure 8.6 shows the marriage rate since 1998. Since the start of the Great Recession, the marriage rate has declined, but that rate was already declining prior to the recession. Contrary to some accounts in the media, there seems to be no major inflexion of the trend in the Great Depression "window" (shaded area in figure). This result indicates that neither of these scenarios seems to be playing out, at least not to any great extent. Alternatively, both scenarios could be operating for different subsets of the population such that they cancel each other. Supplemental analysis (not shown here) reveals no differential trend for states experiencing the recession to a greater or lesser extent. We also carried out analyses parallel to those for fertility in which we compared marriage rates by state and marriage rates by month for the years 2007 to 2009. Again no significant changes were found.[11] Trends seem also to vary little by education or race or ethnic group. Thus, we find little evidence of major recession effects on marriage. Further analysis with future data will be able to answer this question with greater precision.[12]

What about divorce? One might reasonably think that the recession would lead to a decrease in the divorce rate, as divorces can be quite costly, and would also have the additional side effect of disrupting economies of scale. Prosperity, in contrast, may free people to end bad relationships if good times allow them to live and succeed independently. But one could also imagine that economic hardship could disrupt relationships and marriages, leading to a spike in the divorce rate. The academic literature on the subject is fairly scant, with some studies showing that bad economic times lead to increases in marital disruption (South 1985) and others showing that bad times lead to decreases (Hellerstein and Morrill 2010).

What are we actually seeing in the current recession? Figure 8.6 also shows the trend in the divorce rate since 1998. There is some evidence that divorces have become rarer since the beginning of the recession, but the recent decline in the divorce rate also appears to be a continuation of a longer-standing decline in the divorce rate dating back to around 2000. Moreover, we found very little evidence that the basic trends varied much by demographic background or in states hit varyingly hard by the recession. Again, future data will allow for more precise studies of the recession's effects on divorce and will allow for measurement of date of separation (the de facto end of a union).[13] Couples could separate during the recession and legally divorce at a later time; U.S. data show great variation across socioeconomic groups in the interval between separation and legal divorce (see, for instance, McCarthy 1978). So even though we find little evidence that the recession has so far altered trends in marriage and divorce, it is entirely conceivable that its effects may yet unfurl in the future.

Marriage and divorce are legal forms of coupling and decoupling. It is also possible that people might shift their living arrangements in unions more informally, particularly through cohabiting relationships. A recession might be a convenient occasion for a boyfriend and girlfriend in a relationship to move in together and save on rent, food, and utilities. However, economic strains might lead some existing cohabiting unions to split up. Predictions about whether we would expect increases or de-

Figure 8.6   Apparent Lack of Recession's Effect on Marriage Rate, Divorce Rate, and Proportion of Those Age Sixteen and Older Cohabiting

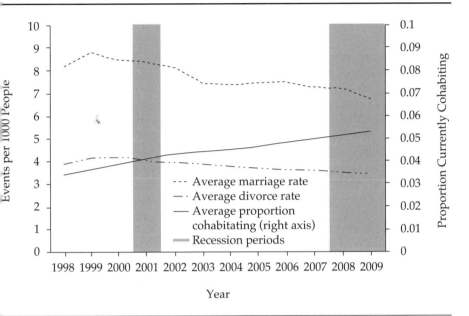

Year

Source: Authors' compilation, based on National Center for Health Statistics (1998–2009) and U.S. Bureau of Labor Statistics (2011b).
Notes: The marriage (divorce) rate is the number of marriages (divorces) per 1,000 total population. The estimates shown here are provisional estimates published by the National Center for Health Statistics in their monthly National Vital Statistics Report. Each point represents the average of the marriage (divorce) rates for all twelve months in each year. The cohabitation rate is the proportion of people age sixteen and older living with unmarried partners. Estimates are based on the monthly Current Population Survey. Anyone who is either a household head with an unmarried partner in the household or an unmarried partner of the household head is counted as "cohabiting." (If neither partner in a cohabiting couple is the household head, then they are not included in the measure.) We calculated the proportion cohabiting each month and then averaged the monthly estimates for twelve months, from January to December of each year.

creases in cohabiting relationships during the recession are risky. To date, research on this topic is virtually nonexistent, perhaps because of the recentness of the secular rise in cohabiting relationships and the relative scarcity of good time series data on entries into and exits from cohabiting unions. A full analysis of how such entries and exits vary with the business cycle is beyond the scope of this chapter, but we are able to provide a glimpse of how cohabitation levels are changing, or not changing, in the current downturn.

Figure 8.6 shows trends from the Current Population Survey in the percentage of people living with an unmarried partner (right axis) from 1998 to 2009. The observed increase in cohabitation would at least partly offset the decline in marriage documented above (also see Bumpass,

Sweet, and Cherlin 1991). However, again we see no inflexion in this trend associated with the Great Recession. We also examined this trend by educational level; at all educational levels cohabitation has increased over the past decade, but there are no noteworthy spikes in this long-standing secular trend since the beginning of the recession. We had reasoned that those with less education and who are doing less well in the labor market might be especially likely to cohabit in response to the economic uncertainty of the recession, but the data show no greater increase in cohabitation among the less-educated than among their more educated peers. This search for disparate effects was repeated with data for race/ethnicity and age. Again we found that increases were pervasive. In sum, to the extent that we can examine union formation and disruption given currently available data, we find virtually no evidence of spikes in union formation and disruption (for the full population or for subgroups) that suggest effects of the Great Recession.[14]

Multigenerational Living Arrangements

Another way that people can deal with a crisis is by relying upon kin support. There is evidence that intergenerational ties and transfers are becoming more important as a result of a range of demographic and societal changes, such the joint survival of parents and children, the increasing risk of marital disruption, and high economic insecurity (see Swartz 2009). One common type of kin support is co-residence. Evidence is clear that most intergenerational co-residence is for the benefit of the child as opposed to the parents (White 2003, 93–94; Swartz 2009, 196). This runs counter to the dominant U.S. cultural expectation that the transition to adulthood involves forming a new family through marriage and parenthood and setting up a separate residence (Hogan and Astone 2003). Substantial evidence shows that with increased income one of the things people buy is greater privacy—they are more likely to live alone or with only a partner and children (White 2003; Costa 1997). Conversely, declines in income and increases in unemployment and economic uncertainty resulting from the recession might well lead to increases in kin living together.

Available evidence suggests that the so-called transition to adulthood has become substantially less orderly over recent decades (Rindfuss 1991; Settersten, Furstenberg, and Rumbaut 2005). What used to be a more carefully and linearly sequenced set of transitions from school to employment and independent living to marriage to children has now become a set of transitions more dissociated from one another, more episodic rather than permanent, and more discontinuous. The transition to adulthood, then, is changing as becoming an independent adult becomes more fraught with uncertainty, leading young people to stray from the familiar pattern. Recessions, especially severe ones such as the Great Recession, are likely to exacerbate this uncertainty, potentially leading more young people to co-reside with their families in response to economic pressures. Younger, less-educated Americans have been hammered disproportionately hard in the recent recession (see chapters 3 and 4 in this volume), which would lead us to expect the recession's impact on young adults' living arrangements to be particularly acute. Note, however, that a variety of factors have been pushing young people back to the nest for some time now even before the recession, including high housing prices, stagnant wages, and the erosion of well-paying middle-level jobs. Therefore we explore possible trends and group differences in people's tendency to co-reside with kin in the current recession. We hypothesized that the difficult job market facing younger Americans, particularly less-educated and minority younger Americans, might lead more younger people to return home and co-reside with kin in order to weather tough times.

Multigenerational living has undergone profound changes over the past seventy years. According to new research by the Pew Research Center, the share of the U.S. population residing in multigenerational households (defined as families that contained at least two adult generations in the same household, or a grandparent and another generational member) decreased from nearly 25 percent of the population in 1940 to only 12.7 percent in 1980. Since 1980, however, this percentage has marched steadily upward, to just over 16 percent in 2008 (Pew Social Trends Staff 2010). These trends have been especially pronounced among the young (age twenty-five to thirty-four) and the old (over sixty-five).

Is this trend accelerating under the economic anxiety fostered by the Great Recession? We used data from the 1998-to-2009 Current Population Surveys for February, June, and October to assess the likelihood that young persons would be living with their parents. We examined four groups—two age groups (nineteen to twenty-four, twenty-five to thirty-four) and married and unmarried for each age group. Figure 8.7 shows that the proportion of young adults co-residing varies sharply by age and marital status: younger and unmarried people are much more likely to live with parents. Regardless of age and marital status, living with parents increased modestly between 2006 and 2009, but increases seem to be greater for the married (from a base of much lower levels). By summer 2009, the proportion of married people living with parents was higher than it had been at any other time since 2001. It is reasonable to attribute these increases to the Great Recession, but this relationship is as yet unproven.

Although we do not show the results here, we examined these data in more detail. Specifically, we focused on the change in the proportion of adults living with parents for 2006 and 2009 by using data for these two

Figure 8.7   **Proportion of Population Living with Their Parents, by Age and Marital Status**

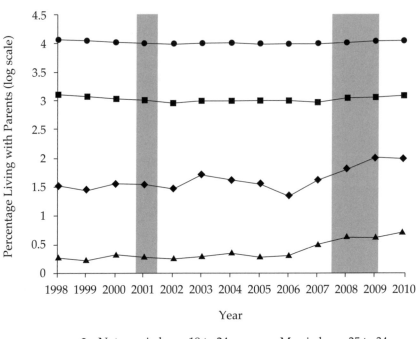

Source: Authors' compilation based on data from U.S. Bureau of Labor Statistics (2011b).
Notes: Estimates are calculated from the basic monthly Current Population Survey conducted by the U.S. Bureau of Labor Statistics (1998–2009). In the Current Population Survey, each household has a designated reference person, which is someone whose name is on the lease or deed. This figure shows the proportion of nineteen-to-twenty-four-year-olds (logged) who are the children or grandchildren of the reference person. We calculated the proportion for each month and then averaged the monthly estimates for March through September.

years to estimate the effects of background factors (race and ethnicity, gender, and education) for the four age and marital status groups. We were looking for evidence of differential change and sought to determine whether these differential patterns are consistent with expectations, given the assumed role of the Great Recession. Specifically, it is usually assumed that rising unemployment and other aspects of a recession affect the more vulnerable—lower socioeconomic—groups most. But for those under thirty-five, the Great Recession increased unemployment rates at all educational levels and for all racial and ethnic groups (see chapter 3, this volume). Also, home foreclosures and stock market losses made the impact of this recession broadly felt. Thus, we are uncertain whether to expect disparate effects on the more vulnerable or pervasive increases.

Overall evidence of differential change was quite modest; in only a few instances were increases in "doubling up" disproportionately strong, and these patterns were not robust across age–marital status groups. For instance, among the young and unmarried group, Hispanics were less likely than non-Hispanic whites to live with parents in 2006 and showed a disproportionate increase so that by 2009 the proportion of Hispanics co-residing with parents more closely approximated the levels observed for whites. There is more limited evidence of disproportionate increases for Hispanics in other age–marital status groups. Again, the main finding was that increases were pervasive, by major demographic characteristics.

We also explored key activity states of young adults: whether they were working, were in school, or were parents. These factors strongly influence the likelihood of living with parents. Specifically, being in school raises the likelihood of co-residence and working and parenthood reduce it. But persons in these groups responded similarly to the beginning of the Great Recession: all groups of young people were more likely to co-reside in 2009 than in 2006.

Discussion

Our analysis of family behavior in the Great Recession has focused on the major decisions family members make: having children, forming and dissolving unions, deciding with whom one lives. But of course recessions can also be a time when family members come together to support one another and help one another get through hard times. Unemployment frees up time for adults formerly in the labor force to pursue leisure time with their spouses and children. Unemployment and economic anxiety can also alter the quality of domestic relations, leading to increases in domestic violence, harsh parenting, or even child abuse and neglect. A brief perusal of stories in the mass media suggests a plethora of possible family effects that may be playing out. For instance, a recent editorial in *Slate* (Bazelon 2009) pondered how marital relationships and gender roles might be changing, given *Slate*'s presumption that men are being hit much harder than women in the labor market. Male unemployment is likely to push up the number and proportion of female-breadwinner homes—for instance, where women are the primary earners in married-couple households. Clearly, this development has the power to challenge conventional gender norms that some people still hold according to which women are the primary providers of housework and child-care. Work has long been central to men's sense of self and self-esteem, and *Slate* also notes many stories of unemployed men falling into depression, anxiety, and anger as a result of their struggles in the labor market. This could lead to marital strain, negative interactions with children, or potentially longer-term upward trends in future divorce. Alarmingly, some anecdotal evidence in the press points to the potential increase in domestic assaults and domestic homicides as reported by family court logs and service providers. Such stories are anecdotal and in part reflect editors' choices; at best they reveal a wide variety of family-related recession stories that we were unable to explore in this chapter.

Another major domain of family life yet to be analyzed is the recession's impacts on parenting and child development. Poverty and material hardship are on the rise for many groups, and millions of children live in households being ravaged by the recession (see, for example, chapter 4 of this volume). As noted, recessions and economic deprivation can harm effective family functioning in these households, with potentially long-lasting consequences for children's well-being. To the extent that growing up in poverty also compromises healthy child development, we could also see much long-term "scarring" effects of the Great Recession on children whose families have been thrown into poverty. A full analysis of the micro-interactional consequences of the recession is beyond the scope of this chapter—suffice it to say that the full story of the consequences of the Great Recession on families awaits further analysis and further data. The purpose of this chapter is to provide a first step in understanding how the current severe economic downturn is shaping American families.

The Great Recession has no doubt influenced family behavior in a host of ways. In some cases, these responses may not have produced measurable "mean effects." For example, individual couples may have been encouraged or discouraged regarding marriage and divorce by the recession, but the effects encouraging one of these events were largely counterbalanced by persons who were discouraged by the recession. In some cases, more detailed data would allow us to model these processes. Also the domains that we have examined have been largely determined by data availability. We were concerned not only that phenomena were well measured but that the measurements were available quickly so that they could be used here.

Available evidence allows us to show that young adults' living arrangements, especially their co-residence with parents, are affected by the Great Recession. Here we were able to look beyond population mean effects and search for diverse responses. We found few such responses—increases in the proportion of children living with their parents were pervasive across socioeconomic groups, whether persons were students, employed, or parents. Available fertility data allowed for interesting analyses of state-level differences. Fertility declined most in states hardest hit by the recession. We also showed that the effect of increased unemployment was affected by the ratio of those who voted for Obama to those who voted for McCain in 2008. We interpret this as a strong indication that the perceived degree of severity of the recession—how long it will last, how robust the upturn will be—depends to some extent on people's political beliefs. Evidence suggests that the Great Recession's fertility effects were greater in "red" states and weaker in "blue" states. Recessions produce behavioral responses both because of underlying material conditions and because the population perceives these conditions as problematic or threatening.

Notes

1. Examination will reveal that the ratio of the TFR to the GFR increases over time. This bias results because the TFR more fully accounts for women's age distribution. Specifically, in the 1970s and 1980s there were larger proportions of the aged fifteen to forty-nine female population of women in their twenties than in the last two decades of the century, when the proportions of women in their thirties and forties increased. The TFR standardizes (or controls for) these differences; the GFR does not. This TFR advantage makes it the preferred estimate for years when it is available.

2. Results available from the authors upon request.

3. Most of the estimates of the Great Recession fertility effects are based on this comparison of 2007 and 2008. See, for instance, Brady E. Hamilton, Joyce A. Martin, and Stephanie J. Ventura (2010a) or Gretchen Livingston and D'Vera Cohn (2010) and media reports based on them (for example, "Birth Rate Down Except for Older Moms," msnbc.com, April 6, 2010, http://www.msnbc.msn.com/id/36195004/ns/health-womens_health; accessed June 2, 2011).

4. The monthly National Vital Statistics Reports (NVSR) available to us when we did this work only counts births by state. We calculated rates using midyear estimates of state populations (U.S. Census Bureau, Population Division 2009). All results described here hold, whether one uses changes in birth numbers or changes in birth rates as the indicator of fertility change. Subsequent NVSR reports provide rates that we have analyzed (Morgan, Cumberworth, and Wimer 2011). These additional analyses support claims made here.

5. A recent Pew report based on data for twenty-five states also finds associations between fertility decline and measures of the severity of the recession in particular states. See Livingston and Cohn (2010).

6. Data for April, May, and June of 2009 have been recently released (see Hamilton, Martin, and Ventura 2010b, 9, 12, 13). Adding data for the second quarter of 2009 and thus analyzing fertility in the first half of the year produces results indistinguishable from those described here.

7. The term "second demographic transition" is in contrast to the first demographic transition. The latter refers to the decline in fertility from high to

low birth rates (large to small families). The second demographic transition refers to postponed marriage and childbearing, increased cohabitation, and rising divorce. See Lesthaeghe and Neidert (2006).

8. See online appendix 8A.1 at http://www.russellsage.org/greatrecession _onlineappendix.pdf.

9. One reviewer pointed out that blue states may have stronger safety nets than red states, which may in turn reduce the link between economic uncertainty and fertility decisions. Our analyses cannot definitively adjudicate between such speculations.

10. Hamilton, Martin, and Ventura (2010a) compare fertility in 2008 to data in 2007 and find evidence that fertility fell for all age groups except women in their forties; they also report that both marital and nonmarital fertility declined by about 2 percent. Note again that we argue that the comparison of these two years as a recession effect is problematic (see figure 8.2).

11. The quality of marriage data in the NVSR (available at: http://www.cdc. gov/nchs/products/nvsr.htm) seems highly suspect. For a number of states there are very large increases or decreases in the number of marriages reported. The count of births is much more consistent.

12. The marriage rate used here does not control well for the population with the likelihood of getting married. A more precise measure would be marriages in a given time period by the years of exposure to marriage for the unmarried adult population. The estimates of the population with a likelihood of getting married in the marriage rate used here are derived from the total population. Surveys collecting retrospective histories of marital unions can provide these more precise estimates, but such data for the period of interest will not be available for several more years.

13. More precise measurement is required for a firm conclusion. A major concern is that data used for the calculation of divorce rates come from vital statistics. The marriage and divorce data have declined in quality in recent years. An additional concern is that divorce events and marital disruption are different concepts. A formal divorce that produces a vital record may come years after the de facto end of a relationship; in fact, the couple may never divorce. Again, retrospective histories available in many social surveys will allow more precise measurement of marital disruption in this period in several years.

14. The indicators of joint living here are not very sensitive to change. A more sensitive indicator would be the number of persons moving into a joint living arrangement in this time period as a proportion of those at risk of such a move. The detailed data required to calculate such precise measures for this recent period are not available as of this writing (summer 2011).

References

Bazelon, Emily. 2009. "Unwashed Coffee Mugs." February 20. Available at: http://www.slate.com/id/2211594; accessed July 8, 2011.

Bongaarts, John, and Griffith Feeney. 1998. "On the Quantum and Tempo of Fertility." *Population and Development Review* 24(2): 271–91.

Bumpass, Larry L., James. A. Sweet, and Andrew J. Cherlin. 1991. "The Role of

Cohabitation in Declining Rates of Marriage." *Journal of Marriage and Family* 53(4): 913–27.

Butz, William P., and Michael P. Ward. 1979. "Will US Fertility Remain Low? A New Economic Interpretation." *Population and Development Review* 5(4): 663–88.

Costa, Dora L. 1997. "Displacing the Family: Union Army Pensions and Elderly Living Arrangements." *Journal of Political Economy* 105(6): 1269–92.

Elder, Glen H., Jr. 1974. *Children of the Great Depression*. Chicago: University of Chicago Press.

Finer, Lawrence B., and Stanley K. Henshaw. 2006. "Disparities in Rates of Unintended Pregnancy in the United States, 1994 and 2001." *Perspectives on Sexual and Reproductive Health* 38(2): 90–96.

Gallup. 2010. "Republicans' Life Ratings Drop While Democrats' Improve: Election, Economy Influenced How Americans Viewed Their Lives in 2009." January 5. Available at: http://www.gallup.com/poll/124928/republicans-life-ratings-drop-democrats-improve.aspx; accessed July 8, 2011.

Guttmacher Institute. 2009a. "A Real-Time Look at the Impact of the Recession on Publicly Funded Family Planning Centers." New York: Guttmacher Institute. Available at: http://www.guttmacher.org/pubs/RecessionFPC.pdf; accessed August 30, 2011.

———. 2009b. "A Real-Time Look at the Impact of the Recession on Women's Family Planning and Pregnancy Decisions." New York: Guttmacher Institute. Available at: http://www.guttmacher.org/pubs/RecessionFP.pdf; accessed August 30, 2011.

Hamilton, Brady E., Joyce A. Martin, and Stephanie J. Ventura. 2010a. "Births: Preliminary Data for 2008." *National Vital Statistics Reports* 58(16). Hyattsville, Md.: National Center for Health Statistics, Division of Vital Statistics, April. Available at: http://www.cdc.gov/nchs/data/nvsr58/nvsr58_16.pdf; accessed May 31, 2011.

———. 2010b. "Births: Preliminary Data for 2009" [online]. Hyattsville, Md.: National Center for Health Statistics, Division of Vital Statistics. Available at: http://www.cdc.gov/nchs/data/nvsr59/nvsr59_03.pdf; accessed July 11, 2011.

Hellerstein, Judith K., and Melinda S. Morrill. 2010. "Booms, Busts, and Divorce." Paper presented at the American Economics Association Annual Meeting. Atlanta (January 2–5).

Hogan, Dennis P., and Nan Marie Astone. 2003. "The Transition to Adulthood." *Annual Review of Sociology* 12(1): 109–30.

Lesthaeghe, Ron J., and Lisa Neidert. 2006. "The Second Demographic Transition in the United States: Exception or Textbook Example?" *Population and Development Review* 32: 660–98.

———. 2009. "U.S. Presidential Elections and the Spatial Pattern of the American Second Demographic Transition." *Population and Development Review* 35(2): 391–400.

Livingston, Gretchen, and D'Vera Cohn. 2010. "U.S. Birth Rate Decline Linked to Recession." Report. Pew Social and Demographic Trends. Washington, D.C.: Pew Research Center, March 6.

Martin, Joyce A., Brady E. Hamilton, Paul D. Sutton, Stephanie J. Ventura. 2009. "Births: Final Data for 2006." *National Vital Statistics Reports* 57(7). Hyattsville,

Md.: National Center for Health Statistics, January 7. Available at: http://www.cdc.gov/nchs/data/nvsr/nvsr57/nvsr57_07.pdf; accessed May 31, 2011.

Martin, Joyce A., Brady E. Hamilton, Paul D. Sutton, Stephanie J. Ventura, T.J. Matthews, Sharon Kirmeyer, J.K. Michelle, and M.H.S. Osterman. 2010. "Births: Final Data for 2007." *National Vital Statistics Reports* 58(24). Hyattsville, Md.: National Center for Health Statistics

McCarthy, James. 1978. "A Comparison of the Probability of the Dissolution of First and Second Marriages." *Demography* 15(3): 345–59.

Moen, Phyllis. 1979. "Family Impacts of the 1975 Recession: Duration of Unemployment." *Journal of Marriage and Family* 41(3): 561–72.

Morgan, S. Philip. 1996. "Characteristic Features of Modern American Fertility." *Population and Development Review* 22(Suppl: Fertility in the United States: New Patterns, New Theories): 19–63.

Morgan, S. Philip, Erin Cumberworth, and Chris Wimer. 2011. "The Partisan (Red/Blue) Fertility Response to the Great Recession." Paper presented to the Annual Meeting of the Population Association of America. Washington, D.C. (March 31–April 2).

National Center for Health Statistics. 1998–2009. "Births, Marriages, Divorces, and Deaths." Washington, D.C.: Centers for Disease Control and Prevention. Available at: http://www.cdc.gov/nchs/products/nvsr.htm; accessed August 30, 2011.

Pew Social Trends Staff. 2010. "The Return of the Multigenerational Household." Washington, D.C.: Pew Research Center. Available at: http://pewsocialtrends.org/2010/03/18/the-return-of-the-multi-generational-family-household/; accessed August 30, 2011.

Rindfuss, Ronald R. 1991. "The Young Adult Years: Diversity, Structural Change, and Fertility." *Demography* 28(4): 493–512.

Settersten, Richard A., Frank F. Furstenberg, and Rubén G. Rumbaut, eds. 2005. *On the Frontier of Adulthood: Theory, Research, and Public Policy*. Chicago: University of Chicago Press.

Sewell, William H. 1992. "A Theory of Structure: Duality, Agency, and Transformation." *American Journal of Sociology* 98(1): 1–29.

———. 2005. *Logics of History*. Chicago: University of Chicago Press.

Smock, Pamela J., and Wendy D. Manning. 1997. "Cohabiting Partners' Economic Circumstances and Marriage." *Demography* 34(3): 331–42.

Sobotka, Tomas, Vegard Skirbekk, and Demeter Philpov. 2010. "Economic Recession and Fertility in the Developed World: A Literature Review." Vienna: Vienna Institute of Demography.

South, Scott J. 1985. "Economic Conditions and the Divorce Rate: A Time-Series Analysis of the Postwar United States." *Journal of Marriage and Family* 47(1): 31–41.

Swartz, Teresa Toguchi. 2009. "Intergenerational Family Relations in Adulthood: Patterns, Variations, and Implications in the Contemporary United States." *Annual Review of Sociology* 35: 191–212.

Sweeney, Megan M. 2002. "Two Decades of Family Change: The Shifting Economic Foundations of Marriage." *American Sociological Review* 67(1): 132–47.

U.S. Bureau of Labor Statistics. 2011a. "Local Area Unemployment Statistics." Available at: http://www.bls.gov/lau/; accessed July 8, 2011.

————. 2011b. "Labor Force Statistics from the Current Population Survey." Washington: Bureau of Labor Statistics. Available at: http://www.bls.gov/cps; accessed July 11, 2011.

U.S. Census Bureau, Population Division. 2009. "National Vital Statistics Report." Available at: http://www.census.gov/popest/states/NST-ann-est.html; accessed July 8, 2011.

White, Lynn. 2003. "Coresidence and Leaving Home: Young Adults and Their Parents." *Annual Review of Sociology* 20(1): 81–102.

Xie, Yu, James M. Raymo, Kimberly Goyette, and Arland Thornton. 2003. "Economic Potential and Entry into Marriage and Cohabitation." *Demography* 40(2): 351–67.

PART IV

The Collective Response: The Government and Charitable Giving

Chapter 9

The Federal Stimulus Programs and Their Effects

GARY BURTLESS AND TRACY GORDON

THE RECESSION THAT began in December 2007 ranks as the longest and deepest economic downturn since World War II. The American government's response to it was also distinctive and aroused intense political controversy. In some ways this should not be surprising, since some of the measures adopted by the Congress, two presidents, and the Federal Reserve helped keep solvent some of the financial institutions whose behavior helped cause the recession. However, most of the money actually spent by the federal government was devoted to policies that would have been familiar to presidents and legislators in earlier recessions, regardless of the political party in control of the government. In this chapter we seek to answer three basic questions about the federal response to the recent recession. What did the federal government do to halt the recession and mitigate its effects? What special protection did it extend to the vulnerable and newly jobless? Which of the adopted measures were unique to the recent downturn and which were standard countercyclical policies in the earlier postwar era? Finally, we offer a tentative answer to the most crucial question of all: How successful were these stimulus policies?

Starting in early 2008, even before it was known that the nation had entered a recession, the U.S. government took a number of steps aimed at dealing with the financial crisis and its expected fallout. As most observers acknowledge, the crisis originated in the nation's real estate and banking industries and then spread to the rest of the economy. Emergency legislation passed by Congress and extraordinary steps taken by the Federal Reserve in late 2008 and early 2009 sought to accomplish a number of goals:

- Prevent the failure of major U.S. financial institutions
- Minimize the impact of financial institutions' weakness on ordinary business and consumer borrowing
- Stimulate consumer spending by raising after-tax household income through temporary tax reductions and increases in government transfers
- Stabilize state and local government budgets to reduce their need to boost taxes and reduce spending during the recession
- Protect the incomes and health insurance of newly laid-off workers and members of other economically vulnerable populations
- Support infrastructure investments and research and development projects in health, science, and efficient energy production

Most of this chapter is devoted to analyzing the last four kinds of policies, which can be classified as conventional fiscal policy. However, the first policies were also important in ensuring that the recession did not metastasize into an even more serious depression. It is worth describing these policies briefly. Starting in late 2007, the Federal Reserve Board began to cut short-term interest rates. Worried by signs of instability in the financial markets, the Federal Reserve Board reduced the federal funds rate—the rate at which banks make overnight loans to one another—from 5.25 percent to 2.0 percent between September 2007 and May 2008. When Lehman Brothers bank declared bankruptcy on September 15, 2008, setting off panic in most of the world's financial markets, the Federal Reserve lowered the federal funds rate still further. By the end of 2008 the federal funds rate had been cut essentially to zero, the lowest level of the modern era. The Federal Reserve Board also extended extraordinary credits to both bank and nonbank institutions in exchange for high-quality collateral. This and related measures were needed to keep credit flowing in markets where ordinary lending had ceased. Without these extraordinary steps, many solvent financial and nonfinancial firms would have been forced either to enter bankruptcy or sharply curtail their operations because of their inability to obtain short-term credit. By keeping credit flowing in the midst of panic and uncertainty, the Federal Reserve kept a financial-market crisis from inflicting even worse damage on the broader economy.

Interventions in the financial market by the George W. Bush and Barack Obama administrations and Congress also played a crucial role in keeping the nation's financial system afloat. Throughout 2007 and 2008, the Bush administration pursued a variety of strategies to stem housing foreclosures, for example the HOPE NOW initiative to facilitate mortgage modifications. It made explicit a previously implicit guarantee of debt issued by the government-sponsored enterprises Fannie Mae and Freddie Mac. During the fateful week of September 15, the Treasury Department and the Federal Reserve Board acted to rescue the American International Group (AIG), establish a temporary guarantee for money-market mutual funds, and launch the Troubled Asset Relief Program, or TARP, which was enacted by Congress on October 3. The goal of this program was to use federal funds to purchase equity or assets from financial institutions in order to keep more of them solvent than would have been possible if they had been forced to rely solely on private capital markets for funds. Congress authorized spending up to $700 billion for this purpose. The Bush administration originally suggested that most of the funds would be used to purchase distressed assets, such as mortgage-backed securities, from struggling financial institutions, providing these institutions with crucial liquidity so they could survive the crisis. The secretary of treasury eventually adopted the more sensible policy of buying preferred equity in all the big banks and in many mid-sized and smaller ones. The share purchases had the effect of recapitalizing these institutions and, in time, increasing the public's confidence in the institutions' chances of survival. Investors' confidence got another boost when the Obama administration and the Federal Reserve Board performed financial "stress tests" on banks in early 2009 to determine whether they had sufficient capital to survive a severe recession. An overwhelming majority of institutions passed these tests, though some critics argued that the tests were too lenient.

The improvement in public confidence meant that most U.S. banks could once again obtain funds in private capital markets and sell equity to new investors. In 2009 and 2010 the federal government was able to sell its equity holdings in most banks at a profit. The ultimate cost of TARP will probably be less than $30 billion after all interest, dividend, and principal payments are received from institutions that obtained funds under the program. A sizable portion of remaining TARP losses are likely to occur in the automobile industry. Government aid to General Motors, Chrysler, and a number of auto parts suppliers was critical in permitting the companies to reorganize their operations and emerge from bankruptcy as smaller but potentially profitable firms. In the absence of federal aid, these auto companies would certainly have been liquidated. No private lender would have stepped forward to serve as the automakers' lender of last resort. The

U.S. auto industry would have shrunk dramatically without the aid provided under TARP.

In the remainder of the chapter we focus on the more conventional fiscal measures taken by Congress to revive the economy, protect household incomes, and strengthen the American social safety net. Aside from the extraordinary measures taken by two administrations, Congress, and the Federal Reserve to shore up the nation's ailing financial system, the government's main instruments for dealing with the crisis were designed to provide direct income assistance and public services to households, to offer fiscal relief to state governments, and to fund or encourage new investments in public infrastructure and research and development. The fiscal response had two main components. The first was the automatic stabilization system already in place, even before Congress and the administration took special steps to respond to the crisis. Automatic stabilization is provided by all government programs that automatically increase their spending or reduce the tax burdens they impose on households and businesses when the private sector shrinks in a recession. The second was the special stimulus measures Congress authorized starting in early 2008. None of the emergency measures will result in permanent changes to the U.S. system of social protection, but a couple of temporary programs represent notable departures from past practice. For example, for the first time Congress authorized generous subsidies so that laid-off workers could continue to receive employer-sponsored health insurance. Most working-age Americans and their families rely on an employer-provided health plan to provide insurance. When they are laid off from their jobs they ordinarily lose the employer subsidy for insurance, and for many workers the loss of the subsidy makes continued insurance coverage unaffordable. By offering to pay 65 percent of the cost of the first fifteen months of post-layoff health insurance premiums, the U.S. government made health insurance affordable for many of the newly unemployed. In another departure from past stabilization policy, Congress appropriated substantial funds for the nation's education system. State governments were given large temporary grants to support primary, secondary, and postsecondary schooling, thus reducing the need for state and local governments to make cuts in educational services. In addition, the federal government appropriated special funds for a large increase in means-tested financial assistance so that low-income students could pay for postsecondary education. Stimulus funds also provided major increases in grants for postsecondary institutions so that they could invest in new buildings as well as basic research in health and energy technologies. It is unusual for the federal government to focus so much of its countercyclical stimulus policy on the education system and on research and development. Finally, state governments were provided generous but temporary general fiscal relief, linked to local economic conditions, so they did not have to cut spending or increase taxes as much as would have been necessary without the emergency federal aid. The federal government had not previously made fiscal relief to state and local governments a cornerstone of countercyclical stimulus policy.

The remainder of the chapter is organized as follows. The next section considers automatic government responses to a recession. These occur without any special action by Congress or the president. The following section examines the fiscal measures adopted by Congress to deal with the recession, with special reference to actions affecting the social safety net. We then focus specifically on the federal transfers to state and local governments, which played an unusually prominent role in the 2009 stimulus package. In conclusion we offer a brief assessment of the U.S. response to economic crisis. How well did these measures perform in reviving the U.S. economy and ensuring social protection to Americans hurt by the economic crisis?

The U.S. Safety Net and Automatic Stabilization

Even if neither the Congress nor the president had taken special actions in response to the recession, a number of federal government programs, including unemployment insurance, social assistance, and the income tax system, would have provided automatic stimulus and protection against shrinking household incomes. The unemployment insurance program undoubtedly shows the biggest proportional change in spending whenever the economy falls into recession. When the economy is growing strongly and unemployment is low, unemployment insurance benefits represent only about 0.3 percent of disposable personal income. In the midst of a recession, that percentage more than doubles, primarily because the number of workers collecting benefits rises steeply. Part of the increase in the number of unemployment insurance recipients is due to special measures passed by Congress. Typically, those measures permit laid-off workers to collect benefits for longer than the standard period of six months, but much of the increase in the number of unemployment insurance recipients and in benefit payments would have occurred even if Congress had failed to provide any additional benefits.

Federal income taxes and social insurance tax payments shrink when the economy contracts. Because the income tax system is strongly progressive, income tax collections decline proportionately much faster than personal and corporate income. The economists Alan Auerbach and Daniel Feenberg (2000) estimate that the consumption response to the decline in federal taxes offsets 8 percent of the initial impact of an adverse shock to U.S. gross domestic product (GDP). Since income tax and payroll tax revenues represent a much bigger share of the U.S. economy than unemployment benefits, the tax system plays a much bigger quantitative role than unemployment insurance in stabilizing the economy.

The tax and benefit system also plays an important role in equalizing incomes and smoothing net income changes across U.S. states and regions. The United States is a large and diverse country. In 2007 the poorest American state, Mississippi, had per capita personal income that was only about half of that of the richest state, Connecticut. Although the United States, unlike most other countries with federalist systems, does not operate an explicit fiscal equalization program, many tax and transfer programs have the effect of reducing disparities among states. The progressive tax system and the progressive formula for determining social insurance and social assistance benefits mean that the difference in net incomes between states is smaller than the difference in their before-tax, before-transfer incomes. States and regions that experience the biggest proportional losses in market income during a recession will generally receive proportionally bigger net gains from their financial transactions with the federal government. Thus, the automatic stabilization that is built into federal taxes and transfer benefits tends to spread the economic pain of a recession more equally across the country than would be the case in the absence of the federal tax and transfer system.

Unemployment Insurance

For American workers the first line of defense against income loss after a layoff is provided by unemployment insurance. Experienced U.S. workers who are dismissed from their jobs can claim unemployment benefits that replace about half of their lost earnings up to a maximum weekly benefit amount. In most American states this maximum amount is roughly half the wages earned by an average worker who is covered by the unemployment insurance system. This means laid-off workers who earn above-average wages collect benefits that replace less than half of their lost earnings. Benefits are taxed as ordinary income by the Internal Revenue Service. Unemployment insurance benefits do not last indefinitely. In ordinary circumstances, benefits are restricted to just twenty-six weeks. Laid-off workers who fail to find work within six months after losing a job will run out of unemployment benefits before they start earning another paycheck. In recent years, between 31 percent and 43 percent of workers who have claimed unemployment benefits have exhausted their eligibility for compensation before they have found a job. The percentage that exhausts benefits is higher when the nationwide unemployment rate is high. In the worst months of the recent recession, about 57 percent of workers who began to collect regular unemployment benefits exhausted them before becoming reemployed. As in other industrialized countries, in the United States there has been a long-term rise in the percentage of unemployed workers who suffer long spells of unemployment. This is reflected in the statistics on the exhaustion of unemployment insurance benefits. In the 1960s the percentage of claimants who exhausted unemployment compensation ranged from 20 percent to 25 percent of all the workers who filed a successful claim for benefits. The exhaustion rate in the 1960s was thus only about two-thirds the rate before the 2008-to-2009 recession.

The Organisation for Economic Co-operation and Development (OECD) has made estimates of the generosity of member countries' programs for replacing earned income after workers lose their jobs. The OECD calculates that in 2005 U.S. workers in single-earner households obtained a net replacement rate of about 56 percent to 62 percent in the case of unemployed workers who earn the average U.S. wage (Organisation for Economic Co-operation and Development 2007). These replacement rates are lower than rates available in most other rich countries, and the gap is particularly large in the case of unemployed workers who have dependents. The gap is even larger for workers with above-average earnings.

Figures 9.1 and 9.2 show the net income replacement rate for laid-off single and married workers in various circumstances who earned the average national wage before losing their jobs. The estimates reflect the unweighted average of replacement rates for heads of family in four kinds of circumstances: single heads of family, married heads of family without any dependent children, single heads of family with two dependent children, married heads of family with two dependent children. The OECD estimates are displayed for twenty-one rich countries ranked according to the replacement rate that unemployed workers received in 2005. Figure 9.1 shows the net income replacement rates during the first six months after a layoff. The United States ranks fourteenth among the twenty-one countries in the chart. Although the net weekly benefits provided by U.S. unemployment insurance are not high by international standards, they are not at the bottom, either. So long as unemployed workers qualify for an unemployment insurance check, American workers obtain replacement rates that are near the average for unemployed workers in the other industrialized countries. Figure 9.2 shows the income replacement rates workers receive during the first five years after a permanent layoff. This estimate takes account of any means-tested unemployment benefits or social assistance benefits workers qualify for after their unemployment insurance benefits end. Judging income replacement rates over this longer time span, the United States only ranks nineteenth out of twenty-one countries, or third from the bottom.

The low U.S. rank in figure 9.2 is the result of two features of the U.S. system of social protection. First, regular unemployment benefits do not

Figure 9.1   Net Income Replacement in the First Year After Job Loss in Twenty-one Countries, 2005[a]

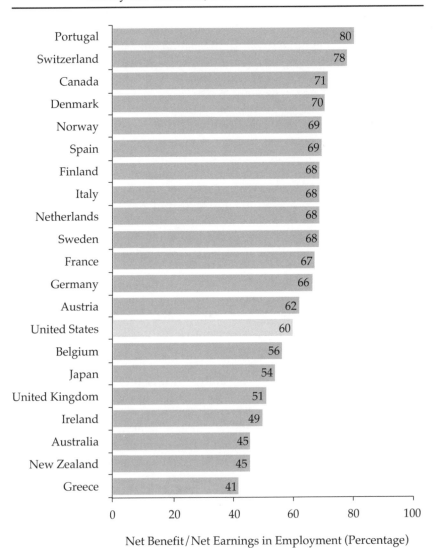

Net Benefit/Net Earnings in Employment (Percentage)

Source: Authors' calculations, based on data from Organisation for Economic Co-operation and Development (2007).
[a] Average replacement rate of workers earning the national average wage in four types of family situations: single and married, with and without children. The estimates reflect income replacement during the first six months after job loss.

Figures 9.2   Net Income Replacement in the First Five Years After Job Loss in Twenty-one Countries, 2005[a]

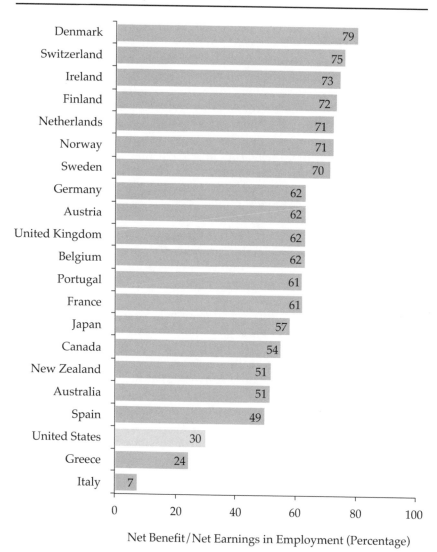

Net Benefit/Net Earnings in Employment (Percentage)

Source: Authors' calculations, based on data from Organisation for Economic Co-operation and Development (2007).
[a] Average replacement rate of workers earning the national average wage in four types of family situations: single and married, with and without children, respectively, during the first six months after job loss.

last as long in the United States as they do elsewhere. Figure 9.3 shows the OECD's estimates of the maximum duration of unemployment insurance benefits available to a fully insured worker in twenty-one rich countries. The United States, offering just six months of benefits, ranks at the bottom of the list. It ordinarily provides unemployment compensation that lasts only one-third as long as the eighteen months of benefits available in the Netherlands. (The Dutch unemployment insurance program offers the median duration of benefits provided in the twenty-one countries included in the chart.) Another reason for the low rank of the United States in figure 9.2 is the meagerness of means-tested assistance available to American workers in long-term unemployment. Most other rich countries offer more generous protection for working-age breadwinners who have been jobless for an extended period. When unemployment benefits are exhausted in the United States, most unemployed workers qualify for very modest public income transfers and then only if they have very low incomes and few assets.

The U.S. unemployment insurance system only replaces the money wages that workers lose when they are laid off. It does not insure workers against the loss of health insurance or other fringe benefits that may have been provided by their former employer. For a private-sector employee, the employer's contribution for health, retirement, and insurance benefits, excluding mandatory social insurance, averages about 16 percent of the worker's money wage (U.S. Bureau of Labor Statistics 2005). The loss of fringe benefits is particularly important for workers who depend on their employers for health insurance. Insurance purchased outside an employer's health plan is so costly that few unemployed U.S. workers can afford it.

When the state or national unemployment rate is high, laid-off workers usually qualify for unemployment compensation in addition to the standard twenty-six weeks of benefits. For the past fifty years the Extended Benefits (EB) program has provided an additional thirteen or twenty weeks of compensation payments for workers in states where the unemployment rate is higher than a threshold, or "trigger," rate.[1] Half the cost of this program is paid with funds from the federal government and the other half is paid by the state in which the program trigger has been met, or "triggered on." (All of the cost of the regular, twenty-six-week package of benefits is paid with payroll taxes raised by state governments.) The EB program has not worked as well in recent years as it did in the 1970s and early 1980s. In the twenty-five years ending in 2008, the program rarely if ever "triggered on" in most states, even when the local unemployment rate was high. For example, in June 2003 when U.S. civilian unemployment reached a nine-year high, EB compensation was available in only three out of the fifty states. Certainly the local unemployment rate was exceptionally high in those three states, but it was also high (more than 6.5 percent) in six other states, including California, Michigan, and Texas. Before the current recession, the EB program had failed to "trigger on" in thirty-three states during any month after the 1981-to-1983 recession, even though the nation experienced two recessions in the period (Vroman 2009).

A number of analysts have attempted to measure the response of the unemployment insurance system when the unemployment rate rises. Recent estimates by economists at the Federal Reserve Board suggest that a one-percentage-point jump in the unemployment rate causes regular and EB unemployment compensation payments to increase by about 0.25 percent of wage and salary income, or roughly 0.10 percent of potential GDP (Follette and Lutz 2010).[2] However, the amount of countercyclical stimulus provided by these unemployment insurance programs drops off after two calendar quarters because laid-off workers start to lose eligibility for further benefits.

Other Transfer Benefits

The Federal Reserve economists also examined the effects of rising unemployment on expenditures in other cyclically sensitive government transfer programs, such as Food Stamps, Medicaid, federally financed welfare, and Social Security retirement and disability benefits. Although benefits in some of these programs are administered and partially funded by state governments, Glenn Follette and Byron Lutz (2010) initially focus on the portion of program costs financed by the federal government. In the case of Food Stamps, all the benefit costs are paid by the federal government. The federal government pays for more than half of the cost of Medicaid, but state governments must pay for a fraction of the costs. At one time the same kind of matching formula was used to pay for cash public assistance benefits to indigent children and their working-age parents, but federal funding for this program was converted into a fixed block grant in 1996. Unless Congress makes a special appropriation to increase intergovernmental transfers in a recession, states must pay for all of the additional cost of these welfare benefits out of their own resources or out of unspent federal block grants from earlier years. The effects of a jump in the unemployment rate on federal spending for these programs are individually much smaller than the impact on unemployment compensation spending. In total, however, the effect is roughly one-half the size of the effect of a rise in the unemployment rate on unemployment compensation payments. Follette and Lutz estimate that a one-percentage-point rise in the unemployment rate increases federal transfer benefits, including unemployment compensation, by about 0.15 percent of potential GDP (Follette and Lutz 2010, 9). They calculate that a cyclical decline of 1 percent in GDP would raise federal transfer program outlays by 0.06 percent of GDP. These estimates exclude the effect of temporary new programs or benefit liberalizations that Congress might establish to deal with a recession. They also exclude the impact of automatic increases in state and local spending on transfer benefits.

As just noted, however, state and local governments administer several important transfer programs, notably those targeting the poor. Spending in some of these programs increases when joblessness worsens. Follette and Lutz (2010) estimate that direct state and local spending on the programs increases by 0.04 percent of potential GDP when the unemployment rate increases by one percentage point. Some of this spending is reimbursed by the federal government; consequently net state and local spending on these programs only increases about half the estimated amount, or 0.02 percent of potential GDP (10).

Overall Impact of Automatic Stabilization

The Federal Reserve economists evaluated the combined impact of automatic stabilization under both federal and state and local policies. Using the Federal Reserve Board's macroeconomic forecasting model, they performed the evaluation by comparing two scenarios. In the first they assumed that a sequence of macroeconomic shocks reduced U.S. GDP by precisely 1 percent as monetary policy remained unchanged. The only fiscal response to the shocks was to permit automatic stabilization to operate in the usual way. Under these assumptions, the Federal Reserve would hold its policy interest rate constant and the nation's tax and transfer system would respond to the economic downturn in the ordinary way. Under the second scenario the Federal Reserve would also leave its policy interest rate unchanged but the automatic stabilizers would fail to respond to the sinking economy. In other words, individual and corporate taxpayers would pay the same taxes as would be owed and transfer recipients would receive the same government benefits as they would have received if the economy had continued to expand steadily. Under the second scenario, Follette and Lutz (2010) find that U.S. GDP would shrink by 1.1 percent four quarters after the adverse shocks to the economy began and would be 1.2 percent smaller eight quarters after the adverse shocks. These results imply that in the absence of automatic stabilization, the effect of the same shocks would be 10 percent worse after four calendar quarters and 20 percent worse after eight quarters.

These estimates do not differ greatly from recent results reported by European economists who have compared automatic stabilization in Europe and the United States (Dolls, Fuest, and Peichl 2010). They found that 19 percent of the impact of a macroeconomic shock that lowers income or boosts unemployment in the United States is automatically offset as a result of lower taxes or increases in transfer spending. This estimate of the U.S. response is similar to the result reported by Follette and Lutz (2010). Mathias Dolls, Clemens Fuest, and Andreas Peichl conclude, however, that the automatic U.S. response is smaller than the average effect of automatic stabilizers in European countries. For this reason there may be a stronger case for discretionary fiscal stimulus in the United States, a topic to which we turn in the next section.

The Stimulus Programs

The Bush and Obama administrations took extra steps in response to the recession, above and beyond the automatic responses built into the nation's tax and social protection systems. The first of these measures, enacted in February 2008, was the Economic Stimulus Act of 2008. The main element of this legislative package was the granting of individual income tax rebates equal to a few hundred dollars per taxpayer. The package also provided tax incentives to spur business investment and permitted an increase in the dollar value of mortgages that could be purchased by government-sponsored enterprises. In June 2008 Congress and the Bush administration established the Emergency Unemployment Compensation (EUC) program, which was later extended and made more generous. The biggest single stimulus package was the American Recovery and Reinvestment Act (ARRA), which passed in February 2009 shortly after the Obama administration took office and a new Congress dominated by Democrats convened. Another large stimulus package, the Tax Relief, Unemployment Insurance Reauthorization, and Job Creation Act of 2010, was passed in December 2010 by a lame-duck Congress that met after Democrats suffered severe electoral losses in the 2010 midterm elections. The 2010 package focused mainly on extending temporary income and payroll tax cuts and providing additional funding for EUC benefits.

Alternative Approaches to Stimulus

Before we discuss provisions of the stimulus packages or their effects, it is useful to distinguish among different kinds of stimulus measures the federal government might adopt. As already noted, the first measure it actually adopted was to provide tax rebates to nearly all low- and middle-income taxpayers. In addition, the first stimulus package offered tax incentives to businesses to spur private investment spending in 2008. The theory behind the first strategy is straightforward. Personal tax reductions, by boosting after-tax household income, can encourage higher personal consumption spending in the near term. The theory behind business tax reductions is that by extending more generous tax treatment to investments that are made in the next year or two, businesses can be induced to accelerate already-planned investment spending or undertake new investment projects that would otherwise be unprofitable. Both increased consumption spending and increased business investment would boost short-term demand for goods and services produced in the United States, offsetting part of the loss in demand that is expected to occur as a result of the shocks that are pushing the nation into recession. Neither of these stimulus measures was novel. Both kinds of actions have been standard elements in postwar stimulus packages, regardless of the political party in control of the White House or Congress.

Congress's next stimulus measure, enacted in June 2008, was to establish a federally funded program to extend the duration of unemployment benefits beyond twenty-six weeks. This action is also a standard U.S. response to higher joblessness. Congress has authorized extra or emergency unemployment benefit extensions in every recession since the late 1950s. Related to this kind of measure is the expansion of other government transfers that boost the incomes of low-income families or households expected to experience extra hardship as a result of a recession. The rationale for these measures is similar to the one for personal tax cuts and rebates. The increase in government outlays on personal transfer payments boosts disposable income and may induce extra household spending on consumption.

Two arguments strengthen the case for targeting the unemployed and economically vulnerable with higher transfers. The first highlights the equity of making special provision for Americans who suffer the biggest income losses as a result of a recession. The losses inflicted by a recession are very unequal. Most pensioners and many workers experience little or no income reduction as a result of higher unemployment. In contrast, laid-off workers may suffer severe earnings losses that can last a year or more. To most voters it seems equitable to help households experiencing serious hardship in preference to households that suffer comparatively little. A second argument is more practical. The unemployed and people with low incomes are more likely to spend immediately whatever extra money the government provides. A basic goal of stimulus policy is to boost consumption and investment, and hence final demand, above the level that would occur in the absence of the stimulus. It thus seems sensible to direct increased government spending to households, businesses, nonprofit organizations, and government agencies most likely to spend the funds quickly.

A third standard stimulus strategy is to boost public investment spending, for example, by increasing planned expenditures on roads, bridges, public transit systems, water and sewage systems, and public buildings. The investments can be selected and managed by federal government agencies, such as the U.S. Departments of Transportation, Energy, or Defense, or by state and local government agencies. In the discussion of the Obama administration's stimulus plan, public infrastructure projects received an outsize share of attention, but these projects received a comparatively small slice of the funding, especially in the first two years after passage of the ARRA stimulus package. Most of the initial increase in the federal deficit caused by the ARRA occurred because of personal income tax cuts, increases in personal transfer payments, and increases in intergovernmental transfers to state and local governments.

A fourth, less conventional, type of stimulus is the provision of direct federal assistance to state and local governments. We label this policy "state and local fiscal relief," or simply "fiscal relief." In one sense the rationale for this kind of measure is the same as the rationale for targeting households with federal tax cuts or extra federal transfers. When the federal government gives extra funds to state and local governments, federal policymakers expect these governments to convert the inter-governmental transfers quickly into additional state and local final government consumption or added public investment spending. Either outcome boosts final demand more than occurs if state and local governments spend less on government consumption or investment. Alternatively, state and local governments might reduce personal and business taxes below what their level would be if the federal government provided no additional aid. In this case, the change in state and local government behavior produces an effect on aggregate demand by inducing households to spend more on personal consumption (because they have more disposable income) or by inducing businesses to invest more or maintain higher payrolls (because their investments or operations yield a higher expected return when their state and local taxes are reduced).

It is conceivable, of course, that state and local governments will do none of these things if they receive larger transfers from the federal government. They may instead add to their reserves or reduce their indebtedness, in which case the balance sheets of state and local governments would improve, but there would be no change in state and local government consumption or investment or in the tax burden imposed on state and local taxpayers. If the sole purpose of fiscal relief is to spur short-term spending on consumption and investment, the decision of state and local policymakers not to spend the intergovernmental transfer will cause the federal policy to fail. Note, however, that the same logic applies to federal stimulus spending that takes the form of personal and business tax cuts or higher unemployment benefits. Many businesses and households that enjoy higher incomes as a result of stimulus measures may save rather than spend the resulting income gains. If the federal government's stimulus spending were entirely saved rather than spent, the balance sheets of households, businesses, and state and local governments would apparently improve, the debt of the national government would rise, but there would be little immediate impact on final demand for goods and services produced in the United States.

Our uncertainty about the response of households, businesses, and state and local governments to federal stimulus measures helps explain the appeal of federal infrastructure spending as an antidote to recession. Infrastructure spending produces a tangible result and directly employs government and private-sector workers, many of whom would be jobless if the public investment were not made. The argument in favor of higher government capital spending as stimulus seems particularly compelling when unemployment is high in the construction and capital goods manufacturing industries. In these circumstances, government capital projects are not taking away or bidding up the cost of resources that would otherwise have been employed by private firms or households. If the government does not employ these resources, they will remain unemployed or underused. In addition, traditional arguments against infrastructure as stimulus—that spending may arrive too late, contributing to inflationary pressures after the recession—are also less compelling in a protracted economic downturn.

The Stimulus Package for Laid-Off Workers

Congress established the temporary EUC program in July 2008. The original legislation authorized payment of an additional thirteen weeks of benefits for unemployed workers in all states after they exhausted their regular benefits. In late fall of 2008, after the severity of the financial crisis had become plain, Congress expanded the program to provide twenty weeks of EUC benefits in all states plus an additional thirteen weeks of compensation in states with high unemployment rates. EUC compensation was further liberalized in November 2009 when Congress funded thirty-four weeks of EUC benefits in all states, plus thirteen additional weeks in states with at least moderate levels of unemployment and an additional six weeks in states with an even higher unemployment rate. All of the cost of EUC benefits was borne by the U.S. Treasury.

In addition to creating the temporary EUC program the Congress also created major incentives for state governments to change the "trigger" rules for the state-federal EB unemployment insurance program. Under the law that was in effect before 2009, one-half the cost of EB payments was financed by states. Under temporary rules established in the February 2009 stimulus package and subsequently extended, Congress authorized the federal government to pay for 100 percent of the cost of EB benefits paid in 2009 through 2011. Because states did not have to pay for any of the benefit costs, they had an incentive to adopt temporarily a lower unemployment rate threshold for triggering EB payments. Over half the states adopted this strategy, making an additional thirteen or twenty weeks of unemployment compensation benefits available to laid-off workers at no cost to employers in the state. Thus, in more than half the states unemployed workers were eligible to receive unemployment compensation for a total of up to ninety-nine weeks, or slightly less than twenty-three months. The first twenty-six weeks of benefits were financed out of state-imposed taxes on the states' employers, and the remaining forty-seven to seventy-three weeks of EUC and EB benefits were funded by the federal government. The twenty-three months of benefit entitlement was the longest duration of unemployment insurance ever offered to laid-off U.S. workers. This benefit duration temporarily placed the United States near the middle of unemployment insurance durations available in industrialized countries (see figure 9.3). Even workers who lost their jobs in states suffering below-average unemployment rates were eligible to receive nearly seventeen months of unemployment benefits. These lengthy benefit durations were, of course, temporary. Federal funding for EUC and liberalized EB payments was scheduled to expire at the end of 2011.

In addition to temporarily extending the maximum period that workers could collect unemployment benefits, Congress also took two other steps to improve the protection provided by unemployment insurance. Between March 2009 and June 2010, it temporarily increased weekly benefit payments by $25, or about 8 percent of the previous average benefit amount. All of the cost of the benefit increase was financed by the federal government. Also, it temporarily eliminated the federal income tax on the first $2,400 per year of unemployment benefits. This step increased the after-tax value of unemployment compensation payments by roughly $240 to $360 per year, because unemployed workers typically face a marginal tax of 10 percent or 15 percent. In no previous recession had Congress increased the value of weekly benefits in this way.

Congress also gave incentives for states to change some of the qualifying conditions for unemployment benefits. The goal was to make benefits available to some unemployed or laid-off workers who had previously been excluded from receiving benefits by state laws. For example, one change in the rules would make it possible for laid-off workers to count wages earned in a more recent qualifying period than the standard period that was used under most states' rules. Another rule change would permit workers who are seeking part-time jobs to obtain unemployment benefits. (Roughly half the states do not permit laid-off workers who are seeking part-time jobs to claim benefits.) Under the terms of the ARRA 2009 stimulus package, the federal government assumed the full cost of the more generous qualifying provisions for the first couple

Figure 9.3   Maximum Duration of Unemployment Insurance in Twenty-One OECD Countries, 2005, in Months

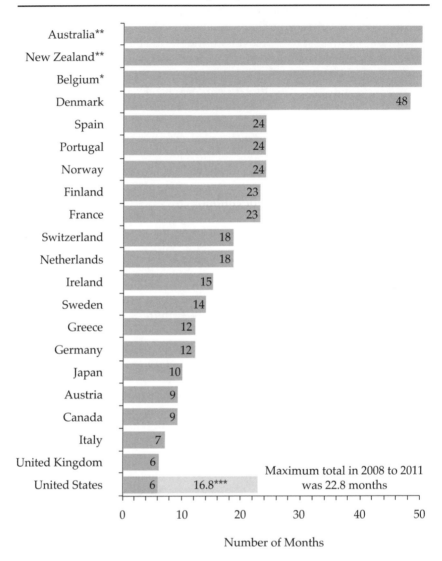

Number of Months

Source: Authors' calculations based on data from Organisation for Economic Co-operation and Development (2007).
* Belgium essentially provides unemployment benefits indefinitely.
** Australia and New Zealand offer only means-tested benefits. If the eligibility test continues to be met, unemployment benefits can last indefinitely.
*** Maximum additional unemployment insurance weeks temporarily made available in 2009 under the Emergency Unemployment Compensation and Extended Benefits programs.

of years after they were adopted. These provisions proved controversial, however. The intention of Congress was to induce states to make permanent changes in their qualifying requirements in exchange for a temporary payment from the federal government. Federal policymakers used the funding formula in the stimulus package to achieve this objective. Some states were nonetheless unwilling to make the required changes. In the end, thirty-eight states adopted a rule permitting workers to use a more up-to-date period in determining whether they are entitled to benefits, and twenty modified their laws or rules to permit part-time job-seekers to obtain benefits.

The most surprising feature of the 2009 stimulus package for laid-off workers was the provision of generous federal subsidies to help unemployed workers pay for health insurance premiums. The subsidy, which was limited to fifteen months per qualifying worker, covered 65 percent of the cost to laid-off workers of continuing their coverage under their former employer's health insurance plan. Workers laid off from a job providing health insurance coverage were eligible for the subsidy if their layoffs occurred between September 1, 2008, and the end of May 2010. Most working Americans who are not poor receive health insurance through their employer or the employer of another wage earner in the family. Employers typically pay for most of the premium costs of this insurance. Workers who are laid off generally lose the employer subsidy. The total unsubsidized cost of health insurance is quite high, around $4,700 a year for single workers and $12,700 for workers with a spouse and child dependents (Vroman 2009). These amounts are 10 percent and 32 percent, respectively, of the average year-round wage of American workers. Not surprisingly, relatively few workers can afford to pay the full cost of these premiums after they are laid off. The result is that many laid-off workers lose their health insurance until they find another job where health insurance is offered as a fringe benefit. Unemployed workers, especially those with child dependents, may become eligible for means-tested public health insurance under the Medicaid and State Child Health Insurance (SCHIP) programs, but working-age families must usually have low incomes and few assets to qualify for public insurance.

Citizens in other rich countries are often shocked to learn that U.S. workers can lose their health insurance coverage when they lose their jobs. In most wealthy countries, health insurance is provided to nearly all the resident population, including the unemployed and their dependents. In the United States, free or low-cost public health insurance is provided to the elderly, to most of the disabled, and to the nonelderly and nondisabled poor population (the population that has an income below a low-income threshold). For nonelderly, nondisabled Americans with incomes above the low-income threshold, inexpensive group health insurance is available only to employees who work for employers providing health insurance and to the dependents of those employees. Of course, many private employers, especially small ones, do not provide health insurance to their workers, so of course their employees do not lose health benefits if they lose their jobs. But for the workers who get health insurance through their jobs, the loss of employment typically causes a much bigger loss than the loss of wage income, since the worker and his or her dependents lose health protection. By providing generous subsidies so these workers could continue their health insurance after they were laid off, Congress dramatically (though only temporarily) expanded the protection available to laid-off workers who lost good jobs.

Temporary Tax Reductions

Each of the large-scale stimulus packages passed in 2008, in 2009, and in 2010 included a sizable and broadly targeted tax cut. These were aimed at providing one-time or short-term income tax reductions to households and, on a smaller scale, to businesses. The first congressional response to the financial crisis occurred in February 2008, when Congress passed a law that gave income tax rebates to households and more generous tax treatment of investments to businesses. The 2008 stimulus package also raised the maximum value of a home mortgage that could be purchased by the Federal National Mortgage Association (Fannie Mae) and the Federal Home Loan Mortgage Corporation (Freddie Mac). Of these measures the most important was the income tax rebate given to taxpayers. Individual taxpayers received a rebate of $600; married couples received $1,200; and taxpayers with child dependents received $300 for each child. Even Americans who had no tax liabilities could receive partial rebates if their earned incomes were at least $3,000. Social Security beneficiaries also received rebates under the 2008 stimulus law. Rebate checks were scaled back for households with gross incomes above certain limits. Single taxpayers with incomes above $75,000 and married taxpayers with incomes above $150,000 saw their rebates reduced by $0.05 for every $1.00 by which their incomes exceeded these limits. Thus, rebates of roughly equal size were received by most Americans in the bottom 90 percent of the income distribution. Only people with virtually no income or with incomes near the top of the distribution received no tax benefits under the plan. The Bureau of Economic Analysis estimates that the tax reductions added about $30 billion to personal transfer income and subtracted about $66 billion from personal taxes paid in 2008, boosting disposable personal income in that year by $96 billion (Landefeld et al. 2010, 15). The miscellaneous tax concessions for business provided estimated tax relief equal to less than one-fifth the amount provided to households through the income tax rebates.

The 2009 stimulus package was more than five times as expensive to the U.S. Treasury as the 2008 package, and it contained a much wider variety of tax and spending provisions. The most costly tax provision, accounting for more than 40 percent of the tax concessions in the stimulus bill, was the "making work pay" tax credit, a credit that was in effect between 2009 and 2010. The credit was modeled closely on a proposal made by President Barack Obama during the 2008 presidential campaign. He pledged to increase the reward for work by giving low-income workers an income tax rebate for part of the payroll taxes they pay. The credit provided workers with a credit equal to 6.2 percent of their earnings, capped at $400 for single taxpayers and $800 for a married couple. This credit rate is equal to the worker's portion of the Social Security payroll tax. The credit was phased out for taxpayers with high incomes, in particular for single taxpayers with incomes above $75,000 a year and married couples with incomes above $150,000 a year. The credit unquestionably reduced the marginal tax rate on earnings received by Americans in the bottom 90 percent of the income distribution, and thus it should have increased taxpayers' willingness to supply labor. In view of the fact that the national unemployment rate ranged between 8.2 percent and 10.1 percent during each of the months the credit was in effect, it seems unlikely the incentive to extra work effort had much effect. Hours worked in the United States were constrained by the extreme weakness in labor demand, not by the reluctance of workers to supply labor. The Congress and administration decided to pay the credit through lower tax withholding rates in the two years it was in effect. Thus, most workers started receiving bigger paychecks in March or April 2009. The tax credit was temporary. When it ended in December 2010 it was replaced by a two-percentage-point cut in the Social Security payroll tax on wage and self-employment income earned in 2011. (The revenue loss to the Social Security Trust Funds was to be made up with a transfer from the U.S. Treasury.)

The 2009 stimulus package contained two notable provisions to liberalize tax credits that are especially important for low-income households with children. One increased the value of the Earned Income Tax Credit (EITC) for households with three or more children. This credit was originally introduced to encourage low-income parents to enter the workforce and increase their annual work effort. For workers with very low earnings it gives families a refundable tax credit equal to either $0.34 or $0.40 for every dollar they earn. There is a maximum annual credit—it is about $3,000 a year for parents with a single child and $5,000 a year for parents with two or more children—and when family income rises above some threshold the credit is phased out. The temporary reforms included in the 2009 stimulus bill provided increased tax credits to parents with three or more children and increased the income levels at which the credit begins to be phased out for married-couple families. Given the relatively low-income population that received tax concessions under this provision, it is likely that a large fraction of the tax reductions were spent soon after they were received.

Another provision in the 2009 stimulus bill altered the child tax credit. This credit provides permanent tax concessions to families containing children. Under the terms of the 2009 stimulus bill, some features of the child tax credit were temporarily changed so that low-income households received bigger tax benefits under the credit. Like the change in the EITC, the temporary change in the child tax credit narrowly targeted low-income working families containing children. In both cases it is likely that a high proportion of the tax benefits was spent soon after the credits were received by families. Since this population includes a high proportion of families with working but poor breadwinners, it is more vulnerable to the effects of a recession than other low-income populations, which may include few working breadwinners. (Pensioners and the disabled are often poor, but poor people in these groups only rarely depend on wage earnings for an important percentage of their support, so they are relatively unaffected by weakness in the job market.)

The second most expensive tax provision in the 2009 stimulus package, at a cost of nearly $70 billion, was a temporary modification in the rules of the "alternative minimum tax." This temporary modification was a technical change in the tax code, but it had important practical effects for people with high incomes or who took large deductions from their taxable incomes. The purpose of the alternative minimum tax, originally enacted in 1969, is to prevent high-income taxpayers from escaping all taxes as a result of claiming a multitude of deductions and exemptions on their income tax returns. How effectively it achieves this goal is a matter of debate. Taxpayers who, under the standard income tax, can claim many deductions are forced to calculate their taxes under simplified (alternative minimum tax) rules that prohibit the use of most of these deductions and exemptions. If the computed tax under the alternative minimum tax is higher than it is under standard tax rules, tax filers must pay the higher tax. A growing percentage of taxpayers are at risk of paying income taxes under the alternative minimum tax rules, even though in many cases these taxpayers do not have particularly high incomes. To prevent middle-income families from paying the alternative tax, the Congress has frequently taken steps to "temporarily" increase the income levels at which the alternative minimum tax begins to apply. The 2009 stimulus package contained a provision that, once again, temporarily achieved this goal, reducing the taxes that otherwise would have been owed by people forced to calculate their taxes under the alternative minimum tax. According to estimates of the Urban Institute and Brookings Institution Tax Policy Center, almost 80 percent of the net benefits from temporarily modifying the alternative minimum tax rules flowed to the richest 20 percent of U.S. households (Altshuler et al. 2009). Viewed as an economic stimulus measure, this was a poor way to target tax concessions. In comparison with low-income taxpayers, high-income households almost certainly spend immediately a smaller percentage of the tax savings they receive from a temporary tax cut.

The 2009 stimulus package also contained a provision that helped students enrolled in postsecondary education. U.S. tax law already contained a permanent "Hope tax credit" that provides students with a tax credit equal to 100 percent of the first $1,200 per year spent on tuition and fees plus 50 percent of the second $1,200 spent on such fees. However, the credit was only provided to students in their first two years of postsecondary schooling. The temporary replacement for the Hope tax credit was called the "American Opportunity credit," and it could be claimed for qualified educational expenses incurred in 2009 and 2010. It provided a credit equal to 100 percent of the first $2,000 spent on tuition, fees, and other expenses plus 25 percent of the next $2,000 spent on those items. Thus, the maximum annual credit was $2,500 as opposed to only $1,800 under the Hope tax credit. The American Opportunity credit covered educational expenses for all four years of postsecondary education. However, like other items in the stimulus package, this was only a temporary tax credit and ended in 2010. When the credit expired, it was replaced by the old Hope tax credit.

The notable feature of the American Opportunity credit is that it targeted Americans investing in higher education to receive temporary tax concessions. It was one of several provisions in the stimulus package aimed at maintaining or increasing Americans' investments in education. In the spending portion of the stimulus package, Congress funded a major expansion of government grants to low-income students so they could pay for postsecondary schooling. These provisions make sense. Between December 2007 and December 2009 the number of wage and salary jobs in the United States dropped by almost 8.7 million. In the same period the number of unemployed job-seekers increased by more than 7.5 million. Because it was hard for unemployed workers to find jobs, it made sense for some of them to stop looking for work and start investing in their own skills to better prepare themselves for work when the job market improved. By providing tax assistance and direct grants to postsecondary students, the federal government encouraged more of the unemployed to adopt this strategy. It was a sensible strategy for many workers, especially for younger unemployed workers.[3] At the same time, the increased incentive for jobless workers to attend college or participate in training programs may have reduced the number of jobless Americans who were seeking immediate employment.

The 2009 stimulus package contained a number of miscellaneous tax provisions, some of them providing tax incentives for businesses to make energy-saving investments. Some business tax incentives, including time-limited tax concessions for capital investments undertaken in a specified period, might have spurred business spending in the short run. Some others, however, probably encouraged spending over such a lengthy period that much of the increased spending might not occur until the recession is past. Some of these tax concessions may have a sound justification quite apart from their success or failure in spurring business investment in the recession. However, to the extent that they cause investment to increase after the recession is over, these tax concessions will do nothing to speed the recovery or to improve the well-being of workers or families during the recession.

Other Direct Income Assistance and Provision of Services

From the perspective of social protection, the most important component of the 2009 stimulus package was direct provision of income assistance and social services to households. We have already described some of the most important measures to offer additional income assistance: temporary extensions in unemployment benefits, a temporary increase in the weekly benefit payment for unemployment compensation, temporary health insurance subsidies for workers who lose their health insurance when they are laid off, tax rebates for most American taxpayers and pensioners, tax concessions targeting working parents who have children, more generous tax credits and means-tested educational grants so that students can afford college.

Congress also took other steps to protect vulnerable populations. It increased for two years the amount of money available in federally funded training programs to pay for retraining unemployed workers and improving the skills of hard-to-employ young people and adults. It provided substantial extra assistance so that states could pay for larger caseloads in the Temporary Assistance for Needy Families (TANF) program, the state-run social assistance program providing cash transfers to indigent children and their parents. The 2009 stimulus package temporarily increased the value of the Food Stamps benefit (now known as the Supplemental Nutritional Assistance Program). This program is essentially a negative income tax program that offers benefits payable in the form of food coupons. As a family's income rises, the value of food coupons provided to the family falls. Families in the top 60 percent of the income distribution are not eligible to receive food coupons. All of the measures just mentioned target for assistance benefits populations that are either directly affected by a weaker job market or are likely to spend higher government transfers relatively quickly.

Effects on Household Disposable Income

Summarizing our discussion of the temporary tax cuts and benefit increases, we can present some estimates of the direct impacts of these measures on Americans' disposable incomes. Our estimates exclude the direct effects of corporate tax changes on business income unless the added income is reflected immediately in personal income. Our estimates also exclude any of the indirect effects of the tax and benefit changes on personal income through their impact on private personal income. We simply measure the reported change in tax revenue or transfer benefit outlays attributable to the 2008 and 2009 stimulus packages and compare these estimates to other measures of income flows going to U.S. households. Estimates of the impact of ARRA on personal tax payments and government transfers to persons have been published by the Bureau of Economic Analysis.[4] We have also made estimates of the effects on personal disposable income of the 2008 stimulus package and various unemployment insurance benefit expansions, using data published by the Bureau of Economic Analysis and the U.S. Department of Labor's Employment and Training Administration. Figure 9.4 displays the direct contribution of the stimulus provisions on disposable personal income in calendar quarters from 2008 through 2010. The estimates reflect the percentage increase in disposable personal income that is due to higher government social benefits to persons and lower personal current taxes authorized by the federal stimulus laws passed between February 2008 and the end of 2010. The initial effect of the stimulus measures occurred in the second quarter of 2008, when tax rebate checks were sent to middle- and low-income families. The effects in the next three quarters were considerably smaller and were primarily due to extensions in eligibility for unemployment insurance. The effects of the ARRA stimulus package are apparent starting in the second quarter of 2009, and these effects grow larger as unemployment compensation payouts under the EUC and EB programs continue to rise. Almost 30 percent of the total estimated increase in disposable personal income attributable to the stimulus was due to various liberalizations of unemployment compensation. In late 2009 and early 2010, when the EUC and EB benefit rolls soared, stimulus spending on unemployment compensation accounted for almost 40 percent of the additions to disposable personal income.

Figure 9.5 puts these estimates in perspective. The chart shows the trend in real per capita U.S. income in the two years before and three years after the onset of the 2008-to-2009 recession. We show three mea-

Figure 9.4   Additions to Disposable Personal Income (DPI) as a Result of Personal Tax and Transfer Provisions of Stimulus Packages, 2008 to 2010

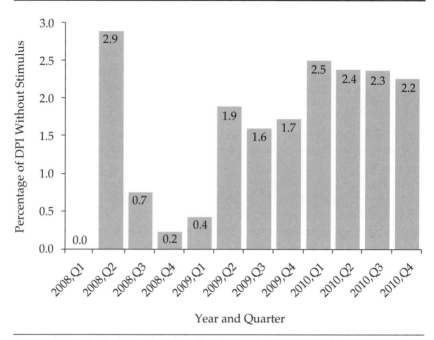

Sources: Authors' calculations based on data from U.S. Department of Commerce, Bureau of Economic Analysis (n.d., 2011) and U.S. Department of Labor, Employment and Training Administration (2011a, 2011b, 2011c).

sures of real per capita income as well as the trend in real per capita consumption expenditures. The first income measure shows the trend in gross private income, that is, total pre-tax private personal income, excluding government social benefits. This measure includes gross wage and salary income; the profits of farms and small businesses; and interest, dividend, royalty, and rent payments (in other words, all the pre-tax private income received by U.S. households). The second income measure subtracts the current income and payroll taxes paid by households but adds the government social benefits they receive, including Social Security, Medicare and Medicaid benefits, unemployment compensation, and means-tested income payments. The effects of the deep recession can be clearly seen in the sharp decline of gross private income after the first quarter of 2008. By the first quarter of 2010, per capita private income was 7.6 percent below what it had been at the end of the previous economic expansion. Because of automatic stabilizers and the stimulus packages, however, the trend in disposable personal income differs markedly from the trend in private income. Per capita disposable in-

Figure 9.5   **Per Capita U.S. Income in Constant 2005 Dollars, 2006 to 2010**

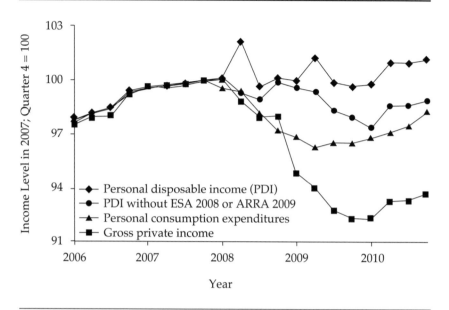

Sources: Authors' calculations, based on data from U.S. Department of Commerce, Bureau of Economic Analysis (n.d., 2011), and U.S. Department of Labor, Employment and Training Administration (2011a, 2011b, 2011c).
Note: ARRA = American Recovery and Reinvestment Act; ESA = Economic Stimulus Act

come hardly declined at all in any quarter after the onset of the recession. The extraordinary stability of disposable income in the face of steep losses in private income is a testament to the powerful effect of automatic stabilizers and the stimulus packages on the after-tax incomes of U.S. households.

A third income line in figure 9.5 shows what the trend in disposable personal income would have been in the absence of the tax cuts and benefit improvements that were authorized by the 2008-to-2010 stimulus packages. This estimate is obtained by subtracting the net income gains that households obtained as a result of the tax cuts and benefit hikes authorized by the stimulus laws. In the first quarter of 2010, for example, our estimates imply that absent the stimulus, real disposable personal income would have been lower than pre-recession disposable income by 2.6 percent.[5] Because households received larger transfers and paid lower taxes as a result of the stimulus laws, their actual disposable incomes were only 0.2 percent lower than their pre-recession incomes.

Note that our estimate of the impact of the stimulus on disposable income understates its full effect. Our calculations assume households' private incomes were unaffected by the stimulus. This seems unlikely, because the personal tax cuts and benefit improvements authorized by the stimulus packages almost certainly induced some households to consume more than they would have in the absence of the stimulus. Their higher consumption would have generated higher private income for the producers who supplied the extra goods and services purchased by consumers. The fourth line in figure 9.5 shows the trend in per capita personal consumption. Note that consumption fell sharply in the early quarters of the recession, mirroring the sharp decline in private incomes. However, the drop in consumption slowed noticeably in early 2009, and real consumption began to rise in the middle of 2009, even though gross private income continued to shrink. It is hard to believe this turnaround would have occurred so soon if the government had not helped stabilize household disposable income through tax cuts and benefit improvements.

Investments in Infrastructure and Research and Development

Even before the extent of the financial crisis became clear, the Bush administration and Congress acted to give tax rebates to low- and middle-income taxpayers and to extend the maximum duration of unemployment benefits. Soon after major financial institutions started to fail, Congress began to discuss other steps to protect the broader economy. A great deal of this discussion focused on alternative investments the government could make to improve the transportation system, reduce greenhouse gas emissions, and improve the energy efficiency of the economy. Debate over this kind of investment dominated the early phase of the public discussion of an appropriate countercyclical stimulus plan, but neither the 2008 nor the 2010 stimulus packages contained noticeable budget allocations for these kinds of investments. The ARRA contained more funding for infrastructure investment, but the actual amounts expected to be spent in 2009 and 2010 were comparatively small.

To understand the level and timing of stimulus spending on infrastructure, we have used Congress's original budget estimates for spending under the 2009 ARRA program. (None of the other stimulus packages included major appropriations for infrastructure spending.) We have divided the various individual components in the ARRA package into three broad categories:

1. Fiscal relief for state governments

2. Benefit increases and tax cuts for households

3. Investments in infrastructure and technology development

Figure 9.6   Predicted Stimulus Spending Under the American Recovery and Reinvestment Act, 2009 to 2019

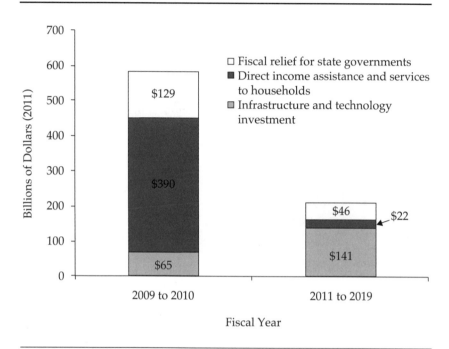

Source: Authors' calculations based on Elmendorf (2009).

Figure 9.6 shows the allocation of resources in the ARRA in these three broad categories, and it further divides the budget totals between two periods, 2009 to 2010 and 2011 to 2019. In much of the discussion up to now we have emphasized the time-limited nature of many of Congress's actions. In the case of the ARRA, most tax concessions were limited to the tax years 2009 and 2010. Nearly all the transfer program benefit increases in ARRA were scheduled to terminate by the end of 2010.[6] Even counting the extensions in tax cuts and unemployment benefit hikes enacted in 2010, all the benefit increases and tax cuts are expected to be phased out in 2011 or 2012. Nonetheless, a surprisingly large percentage of the total costs of the ARRA package will be incurred after 2010. An overwhelming fraction of the late-period costs of ARRA are for infrastructure and technology investment projects. In the case of tax concessions, benefit increases, and state fiscal relief packages, it is straightforward for the federal government to start spending and to stop it. It is much harder to obtain worthwhile results from an investment in infrastructure or a research and development project if the government is committed to obtaining results within a very short period of time. It

Figure 9.7   Predicted Stimulus Spending Under the American Recovery and Reinvestment Act, 2009 to 2015

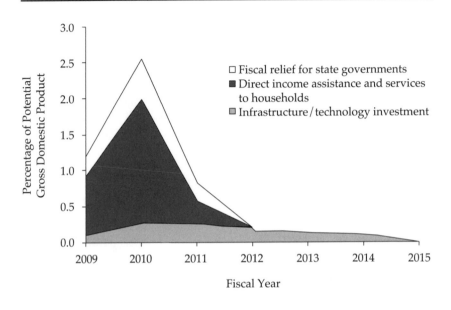

Sources: Authors' calculations, based on Elmendorf (2009) and U.S. Congressional Budget Office (2009).

takes time to plan a well-designed project and even more time to assemble and carefully manage the resources needed to complete it. A rule of thumb is that only one-quarter of spending on an infrastructure project occurs within its first year. Indeed, this is one of the traditional arguments against infrastructure as economic stimulus. In the 2008-to-2009 recession, however, this argument was weakened by policymakers' expectation that the downturn would be severe and long-lasting.

The different time horizons of the three kinds of stimulus activities are plain in figure 9.7. It shows predicted stimulus spending in the years between 2009 and 2015 measured as a percentage of the U.S. Congressional Budget Office's estimate of potential GDP in those years (U.S. Congressional Budget Office 2009). At the peak of the funding authorized by the ARRA, in fiscal year 2010, total spending was expected to be slightly more than 2.5 percent of potential GDP. Only a small portion of the funds in that year were to be spent on infrastructure or research and development projects. An overwhelming share was devoted to direct income assistance and to state fiscal relief. The funding for infrastructure and research and development projects will be spread fairly evenly over most of the next six years. Even if the projects ultimately prove to have high value, their value as countercyclical stimulus might be questioned. Only a small percentage of funds devoted to the projects was spent in 2009 and 2010, when the gap between potential and actual U.S. GDP was expected to be greatest.

The Obama administration and Congress were aware of the practical limits on spending infrastructure investment dollars quickly. This may have led to the relatively small allocation of total ARRA spending to infrastructure projects. The fact that government infrastructure investment was not very visible in the first two years after ARRA passed was entirely predictable. It was the result of allocating most early ARRA spending to tax cuts, transfer benefits, and fiscal relief to state governments. It was also an inevitable consequence of the early decision to require federally funded capital projects to be operated under normal procurement and administrative rules. These rules might have ensured that capital projects were reasonably well selected and that contractors were chosen in compliance with strict regulations, but they also slowed the process of converting appropriated federal dollars into active construction sites and completed public projects.

Fiscal Relief for State Governments

By our estimate a little more than one-fifth of the 2009 stimulus package, or about $175 billion, was devoted to providing fiscal relief to state governments. This relief was provided in a variety of forms. For example, a little less than $3 billion in federal grants was authorized to help pay for local law enforcement, and nearly $30 billion was authorized to pay for aid for particular aspects of state and local education. Some ARRA spending for education targeted the economically disadvantaged and children with learning or other disabilities. Since most educational spending is fungible, however, it is likely that the extra federal funds freed up state and local resources for other purposes.

Congress created two temporary programs to provide general fiscal relief to the states. One gave almost $50 billion to be divided among the states "in order to minimize and avoid reductions in education and other essential services." In exchange for the generous grants, state governments had to show they were "(1) making improvements in teacher effectiveness and in the equitable distribution of qualified teachers for all students, particularly students who are most in need; (2) establishing pre-K-to-college-and-career data systems that track progress and foster continuous improvement; (3) making progress toward rigorous college- and career-ready standards and high-quality assessments that are valid and reliable for all students, including limited English proficient students and students with disabilities; and (4) providing targeted, intensive support and effective interventions for the lowest-performing schools" (U.S. Department of Education 2009, 1). For most states, no changes in their education policies were needed to obtain the generous but temporary federal assistance.

The other important form of fiscal relief was provided through a temporary change in the funding formula for Medicaid. The Medicaid program is administered by state governments, but most of its costs are financed with large federal grants to state governments. If a state maintains a qualifying public insurance program for its indigent population, the federal government pays for a percentage of the state's program costs. The fraction of costs paid by the federal government, known as the Federal Medical Assistance Percentage (or FMAP), is determined by a formula that links the state's federal reimbursement rate to its per capita income. States with high average incomes get 50 percent of their Medicaid program costs reimbursed, and states with low average incomes receive a higher federal subsidy rate. Medicaid is one of the most costly government programs: in 2007, benefit payments under the program represented 2.8 percent of GDP. This means that the federal government's Medicaid grants to state governments are a major source of state revenues. By changing the FMAP formula, the federal government can dramatically raise or lower total state revenues. The 2009 stimulus package temporarily changed the FMAP formula to make it more favorable to states. All states were guaranteed that the percentage of Medicaid costs borne by the federal government would rise by at least 6.2 percentage points (reducing the percentage of program costs borne by the state by an equivalent percentage). In addition, Congress authorized even bigger increases in the federal match rate for states experiencing large increases in their unemployment rates. The legislation also held harmless states that would have seen reductions in their FMAP because incomes were rising before the recession. These changes in the FMAP formula were effective for the period from October 2008 through December 2010. The cost of this temporary formula change to the U.S. Treasury was originally estimated to be $90 billion, spread over three years. In August 2010, the president and Congress provided an additional $10 billion for education-related jobs and extended the increased FMAP through June 2011, at a cost of another $26 billion.

Both of these temporary measures provided immediate relief to state governments. Nearly all state governments in the United States operate under balanced-budget rules. Although these rules differ across states, they generally mean that the planned operating budget of the state (excluding the budget for capital investment) must be fully financed with current revenues. These rules, which are usually included in state constitutions, mean that a shortfall in expected revenues must be matched within a few months by an equivalent reduction in the state's planned spending. Unlike the federal government, which can borrow unlimited funds to pay for its operations, state governments must generally plan to cover the operating cost of their programs with current tax revenues, fees, or grants from the federal government. The provision of generous fiscal relief in the recent recession meant that state governments did not have to cut spending or increase taxes as much as they would have been forced to do in the absence of the federal aid.

Federal fiscal relief to the states is particularly important for education and for maintaining social protection of the poor. In the United States, education is primarily the responsibility of state and local governments. The federal government typically pays for only about 10 percent to 12 percent of the total cost of public primary and secondary schools, and state and local governments pay for the rest. Since balanced-budget rules make state and local budgets somewhat pro-cyclical, state legislatures face pressure to reduce school budgets during recessions. The federal government pays for most of the cost of social-safety-net programs for the poor, but state governments still pay for a substantial share of their costs. Equally important, state governments are responsible for administering some of the biggest means-tested programs, including Medicaid and TANF. State governments make the rules that help determine who is eligible for benefits and the amount of benefits. Even though they do not pay for the full cost of the programs, when a recession occurs many states are tempted to curtail eligibility or cut benefits. This is the opposite policy from the one urged by most economists, who think it is important for benefits to be maintained or even improved during a recession.

State and local governments were hit hard in the recession. States in particular suffered historic revenue declines, with revenues plummeting 17 percent in the second quarter of 2009 compared to a year earlier (figure 9.8). Local revenues held steadier but are expected to dip as property tax assessments increasingly reflect depressed market values. Compared with local governments, states tend to rely on more volatile revenue sources such as income and sales taxes. States with progressive income tax systems are particularly vulnerable to recessions because they depend on collections from high-income individuals, whose earnings themselves are more volatile because they include non-wage sources such as interest and capital gains. In the recent recession, sales taxes were the first to fall but income taxes plunged farther and faster. By the second quarter of 2009, they were 29 percent below their level one year earlier.

At the same time, service demands in states continued unchanged or escalated. In particular, states faced rising enrollments for social-safety-net programs. Medicaid caseloads grew by 7.6 million, nearly 18 percent, from December 2007 to June 2010, with most of the enrollment

Figure 9.8   Change in State Tax Revenues Compared with One Year Earlier, 1989 to 2010

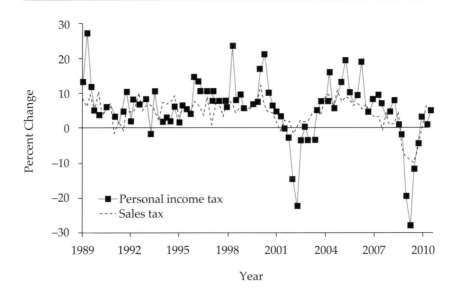

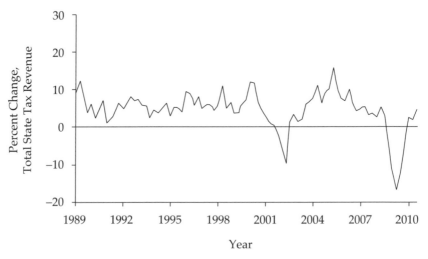

Source: Authors' calculations based on data from U.S. Census Bureau (2011).

growth coming from increases in the number of insured children (Kaiser Family Foundation, Kaiser Commission on Medicaid and the Uninsured 2010, 2011). Enrollment also climbed in K–12 and public postsecondary institutions, especially community colleges. The result was massive state budget shortfalls or gaps between projected revenues and expenditures. The National Conference of State Legislatures (2010) reports more than $400 billion in cumulative state funding gaps from fiscal years 2009 to 2011. They anticipate another $150 billion shortfall before the end of fiscal year 2013. State budgets generally take two to three years to recover from a recession, and this recession was particularly destructive to employment as well as company and household balance sheets. Although ARRA was helpful, it is estimated to have covered no more than 40 percent of total state budget gaps. Moreover, after receiving more than $107 billion in fiscal 2010 and $89 billion in fiscal 2011, states will receive only $23 billion in fiscal relief in fiscal year 2012, as they confront what could be their most difficult budget cycle yet.

As noted, states and localities are generally required to balance their budgets and must therefore raise taxes or cut spending in a recession, yet these actions can harm vulnerable populations as well as the larger economy. For example, the failure to coordinate national and subnational fiscal policy is thought to have compounded the Great Depression in the United States and Japan's Lost Decade in the 1990s (Brown 1956; Kuttner and Posen 2001). This is a particular danger in the United States, where state and local governments are major contributors to the economy, employing one out of seven workers and generating an average of 0.33 percentage points in real annual GDP growth. Federal policymakers thus often seek to provide antirecessionary aid to states in a downturn. In the early 1970s, Congress offered the states added infrastructure and job training funds through the Antirecession Fiscal Assistance, Local Public Works, and Comprehensive Employment and Training Act programs. More recently, the federal government dispersed $10 billion in enhanced Medicaid payments through the Jobs and Growth Tax Relief Reconciliation Act of 2003 (JGTRRA).

The ARRA in 2009 contained elements of past programs but also charted new territory. In particular, it directed significantly more resources ($282 billion, including fiscal relief and project-based aid) to states and localities than had occurred in earlier recessions. Under ARRA, federal grants to states and localities reached a historic peak in nominal terms and as a share of GDP (4.5 percent in federal fiscal year 2010, compared to an average of 3.3 percent annually from 2005 to 2007). Beyond the size of state and local transfers, ARRA included several innovations in the delivery of funds. It provided more discretionary aid than previous antirecessionary efforts, such as JGTRRA in 2003. The 2009 federal stimulus package also improved the targeting of funds to states suffering higher than average unemployment. By contrast, JGTRRA transferred funds on a per capita basis, adjusted to provide minimum funds for smaller states. At the same time, ARRA sought to leverage federal dollars to achieve policy innovations in education and infrastructure, including clean energy. It imposed new systems of control and accountability, including strict deadlines for committing funds to particular projects and new recipient information and reporting requirements, all in service to the president's goal of establishing a higher standard of transparency and accountability.

Although ARRA's fiscal relief package for state and local governments will be studied for years to come, the most pressing question is: Did it work? To date, most public and private assessments have focused on employment, income, and consumption outcomes, primarily by applying previously estimated multipliers to aggregate federal spend-out rates rather than directly estimating state and local government responsiveness to federal grants.[7] An alternative method is simply to count the number of jobs created on the basis of so-called Section 1512 reports that recipients must file quarterly with the Recovery Accountability Transparency Board. "Recipients" are defined as any state or entity other than an individual that receives funds directly from the federal government. Although the focus of many popular debates, these reports cover only about one-fifth of ARRA's cost to the federal government (including direct spending and revenue losses). In particular, the reports do not cover payments to individuals through Medicaid and unemployment insurance. The reports also exclude secondary jobs created by subcontractors and indirect effects such as higher consumption spending induced by these wages (see U.S. Congressional Budget Office 2011).

One of the first assessments of ARRA's effect on state and local government spending was by Joshua Aizenman and Gurnain Kaur Pasricha (2010). They found that ARRA did not significantly boost either government consumption and gross investment, as defined in the National Income and Product Accounts, or total government expenditures (including government consumption and gross investment plus transfer payments to individuals). The authors attribute this result to state and local budget cuts offsetting increased federal spending. A limitation of this study, however, is that it ended in the third quarter of 2009,[8] by which point the federal government had disbursed only $38 billion, or less than 30 percent of total funds earmarked for state fiscal relief. Most states were just starting fiscal year 2009-to-2010 and their first full budget cycle of the recession. Many states still had ample rainy-day funds and were relying on temporary solutions to their funding shortfalls, including internal borrowing, fund shifts, and deferrals. More important, the Aizenman and Pasricha result depends critically on the definition of a baseline or counterfactual for the path of state spending without ARRA. The authors specify a baseline using time-series methods—that is, a model in which current expenditures reflect experience in the past. This approach is not well suited to assessing a revenue shock outside the range of historical experience.

By contrast, other authors have followed an approach pioneered by the late Edward Gramlich. In a series of papers starting in the 1970s, he and his coauthors sought to explain how state and local government finances, including spending, taxes, and fund balances, responded to federal grants as well as income, costs, demographics, and prior balances. An advantage with his approach is that it can detect spillovers across budget categories (for example, federal grants that are spent on tax cuts) as well as responses over time (for example, if states initially save but later spend federal grants). For example, Gramlich and Harvey Galper (1978) found that each dollar of unrestricted federal aid stimulated $0.25 in state and local spending in the near term and $0.43 in added spending in the longer term.

In this vein, John F. Cogan and John B. Taylor (2010) estimate a behavioral model of state and local government responses to ARRA. They relate government consumption and gross investment as just described, other expenditures (including transfer payments), and net lending or borrowing to ARRA funds and other revenues (such as tax receipts) in a joint regression framework. The authors conclude that ARRA did not increase direct government purchases but did boost other expenditures. The net effect on total spending was close to zero. They attribute this result to the effectiveness of federal requirements that states at least maintain previous levels of spending on Medicaid. In contrast, Cogan and Taylor detect a strong positive effect, nearly one-for-one, of ARRA funds on state and local savings. They do not consider effects on revenues. Gerald A. Carlino and Robert P. Inman (2010) obtain a similar, though more muted, savings response using data on all federal grants from 1979 to 2005 and allowing for changes in revenues as well as spending. These results are consistent with findings from Gramlich and Galper (1978) as well as more recent results for a sample of large U.S. municipalities (Buettner and Wildasin 2006). They also mirror limited consumer spending responses to tax rebates (see, for example, Sahm, Shapiro, and Slemrod 2009).

In sum, the Great Recession was particularly hard on state and local governments. Concerned about potential negative spillovers to the larger economy, federal policymakers enacted unprecedented state fiscal relief in addition to project-based aid. Critics have argued that these fiscal relief payments were ineffective, pointing to flat or negative state and local government purchases as well as higher net saving (see Cogan and Taylor 2010). However, a key question in interpreting these results is "compared with what?" State revenues, including investment income as well as tax receipts, plummeted 30 percent in 2009. Extrapolations from historical experience may therefore provide an inadequate basis for comparison.

At the same time, ARRA pursued many goals, including state and local budget stabilization and prevention of harm to the most disadvantaged, in addition to countercyclical stimulus. Federal policymakers sought to direct aid to the most distressed states while also limiting incentives for moral hazard or diminished fiscal prudence. In this regard, ARRA fiscal relief for state and local governments was not unlike previous, flawed efforts at redistribution through a federalist system. The withdrawal of federal fiscal relief after 2010 will provide some additional information about state and local government responses to the generous intergovernmental transfers they received in 2009 and 2010.

Did the Stimulus Programs Work?

In past recessions federal stimulus programs have emphasized extra spending on unemployment benefits, temporary tax cuts to boost consumer spending and encourage business investment, and increases in infrastructure investment. In the recent recession, most spending was devoted to these same items, with personal tax cuts and unemployment compensation and other benefit hikes absorbing the lion's share of funds. Infrastructure investment projects received comparatively small allocations through the end of 2010.

Before the 2008-to-2009 recession, fiscal relief of states and temporary incentives for human-capital investment seldom played a big role in stimulus packages. As a result, policymakers had little evidence to assess the short-term impact of these measures on government and household consumption and investment. We will learn more about the countercyclical effectiveness of these two kinds of policies from future evidence on state spending patterns and postsecondary education investments. One encouraging sign is that payroll employment in state and local government and in education was not hurt noticeably by the recession, at least initially (figure 9.9). In spite of the sharp decline in state and local tax revenues, state and local governments were able to maintain or even increase their pre-recession employment levels in the early months of the recession. In many states and localities, employees' annual wages and benefit costs were trimmed, as some governments forced their workers to accept unpaid furloughs. However, the payroll employment statistics provide little evidence of a massive cutback in the number of state and local employees in the first two years after the recession began. The drop in government employment was larger and more worrisome in 2010 and early 2011, just as private employment began to rebound. Government employment came under pressure as a result of the cumulative effect of the recession on state and local revenues and the expected end of federal fiscal relief.

Considerable evidence suggests that the federal government's efforts to support education and human capital investment were successful. Many public and private postsecondary institutions reported continued

Figure 9.9   **Percent Change in Payroll Employment in State and Local Government and Private Sectors, December 2007 to December 2010**

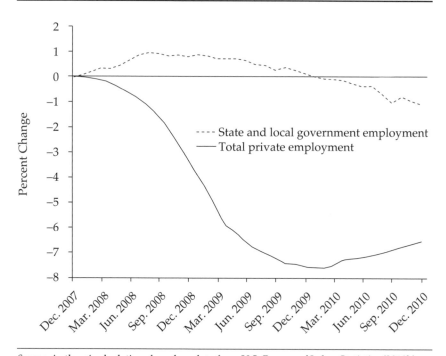

Source: Authors' calculations based on data from U.S. Bureau of Labor Statistics (2010b).

strong demand for places in entering classes throughout the recession. In fall 2009, almost two years after the recession began, college enrollment rates of new high school graduates reached a record high (U.S. Bureau of Labor Statistics 2010a). Community college enrollments increased 17 percent between fall 2007 and fall 2009, and they increased another 3 percent in fall 2010 (Phillippe and Mullin 2011). School enrollment data published by the Census Bureau show accelerated growth in enrollment rates between 2007 and 2009 for every age group past age seventeen. The gains were particularly impressive for young adults between age eighteen and twenty-four.[9] The ARRA provisions that helped Americans pay for college and helped fund states' higher-education budgets evidently strengthened both demand for and supply of postsecondary schooling.

The most tangible sign of a payoff from the government's stimulus program was the comparative strength in consumer spending. The severity of the recession caused private incomes to plunge (see figure 9.5).

Federal government programs and stimulus dollars cushioned the massive blow to private family incomes. In no quarter after the recession began did real per capita disposable income fall more than 0.5 percent below its pre-recession level. During three of the quarters in which GDP was shrinking, disposable income was actually higher than it was in the months before the recession began. Reduced federal taxes and increased government benefit payments, partly funded out of the stimulus packages, kept Americans' spendable incomes from falling when their private incomes plunged. Household consumption fell in the recession, in spite of the massive swing in taxes and public transfers, but consumption began to rise even as private incomes continued to fall. Many Americans were made cautious by the drop in their personal wealth and fear of losing their jobs. But higher government benefits helped boost the spending of the unemployed and poor, and lower taxes helped insulate middle-class families from some of the effect of the loss in their wealth. By the end of 2010, per capita personal consumption spending was within 1.6 percent of its pre-recession level.

Other analysts agree that the stimulus programs helped boost the economy. A provision of the 2009 ARRA required the Congressional Budget Office (CBO) to comment on required reports from recipients of ARRA funds. The CBO went beyond this mandate and issued periodic updates of its own estimates of the impact of ARRA on national output, employment and unemployment, and total hours worked. Rather than providing point estimates of ARRA's effects, CBO analysts produced a range of estimates of several kinds of impact under pessimistic and optimistic views of the multiplier effect of tax cuts, benefit increases, and other government outlays on economic activity. In its February 2011 report, the CBO estimated that the ARRA stimulus program boosted U.S. GDP in 2010 by between 1.5 percent and 4.1 percent and increased full-time-equivalent employment by between 1.9 million and 4.8 million workers (U.S. Congressional Budget Office 2011). Alan Blinder and Mark Zandi (2010) offered a more comprehensive assessment of the government's actions in 2008-to-2010, including the extraordinary measures to shore up the financial system. Focusing on just the stimulus measures, including the tax cuts and unemployment compensation liberalizations that occurred outside the ARRA, the two economists estimate the stimulus added 3.4 percent to 2010 GDP and boosted 2010 employment by 2.7 million jobs.

Though the government's countercyclical policies were generally successful, the public regarded them with deep skepticism. A CNN poll in January 2009 showed that about three-quarters of Americans thought half or more of the stimulus spending was wasted. Forty-five percent thought "most" or "nearly all" of the stimulus dollars had been wasted.[10]

This harsh verdict was unjustified, but it affected the political climate in Washington. Congress became disinclined to pass a major expansion or extension of the stimulus, especially if stimulus required any increase in federal outlays.

The recession was severe. Unemployment rose more steeply than in any other postwar recession, and it declined very slowly in the first year and a half of the recovery. Two presidents and the Congress put into place a number of countercyclical policies that helped protect the incomes, health insurance, and educational prospects of Americans who would otherwise have suffered grievous harm from the downturn. These policies helped prevent a serious recession from worsening into a deep depression. A key question in assessing the economy after implementation of the stimulus program is "What would have happened without the stimulus?" In giving a failing grade to the government's stimulus programs, many voters and opposition lawmakers implicitly compared the bad times in 2008-to-2010 with the much stronger economy of 2005-to-2007. Most informed observers recognize that this is a wildly implausible benchmark. After the near collapse of major financial institutions in 2008, it was inevitable that Americans' employment and earned incomes would fall. The stimulus program reduced the income losses that vulnerable Americans suffered as a result of the recession and made the downturn less severe than it otherwise would have been. Unfortunately for the policymakers who sponsored or supported the stimulus programs, "It could have been worse" is rarely a winning slogan in a political campaign.

The authors are grateful for the helpful research assistance of Sveta Milusheva. All views in this chapter are the authors' alone and should not be attributed to the Brookings Institution or the School of Public Policy, University of Maryland.

Notes

1. Federal law provides states with the option of selecting one or more alternative unemployment rates. Details of the trigger mechanism can be found in U.S. House of Representatives, Committee on Ways and Means (2000), Section 4.
2. "Potential GDP" is the dollar value of goods and services that can be produced by the economy when it is operating at full employment. In recent years, economists estimate that full employment is attained when the unemployment rate is somewhere between 4.5 percent and 5 percent.
3. Contrary to the widespread impression that the payoff to college has declined, it has in fact improved almost without interruption since the late 1970s. See Burtless (2007).

4. See U.S. Department of Commerce, Bureau of Economic Analysis (n.d., 2011).

5. Recall that this estimate includes only the direct impact of extra transfer payments and lower personal tax liabilities authorized by the stimulus laws. It ignores the indirect effects of larger federal transfers to state and local governments, which may have induced some states to pay higher transfer benefits or impose lower taxes on state and local residents. It also ignores the indirect effects of the stimulus on private income, which may have increased as a result of the stimulus because consumption was maintained at a higher level than would have been the case without the stimulus.

6. In figures 9.6 and 9.7 we do not divide up "direct income assistance and services to households" between the part that is derived from tax cuts and the part that is due to increases in transfers because in many cases the distinction is not easy to make. (Only a very small percentage of ARRA spending was allocated to an increase in the provision of direct federally funded government services.) In the Department of Commerce's National Income and Product Accounts, an income tax cut that is larger than a household's tax liability and that is refundable to the taxpayer is treated as a transfer to the extent that the cut exceeds the taxpayer's tax liability. Thus, the cost to the Treasury of some income tax cuts and tax credit liberalizations in ARRA was treated partly as a reduction in personal current taxes and partly as an increase in government transfer payments. In either case, the tax cuts and more generous income tax credits were reflected as an increase in disposable personal income.

7. See, for example, Alan Blinder and Mark Zandi (2010) and U.S. Congressional Budget Office (2011). Two recent papers implement an alternative strategy of estimating multipliers directly using cross-state variation in ARRA spending. Daniel J. Wilson (2010) examines the portion of spending that was determined by previously existing federal funding formulas, a so-called instrumental variable that is related to total spending but unrelated to current economic conditions or other factors that could bias results. James Feyrer and Bruce Sacerdote (2011) follow a similar approach, using the average seniority of a state's delegation to the U.S. House of Representatives as their instrumental variable. Both papers find heterogeneous responses but are not inconsistent with the range of estimates described by the Congressional Budget Office.

8. In a subsequent paper, Aizenman and Pasricha (2011) show that state and local "pure fiscal expenditure" declined even further in 2009 than it did in 2008. Again, however, this measure excludes spending on individual transfer payments and tax cuts.

9. For example, the school enrollment rate of Americans between twenty and twenty-one increased 3.3 percentage points, to 51.7 percent. If the enrollment rate in this age group had risen at the trend rate observed from 1995 to 2007, the 2009 enrollment rate would have been only 50.0 percent, or 1.7 percentage points lower than it actually was. Among young adults between twenty-two and twenty-four, the school enrollment rate increased 3.1 percentage points between 2007 and 2009, more than four times the enrollment gain that would have been predicted on the basis of the trend

from 1995 to 2007. See U.S. Census Bureau, "Table A-2. Percentage of the Population 3 Years Old and Over Enrolled in School, by Age, Sex, Race, and Hispanic Origin: October 1947 to 2009," http://www.census.gov/popula tion/socdemo/school/TableA-2.xls; accessed June 3, 2011.

10. See CNN Opinion Research, Poll, press release, January 25, 2010, http:// i2.cdn.turner.com/cnn/2010/images/01/25/rel1g.pdf; accessed June 3, 2011.

References

Aizenman, Joshua, and Gurnain Kaur Pasricha. 2010. "On the Ease of Overstating the Fiscal Stimulus in the US, 2008–9." NBER Working Paper No. 15784. Cambridge, Mass.: National Bureau of Economic Research.

——. 2011. "Net Fiscal Stimulus During the Great Recession." NBER Working Paper No. 16779. Cambridge, Mass.: National Bureau of Economic Research.

Altshuler, Rosanne, Leonard Burman, Howard Gleckman, Dan Halperin, Ben Harris, Elaine Maag, Kim Rueben, Eric Toder, and Roberton Williams. 2009. *Tax Stimulus Report Card: Conference Bill as of February 13, 2009.* Washington, D.C.: Urban Institute and Brookings Institution Tax Policy Center. Available at: http://www.urban.org/UploadedPDF/411839_conference_reportcard.pdf; accessed June 2, 2011.

Auerbach, Alan, and Daniel Feenberg. 2000. "The Significance of Federal Taxes and Automatic Stabilizers." *Journal of Economic Perspectives* 14(3; Summer): 37–56.

Blinder, Alan, and Mark Zandi. 2010. "How the Great Recession Was Brought to an End." Available at: http://www.economy.com/mark-zandi/documents/ End-of-Great-Recession.pdf; accessed June 2, 2011.

Brown, E. Cary. 1956. "Fiscal Policy in the 1930s: A Reappraisal." *American Economic Review* 46(December): 857–79.

Buettner, Thiess, and David E. Wildasin. 2006. "The Dynamics of Municipal Fiscal Adjustment." *Journal of Public Economics* 90(6–7): 1115–32.

Burtless, Gary. 2007. "Comment." In *Labor Supply in the New Century*, edited by Katherine Bradbury, Christopher L. Foote, and Robert K. Triest. Boston, Mass.: Federal Reserve Bank of Boston.

Carlino, Gerald A., and Robert P. Inman. 2010. "State Fiscal Policy and the Economic Crisis: Does the Obama Stimulus Make Sense?" 46th Annual American Real Estate and Urban Economics Association Conference Paper. November 29.

Cogan, John F., and John B. Taylor. 2010. "What the Government Purchases Multiplier Actually Multiplied in the 2009 Stimulus Package." NBER Working Paper No. 16505. Cambridge, Mass.: National Bureau of Economic Research.

Dolls, Mathias, Clemens Fuest, and Andreas Peichl. 2010. "Automatic Stabilizers and Economic Crisis: U.S. vs. Europe." NBER Working Paper No. 16275. Cambridge, Mass.: National Bureau of Economic Research.

Elmendorf, Douglas. 2009. "A Year-by-Year Estimate of the Economic Effects of the American Recovery and Reinvestment Act of 2009 (ARRA, Public Law 111-5)." A letter to Senator Charles E. Grassley from CBO Director Elmendorf,

March 2, 2009. Available at: http://www.cbo.gov/ftpdocs/100xx/doc10008/03-02-Macro_Effects_of_ARRA.pdf; accessed February 22, 2011.

Feyrer, James, and Bruce Sacerdote. 2011. "Did the Stimulus Stimulate? Real Time Estimates of the Effects of the American Readjustment and Recovery Act." NBER Working Paper No. 16759. Cambridge, Mass.: National Bureau of Economic Research.

Follette, Glenn, and Byron Lutz. 2010. "Fiscal Policy in the United States: Automatic Stabilizers, Discretionary Fiscal Policy Actions, and the Economy." Finance and Economics Discussion Series No. Paper 2010-43. Washington: Federal Reserve Board, Divisions of Research and Statistics and Monetary Affairs.

Gramlich, Edward M., and Harvey Galper. 1978. "State and Local Fiscal Behavior and Federal Grant Policy," *Brookings Papers on Economic Activity* 1978(1): 15–65.

Kaiser Family Foundation, Kaiser Commission on Medicaid and the Uninsured. 2010. "Medicaid Enrollment: December 2009 Data Snapshot." Medicaid Facts (website). Washington, D.C.: Kaiser Family Foundation, September. Available at: http://www.kff.org/medicaid/upload/8050-02.pdf; accessed August 24, 2011.

———. 2011. "Medicaid Enrollment: June 2010 Data Snapshot." Medicaid Facts (website). Washington, D.C.: Kaiser Family Foundation, February. Available at: http://www.kff.org/medicaid/upload/8050-03.pdf; accessed August 24, 2011.

Kuttner, Kenneth N., and Adam S. Posen. 2001. "The Great Recession: Lessons for Macroeconomic Policy from Japan," *Brookings Papers on Economic Activity* 32: 93–186.

Landefeld, J. Steven, Brent R. Moulton, Joel D. Platt, and Shaunda M. Villones. 2010. "GDP and Beyond: Measuring Economic Progress and Sustainability." *Survey of Current Business* 90(April): 12–25.

National Conference of State Legislatures. 2010. "State Budget Update: November 2010." Report. Available at: http://www.ncsl.org/documents/fiscal/november2010sbu_free.pdf; accessed June 2, 2011.

Organisation for Economic Co-operation and Development. 2007. "Benefits and Wages: OECD Indicators, 2007." Paris: OECD.

Phillippe, Kent, and Christopher M. Mullin. 2011. "Community College Estimated Growth: Fall 2010." Report. Washington, D.C.: American Association of Community Colleges.

Sahm, Claudia R., Matthew D. Shapiro, and Joel Slemrod. 2009. "Household Response to the 2008 Tax Rebates: Survey Evidence and Aggregate Implications," Finance and Economics Discussion Series Working Paper No. 2009-45. Washington: Federal Reserve Board.

U.S. Bureau of Labor Statistics. 2005. "Employer Costs for Employee Compensation, March 2005." News release. Publication No. USDL 05-1056. Washington: U.S. Bureau of Labor Statistics.

———. 2010a. "College Enrollment and Work Activity of 2009 High School Graduates." Economic news release. USDL 11-0462. Washington: U.S. Bureau of Labor Statistics.

———. 2010b. *Current Employment Statistics* Survey (National). Available at: http://stats.bls.gov/data/#employment; accessed January 18, 2011.

U.S. Census Bureau. 2011. "Quarterly Summary of State and Local Government Tax Revenue." Available at: http://www.census.gov/govs/qtax/; accessed February 2, 2011.

U.S. Congressional Budget Office. 2009. "Selected Tables." Available at: www .cbo.gov/ftpdocs/99xx/doc9957/selected_tables.xls; accessed June 20, 2011.

————. 2011. "Estimated Impact of the American Recovery and Reinvestment Act on Employment and Economic Output from October 2010 through December 2010." Washington: Congressional Budget Office.

U.S. Department of Commerce, Bureau of Economic Analysis. n.d. "Effect of the ARRA on Selected Government Transactions." available at: http://www.bea .gov/recovery/pdf/arra_impact_table_01.pdf; accessed February 4, 2011.

————. 2011. "National Income and Product Accounts Table 2.1: Personal Income and Its Disposition." Available at: http://bea.gov/national/nipaweb/ TableView.asp?SelectedTable=58&Freq=Qtr&FirstYear=2006&LastYear=2010; accessed February 4, 2011.

U.S. Department of Education. 2009. "Guidance on the State Fiscal Stabilization Fund Program." Available at: http://www.ed.gov/programs/statestabiliza tion/guidance.pdf; accessed June 2, 2011.

U.S. Department of Labor, Employment and Training Administration. 2011a. "Emergency Unemployment Compensation 2008 Data: National Data by Month by Tier." Available at: http://www.workforcesecurity.doleta.gov/un employ/docs/euc/euc_activity.xls; accessed February 22, 2011.

————. 2011b. "Federal-State Extended Benefit Program: National Data by Month." Available at: http://www.ows.doleta.gov/unemploy/docs/eb/ eb_activity.xls; accessed February 22, 2011.

————. 2011c. "Federal Additional Compensation Disbursements." Available at: http://workforcesecurity.doleta.gov/unemploy/fac.asp; accessed February 22, 2011.

U.S. House of Representatives, Committee on Ways and Means. 2000. *The 2000 Green Book: Background Material and Data on Programs within the Jurisdiction of the Committee on Ways and Means.* Washington: U.S. GPO.

Vroman, Wayne. 2009. "Unemployment Insurance in the American Recovery and Reinvestment Act (HR1)." Washington, D.C.: Urban Institute. Available at: http://www.urban.org/publications/411851.html; accessed June 2, 2011.

Wilson, Daniel J. 2010. "Fiscal Spending Multipliers: Evidence from the 2009 American Recovery and Reinvestment Act." Working Paper No. 2010-17. San Francisco: Federal Reserve Bank of San Francisco.

Chapter 10

Has the Great Recession Made Americans Stingier?

Rob Reich, Christopher Wimer, Shazad Mohamed,
and Sharada Jambulapati

Americans have long been, and continue to be, a particularly charitable people. Whereas Europeans have well-developed and comprehensive welfare states, the United States has always relied more on private charity to support a multitude of causes, including aid and assistance to the poor (Alesina and Glaeser 2004). But how does this proclivity to engage in charity play out during economic downturns? Does it increase as well-off Americans respond to the rising needs that a recession spawns? Or have Americans and American institutions tightened the purse strings during hard times, despite rising needs? In this chapter we examine such questions by examining data from the Great Recession and comparing them to earlier time periods.

Marshaling data from a variety of sources, we document substantial drops in charitable giving since the beginning of the recession in late 2007. These declines have come from all sources (individuals, corporations, foundations) and have hit virtually all types of nonprofits (human services organizations, arts organizations, education organizations). Our most significant finding, therefore, is that Americans are not responding to the greater needs of citizens during the Great Recession by increasing their charitable giving; this is true even when we isolate giving to the human and social service organizations whose mission is to provide for people's basic needs.

There are two notable exceptions to the downturn in giving. The most prominent of these is giving to religious organizations, which have fared comparatively well in the current recession and indeed have seen an increase in giving (not included in the category of religious organizations are faith-based social service organizations, which are considered part of the human and social service category). The other exception is giving to the nation's major food banks, which have seen continued and accelerated increases in giving so far in the recession. This trend has not previously been documented and suggests at least one area of increased giving targeting the increased number of hungry Americans suffering during the downturn.

We next document how the declines in giving in the current recession mirror changes in past severe economic downturns and show how nonprofits are struggling and adapting to scarcer times. There is some evidence that the downturn in giving during this recession is greater than in previous recessions.

Finally, we take a look at non-pecuniary forms of giving, namely volunteering, and show that among younger demographic groups we may be seeing a shift toward increased volunteering that stands in contrast to the decline in monetary gifts.

Overall, however, the nonprofit sector is facing declining resources during the Great Recession. This contraction has profound implications for the well-being of the poor and the dislocated segments of American society, who more than their counterparts elsewhere in the developed world rely heavily on nonprofit organizations in civil society, which in turn depend on charitable donations to meet societal needs.

Before turning to an exploration of this contraction, it is worth noting the paucity of high-quality social science research on the charitable sector in general and the near absence of any research on trends in the charitable sector during economic downturns and recessions. The standard reference text for research on the nonprofit sector (Powell and Steinberg 2006) includes no discussion about charity during downturns. We uncovered a few scattered reports on the topic, all of which reach the unsurprising conclusion that charitable giving drops during economic downturns (Giving USA Foundation 2008; Mohan and Wilding 2009; Sherlock and Gravelle 2009). When individuals have fewer resources, because of either wage stagnation or loss of income through job loss or fewer hours of available work, individuals cut back on their charitable giving.

We attempt to go further than restating this commonsensical finding in this chapter by examining, when possible, the precise amount by which giving drops and the types of giving that are most affected.

To gain purchase on the problem, we begin by considering that charitable giving in the United States comes from four sources: individual giving, individual charitable bequests, foundation giving, and corporate giving. Individual giving by live and dead donors is by a significant margin the largest of the three sources, accounting for roughly 80 percent of all charitable dollars. The consequence is that trends in charitable giving are driven mainly by actions of individual donors, and individual donors turn out to be sensitive to dramatic changes in the economy that affect their income and wealth. This is true, it turns out, of foundations and corporate giving as well, but our primary focus here is on individual giving because it accounts for the vast majority of charitable giving.

Data and Methods

The chief source of data on charitable giving over time is the Giving USA Foundation, an organization devoted to promoting research, education, and public understanding of philanthropy. Giving USA estimates, for every year since 1968, the amount of giving for four different types of giving sources and nine types of giving recipients. We now turn to a description of how these data were collected and estimated. (For a more detailed description of the methods employed to generate the trends discussed here, see Giving USA Foundation 2010).

The 2009 information for giving by individuals uses Internal Revenue Service (IRS) data on itemized deductions from individual tax returns for 2007. Estimated changes in charitable contributions by households that itemize and don't itemize their contributions are then added for 2008 and 2009. The estimate for non-itemized contributions was derived from the Center on Philanthropy Panel Study (COPPS), which determines information on charitable contributions based on a survey of 7,800 households (Giving USA Foundation 2010). Initial estimates on giving developed based on COPPS data in 2004 have been subsequently adjusted for changes in income and the number of households that do not itemize their deductions since 2005. Estimates for changes in individual giving incorporate information regarding changes in individual income, tax rates, and market movements on the basis of the value of S&P 500 Index. Individual income is estimated using data on "Personal Income and Outlays" from the Department of Commerce, Bureau of Economic Analysis (Giving USA Foundation 2010). Changes in the year-end S&P 500 index are added to account for wealth effects of high-income individuals, who tend to be major charitable donors. The current maximum tax rate is incorporated to account for the effect that changes in tax rates have on predicated levels of giving.

The estimates for giving by bequest are based on data collected by the Council for Aid to Education on bequests to institutions of higher education (Giving USA Foundation 2010). The data are then used to estimate bequests to all charities, extrapolating from estates that file estate tax returns. The estimate is then added to a number that represents bequests on behalf of estates below the tax filing level. The 2009 numbers are based on bequests reported from 2008 and 2009. Historically, Council for Aid to Education data have represented 13.7 percent of bequests made to all charities, as calculated from estate tax returns. The number generated from this calculation is then added to additional amounts estimated to have been filed on tax returns in 2009, inferred from announced gifts from 2007. The process of reporting major gifts on returns generally takes two years. For estimates on bequests below the estate tax level of $2 million required for federal estate tax reporting, the following information is used to determine the value added to the described formula: the number of deaths of adults age fifty-five and over, average net worth in that age group, and average percentage of assets left to charity in that age group.

The figures for foundation giving are calculated from Foundation Center data for giving levels in 2009 (the data do not include money given by Warren Buffett to the Bill & Melinda Gates Foundation). The estimate is based on a survey sent out by the Foundation Center to 5,000 corporate and community foundations to determine levels of giving for 2009. The results were compiled from 1,225 responses received from the survey (Giving USA Foundation 2010).

Giving by corporations includes itemized contributions by companies as reported on IRS tax returns. Those figures are modified by deducting corporate contributions to corporate foundations and incorporating giving by corporate foundations to beneficiaries. Giving to corporate foundations is based on the Foundation Center's survey of foundations used to estimate relative levels of corporate foundation giving in 2009. Additional estimates are based on changes in the corporate tax rate to estimate the level of giving based on the relative change in maximum tax levels. Increases in gross domestic product (GDP) are also factored into the estimate derived (Giving USA Foundation 2010).

Giving to religion is based on a baseline of $50 billion of estimated giving in 1986 to religious organizations. The number is then modified based on the percentage change in giving using data by the National Council of Churches of Christ of USA and the Roman Catholic Church on the basis of surveys, and amounts reported by the Evangelical Council for Financial Accountability. The amount given to Protestant groups is based on data compiled from the *Yearbook of American and Canadian Churches* (Giving USA Foundation 2010). Giving to nonreporting groups is based on estimated per capita averages, and giving to other religious groups is estimated based on the availability of data making use of Protestant per capita averages where no data are available. Data for each year are based on the average inflation-adjusted change over a period of three years. The multiyear average is determined as the final estimate for changes in year-over-year giving.

Figure 10.1   Charitable Giving Declines with Economic Downturn

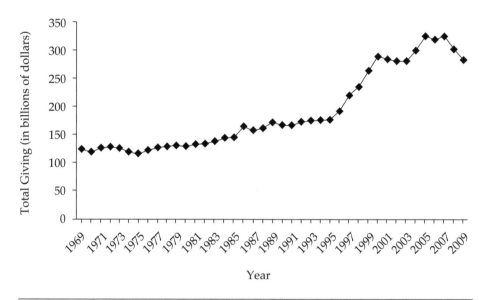

Source: Authors' compilation based on data from Giving USA Foundation (2010).
Note: Amounts are in inflation-adjusted dollars.

Estimates in giving to each subsector are derived from the method used to determine individual levels of giving. The estimate is based on the projected change in giving based on personal income, the S&P 500 index, lagged giving from previous years, and previous subsector contributions. The estimate is then combined with the previous year's data to determine the 2009 total estimated giving per subsector. Taken together, the Giving USA data provide the most comprehensive and reliable data available on long-term trends in charitable giving. Though individual assumptions used to generate estimates may be debated, these data nevertheless represent the most accurate picture of changes over time in overall giving, giving by source, and giving by recipient type. We turn to these results now.

Trends in Overall Giving

The economic downturn of 2008 has given rise to one of the largest year-over-year declines in charitable giving since the late 1960s (see figure 10.1). Total giving in 2008 fell by 7 percent in inflation-adjusted dollars, from $326.57 billion to $303.76 billion. In 2009, things got yet worse, with charitable giving dropping another 6.2 percent, to approximately $284.85

Figure 10.2   Declines in Giving Attributable Mostly to Declines in Available Money

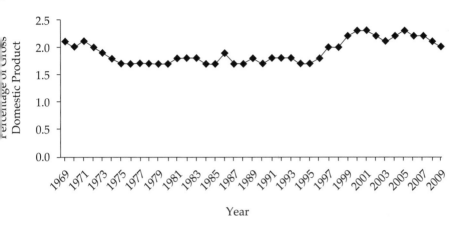

Source: Authors' compilation based on data from Giving USA Foundation (2010).

billion. Estimated giving in 2010 was $290.89 billion, a modest uptick reflecting, we suspect, a modestly improved economy. Overall, charitable giving has dropped 4.2 percent between 2008 and 2010. Despite this drop, charitable giving remains at extraordinarily and historically high levels, with only 2005 to 2007 showing higher levels of overall giving.

Such a large reduction might not indicate that Americans are giving a smaller proportion of their income than they used to. Can this reduction in giving be understood as merely reflecting the economic decline and hence the smaller amount of money that is available for charitable purposes? Are we giving the same proportion of (declining) GDP to charitable causes?

The answer is a resounding "almost." Giving as a percentage of GDP has fallen only slightly in the last year, declining from 2.1 percent in 2008 to 2.0 percent in both 2009 and 2010, declining from an all-time high of 2.3 percent in 2005 (see figure 10.2). Thus, the recent decline in absolute giving is tracking overall downward trends in the broader economy. Figure 10.2 shows that total charitable giving as a percentage of GDP has fluctuated within a relatively narrow band, from 1.7 percent to 2.3 percent, over the past forty years. Although not shown here, the stability of relative giving levels is further indicated by trends in charitable donations as a percentage of either individual disposable income or essential personal outlays. In both cases, there is little or no change over the past two years, again suggesting that declines in giving are attributable to declines in available money, not to some ratcheted-up selfishness that kicks in during economic hard times. Indeed, two recent Harris Interactive polls, conducted in January 2009 and September 2010, confirm that, as a result of the current economy, Americans are giving smaller amounts to charities (31 percent in both polls), and to fewer organizations (24 percent and 19 percent, respectively)—evidence that is consistent with the idea that charitable giving is contracting due to economic belt-tightening (Krane 2010). There is evidence, moreover, that some people have stopped giving altogether, as 12 percent of those surveyed in the 2010 survey reported giving nothing, up from 6 percent in 2009. We might expect that, as the economy emerges from recession, these people will return to giving at pre-recession levels.

Charitable giving, then, appears to operate in something approaching a cyclical manner, contracting during hard times and expanding as incomes rise. Need is countercyclical, not surprisingly, increasing as the economic pie contracts.

Giving by Source

The four main sources of giving are individuals, charitable bequests, corporations, and foundations. Have any of these sources been immune to the overall trends presented above? We might not expect any major differences by source given that individuals, corporations, and foundations alike have all suffered greatly in the Great Recession, albeit in different ways. Whereas individuals and corporations have suffered because economic activity is down (thereby affecting earnings, employment, profits), foundations and bequests suffer as a result of losses in the stock market and other investments.

And indeed, as expected, all four sources have been affected by the downturn, albeit in different ways (see figures 10.3 and figure 10.4). Giving by individuals, by far the largest source of charitable contributions, saw a decline to $216.7 billion in 2008, an 8.3 percent decline compared to 2007. In 2009, individual giving declined a further 3.6 percent. In 2010 we see a modest recovery of an estimated 2.7 percent, with the result of a modest 2008 to 2010 cumulative change of –1.0 percent in individual giving. Charitable bequests, the most volatile of all sources of giving, jumped by more than $7 billion in the first year of the recession but then fell by a whopping 38.5 percent in 2009. In 2010, bequests rose an estimated 16.9 percent, with the result being a cumulative change of –21.6 percent in giving by bequest from 2008 to 2010. Contributions by corporations continued a multiyear decline in 2008, falling 16 percent to $12.6 billion. But corporate giving picked up in 2009 by nearly 12 percent, to $14.1 billion, and rose again in 2010 by nearly 9 percent, to $15.3 billion.

Figure 10.3   Decline in Individual Giving in 2008

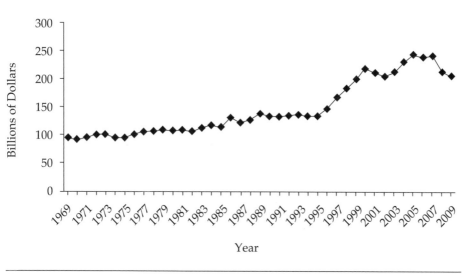

Source: Authors' compilation based on data from Giving USA Foundation (2010).

The decline up to 2009 extends a trend that has played out since the major spike in donations following the Indian Ocean tsunami in 2004.

Although giving by foundations inched upward from 2007 to 2008, foundation giving dropped by 2.4 percent in 2009 and continued an estimated modest decline of 1.8 percent in 2010. Foundation spending is governed by strict payout and operating rules that typically reflect changes in market conditions across multiple years rather than an immediate reaction to developments in any single year. Although such averaging formulas likely served to protect against a sudden drop in 2008, they offered less protection as the downturn protracted into 2009. As we show later, many of the nonprofits relying on foundation funding have found 2009 to be even more challenging than 2008, which is consistent with the portrait painted by the Giving USA data. The Foundation Center has noted that things could have been much worse in 2009 if not for the Bill & Melinda Gates Foundation increasing its giving to cope with the recession, and for other foundations slashing their operating funds in order to maintain as high giving levels as possible.

While foundation funding dropped in 2009, some research suggests that foundations also shifted strategy as the recession deepened, and in ways that intelligently directed resources to areas hardest hit by the crisis (see Preston 2010). Douglas Holtz-Eakin, the former director of the

Figure 10.4   **Corporate, Bequest, and Foundation Funding Drop During Great Recession, 2007 to 2009**

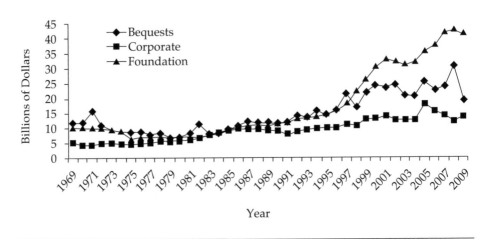

Source: Authors' compilation based on data from Giving USA Foundation (2010).

Congressional Budget Office, and Cameron Smith, harnessing data from a sample of 2,672 foundation grants made between 2008 and 2010, found that in 2009 and 2010 foundations directed a greater proportion of their grants to areas with high levels of unemployment and high levels of mortgage delinquency rates (Holtz-Eakin and Smith 2010). For example, in 2008, 563 grants totaling $126 million went to low-unemployment states, while high-unemployment states received only 422 grants worth $29.9 million. But in 2009 the pattern reversed, with high-unemployment states receiving 803 grants worth $200 million and low-unemployment states receiving 706 grants worth $112 million. In general, as the recession deepened, states and localities with larger problems began receiving a larger share of foundation funding, suggesting a certain level of adaptiveness among American foundations (Preston 2010).

It appears that charities are also being hurt by reduced giving from cash-strapped state and local governments. According to a recent report by the National Council of Nonprofits (2010) that examined state and local budget trends, governments are increasingly cutting programs similar to programs that nonprofits run and expecting nonprofits to pick up the slack, withholding contract payments for services already rendered by nonprofits, and imposing new fees and taxes on nonprofits that further drain these nonprofits' operating funds. Thus, in addition

Figure 10.5   Declines in Giving Experienced by Most Types of Charitable Organizations, by Category, Part One

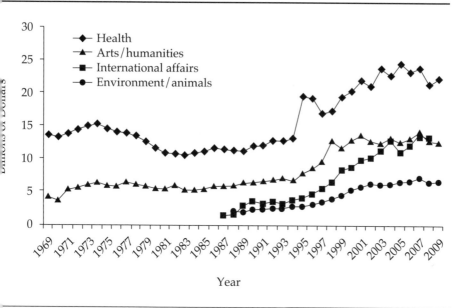

Source: Authors' compilation based on data from Giving USA Foundation (2010).

to receiving less from all forms of donors, nonprofits are also being challenged by the actions of strapped state and local governments.

Have All Recipients Been Equally Harmed by the Recession?

So far, we have seen that giving has dropped across the board from all sources, but we can also look at whether all types of recipients have experienced comparable declines in funding. In other words, are some types of recipient organizations more protected than others in recessionary times? Figures 10.5, 10.6, and 10.7 show that seven out of nine subsectors tracked by the Giving USA Foundation (2010) saw declines in funds raised between 2007 and 2008. As can be seen in figure 10.5, giving to health-related organizations (hospitals, clinics, and other institutions) fell 10 percent from the previous year, to $21.55 billion, before rebounding a bit in 2009. Donations to arts and humanities organizations also saw a decline of 10 percent, to $12.59 billion, and fell a more modest 2 percent in 2009. Contributions to environment and animal-welfare and

Figure 10.6   Declines in Giving Experienced by Most Types of Charitable Organizations, by Category, Part Two

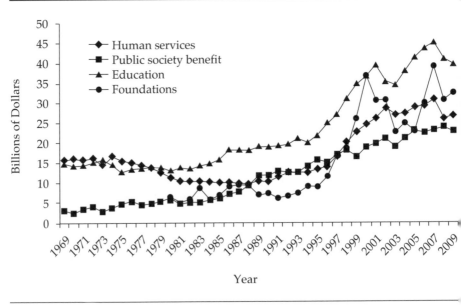

Source: Authors' compilation based on data from Giving USA Foundation (2010).

Figure 10.7   The Persistence of Giving to Religious Organizations

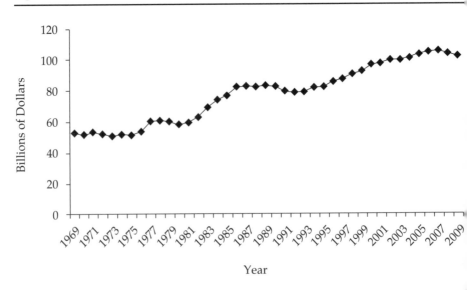

Source: Authors' compilation based on data from Giving USA Foundation (2010).

conservation groups managed to rise by approximately 9 percent in 2008 but then fell 9 percent, to $5.99 billion, in 2009. Giving to international affairs organizations, which includes charities focusing on international development, aid, and relief, saw a decline of only 3 percent, to $13.5 billion, in 2008, before rebounding and rising 3 percent to $13.9 billion in 2009 and then growing to an estimated $15.8 billion in 2010. This is the largest growth category in all of charitable giving and reflects an increasing interest in international causes by individual donors and, especially, by foundations.

Giving to education fell 6.7 percent to $42.5 billion in 2008 and then another 5.3 percent to $40.25 billion in 2009 (see figure 10.6). Donations to human services organizations—which include organizations focused on vocational and educational training, food and nutrition, public safety and housing—saw a decline of 15.9 percent, to $26.22 billion, in 2008, before rebounding slightly (2.6 percent) to $26.9 billion in 2009. Giving to foundations declined by 21 percent from 2007 to 2008, reversing a significant rise in contributions starting in 2005. But giving to foundations rebounded in 2009 by nearly 6 percent, to $32.9 billion. As mentioned, this net decline over the period portends bad things for foundation giving in coming years, since such giving is largely determined by multiyear formulas that have not yet taken into account 2009 portfolios.

Giving to religious organizations—which includes houses of worship and governing bodies of faith groups and excludes faith-based charities and service organizations—fell by a modest amount in 2008, 3 percent, to $101.25 billion (see figure 10.7). In 2009, giving to religious organizations barely changed. Indeed, a separate study of the financial statements of 1,148 religious organizations by the Evangelical Council for Financial Accountability found that contributions declined by just 0.1 percent from 2007 to 2009, though declines were larger for groups with smaller budgets (Hall 2010). Giving to religious organizations is, by a large margin, the biggest category of charitable giving in the United States, accounting for more than a third of all giving. While such giving might be thought to be directed at the needy, since some religious congregations provide benefits for the needy outside of religious services, studies indicate that only about 10 percent of the funds of religious organizations go to the provision of social services (Wuthnow 2004, 94).

Thus, religious organizations seem to be faring fairly well in the current recession, while organizations devoted to providing human services, providing education, or attending to people's health have all seen steep drops in funding levels.

The last subsector tracked by Giving USA consists of "public society benefit" organizations (see figure 10.6), a category that includes organizations such as the United Way, Jewish federations, and others. Giving to public society benefit organizations also comprises contributions for research in biological, physical, and social sciences as well as public policy research funding, community and economic development, voter education, and consumer protection groups. Giving to public society benefit organizations rose 1.6 percent from 2007 to 2008 but then fell in 2009 by approximately 4.4 percent, to $23.2 billion. In summary, then, when we divide charitable giving by recipient type, we see that the organizations suffering the most are those, such as human services organizations, whose clear mission is to serve the neediest among us, and organizations targeting more niche or "luxury" concerns such as arts and environmental organizations. Religious institutions and public society benefit organizations have fared relatively better.

Food Banks in the Great Recession— A Silver Lining?

Giving USA only measures broad categories of recipients, which makes the data an imperfect barometer of how sensitive donors are to causes geared toward the needy as opposed to other causes. Then we read an article in *The Chronicle of Philanthropy* noting that the national Feeding America organization was experiencing surging levels of giving, up more than 50 percent in the final quarter of 2009 over the same quarter the year before (Preston 2010). We decided to examine food banks in America's largest cities to find out whether they were seeing comparable surges in giving.

To explore this, we developed a list of the fifty largest cities, by population size, and identified the largest food bank in each city. We then attempted, for each food bank, to collect data for each year from at least 2007 to 2009 on contributions and grants. Our information sources were annual reports, financial statements such as IRS 990 forms (on which nonprofits report total grants and contributions), and archived information in Charity Navigator (http://www.charitynavigator.org) and the GuideStar database (http://www.guidestar.org). We were able to obtain complete data to 2009 for forty of these fifty cities (the results are shown in figure 10.8).[1] Total funding to food banks in these cities rose 2.2 percent from 2007 to 2008, with approximately two-thirds of food banks showing increases over this period. Funding then surged from 2008 to 2009, as the recession deepened, by a staggering 31.9 percent despite deepening problems in the labor market. Increases in donations were found across all but one of the forty food banks. The average food bank in our sample gained $637,176 in contributions and grants between 2007 and 2008 and gained nearly $9.4 million in contributions between 2008 and 2009. Feeding America estimates the cost per meal provided by its network of food banks to be approximately $1.93, meaning that (if all funds had gone directly toward meal provision) the average food bank

Figure 10.8   **The Surge in Total Food Bank Donations in Forty of the Largest U.S. Cities, 2009**

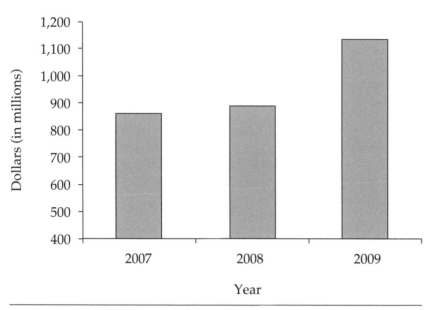

Year

Source: Authors' tabulations based on data collected by the authors from multiple sources, including contribution and grant records from food banks' annual reports, Internal Revenue Service Form 990s, and GuideStar/Charity Navigator records.

in our sample was able to provide roughly 4.87 million additional meals in 2009 thanks to increased levels of contributions.

The Great Recession Versus Prior Downturns

It is perhaps unsurprising that overall giving levels have declined during the current recession. Have these declines been more or less extreme than those experienced in past severe economic downturns? One way to approach this question is to look at what happened during the greatest economic collapse in modern American history, the Great Depression. In 1950, in *Philanthropic Giving*, a pioneering study of philanthropy, Frank Emerson Andrews (1950) published data on philanthropic giving by living donors from 1929 to 1949 (Andrews was the director of publications at the Russell Sage Foundation). This compilation helped shed light on the question of earlier giving patterns. Though the data must be interpreted with caution given changes in income tax reporting over this period, Andrews shows that giving dropped substantially during the early years of the Great Depression before recovering as the economy exited

Figure 10.9   Percent Change in Giving and Unemployment After Three Economic Shocks: 1930, 1974, and 2008

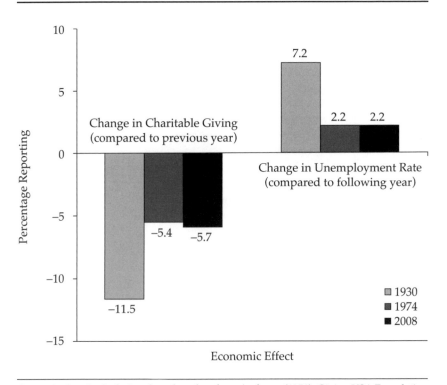

Source: Authors' calculations based on data from Andrews (1950), Giving USA Foundation (2010), and U.S. Bureau of Labor Statistics (2011).

recession, only to fall again as the country experienced a "double dip" in 1937 (Andrews 1950). Giving also declined in the economic slump after 1973, following the economic crisis spurred by the food and oil crises of that year. On the flip side, neither the severe recession of the early 1980s nor the milder recession of the early 1990s led to dips in giving, but dips in giving followed the Savings and Loan crisis in the late 1980s and the recession of the early 2000s. In general, then, it appears that charitable giving does contract substantially in recessionary years, especially in recessions generated by large shocks to the economy and the market.

Figure 10.9 provides a closer look at three severe downturns in the economy: 1930 (following the stock market crash of 1929 that sent the United States into the Great Depression), 1974 (following the food and oil shocks of 1973), and 2008 (following the turmoil generated by the subprime mortgage crisis and near collapse of the financial industry). In the left panel of figure 10.9, we show the changes in charitable giving in the year immediately following these economic shocks. In the right panel, we show the increase in unemployment during that same year. The results starkly demonstrate the similarities between these three years in terms of the proportional change in unemployment and in charitable giving.

Large Donors

Many of the major accomplishments of the nonprofit sector were made possible by large donations. Extremely large donations create foundations, launch major new initiatives, and push nonprofits toward high-profile ventures with the potential for bringing about meaningful change. Of course, extremely large donations typically come from the extremely wealthy. Wealth at the very top has taken a big hit because of declines in the stock market and in real estate wealth (see chapter 5 of this volume, by Edward N. Wolff, Lindsay A. Owens, and Esra Burak). Has this led to similar drops in the number or size of the very largest donations? Between 2000 and 2009, the number of donations of more than $100 million each dropped by 38 percent, from twenty-one to thirteen. Although thirteen is still high by historical standards, this is a substantial drop-off from recent years. Large donations have also dropped in size. Since 2000, the news organization *Slate* has been tracking the Slate 60, or the top sixty philanthropic givers and the size of their gifts each year. According to our analysis of their data, both the total contributions of the Slate 60 and the average Slate 60 gift amount dropped markedly in 2009. This is confirmed by a recent study published by the Center on Philanthropy at Indiana University (2010), which found that high-net-worth households' average annual gift amounts fell by approximately 35 percent between 2007 and 2009.

The Nonprofit Sector: Survival and Adaptation

As delineated in the methodology section, the Giving USA data rely on a set of assumptions partially based on projections forward from data collected prior to the onset of the recession. A skeptic might wonder whether these assumptions are defensible and whether we can trust evidence of the declines in giving documented in these data. It's useful in this context to consider how nonprofit organizations see their situations. Are nonprofits "feeling" the challenges that the dips suggested by the Giving USA data entail?

The short answer is yes. An online survey of 2,279 charities and foundations (92 percent and 8 percent of the sample, respectively) conducted by the nonprofit research firm GuideStar found that over two-thirds of nonprofits in that survey and in a similar survey roughly six months earlier reported smaller individual gifts, and roughly the same fraction reported fewer individual gifts (McLean and Brouwer 2009). Over a third reported smaller corporate and foundation gifts as well. Smaller, but still significant, numbers of nonprofits reported discontinued gifts and grants, smaller and discontinued government grants, and smaller and discontinued government contracts. Overall, then, nonprofits confirm that they are facing a severely challenging environment with reduced funding from a variety of sources.

How are nonprofits responding to this harsher funding environment? The same two surveys show that nonprofits are adapting in a variety of ways that in general would be likely to result in decreased capacity to meet the needs of their clientele, especially at a time when those needs have increased considerably. Over half of nonprofits reported reducing program services in response to economic challenges, and nearly half reported freezing staff salaries. Approximately a third reported freezing their hiring, and nearly a third reported laying off staff. Smaller, but again still substantial, percentages of organizations reported reducing salaries, reducing employee benefits, and reducing operating hours. Thus, the array of adaptation strategies adopted by nonprofits is likely to have resulted in decreased capacity for services as well as decreased employment and pay in the nonprofit sector as a whole.

Volunteering

Up to this point, we have treated charitable giving solely in terms of dollars and cents, but people can make charitable gifts of their time as well as their money, and there are at least two good reasons why we might expect volunteering to increase during the Great Recession. First, as people struggle to find work and as people lose work, more people have time on their hands. Volunteering provides a good potential to find paid employment and to polish one's résumé. Second, workers who find themselves unable to financially contribute as they once did may choose to give of themselves in other ways, most obviously by giving their time. To try to quantify this trend we looked at data for volunteering rates up to 2009. Data came from the Corporation for National & Community Service's Volunteering in America database, which in turn is based on annual data on volunteering collected in the Current Population Survey (CPS) September Volunteer Supplement (U.S. Bureau of Labor Statistics 2010).

From 2007 to 2008, the CPS data show small though marked increases in rates of volunteering on the part of younger people and immigrants.

From 2008 to 2009, rates of volunteering rose again, this time primarily driven by adult women, particularly black women. Though modest in nature, these increases suggest that more Americans were volunteering in their communities as the recession deepened. Further analysis will be necessary to unpack why the uptick in volunteering has been confined to these demographic groups.

What It All Means

The purpose of this chapter was to find out whether the Great Recession, which has affected so many Americans, has induced us to scale back on our long-standing generosity and tend to our own needs. Have Americans, in response to economic duress, drawn inward and become (understandably) self-interested? There is little evidence of such an effect. Although total giving has declined, we are still giving at extremely high levels and at nearly the same proportion of income, or GDP, as before. Much as they always have, Americans are contributing an impressive proportion of their available funds, the main difference being that such "tithing" now applies to a smaller base of money and hence entails a decline in the absolute amount of giving. This overall reduction in absolute giving is occurring at a time when overall need is increasing—a particular and unfortunate countercyclical feature of the way this country deals with poverty and other social needs. Innovation in the nonprofit sector is likely to be stymied as nonprofits struggle merely to survive and as large donations shrink and dry up. Nonprofits, for their part, report that they are indeed feeling the pinch of the contracting economy and that they are cutting services and slashing payrolls in order to stay afloat. Although some segments of the population, notably young people, are pitching in with increased volunteering, the nonprofit sector is clearly stretched in the face of increasing needs.

In thinking about the likely patterns of giving in the future, it is important to recognize several political realities that may affect charitable giving. President Barack Obama proposed in 2009, in 2010, and again in early 2011 that the tax incentive for charitable donations—the charitable contributions deduction—be capped at 28 percent for the highest income earners, down from the current 35 percent for those in the 35 percent tax bracket. The proposal has two motivations: first, to limit the deduction in order to generate more revenue in order to close the deficit; and second, President Obama sees capping the deduction as a matter of fairness, attempting to level the incentive for all income earners rather than providing a larger incentive to the wealthiest Americans. Were this policy to be adopted, the incentive to give would drop, and giving by the wealthiest Americans might also drop. As a consequence, it is possible that wealthy Americans front-loaded their giving in 2009 and 2010, taking advantage of the full charitable contributions deduction while it was still available. As of this writing, President Obama's proposal had not been made into law.

In late 2010, several bipartisan commissions were formed for the purpose of making recommendations about how to reduce the deficit faced by the United States. Some of these recommended, among a battery of other measures, that the charitable contribution deduction be eliminated altogether or reduced more than President Obama had proposed. We don't know whether such recommendations will be adopted, but if they are, the short-term effect on giving by the wealthy will probably be significant. In the meantime, absent change in the tax incentive structure, a turnaround in the levels of charitable giving likely will await a significant turnaround in the economy.

We would like to thank the authors of all the other chapters in this book for their helpful feedback and suggestions. We would also like to thank Samri Tessema, Kendall Ernst, Nadiv Rahman, and Katie Rosman for their able research assistance in compiling trends on giving to food banks.

Note

1. We were able to obtain complete data for forty of the fifty cities. For the majority of the remaining ten cities, 2009 data were unavailable at the time of analysis. For others, data for one year in the 2007-to-2009 range were unavailable. The ten largest cities whose data were unavailable are Tulsa, Oklahoma; Omaha, Nebraska; Fresno, California; San Antonio, Texas; Philadelphia, Pennsylvania; San Diego, California; Houston, Texas; Jacksonville, Florida; Memphis, Tennessee; and Las Vegas, Nevada.

References

Alesina, Alberto, and Edward L. Glaeser. 2004. *Fighting Poverty in the US and Europe: A World of Difference.* Oxford: Oxford University Press.

Andrews, Frank Emerson. 1950. *Philanthropic Giving.* New York: Russell Sage Foundation.

Center on Philanthropy at Indiana University. 2010. *The 2010 Study of High Net Worth Philanthropy: Issues Driving Charitable Activities Among Affluent Households.* Indianapolis: Bank of America Merrill Lynch.

Giving USA Foundation. 2008. "Giving During Recessions and Economic Slowdowns." *Giving USA Spotlight*, no. 3.

———. 2010. *Giving USA 2010: The Annual Report on Philanthropy for the Year 2009.* Glenview, Ill.: Giving USA Foundation.

Hall, Holly. 2010. "Religious Groups Fared Better than Other Charities in the

Recession." *The Chronicle of Philanthropy Online Journal*, November 10, 2010. Available at: http://philanthropy.com/article/article-content/125338; accessed December 12, 2010.

Holtz-Eakin, Douglas, and Cameron Smith. 2010. "Responding in Crisis: An Early Analysis of Foundaitons' Grantmaking During the Economic Crisis." Report. Washington, D.C.: The Philanthropic Collaborative.

Krane, David. 2010. *The Harris Poll #135*, November 4, 2010. New York: Harris Interactive.

McLean, Chuck, and Carol Brouwer. 2009. "The Effect of the Economy on the Nonprofit Sector: March–May 2009." Report. Williamsburg, Va.: GuideStar.

Mohan, John, and Karl Wilding. 2009. "Economic Downturns and the Voluntary Sector: What Can We Learn from the Historical Evidence." *History and Policy* (online journal). Available at: http://www.historyandpolicy.org/papers/policy-paper-85.html; accessed June 6, 2011.

National Council of Nonprofits. 2010. "State Budget Crises: Ripping the Safety Net Held by Nonprofits." Special report. Washington, D.C.: National Council of Nonprofits (March 16).

Powell, Walter W., and Richard Steinberg. 2006. *The Non-Profit Sector: A Research Handbook*. New Haven: Yale University Press.

Preston, Caroline. 2010. "Foundations Get High Marks for Response to Economic Crisis." *The Chronicle of Philanthropy* (online journal), May 6. Available at: http://philanthropy.com/article/Foundations-Get-High-Marks-for/65423/?sid=&utm_source=&utm_medium=en; accessed June 6, 2011.

Sherlock, Molly, and Jane Gravelle. 2009. "An Overview of the Nonprofit and Charitable Sector." CRS Report for Congress. Washington, D.C.: Congressional Research Service, November 17.

U.S. Bureau of Labor Statistics. 2010. "News Release: Volunteering in the United States—2009." Available at: http://www.bls.gov/news.release/archives/volun_01262010.pdf ; accessed July 7, 2011.

———. 2011. "Labor Force Statistics from the Current Population Survey." Washington: Bureau of Labor Statistics. Available at: http://www.bls.gov/cps; accessed July 11, 2011.

Wuthnow, Robert. 2004. *Saving America? Faith-Based Services and the Future of Civil Society*. Princeton: Princeton University Press.

Index

Boldface numbers refer to figures and tables.

ACS (American Community Survey), 11, 76

adjustable-rate mortgages (ARMs), 41–42, 140

affluent Americans. *See* rich Americans

African Americans: consumer confidence, 174; foreclosures, 140; government role views, 211–12; mortgage delinquency, 136; personal financial situation perceptions, **175,** 176; underwater mortgages, 135; unemployment, 61, 75–76, 85

age analyses: consumption decisions, 178, **179**; mortgage delinquency, 137; personal financial situation perceptions, **175**; underwater mortgages, 135

Aguiar, Mark, 169–70

AIG (American International Group), 5, 26, 251

Aizenman, Joshua, 284, 290n8

Alabama: credit card debt, 142

Alaska: credit card debt and delinquencies, 141

Alt-A loans, **33,** 36–37, 47

alternative minimum tax (AMT), 270–71

American Community Survey (ACS), 11, 76

American International Group (AIG), 5, 26, 251

"American Opportunity credit," 271–72

American Recovery and Reinvestment Act (ARRA) (2009): anti-poverty efforts, 95, 98; components of, 276–77; enactment, 28, 261; federal deficit caused by, 263; overview of, 5; tax reductions, 269–72; unemployment insurance benefits, 97. *See also* federal stimulus programs

American Time Use Survey (ATUS), 170

Ameriquest, 43

AMT (alternative minimum tax), 270–71

Andrews, F. Emerson, 307–8

animal-welfare organizations, 303

anti-poverty programs, 95, 97–98

Antirecession Fiscal Assistance, Local Public Works, and Comprehensive Employment and Training Act, 283

apparel, consumer spending on, 169

Arizona: bankruptcies, 144–45; credit card delinquencies, 141; housing crisis, 23–24, 28, 40, 140

ARMs (adjustable-rate mortgages), 41–42, 140

ARRA (American Recovery and Reinvestment Act) (2009). *See* American Recovery and Reinvestment Act (ARRA) (2009)

arts and humanities charitable organizations, 303

asset price changes, 128, 131–32. *See also* housing prices

Associated Press: bankruptcies, 144

Atkinson, Anthony, 121n14
ATUS (American Time Use Survey), 170
Aubry, Jean-Pierre, 108
Auerbach, Alan, 253
automatic stabilization system, 252, 253–61
automobile industry, 26, 66, 165, 168–69, 251–52
Autor, David, 85, 86–88

baby boomers, 79
Bank of America, 26, 38, 45, 128, 147, 150
bankruptcy, 128, 143–45, 151
banks and banking: deregulation, 34, 66, 79; public opinion of, 201–4, 216; stress tests, 251; Troubled Asset Relief Program, 5, 26, 251–52. *See also* investment banks; mortgages; *specific banks*
Barber, Mike, 144
BEA (Bureau of Economic Analysis). *See* Bureau of Economic Analysis (BEA)
Bear Sterns, 5, 26, 34, 38, 44
bequests, 296–97, 300, **302**
Bernanke, Ben, 5, 42
Bill & Melinda Gates Foundation, 297, 301
Black Americans. *See* African Americans
Blank, Rebecca M., 89–91, 99
Blinder, Alan, 288, 290n7
BLS (Bureau of Labor Statistics). *See* Bureau of Labor Statistics (BLS)
blue states, recession perceptions, 226–32, 241
bonds, 154
border control, 77
Boston University, Center for Retirement Research, 128, 145, 146–47
Broda, Christian, 190n8
Brookings Institution, 271
Burak, Esra, 69, 82, 127
Bureau of Economic Analysis (BEA): ARRA's impact on personal tax payments and government trans-

fers, 273; income effects of federal stimulus, **274**; tax rebates, 268. *See also* National Income and Product Accounts (NIPA)
Bureau of Labor Statistics (BLS): construction industry employment, 69; Consumer Expenditure Survey, 11, 161, 177–86; government employment, **287**; labor force growth, 78–79; multigenerational living arrangements, **238**; prime-age employment ratio, **67**; private employment, **287**; unemployment and charitable giving, **308**; unemployment and fertility, **224**, **229**; unemployment by education, **74**, **77**; unemployment by race and ethnicity, **75**; unemployment duration, 84
Burkhauser, Richard, 84, 101, 121n12
Burtless, Gary, 249
Bush (George W.) administration: foreclosure prevention programs, 251
business. *See* corporations
Butrica, Barbara A., 145
Butz, William P., 221

California: bankruptcies, 145; housing crisis, 23–24, 40, 140
Capgemini, *World Wealth Report*, 11, 128, 130–31, 150
capital, share of income from, 114–17
Carlino, Gerald A., 285
Case-Schiller Home Value Index, 132
"cash for clunkers" program, 165
CBO (Congressional Budget Office). *See* Congressional Budget Office (CBO)
CDOs (collateralized debt obligations), 31, 49–50
Census Bureau, U.S.: income inequality, 101–2; income measurement, 118; poverty, 89, **90, 92, 94**, 95, 120n5; school enrollment rates, 287; state tax revenues, **282**; unemployment insurance, 98
Center on Philanthropy Panel Study (COPPS), 296

CEO compensation, 116
CEX (Consumer Expenditure Survey), 11, 161, 177–86, 188–89
charitable giving, 294–313; data sources and methodology, 296–98; during Great Recession vs. previous recessions, 307–9; introduction, 294–96; large donations, 309; nonprofits' response to reduced giving, 309–10; by recipient organization category, 295, 303–7; by source, 300–303; tax deduction for, 311–12; trends in overall giving, 298–300, 311; volunteering, 310–11
Charity Navigator, 306
child development, 240
child poverty rates, 91, 95, 100
child tax credit, 98, 270
The Chronicle of Philanthropy, 306
Citibank, 38, 39, 42, 45
Citigroup, 44
civil engagement, 10
Cogan, John F., 285
cohabitation, 234–36
collateralized debt obligations (CDOs), 31, 49–50
college education: education bill (2010), 117; and employment rates, 84; financial aid, 252, 271; gender gap, 117; mortgage delinquency rates, 136; stimulus program's enrollment impact, 287; tax credits, 271–72; and unemployment rates, 73–75, 76, 85
Commerce Department, U.S.: income effects of federal stimulus, **274**
community colleges, 287
computers, 66–68
conduits, 34–36, 38, 48
Congress, 204
Congressional Budget Office (CBO): federal stimulus reports, 288; federal stimulus spending, **278**; housing prices and consumer spending, 192n31; income inequality, 102–5; income measure, 118–19; poverty rate forecast, **99**; unemployment rate forecast, 16

conservation groups, 303
conservatives, 18, **215,** 217, 226–32, 241
construction industry: credit availability, 73; employment trends, 86; men employed in, 78; new construction figures, 132; unemployment, 69–70
consumer confidence, 27, 162, 171–74
consumer credit: contraction of, 162, 178, 186; credit card debt exposures and delinquencies, 141–43, 151
Consumer Expenditure Survey (CEX), 11, 161, 177–86, 188–89
Consumer Financial Protection Agency, 152
Consumer Price Index (CPI), 131, 163, 177
consumer spending: on durables, nondurables, and services, 164–70; federal stimulus program impact, 287–88; job loss impact, 59; as percentage of GDP, 161; and personal disposable income trends, 163–64; survey responses, 147
consumption, 161–95; across sociodemographic groups, 177–83; consumer spending and personal disposable income comparison, 163–64; and consumer uncertainty, 170–77, 187–88; data sources, 161, 191n17; federal stimulus effects, 276, 287–88; Great Recession features, 161–62, 186; in Great Recession vs. other postwar recessions, 165–68; inequality, 183–84; mobility, 184–86; price effects, 188; research considerations, 161–62; trends, 187; wealth effect, 162, 181–82, 187
COPPS (Center on Philanthropy Panel Study), 296
co-residence, 236–39
Corporation for National & Community Service, Volunteering in America database, 310
corporations: business tax incentives, 272; charitable giving, 297, 300, **302;** executive pay, 116; profitability, 106; public opinion of, 201–4, 216
Council of Aid to Education, 296–97

Countrywide Financial, 34, 38, 43, 49
Cowen, Tyler, 115
CPI (Consumer Price Index), 131, 163, 177
CPS (Current Population Survey). *See* Current Population Survey (CPS)
credit card debt exposures and delinquencies, 141–43, 151
credit crunch, 162, 178, 186
credit default swaps, 52
credit markets, 5, 43–44, 45, 186, 187, 250
credit rating agencies, 40, 42
cross-national comparison: automatic stabilization, 260–61; income replacement rates, 255–58
cultural effects. *See* social and cultural effects
Cumberworth, Erin, 59, 220
Current Population Survey (CPS): cohabitation rate, 235–36; fertility, 221; income inequality, 83; income measure, 108; introduction, 11; multigenerational living arrangements, 237; unemployment rate, 61–62

data sources: charitable giving, 296–98; consumption decisions, 161, 191n17; family issues, 221; foreclosures, 128; housing prices, 128; inequality, 83; job loss and unemployment, 61; overview of, 11; public opinion changes, 197–98; underwater mortgages, 128; unemployment, 61; wealth losses, 128–29. *See also specific sources*
debt-service ratio, 142, 190n13
debt-service-to-income ratio, 37
deficit, federal, 31–32, 263, 311–12
deficit spending, 59
defined contribution plans, 145, 153. *See also* retirement accounts
demand, for workers, 88
Democrats, 212–16, 217, 232, **233**
DeNavas-Walt, Carmen, **90, 102, 103**
deregulation, 34, 66, 79
Deutsche Bank, 34

direct income assistance and service provisions, 272–73, **277**
disposable income: and consumption, 163–64; defined, 189n1; federal stimulus impact, 273–76; government transfer impact, 262; trends, 15, 288
divorce, 136, 234
Dolls, Mathias, 261
Dorn, David, 88
Dow Jones Industrial Average, 4, 28
durable goods, 164–69

Earned Income Tax Credit (EITC), 96, 97, 98, 269–70
earnings, 105–16. *See also* income
EB (Extended Benefits) program, 5, 97, 258–59, 262, 264–65
economic effects: Great Recession vs. other postwar recessions, 16–17; overview of, 6–7. *See also* income inequality; poverty; unemployment and job loss; wealth and wealth losses
economic growth, 16
economic model, of Reagan administration, 73
economic recovery, 78–80, 130
Economic Stimulus Act (2008), 261. *See also* federal stimulus programs
Economist Intelligence Unit, 99
education: charitable giving to organizations, 305; employment trends, 85; public school enrollment increases, 282–83; stimulus funding, 252, 279–80, 281, 286–87; tax credits, 271–72. *See also* college education
educational attainment and: employment rates, 84; financial dissatisfaction during recessions, 201; mortgage delinquency rates, 136–37; party identification, 216; poverty rates, **92**, 93; unemployment, 73–75, 76, 85
EITC (Earned Income Tax Credit), 96, 97, 98, 269–70
elderly Americans: poverty rate, 92;

retirement accounts, 108, 128–29, 145–50

Elmendorf, Douglas, **277**, **278**

Emergency Unemployment Compensation (EUC) program, 261, 264–65

employment: federal stimulus impact, 286, **287**, 288; full-time employment trends, 85–88, 288; prime-age employment ratio, 64–68. *See also* unemployment and job loss

employment-to-population ratio, 62, 64, 83

energy-saving investments, tax credits for businesses, 272

Engemann, Kristie M., 84

environmental organizations, 303

ethnic differences. *See* racial-ethnic differences

EUC (Emergency Unemployment Compensation) program, 261, 264–65

Evangelical Council for Financial Accountability, 297, 305

Extended Benefits (EB) program, 5, 97, 258–59, 262, 264–65

fairness, public opinion of, 205–8, 217

faith-based organizations, 295, 297, 305

family issues, 220–45; cohabitation, 234–36; data sources, 221; divorce rates, 234; fertility rates, 221–32, 241; gender roles, 239–40; marriage rates, 233–34; multigenerational living arrangements, 236–39, 240; parenting and child development, 240; research considerations, 220–21

family planning services, 225–26

Fannie Mae, 5, 26, 32, 251, 268

federal deficit, 31–32, 263, 311–12

federal funds rate, 250

Federal Housing Administration (FHA) loans, **33**

Federal Housing Finance Agency, 136

federal income tax: alternative minimum tax, 270–71; automatic stabilization, 253–54; rebates (2008), 261;

unemployment insurance exemption, 265

federal job training programs, 272

Federal Medical Assistance Percentage (FMAP), 280

Federal Reserve Board: automatic stabilizer system impact, 259, 260; credit card debt, 142; financial crisis responses, 26, 44, 46, 249, 250, 251, 252; Flow of Funds, 131–32, 145, 152; Great Recession responses, 250, 251; housing bubble, 37, 39–40, 49; income measure, 118; interest rates, 39–40, 250; mortgage-backed securities, 51–52; role of, 63

federal stimulus programs: approaches, 261–64; and automatic stabilization system, 252, 253–61; direct income assistance and service provisions, 272–73; evaluation of, 286–89; fiscal relief, 263–64, **277**, 279–86; goals of, 250; household disposable income effects, 273–76; infrastructure investments, 262–63, 276–79; introduction, 249–53; for laid-off workers, 264–68; legislative package, 261; temporary tax reductions, 268–72. *See also* American Recovery and Reinvestment Act (ARRA) (2009)

Feeding America, 306

Feenberg, Daniel, 253

fertility rates, 221–32, 241

Feyrer, James, 290n7

FHA (Federal Housing Administration) loans, **33**

financial aid, 252, 271

financial crisis (late 2000s): causes of, 39–46; events of, 4–5; myths about, 46–51; stock market impact, 4

financial institutions. *See* banks and banking

financial instruments, complexity of, 49–50, 51

financial situations, perceptions of, 174–77, 199–201, 232

financiers, influence of, 115–16

fiscal relief, 263–64, **277,** 279–86
Fischer, Claude S., **63**
Fligstein, Neil, 21, 73
Florida: credit card delinquencies, 141; housing crisis, 24, 28, 40, 140
FMAP (Federal Medical Assistance Percentage), 280
Follette, Glenn, 259–60, 261
food, consumer spending on, 169–70
food banks, 295, 306–7
food stamps, 96–98, 100, 164, 259–60, 272–73
Forbes 400, 128, 129–30, 150
foreclosures: data sources, 128; federal prevention programs, 152, 251; trends, **25,** 28, 137–41, 151
foreign-born workers, unemployment rates, 61, 76–77
Foundation Center, 297, 301
foundations, 297, 301–2, 305
401(k) plans, 118, 119, 145, 152, 153. *See also* retirement accounts
fraud, mortgage, 46, 47–48
Freddie Mac, 5, 26, 32, 251, 268
Fuest, Clemens, 261
full-time employment trends, 85–88, 288
furniture, consumer spending on, 168

Gallup, 232, **233**
Galper, Harvey, 285
Gangl, Markus, 69
gasoline, 162, 169, 176, 188
GDP (gross domestic product). *See* gross domestic product (GDP)
Geithner, Timothy, 5
gender differences: financial dissatisfaction during recessions, 201; prime-age employment ratio, 64–68; retirement postponement, 148; unemployment, 61, **63**
gender roles, 239–40
general fertility rate (GFR), 222–25
General Social Survey (GSS), 11, 197–216
Ghilarducci, Teresa, 153
Gini coefficient, 101–2, 114
Ginnie Mae, 32

Giuliano, Paola, 197
Giving USA, 11, 296, 298, **302,** 303, **304, 308**
Glass-Steagall Act, 34
global issues, 23, 53n1
GNP (gross national production), **107**
Goldman Sachs, 38, 45, 47
Goldstein, Adam, 21, 73
Gordon, Tracy, 249
Gorton, Gary, 46
government employees: consumer spending, **179,** 180; employment trends, 59–60, 286, **287;** unemployment, 71
government regulation, 34, 66, 79
government responses: and institutional reform, 9; overview of, 4–5; public opinion, 209–12, 217. *See also* federal stimulus programs
government role, public opinion of, 209–12, 217
government spending, 59, 262–63
government-sponsored enterprises (GSEs): Bush administration initiatives, 251; government takeover, 5, 26; maximum value of home mortgage purchased by, 268; mortgage-backed securities, 32; subprime loans, 33
government transfers, 96–97, 164, 182–83, 259–60, 262. *See also specific programs*
Gramlich, Edward, 49, 284–85
GRAs (Guaranteed Retirement Accounts), 153–54
Great Depression, 9, 62, 196, 307–8
Great Recession: collective responses to, 8–10; economic effects overview, 6–7; events leading up to, 23–27; features of, 3–5; methodology, 10–11; research considerations, 5–6; severity vs. other postwar recessions, 3–5, 16–18, 62–69, 165–68; social and cultural effects overview, 7–8. *See also specific index topics*
Greenspan, Alan, 37, 40
gross domestic product (GDP): and automatic stabilization system, 260;

charitable giving as percentage of, 299; consumer expenditures as percentage of, 161; federal stimulus impact, 278–79; and income distribution, **107**; labor market impact, 16
gross national production (GNP), **107**
Grusky, David B., 3
GSEs (government-sponsored enterprises). *See* government-sponsored enterprises (GSEs)
GSS (General Social Survey), 11, 197–216
Guaranteed Retirement Accounts (GRAs), 153–54
GuideStar, 306
Gustman, Alan L., 150
Guttmacher Institute, 225

HAFA (Home Affordable Foreclosures Alternatives Program), 152
Haig, Robert M., 108
Hamilton, Brady E., 242n10
Hamilton, James D., 169
HAMP (Home Affordable Modification Program), 152
Harris Interactive, 300
Haverstick, Kelly, 145
Health and Retirement Study, 191n17
health care industry, influence of, 116
health care reform, 17
health care spending, 170
health care workers, employment trends, 85–86
health insurance, 252, 267–68
health-related charitable organizations, 303
Heathcote, Jonathan, 120n11, 183
high school dropouts: employment rates, 84; mortgage delinquency rates, 137; poverty rates, **92**, 93; unemployment, 85
high school graduates: employment rates, 84; mortgage delinquency rates, 136; poverty rates, **92**, 93
Hispanics: mortgage delinquency, 136; multigenerational living arrangements, 239; personal financial situation perceptions, **175**, 176;

underwater mortgages, 135, 180; unemployment, 178
Holtz-Eakin, Douglas, 301–2
Home Affordable Foreclosures Alternatives Program (HAFA), 152
Home Affordable Modification Program (HAMP), 152
home equity loans, **33**, 36
Homeland Security Department, 76–77
homeownership, 128
HOPE NOW, 251
"Hope tax credit," 271
hot potato theory, 46–49
household debt service ratio, 142, 190n13
household debt-service-to-income ratio, 37
Housing and Urban Development Department, **25**, 128, 139, 140
housing bubble: causes of, 21–22; early recognition and warnings about, 49; events of, 4, 23–26, 28, 39–42; global implications, 23; government responses, 5; research considerations, 22–23; and securitization, 52. *See also* subprime mortgage crisis
housing prices: consumer spending impact, 192–93n31; data sources, 128; trends, 4, 23–24, **25**, 28, 100–101, 108, 132–33, 151
Hout, Michael, 59, **63**
human capital, 117. *See also* educational attainment
human service organizations, 305
Hurst, Erik, 169–70
hybrid adjustable-rate mortgages (ARMs), 41–42

ICS (Index of Consumer Sentiment), 11, 27, 171–74
ideology, political, 212–16, 217, 226–32
illness, as mortgage default cause, 136
immigrants, unemployment rates, 61, 76–77
immigration reform, 77
income: from capital vs. labor, 114–17; and consumer confidence, 174; and

income (*cont.*)
  consumption decisions, **179**, 180–81;
  federal stimulus effects, 273–76,
  287–88; loss of as mortgage default
  cause, 136; measures of, 118–19; and
  mortgage delinquency rates, 137;
  and retirement postponement decisions, 148–49; sources of, 105–17;
  and underwater mortgages rates,
  135. *See also* disposable income
income assistance, 272–73, **277**
income inequality, 16–17; capital vs.
  labor sources, 114–17; data sources,
  83; public opinion of, 205–8, 217;
  research considerations, 83; trends,
  100–105; unemployment effects, 83–
  88; wealth vs. labor sources, 105–14
income taxes: alternative minimum
  tax, 270–71; automatic stabilization
  system, 253–54; Great Recession's
  impact on state revenues from, 281,
  282; rebates (2008), 261; unemployment insurance exemption, 265
Independents, recession perceptions,
  232, **233**
Index of Consumer Sentiment (ICS),
  11, 27, 171–74
Indiana: foreclosures, 140
Indiana University, Center on Philanthropy, 309
individual giving, 296, 300, **301**
individualism, 10
individual retirement accounts (IRAs),
  118, 145, 153. *See also* retirement accounts
industry analysis, of job loss and unemployment, 69–71
Indy Mac, 26, 34, 39
inequality of consumption, 183–84
inequality of income. *See* income inequality
infrastructure, government spending
  on, 262–63, 276–79
Inman, Robert P., 285
institutional reform, 9, 17, 18
interest rates, 40, 51–52, 250
Internal Revenue Service (IRS), 106,
  296, 297
international affairs organizations, 305

investment banks: financial crisis, 5,
  26; mortgage securitization role,
  30–34, 38, 39, 40. *See also* mortgage-
  backed securities (MBS); *specific
  banks*
Iowa: credit card debt, 142
IRAs (individual retirement accounts),
  118, 145, 153. *See also* retirement accounts
IRS (Internal Revenue Service), 106,
  296, 297
Isaacs, Julia, 100
Issa, Philip, 145

Jambulapati, Sharada, 294
Japan, economic situation, 80
Jappelli, Tullio, 185
job creation, 78, 88, 284
job loss. *See* unemployment and job
  loss
Jobs and Growth Tax Relief Reconciliation Act (JGTRRA) (2003), 283
job searches, 60
job training programs, 272
JP Morgan, 26, 34, 45, 47
jumbo loans, **33,** 36
Juster, Thomas F., 193n31

Kendall, Leon T., **30**
Kenworthy, Lane, 18, 196
King, Miriam, **63, 74, 77**
Krueger, Dirk, 120n11, 186

Labor Department, 273
labor income, 105–17, 119
laid-off workers, federal stimulus
  programs for, 264–68. *See also* unem-
  ployment and job loss
Larrimore, Jeff, 84, 101
Las Vegas, Nev.: housing crisis, 4
Latinos. *See* Hispanics
law enforcement, 279
laws and legislation: Antirecession
  Fiscal Assistance, Local Public
  Works, and Comprehensive Em-
  ployment and Training Act, 283;
  Economic Stimulus Act (2008), 261;
  Glass-Steagall Act, 34; Jobs and
  Growth Tax Relief Reconciliation

Act (JGTRRA) (2003), 283; Patient Protection and Affordable Care Act, 17; Tax Relief, Unemployment Insurance Reauthorization, and Job Creation Act (2010), 5, 97, 98, 261. *See also* American Recovery and Reinvestment Act (ARRA) (2009)

Lehman Brothers, 5, 26, 34, 38, 250

Lesthaeghe, Ron J., 228–29, 230

Levanon, Asaf, 59, 82

leveraging, 45

liberals, **215,** 217, 226–32, 241

loan pools, 47–48

loans, mortgage. *See* mortgages

local governments, fiscal relief for, 263–64

Los Angeles Times: foreclosures, 138–39

low-documentation loans, 47–48

low-income Americans: college student loans and grants, 252, 271; consumer confidence, 174; Earned Income Tax Credit, 96, 97, 98, 269–70; retirement savings, 153. *See also* poverty

Ludvigson, Sidney, 191n16

Lutz, Byron, 259–60, 261

Mackenzie, Donald, 49

macroeconomic policy, 63

"making work pay" tax credit, 269

managerial workers: employment trends, 85; unemployment, 72–73

manufacturing industry: future employment prospects, 86; recovery after recession (1980-82), 66–68; unemployment, 71; value added by, 71

marriage rates, 233–34

married couples: multigenerational living arrangements, 237, **238;** tax cut phaseout, 268, 269; underwater mortgages, 135

Martin, Joyce A., 242n10

Massey, Douglas, 77

MBA (Mortgage Bankers Association), 137, 139

MBS (mortgage-backed securities). *See* mortgage-backed securities (MBS)

McDaniel, Raymond, 42

MCI (more complete income), 107–14, 118

media, 203, 208

Medicaid, 259–60, 280, 281, 283

men: construction industry employment, 78; employment in contracting occupations, 86; Great Recession's impact on, 7, 78, 239–40; prime-age employment ratio, 64, 66, **67,** 68; unemployment of undereducated, 85. *See also* gender differences

Mercer Oliver Wyman, 37–38

Merrill Lynch: Bank of America's purchase of, 26; mortgage-backed securities, 34, **35;** subprime loans, 38, 42; *World Wealth Report,* 11, 128, 130–31, 150

methodology, overview of, 10–11

Mexican immigrants, 76–77. *See also* Hispanics

Meyer, Daniel R., 96

Miami, Fla.: housing crisis, 4

Mian, Atif, 187

Michigan: foreclosures, 140

middle class, 86–88, 117, 135, 209–11

mobility, consumption, 184–86

Mohamed, Shazad, 294

Monea, Emily, 99, 100

Monk, Courtney, 145

Moody's, 42

more complete income (MCI), 107–14, 118

Morgan, S. Philip, 220, 231

Morgan Stanley, 34, 38, 45

Morin, Rich, 147, 148

mortgage-backed securities (MBS): conduits for, 34–36; financial crisis role, 5, 21–23, 42–52; growth of, 32–39, 51–52; history of, 31–32; and housing bubble, 39–42; risk management, 47, 52; SEC requirements, 48; securitization process, 29–31; underwriting standards, 47–48

Mortgage Bankers Association (MBA), 137, 139

mortgage delinquency rates: and ARMs, 140; by household characteristics, **134,** 135–37; and house price appreciation, **26;** trends, 28, 151 mortgage modification programs, 152, 251

mortgage originators, 29–30, 34, 35–39, 46

mortgages: Alt-A loans, **33**, 36–37, 47; ARMs, 41–42, 140; finance approach shift, 29, 45–46; foreclosures, **25**, 28, 128, 137–41, 151, 251; home equity loans, **33**, 36; jumbo loans, **33**, 36; market for, 32–34; origination by product type, **33**, 37; top originating firms, **35**; underwater mortgages, 28, 128, 133–37, 151, 180; underwriting standards, 11, 46, 47–48. *See also* mortgage-backed securities (MBS); subprime loans

Mozilo, Angelo, 49

multigenerational living arrangements, 236–39, 240

Munnell, Alicia, 108

National Academy of Sciences (NAS), poverty measurement, 89, 94–95

National Association of Realtors, 128, 131, 151

National Bureau of Economic Research (NBER), 11, 27, 82, 198

National Center for Health Statistics: fertility rates, **223**, **224**, 226, **229**, 241n4; marriage and divorce rates, 235, 242n11

National Conference of State Legislatures, 283

National Council of Churches of Christ of USA, 297

National Council of Nonprofits, 302–3

national income, **107**

National Income and Product Accounts (NIPA): vs. CEX, 188–89; consumption, 161, 162; income and asset projections, 108; introduction, 11; savings rate, 147

National Opinion Research Center, General Social Survey (GSS), 11, 197

National Vital Statistics Reports (NVSR), 11, 221, 222

NBER (National Bureau of Economic Research), 11, 27, 82, 198

negative home equity. *See* underwater mortgages

Neidert, Lisa, 228–29, 230

Netherlands: unemployment insurance, 258

net worth: of rich Americans, 128, 129–30; trends, 143. *See also* wealth and wealth losses

Nevada: bankruptcies, 145; credit card delinquencies, 141; housing crisis, 23–24, 28, 40, 140

New Century Financial, 26

New York Times: credit card delinquencies, 141

NIPA (National Income and Product Accounts). *See* National Income and Product Accounts (NIPA)

nondurable goods, 164–70, 183

non-farm employment, 68

nonprofits: and government program cuts, 302–3; response to reduced giving, 309–10; role in Great Recession management, 9–10. *See also* charitable giving

North Dakota: credit card debt exposure and delinquencies, 141, 142

NVSR (National Vital Statistics Reports), 11, 221, 222

Obama, Barack: charitable giving tax deduction, 311–12; consumer confidence impact, 174; homeowner protection programs, 152; "making work pay" tax credit, 269; manufacturing unemployment, 71; universal IRAs, 153

occupational analysis: consumption decisions, **179**, 180; full-time employment, 85–86

OECD (Organisation for Economic Co-operation and Development), 255–58, **266**

Office of Management and Budget, 99

Office of the Comptroller of the Currency, 137

Ohio: foreclosures, 140

older Americans: poverty rate, 92;

retirement accounts, 108, 128–29, 145–50
opportunity, economic, public opinion of, 205–8, 217
Organisation for Economic Co-operation and Development (OECD), 255–58, **266**
originate-to-distribute hypothesis, 46–49
Owens, Lindsay, 18, 69, 127, 196

Panel Study of Income Dynamics (PSID), 11, 128, 135–36, 151, 191n17
parenting, 240
Parker, Jonathan, 106, 121n12, 190n8, 192n26
party identification, 212–16, 217, 232–33
Pasricha, Gurnain Kaur, 284, 290n8
Patient Protection and Affordable Care Act, 17
Paulson, Henry, 5
payroll taxes, 96, 253–54, 269
Peichl, Andreas, 261
pensions. *See* retirement accounts
per capita income, 273–75, 288
Perri, Fabrizio, 120n11, 183, 186
personal disposable income. *See* disposable income
personal financial situations, perceptions of, 174–77, 199–201, 232
Petev, Ivaylo, 161
Pew Research Center, 147–48, 197–216, 237
pharmaceutical industry, 116
Philanthropic Giving (Andrews), 307–8
Piketty, Thomas, 121n14
Pistaferri, Luigi, 161, 185
Plotnick, Robert D., 120n7
political ideology, 212–16, 217, 226–32
political parties, identification with, 212–16, 217, 232–33
Political Values and Core Attitudes Survey, 11
Poterba, James, 192–93n31
poverty: anti-poverty policy impact, 95, 97–98; future forecasts, 88, 98–100; measurement of, 89, 93–96; par-

enting impact, 240; tax and transfer effects, 96–97; trends, 89–93; unemployment effects, 83–88
poverty line, 89
predatory lending, 152
presidency, 204
prices, 162, 169, **175**, 176, 188. *See also* housing prices
prime-age employment ratio, 64–68, 74
prisoners, 75, 85, 93
Proctor, Bernadette, **90, 102, 103**
professionals: employment trends, 85; unemployment, 72–73
progressive taxes, 254
PSID (Panel Study of Income Dynamics), 11, 128, 135–36, 151, 191n17
public employees. *See* government employees
public investment spending, 262–63, 276–79
public opinion, 196–219; adverse effects of economic downturns, 198–201, 216; business and financial institutions, 201–4, 216; conclusions, 216–18; data sources, 197–98; fairness, opportunity, and inequality, 205–8, 217; federal stimulus, 288; government, 204–5, 209–12, 217; job security, 78; noticing economic downturns, 198–99, 216; party identification and political orientation, 212–16, 217; research considerations, 196–98
public school enrollment rates, 282–83
public society benefit organizations, 305–6

racial-ethnic differences: consumption decisions, 178–80; financial dissatisfaction during recessions, 201; personal financial situation perceptions, **175**; underwater mortgages, 133–35; unemployment, 61, 75–76, 85
Ranieri, Louis, 32
Reagan administration: economic recovery, 66–68, 79

real estate bubble. *See* housing bubble

RealtyTrac foreclosure data, 11, 28, 128, 138, 151

recessions: 1929-33, 62; 1973-75, 70, 167, **199, 206, 208, 223**; 1980s, 66–68, 70, 73, 79, 167, 172, **199, 206, 208, 213, 223**; 1990-91, 70, 167–68, 182–83, **199,** 202, **206, 208, 212, 213, 223**; 2000-01, 187, **199,** 203, **206, 208, 212, 213, 223**; definitions of, 6; management of, 8–9; severity of Great Recession vs. other postwar recessions, 3–5, 16–18, 62–69, 165–68

The Recovery Act. *See* American Recovery and Reinvestment Act (ARRA) (2009)

recreation, consumer spending on, 170

redistributive effects, 178–83

red states, recession perceptions, 226–32, 241

regional analyses: bankruptcies, 144–45; credit card debt exposure and delinquencies, 141–42; foreclosures, 140; housing prices, 132–33; poverty rates, 91

Reich, Rob, 294

Reich, Robert Bernard, 4

religious organizations, 295, 297, 305

Republicans, 212–16, 217, 232, **233**

research and development, 252, 276–79

research considerations: charitable giving, 295; consumption, 161–62; family issues, 220–21; housing bubble, 22–23; income inequality, 83; overview of, 5–6; public opinion, 196–98; unemployment and job loss, 60–61; wealth losses, 127–29

research methodology, overview of, 10–11

restructuring, 73, 79

retail industry, future employment prospects, 86

retirement accounts: average rates of return, 108; Great Recession losses, 128–29, 145–50, 152; policy recommendations, 153–54

retirement age, 147–48

rich Americans: charitable giving, 309; consumer confidence, 174; influence of, 115–16; personal financial situation perceptions, 176; retirement age, 147; wealth losses, 128, 129–32, 150

risk management, 47

Roman Catholic Church, 297

Sacerdote, Bruce, 290n7

Saez, Emmanuel, 106, 121n14

sales taxes, 281

Salomon Brothers, 32, 34

Saporta-Eksten, Itay, 161

Sass, Steven A., 145

savings, 147, 176–77, 190n13

savings-and-loan industry, 79

Sawhill, Isabel, 99, 100

SCF (Survey of Consumer Finances). *See* Survey of Consumer Finances (SCF)

schooling. *See* educational attainment

Section 1512 reports, 284

securities, 132, 145. *See also* mortgage-backed securities (MBS)

Securities and Exchange Commission (SEC), 40, 48

securitization: originate-to-distribute hypothesis, 46–49; process, 29–31. *See also* mortgage-backed securities (MBS)

self employment, **179,** 180

services: consumer spending on, 164–68, 170; future employment prospects, 86

shareholder model, 73

Sherman, Arloc, 98, 120n9

Shorrocks index, 184–85

short sales, 138

Simons, Henry, 108

single-parent households, poverty risk, 117

single women: mortgage delinquency, 136; underwater mortgages, 135

Slate: charitable giving, 309; family effects of Great Recession, 239–40

Smeeding, Timothy M., 82, **90,** 106, **110, 111, 112, 115**
Smith, Cameron, 302
Smith, Jessica C., **90, 102, 103**
SNAP (Supplemental Nutrition Assistance Program), 96–98, 100, 164, 259–60, 272–73
social and cultural effects: Great Recession vs. other postwar recessions, 17–18; literature review, 8; overview of, 7–8. *See also* consumption; family issues; public opinion
Social Security, 259–60
South Dakota: credit card delinquencies, 141
spending, consumer. *See* consumer spending
spending, government, 59, 262–63
Spilimbergo, Antonio, 197
states: budget shortfalls, 281–83, 285; fertility rate differences, 225, 226–31; fiscal relief, 263–64, **277,** 279–86; income differences, 254
Steinmeier, Thomas L., 150
stimulus programs. *See* federal stimulus programs
stock, 132, 145
stock market, 4, 17, 28, 145, 150
stock options, 116
subprime loans: default rates, 24–26; definition of, 155n13; delinquency rates, 28; features of, 33; foreclosure rates, 139–40; growth of, 24, 40; originations, **33**; as percentage of mortgages, 139; top originating firms, **35**
subprime mortgage crisis: early recognition and warnings about, 49; events of, 36–46; financial institution impact, 26; as Great Recession cause, 21–23
Sufi, Amir, 187
Supplemental Nutrition Assistance Program (SNAP), 96–98, 100, 164, 259–60, 272–73
Survey of Consumer Finances (SCF): bankruptcy, 143; income inequality, 83, 106, 107–8, **113**, 114, 118; introduction, 11; retirement account losses, 145–46, 152; underwater mortgages, 151; wealth, 128–29, 131–32, 192n27
Survey of Consumers, University of Michigan, 161
surveys. *See* public opinion

Tabatabai, Nahid, 150
take-up rates, 164
TANF (Temporary Assistance for Needy Families), 98, 164, 272
TARP (Troubled Asset Relief Program), 5, 26, 251–52
tax credits: child tax credit, 98, 270; college education, 271–72; Earned Income Tax Credit, 96, 97, 98, 269–70; federal stimulus programs, 269–70; "making work pay" tax credit, 269; poverty impact, 96–97, 98; and poverty measurement, 89, 93, 94; retirement savings proposal, 153
tax cuts: federal stimulus programs, 5, 263, 268–72, 276–77; GDP impact, 288; Reagan era, 66
tax deductions, 153, 311–12
taxes: payroll taxes, 96, 253–54, 269; sales taxes, 281. *See also* income taxes
tax rebate (2008), 189–90n8, 261–62, 268
Tax Relief, Unemployment Insurance Reauthorization, and Job Creation Act (2010), 5, 97, 98, 261
Taylor, John B., 285
Tea Party, 18
Temporary Assistance for Needy Families (TANF), 98, 164, 272
Tennessee: credit card debt, 142
Tett, Gillian, 44
Thompson, Jeff E., 106, **110, 111, 112, 115**
Thompson, Jeffrey P., 82
total fertility rate (TFR), 221–24
tranches, 31

transportation, 170, 262–63
TransUnion, 141, 142
Treasury, U.S., 264, 269, 280
Troubled Asset Relief Program
  (TARP), 5, 26, 251–52

UI (Unemployment Insurance). *See*
  Unemployment Insurance (UI)
uncertainty, 170–77, 187–88
underclass, 88
underemployment, 62
underwater mortgages: data sources,
  128; and mortgage delinquency
  rates, 136–37; racial-ethnic differences, 135, 180; trends, 28, 133–36,
  151
underwriting standards, 11, 46, 47–
  48
undocumented immigrants, 76–77
unemployment and job loss, 59–81;
  charitable giving impact, 308; consequences of long-term employment, 68–69; consumer spending
  impact, 59; data sources, 61; by
  educational level of workers, 73–
  75, 76, 84; fertility rate impact, 224–
  25; future projections, 16, 78–79;
  gender differences, 61; Great Recession vs. other postwar recessions,
  4, 69–69; Hispanics, 178; immigrants, 61, 76–77; by industry,
  69–71; measurement of, 61–62;
  mortgage default rate impact, 136;
  by occupation, 71–73; poverty effects, 83–88; public opinion in
  response to, 199–201; racial-ethnic
  differences, 61, 75–76; research considerations, 60–61; retirement account withdrawals during, 150;
  and transfer benefits, 259–60;
  trends, 3, 27–28, 60, 77, 82–83; and
  Unemployment Insurance response,
  259
unemployment duration: by educational level, 74–75; Great Recession
  vs. other postwar recessions, 68;
  trends, 84
Unemployment Insurance (UI): ARRA

provisions, 97, 265; automatic stabilization system, 253; and disposable
  income stability, 164; eligibility,
  265–67; Emergency Unemployment
  Compensation (EUC) program, 261,
  264–65; exhaustion of benefits rate,
  254–55; extended benefits, 5, 97,
  258–59, 262, 264–65; government
  spending on, 189n6; income tax
  exemption, 265; take-up rates, 164;
  underskilled workers' ineligibility,
  85; U.S. system, 254; U.S. vs. OECD
  countries, 255–58, **266**
unemployment-job vacancy ratio, 62,
  64
universal pension programs, 153–54
University of Michigan: Index of Consumer Sentiment, 11, 27, 171–74;
  Survey of Consumers, 161
unmarried women, births to, 222
Urban Institute, 145, 271

Ventura, Stephanie J., 242n10
Violante, Giovanni, 120n11, 183
Vissing-Jorgenson, Annette, 106,
  121n12, 192n26
volunteering, 310–11

Wachovia, 26
Wall, Howard J., 84
Wallace, Geoffrey L., 96
Ward, Michael P., 221
Washington Mutual, 34
wealth and wealth losses: bankruptcy,
  128, 143–45, 151; consumption decision impact, 162, **179**, 180–82, 187;
  credit card debt exposure and delinquencies, 141–43, 151; data sources,
  128–29; from housing, 132–41, 151;
  and income inequality measurement, 105–17; policy recommendations, 152–54; research considerations, 127–29; retirement accounts,
  128–29, 145–50, 152, 153–54; of rich
  Americans, 128, 129–32, 150
wealthy Americans. *See* rich Americans
welfare benefits, 98, 259–60, 272

welfare reform, 211
Wells Fargo, 26, 34, 38, 45
Western, Bruce, 3, 75
West Virginia: credit card debt, 142
whites: mortgage delinquency, 136; personal financial situation perceptions, **175,** 176; underwater mortgages, 135
Wilcox, James, **24**
Wilson, Daniel J., 290n7
Wimer, Christopher, 3, 220, 294
Wolff, Edward N., 69, 127, 178, 180, 181, 192n127
women: employment in expanding occupations, 86; prime-age employment ratio, 65, **67,** 68; retirement

postponement, 148. *See also* gender differences
working poor, 91–92
World Wealth Report, 11, 128, 130–31, 150
Wyoming: bankruptcies, 145

Yearbook of American and Canadian Churches, 297
young adults: employment rates, 84; living with parents, 236–39, 240; poverty rates, 91, 92–93; unemployment, 85

Zandi, Mark, 288, 290n7
Zuckerman, Ezra, 49